Praise for

BRANDO'S SMIL

"An important and meticulously researched volume that shines long-overdue light on the method and madness of one of America's true visionary rebels. Somewhere Brando is smiling."
—John Zorn

"The characterization of Brando, here, is rich with deft and thorough analyses of his films. . . . A great achievement."
—Alexander Norcia, *Slant Magazine*

"Susan Mizruchi's superb new book (so knowingly called *Brando's Smile*) leaps off its pages at a snorting full gallop, scattering numberless fresh discoveries about her passionate, generous, suspicious, elusive, eternally testing subject, Marlon Brando."
—Stewart Stern, screenwriter of
The Ugly American and *Rebel Without a Cause*

"There is much to enjoy here for the confirmed Brando fan."
—*Mail on Sunday*

"Biographers have often highlighted Marlon Brando's eccentricities. But in this sympathetic portrait, Mizruchi plays up his intellectualism: Brando was an autodidact with a library of 4,000 books, not to mention a great editor of his own lines."
—Rebecca Rose, *Financial Times* Best Books of 2014

"*Brando's Smile* is so many things in a single volume: a deeply respectful biography of Marlon Brando; a fascinating study of the art of acting as practiced by perhaps the most important actor of his time and ours; a brilliant testimony of the potency of the acting techniques of my grandmother, Stella Adler, and her Yiddish Theatre/Group Theatre lineage. I admire also the clarity with which Mizruchi connects Brando's acting with his social conscience and engagement as well as his love of humanity and all of the arts."

—Tom Oppenheim, artistic director and president,
Stella Adler Studio of Acting

"Engrossing biography. . . . Some great photos, too."

—*The Bookseller*

"Renowned cultural scholar . . . Susan L. Mizruchi explores the Brando that was not visible to the world in order to better understand the one that was—a Brando that was independent of the public persona and often at odds with it."

—*Examiner*

BRANDO'S
SMILE

BRANDO'S
SMILE

HIS LIFE, THOUGHT, AND WORK

SUSAN L. MIZRUCHI

W. W. NORTON & COMPANY

New York • London

To Saki

Because this page cannot legibly accommodate all the copyright notices,
page 429 constitutes an extension of the copyright page.

For information about Alexander Khochinskiy's collection, please contact him at
alexanderkhochinskiy@gmail.com., 212-346-0803, or 917-332-8953.

For information about permission to reproduce selections from
this book, write to Permissions, W. W. Norton & Company, Inc.,
500 Fifth Avenue, New York, NY 10110

For information about special discounts for bulk
purchases, please contact W. W. Norton Special Sales at
specialsales@wwnorton.com or 800-233-4830

Manufacturing by Courier, Westford
Book design by Chris Welch Design
Production manager: Julia Druskin

Library of Congress Cataloging-in-Publication Data

Mizruchi, Susan L.
Brando's smile : his life, thought, and work / Susan L. Mizruchi. — First edition.
pages cm
Includes bibliographical references and index.
ISBN 978-0-393-08286-9 (hardcover)
1. Brando, Marlon. 2. Motion picture actors and actresses—United States—
Biography. I. Title.
PN2287.B683M49 2014
791.4302'8092—dc23
[B]
                                        2014008362

ISBN 978-0-393-35120-0 pbk.

W. W. Norton & Company, Inc.,
500 Fifth Avenue, New York, N.Y. 10110
www.wwnorton.com

W. W. Norton & Company Ltd., Castle House,
75/76 Wells Street, London W1T 3QT

1 2 3 4 5 6 7 8 9 0

CONTENTS

List of Illustrations   ix

INTRODUCTION   HIS SMILES   xiii

CHAPTER ONE   LESSONS OF THE MIDWEST   1

CHAPTER TWO   MANHATTAN SCHOOLING   32

CHAPTER THREE   BUILDING THE REPERTOIRE   68

CHAPTER FOUR   THE EPIC MODE, 1960-1963   139

CHAPTER FIVE   POLITICAL FILMS, 1963-1969   180

CHAPTER SIX   ANNUS MIRABILIS, 1972   219

CHAPTER SEVEN   VILLAINS AND SUPERMEN   255

CHAPTER EIGHT   CITIZEN OF THE PLANET   310

EPILOGUE   LYING FOR A LIVING   349

Acknowledgments   363
Appendix: Brando's Plays and Films   365
Notes   367
Permissions   429
Index   431

LIST OF ILLUSTRATIONS

Playing bongos, Paris, France, 1950s   *xxi*

With Jane Goodall, ca. 2001   *xxxvii*

Great-Aunt June in the Midwest, photographed by Brando, 1950s   *3*

With sisters Jocelyn and Franny in Omaha, 1927   *8*

Dodie Brando, Omaha Playhouse, 1925   *10*

With Grandmother Bess Myers while filming *The Men*, 1949   *11*

On pony with sister Franny, Evanston, 1932   *12*

Lincoln Elementary School, Evanston, 1935–1936   *14*

Brando's first mash note, 1936   *15*

With his mother picnicking, 1930s   *17*

Marlon Brando Sr., 1930   *18*

Schoolboy, Evanston, 1934   *19*

Cowboy, Evanston, 1932   *19*

Marlon Brando Sr. playing chess on *One-Eyed Jacks* set, ca. 1959   *20*

The young acting student, ca. 1944   *47*

Posing, 1940s   *50*

Applying makeup for *Teahouse of the August Moon*, 1956   *54*

Applying makeup in *On the Waterfront*, 1953   *55*

The Ugly American with mustache and cigar, 1963   *56*

Original program for *A Flag Is Born*, 1946   *61*

A Flag Is Born, 1946   *65*

Stanley Kowalski, 1948   *77*

Rehearsing for *The Men*, 1949   *86*

With Birmingham VA Hospital veterans, 1949   *87*

Emiliano Zapata, ca. 1908   *89*

Brando's Zapata before his assassination, 1952   *95*

Playing chess on the set of *Julius Caesar*, ca. 1952   *98*

On roof with dead pigeon in *On The Waterfront*, 1954   *113*

Golden Globe Awards ceremony, February 24, 1955   *115*

As Napoleon, on the set of *Désirée*, 1954   *122*

Greeting Irwin Shaw in Paris, 1957   *134*

Scriptwriting on *One-Eyed Jacks*, ca. 1959   *148*

Handshake with Dad Longworth in *One-Eyed Jacks*, 1961   *151*

Mona Lisa with card from *One-Eyed Jacks*, 1961   *152*

Reading on the *Bounty*, ca. 1961   *166*

Flirting on the set of *Mutiny*, ca. 1961   *170*

Climbing *Bounty*'s rigging, ca. 1961   *172*

Playing chess on the *Bounty*, ca. 1961   *175*

On Tetiaroa, 1970s   *178*

Brando's revised script page from *The Ugly American*,
    1962   *189*

Using wife's toes as letter holder, *The Ugly American*, 1963   *190*

On the set of *The Chase*, 1965   *194*

With Elizabeth Taylor on the set of *Reflections in a Golden Eye*,
    1966   *203*

With John Huston on the set of *Reflections in a Golden Eye*,
    1966   *204*

Playing chess on the set of *Burn!*, ca. 1969   *213*

Paul in anguish, *Last Tango*, 1972   *229*

Paul in dance hall, *Last Tango*, 1972   *231*

The Don in wedding attire, 1972   *244*

The Don's death scene, 1972   *247*

With Dick Cavett in New York City, June 1973   *252*

Robert E. Lee Clayton in *Missouri Breaks*, 1976   *258*

Singing on the *Breaks* set with Jack Nicholson, Kathleen Lloyd, and Harry Dean Stanton, 1975   *259*

On the *Apocalypse Now* set in the Philippines, 1976   *269*

At home with white cat, ca. 1955   *290*

With father on Edward R. Murrow's *Person to Person* show, 1955   *291*

With son Christian during trial, 1990   *292*

With Nelson de la Rosa on the set of *Dr. Moreau*, 1995   *300*

Conversing with a parrot during filming of *Dr. Moreau*, 1995   *302*

With Mira Sorvino in *Free Money*, 1998   *306*

With Robert De Niro in *The Score*, 2001   *307*

Brando as Mrs. Sour, 2004   *309*

With Buddha statue in Bangkok, ca. 1956   *312*

Sample of Brando's annotations on a book about American Indians, ca. 1962   *319*

At "fish-in" with Robert Satiacum, March 2, 1964   *320*

Giving forty acres in Liberty Canyon to Indians, 1974   *323*

Speaking at civil rights event with Martin Luther King Jr., ca. 1963   *332*

With James Baldwin at March on Washington, August 28, 1963   *334*

Praying with children in Thailand, 1950s   *341*

Screening film on hunger at UNICEF headquarters, ca. 1967   *343*

Brando's island, Tetiaroa, ca. 2004   *344*

On *The Dick Cavett Show*, June 1973   *353*

Brando as Brando, 1997   *361*

HIS SMILES

Marlon Brando loved watching people, a habit that supported a genius for impersonation and characterization. Though it came naturally, he pursued it with an almost scientific zeal. "The face is an extraordinarily subtle instrument," he noted. "I believe it has 155 muscles in it. The interaction of those muscles can hide a great deal, and people are always concealing emotions. Some people have very non-expressive faces. ...In such cases I try to read their body posture, the increase in the blink rate of their eyes, their aimless yawning or a failure to complete a yawn—anything that denotes emotions they don't want to display."[1] Brando made a lifelong study of emotions and the differences of personality and culture that inhibited their expression, which he managed to exploit in a remarkable variety of film roles.

His interest in human faces went beyond their function as measures of diversity. He was also aware of how they revealed, in profit-driven Hollywood, an actor's marketability, or the lack thereof. The smiles accorded celebrities by the local cognoscenti were calibrated to their earning power. "You can figure which salary bracket a Hollywood actor is in by the kind of smile he gets. When I first came out here I got $40,000 a picture. The smiles people gave me showed two teeth. Now, I'm paid around $125,000 and more, I get both uppers and lowers, but they're locked together. The smile goes up at the corners, but the teeth are set. I'll never get the kind of big fat grins that go with $250,000 a picture. They only pay that kind of money to cowboy stars."[2] Brando's sense of what smiles could expose explains why he was sparing with them on camera.

When you think of Brando, you don't think of a smile. Granted, comedy was not his forte and most of the characters he played were unaccustomed to happiness. But equally important was his understanding of smiles as indices of vulnerability or manipulation. When he does smile in films, it's usually compromised in some way—it's a half-smile, or an ironic smile, or a smile threatening to collapse into something sad or sinister.

Consider Stanley Kowalski of *A Streetcar Named Desire*, covered with automobile grease, shooting an uncharacteristically diffident grin at his wife, Stella, hoping to reassert, against her sister Blanche's scheming, his masculinity and erotic appeal. The wistful smile of Terry Malloy in *On the Waterfront*, as he straightens his nose with a finger to remind Edie of his early profile before the boxing career, before he had compromised himself by betraying her brother. The unctuous smile of the splendidly arrayed Lieutenant Fletcher Christian of *Mutiny on the Bounty*, accompanied by paramours as he meets the unsophisticated captain whom he considers beneath him. The Godfather's wedding-photograph smile, classic Brando, on the verge of a grimace; Paul's smirk in *Last Tango in Paris*, responding to his lover's exasperated speech: "Do you really think that an American sitting on the floor in an empty flat eating cheese and drinking water is interesting?" Or the desperate at-your-service smile of Max in *The Score*, barely a step ahead of the mob.

Brando carefully controlled his smiles: he knew their price. He knew the commodity status of body parts, none more so than his own. As soon as he achieved fame on Broadway, he saw that an actor, like an athlete, could become a slave to his image. Smiles, he recognized, were never free.

His reading of body language was so adept, according to his nephew, that "it was almost supernatural. He would know more about you than you could imagine just by the way you sat down in a chair."[3] Once at a social gathering, Brando asked a woman her age, and she demurred. "It doesn't matter," he responded, "I can tell from your teeth." He guessed accurately. He honed these skills with such habits as frequenting the criminal courts in Brooklyn for the human spectacle they provided. Another New York pastime was sitting in the Optima Cigar Store phone booth watching people walk by, and he was "wrecked," a friend recalled, when his freedom to observe was ruined by the fact that *he* had become an object of scrutiny.[4]

Both the actor and the man were obscured by this public obsession. He created characters so powerfully authentic that audiences refused to believe that these creations were not real. While many considered him a great actor, they missed how denying him distance from his roles qualified that greatness. Even the most astute analysts overlook the conscious observant mind behind the work. It has been difficult for us to see how much more the actor was than any one part, and how different the man was from all of them. As the actor and idol who made it all right for men to be tongue-tied or incoherent, he became so synonymous with an inarticulate masculinity that it was impossible for audiences to accept that the physique was inseparable from an equally formidable intellect.

Brando has been a victim of sexism. Because he was so charming and physically appealing, his equally energetic mind tended to be negated. So dazzled are his most admiring critics that they can't reconcile his attractiveness with the idea of a man who loved language let alone owned a book collection that outstripped those of most academics.[5] Thus, Daphne Merkin opened a 2004 obituary with her memory of being "struck by libidinal lightning" after first seeing Brando on screen, and pronounced him "an untutored *philosophe* who liked to dabble in half-baked political stands." And Camille Paglia celebrated a "Brando, mumbling and muttering and flashing with bolts of barbaric energy, [who] freed theatrical emotion from its enslavement by words." Neither portrait can accommodate the fact that the fantasy hunk took books to bed and undoubtedly (given the limits of even his body) spent more time there reading than engaging in what Paglia called "epic womanizing."[6]

This is not to deny Brando's attractiveness or his womanizing. One of his friends described Brando as having "the kind of face artists are always interested in.... It was as if a klieg light had been shoved up his ass and was shining out his pores."[7] Though it's worth emphasizing that Brando considered himself only "reasonably attractive," attributing his magnetism to his energy and strangeness as a Nebraska farm boy in cosmopolitan settings. But our preoccupation with the looks that helped to bring Brando fame and fortune has clouded our appraisal of his contributions as an actor and as a public citizen who took to heart Hannah Arendt's ideal of independent thinking. The excessive focus on his romantic affairs—what was most common about him—has limited our appreciation of what was most unique and enduring.[8]

Among celebrities with iconic status, those whose single name alone conjures an image—Garbo, Marilyn, Sinatra, Michael, Olivier—Brando is distinctive for his ambiguity. Garbo in profile, Michael moonwalking, Sinatra crooning, Marilyn above a subway grate in billowing white skirt, Olivier in evening dress. The name Brando invites a question: Is he the charismatic brute in a white tee; the biker in a black leather jacket and gray cap; the Godfather; the father of Superman; or the bald phantom of the Vietnamese jungle in *Apocalypse Now*? There are *many* Brandos, early and late. In contrast to most cultural icons, he eludes the prospect of a *persona*. Brando was more fluid, more wily than others who achieved comparable fame. This is attributable to the diverse identifications of a lead actor who preferred character roles and foiled expectations in choosing film parts. He had a wide-ranging curiosity and was suspicious of absolutes and rigidity of any kind, rejecting the pressure to conform to a single likeness.

While some have suggested that Brando's disdain for the celebrity that transformed his life was motivated by self-hatred, its more obvious roots were his bohemian tendencies and democratic politics. Along with Zapata, whom he played in a movie, Brando believed that the masses were doomed when they projected their own power onto idealized objects of worship. No one was worthy of such idolatry, least of all actors and entertainers. What has been overlooked is the seriousness of his thinking on these subjects, how deeply he lamented the adulation that he considered so misplaced. Partial to Talmudic wisdom, Brando surely would have appreciated the aphorism, "If you want truth, shun fame."[9]

"The worst thing that can happen when someone becomes famous," Brando observed, "is for him to believe the myths about himself—and that, I have the conceit to say, I have never done. Still, I am stung by the realization that I am covered with the same muck as some of the people I have criticized because fame thrives in the manure of the success of which I allowed myself to become a part."[10] Celebrity was a dirty business, Brando recognized almost as soon as he achieved it at twenty-three, and he never came to terms with its consequences. The invasion of his privacy, the constant distortions of his views in the press, and the conviction on the part of so many that they *knew* him—his resentment toward these downsides of celebrity remained surprisingly fresh until he died at the age of eighty.[11]

According to friends from *Streetcar* days, after the play's sensational opening on December 3, 1947, his image was plastered throughout Manhattan, and it became difficult for Brando to go anywhere undisguised without attracting attention. By the 1950s, his detection in public could elicit mobs. Meeting Brando at their seats in a theater, his date heard a roar from the lobby when admirers discovered him. Another time at a hotel, the police had to handle a sea of unruly people when word spread that Brando was there.[12] Brando himself recalled a crowd so ferocious at the premiere of *Guys and Dolls* that he feared it might tear him apart limb by limb. But he was calm when fans swarmed his limousine en route to a day of filming for *The Fugitive Kind*. "You know," he said to costar Maureen Stapleton, who was trembling beside him, "they feel about me the way you and I feel about Adlai Stevenson."[13] As Brando told Truman Capote, he had been roused from the troubled self-absorptions of a very young man to find himself "sitting on a pile of candy."[14] There is wonder as well as contempt in Brando's realization that his discharges have become sweet rather than foul.

Throughout his life, Brando struggled to use his fame as a way of cleansing fame's "muck." He gave interviews on talk shows when he had a cause to support, such as black civil rights, or compensation for the violation of US–Indian treaties. But sometimes he appeared because a film contract had stipulated it, and in these encounters he did his best to turn the camera back on his interviewers. In *Meet Marlon Brando* (1966), the Maysles brothers, documentary filmmakers who gained renown in 1964 for a film on the Beatles, recorded Brando's stratagems as he promoted *Morituri*, his 1965 film about espionage in World War II. By exposing the profiteering aims of movie star and journalists, he managed to turn the discussion into a critique of publicity. Brando's goal in the Maysles film is captured by a Yiddish phrase he often used, "*Tuches afn tish*"—literally, "behind on the table," or "show your cards."[15]

"Every time we get in front of the television, everybody starts hustling," he says conspiratorially to a reporter. "I don't think we should sneak around it. I think we ought to say we're here as hucksters. He's a newsman, and I'm a huckster, and I'm thumping the tub for a picture called *Morituri*." Audiences, with their craven appetites for details of the private lives of stars, unwittingly fuel this cycle of corruption. "People don't realize that a press item, a news item is money, and that news is hawked in the same way that shoes are or toothpaste or lipstick or hair tonic or anything else. And if you put something in the paper about Elizabeth Taylor or Richard Burton everybody's gonna buy it, everyone wants to know about that. It becomes an item and it becomes a sellable item, and the merchandising aspect of the press is not really fully recognized I think by the public. And when you don't cooperate with those merchandising systems, people that sell news...it's sort of an unwritten code that if you don't cooperate with those people and tell them about the intimacies of your personal life then you've broken the rule and have to be publicly chastised for it. Or chubicly clastized for it, if you like."[16]

The Maysles film reveals methods Brando had been using for years to counter a limelight he despised. On Broadway, he responded playfully to the personalization of actors that from the start irked and increasingly oppressed him, fabricating details for playbills. Biographies for *I Remember Mama* (1944), *Candida* (1946), and *A Flag Is Born* (1946) stated, respectively, that he "was born in Calcutta, India, where his Father was engaged in geological research...in Bangkok while his father was engaged in zoological research...in Bangkok, Siam, the son of an etymologist now affiliated with the Field Museum in Chicago, Mr. Brando spent his early years in Calcutta, Indo-China, the Mongolian desert and Ceylon." By the 1980s he was branding himself in letters as "Bran Dough" and "Branflakes."[17] Enlisted to promote his autobiography for Random House, he appeased himself by writing pages of his own parody interviews.[18]

Brando's sister Jocelyn, who died a year after him, wrote a dirge for his funeral that summarized his lifelong struggle with the engine of publicity.

> *They are scattering you tonight or tomorrow*
> *And I am with you every breath of the way*
> *I hope there is a brisk wind that will take you far and wide*
> *Everyone in the world wanted a piece of you*
> *Now you can accommodate them all*
> *Land lightly on their greedy brows*
> *Or blur their eyes with your gritty essence*
> *Or if we could conjure up a gale*
> *You could choke them all to death*

"How's that for a dirge, old man," she concludes the poem, which, she said, "I think he would have liked."[19]

HIS PASSIONS

This book explores the Brando that was not visible to the world in order to better understand the one that was. This Brando was independent of the public persona and often at odds with it. The Brando described here knew a loneliness that felt, he said, as if he were "out on a limb, . . . and none of the other birds will talk to you."[20] He was as drawn to the way that people mouthed words as he was to the words that came out. He was not only a devoted drummer who could hold his own with professional musicians, he was also knowledgeable about an extraordinary range of music. In the 1950s, when he used to go to jazz clubs like Small's Paradise in Harlem with his friend Quincy Jones, Brando would say, "It's time to go jiggle some molecules."[21] He had an extensive collection of jazz and classical records as well as many books on

Brando playing bongos at Club Saint-Germain, Paris. © Herman Leonard
Photography, LLC, www.hermanleonard.com.

music, and his sound equipment was always cutting edge. A note to him during the making of *The Chase* confirms his eclectic taste (and concern for keeping an organized collection): "Marlon—all of your records are in order here—all in order and all in their correct jackets. There are five records missing but I believe they are with you...Bach...The Beat of Tahiti...Exotica with Martin Denny."[22] Despite his resistance to schooling (he never graduated from high school), he was a reader from youth, and the library he amassed over time, a significant portion of it annotated, suggests a profoundly inquisitive mind.

The image presented here will help to explain what has until now seemed contradictory or accidental in his life and work—why it was, for instance, that his plays and films so often featured music by serious composers—a devotee of music, Brando told close friends, "If you want to know me, listen to Miles Davis's *Sketches of Spain*"—and stories and scripts by major Anglo-American writers, including Tennessee Williams, John Steinbeck, Carson McCullers, Henry James, Joseph Conrad, and H. G. Wells.[23]

It is not unusual for someone lacking an education to esteem those who have one. With Brando the situation is more complicated. He was comfortable among intellectuals, and, as his book marginalia reveal, developed a high opinion of his own talents and qualities of mind. His comment in *The Indian Tribes of the United States: Ethnic and Cultural Survival* (1962) displays a typical combination of skepticism and respect toward academics. Next to the passage "Individual Indians who dress and speak and act like any contemporary American, still play ordained roles as clansmen, as members or even as heads of ritualistic societies and as upholders of an older social order," he wrote, "Harvard Proff"—the misspelling exposes the lifelong foible that led people to underestimate him; the insight that tribal behavior is similar everywhere shows sophisticated awareness.[24] His confidence and avidity are illustrated by his practice of phoning authors of books he admired and arranging to meet them. When he was living above Carnegie Hall, for instance, he invited Margaret Mead over for dinner after reading her *Coming of Age in Samoa*. He asked his mentor Stella Adler to join them, because he thought these two formidable woman would get along—they didn't.[25]

Equally complex is the issue of his attitudes toward acting. In interviews given throughout his life, he seemed disparaging, insisting it was instinct: Everyone acted, some just did it better than others. He had fallen into acting, and stuck with it because he had never decided what he really wanted to do. Such statements contradict basic facts. Brando prepared deliberately and extensively for film roles early to late, in a manner that would have been familiar to Stanislavski and to Stella Adler. He read books about the world of his characters, wrote pages of notes highlighting questions and problems in his film scripts, and revised numerous scenes and dialogues. As Brando observed late in his career, "In almost all my films I've rewritten my parts. Sometimes I've written them entirely, but I never asked for any credit."[26]

Most belying an indifference to acting is the fact that Brando kept the materials related to his career. Visitors to his home regularly remarked on the few signs of his profession. Little within (a framed portrait from *The Wild One* on his desk; a mounted still in his study of him embracing Rita Moreno in *The Night of the Following Day*) disclosed that the inhabitant was a major American actor. But in a shed on his estate there were piles of carefully preserved scripts, notes, papers, and memorabilia from each of his films—every one a time capsule with preparations for the specific movie and evidence of the ordinary life that continued while making it.[27] The contents of the career were separated from his home, yet these contents, meticulously cataloged, remained part of the property. Their existence reinforces another striking fact—that Brando made films until the very end. Brando kept acting until he could barely breathe. Less than a month before he died from pulmonary fibrosis, with an oxygen tank nearby, he played a most improbable final role as the voice of a candy-store owner, Mrs. Sour, a dowager with a blonde wig, in *The Big Bug Man*, an animated film.

Though he enjoyed imagining other careers for himself, Brando also knew that acting was the thing that he could do. His singular ability to impersonate, ennoble, and delight had earned him accolades that would extend far beyond his death. Peers turned out for the sale of his books, papers, and personal memorabilia in greater numbers than curators had seen for other actors' estates—a tribute to his standing among actors.[28] During the 2008 presidential campaign, when asked to identify their favorite movies, both John McCain and Barack Obama named Brando films. That the two candidates could not have been more different—from a cultural, class, and generational standpoint—was a tribute to Brando's iconic longevity as well as his wide-ranging appeal. This was underlined by their choices: McCain cited *Viva Zapata!*, reflecting that Republican's multiculturalism and personal ethic of self-sacrifice; Obama picked *The Godfather*, affirming the broad appeal of the film's patriarchal mythology, that a black boy raised by a single white mother in Hawaii could cherish the same compromised familial ideal as any other American.[29]

Their responses illustrate the continuing importance of an actor whose contributions to theater and film have been widely recognized by other actors and appreciated by large audiences but rarely well understood. For much of his career, Brando was favored by history and his enormous talent was enabled by a combination of factors. Brando's historical afterlife may prove equally propitious, for there is no actor whose performances are more susceptible to the close study afforded by new technology.

HIS ACTING

One factor that makes Brando's acting enduring and explains its importance for fellow actors is the sheer heterogeneity of the roles he played. In some films, such as *Viva Zapata!, The Teahouse of the August Moon, The Young Lions, Candy, The Godfather,* and *The Formula,* he was virtually unrecognizable, playing characters from other cultures—Mexico, Okinawa, India—or wearing makeup that almost completely altered his features. He experimented with accents and labored, through imitation or research, at the specifics of each one: the Southern accents, all of them distinctive, he used for *Sayonara, The Chase,* and *Reflections in a Golden Eye*; the German accents of *The Young Lions* and *Morituri*; the Irish accents of *The Nightcomers* and *The Missouri Breaks*; the British accents of *Désirée, Mutiny on the Bounty, Burn!,* and *A Dry White Season.*

Though he is somewhat notorious for playing uneducated drifters, the actual number of these figures—Johnny Strabler (*The Wild One*), Terry Malloy (*On the Waterfront*), Val Xavier (*The Fugitive Kind*), Rio (*One-Eyed Jacks*), Matt Fletcher (*The Appaloosa*), Bud (*Night of the Following Day*)—is quite small. Indeed, his characters in general are rather bookish. Sky Masterson (*Guys and Dolls*) knows The Good Book better than the missionaries: "The only thing that's been in more hotel rooms than I have is the Gideon Bible." Sakini (*The Teahouse of the August Moon*) is conversant with Eastern and plenty of Western philosophy. Sheriff Calder (*The Chase*) notes condescendingly that the drunken townies would all be "better off at home reading a book...if they can read."[30] And Lee Clayton (*The Missouri Breaks*) takes bird-watching breathers from his work as a hired assassin, usually with a field guide in hand. In keeping with this postwar era,

Brando's repertoire is full of military figures, though his tended to be more offbeat than usual. He was among the first major actors to play a closeted homosexual (*Reflections in a Golden Eye*)—in this case a Southern officer teaching at an army base. And by the time he makes his first appearance, Brando's Colonel Kurtz of *Apocalypse Now* is dangerously at odds with his vocation. He was frequently outside or above the law, playing outlaws, gamblers, adventurers, mobsters, and thieves, but he also played lawmen, doctors, lawyers, ambassadors, and other officials, including Napoleon and Torquemada.[31]

In each of these roles, Brando created a distinct character with his own particularities of face, gesture, voice, accent, and gait. Even in *A Countess from Hong Kong*, where he delivers a wooden performance on a tedious script, with improvisation barred by director Charlie Chaplin, Brando is memorable. He draws the stifling of his own acting into the characterization: Ogden Mears's rigid movements and tight mouth are natural responses to a life constricted by his father's oil wealth and a cold, demanding wife. Similarly, Brando's Mark Antony is a subtle opportunist. A bit too quick in satisfying Caesar—moving to the side of his better ear or darting off on an errand—he displays a cunning that foreshadows his smirk as he turns away from the crowd he has aroused. His Napoleon is quiet and restrained, his ambition conveyed subtly through humorlessness and disinterest in other human beings. There is little here that points back to Stanley Kowalski or forward to Colonel Kurtz.

What is continuous from role to role is technique, as in Brando's exemplary use of objects. This was understood by David Foster Wallace, who wrote in *Infinite Jest* that Brando "studied objects with a welder's eye for those strongest centered seams... touched whatever he touched as if it were part of him."[32] Among the effective moments in *The Wild One* is an improvisation with a quarter. Brando's costar Mary Murphy recalled the way he toyed catlike with the payment for his beer, pushing it toward her across the counter and then retracting it on the point of contact. This unscripted exchange encapsulated the character's foundational ambivalence: the playfulness countered by aggression toward the alien world of good citizens.[33]

"Every object you bring on stage has to tell you about the circumstances of the character you're playing and the world in which he lives," Stella Adler exhorted decades of acting students. No one took this more to heart than Brando. This was one of the many insights Adler developed over her enormously influential career as a teacher of actors. Trained in the Yiddish theater, and committed to a pure interpretation of realist acting techniques acquired firsthand from Stanislavski in Paris, Adler's encounter with Brando in 1943–44 was a meeting of perfectly attuned minds. She was his ideal teacher, he her model student. Some moments in his films seem filmic realizations of her classes. Consider Adler lecturing on hats: "The person who wears a high hat has to know how it lives.... Do you know you have to use both hands to put it on? It's made to be worn straight. The person who wears it has a controlled speech, a controlled walk, a controlled mind." Now, go watch how Brando, as the aristocratic ship's officer Fletcher Christian, puts on his hat in the first scene of *Mutiny on the Bounty*.[34]

Brando had a knack for making whatever he learned appear instinctive. In the climax of *One-Eyed Jacks* (the only film Brando directed), Karl Malden as "Dad" Longworth, the former friend and protector of Brando's "Kid" Rio, pronounces Rio's gunslinging days "over," promptly smashing his right hand with a gun butt. Recuperating by the ocean, Rio broods, threading a necklace, recently returned by Louisa, Dad's stepdaughter, through his maimed fingers. At a certain point he stops, noticing that his fingers bend with the necklace supporting them. In the next scene, a leather contraption has replaced the necklace, as Rio flexes his hand and then takes up his gun again. By the film's end, the gun hand works well enough for Rio to kill Longworth in a shootout, before riding off with Louisa.

Here, too, Brando manages to illuminate pages worth of characterization and plot through his work with objects. One subtle material detail serves to highlight the character's ingenuity and instinct for survival, the redemptive aspect of his romantic nature (Rio's inability to forget the girl yields the "cure"), and the desolation of the nineteenth-century West, so at odds with the American 1950s, where people have so few possessions that *everything* has to be *utilized*.

Robert Duvall and Arthur Penn, who worked with Brando in *The Chase*, recalled watching him create the environment for his character, carefully selecting the props for Sheriff Calder's office and living room.[35] Widely viewed as the lackey of the local oil baron, Calder is slow to counter threats of violence, until all hell breaks loose. Brando's Calder is forever polishing (a saddle, his shoes) and wiping his hands, physical activity that reinforces his interpretation. In one scene, having just been accused of obsequiousness toward the oil baron, Calder grabs a pipe off the mantel and, deep in thought, rubs the bowl across each cheek in turn, inspecting the residue with care. It's not clear what he expects to find there, but oil, as in "mineral" and "ingratiating," is a strong possibility. Robert Duvall also learned from Brando during filming to deemphasize the idea of a beginning. With Brando, Duvall noted, there was no deliberate start to a performance, no end; he talked as he moved onto the set, as if the scene were part of an ongoing conversation.[36] He eliminated the border between behaving and acting.

"The great moments of emotion are signalized by some ordinary, small, natural movement," writes Stanislavski in *An Actor Prepares*. Advancing a technique that is "natural, intuitive, and complete," he asserts that "strong tragic moments" are reached "through the truth of physical actions."[37] Brando owned this book and others by Stanislavski and referred to them on occasion.[38] But he seems to have encountered such ideas, as he did much of what Stella Adler taught, as confirmation of deep convictions. The seeds were there; they just needed watering.

To those who knew him well, he gave the impression, beyond the energy and impulsiveness, of wisdom. If there was such a thing as an actor type, he was it: a close observer of all forms of life, a night owl who hated getting up before noon, sexually promiscuous, resistant to authority and convention. And he had what is referred to as "the actor's mask"—a high forehead accentuated over time by a receding hairline, with eyes set wide apart and back beneath the brow. This physiognomic detail made Brando's eyes at once more noticeable and more mysterious. People occasionally mistook them for brown or hazel. Truman Capote, who prided himself on his photographic memory, recalled Brando's eyes as *caffè-espresso* color." In fact, they were a striking blue-gray, their depth and richness making them uniquely hospitable to photography and film.[39]

It is a notable coincidence that Paul Klee's famous work *Actor's Mask* was painted in 1924, the year of Brando's birth. The actor's mask, according to Klee, reflects both blankness and turmoil. The face discloses little, but the lines suggesting a variety of frequencies confirm much activity within. As Klee wrote, "The mask represents art, and behind it hides man."[40] Brando would have understood this. He was fascinated by masks and studied them for the acting classes he gave in 2001, distinguishing "the masks we wear without masks" from the elaborate ritual apparel worn across time and place.[41] He observed a decade earlier that "storytelling is a basic part of every human culture—people have always had a need to participate emotionally in stories—and so the actor has probably played an important part in every society. But he should never forget that it is the audience that really does the work...every theatrical event, from those taking place in Stone Age caves to Punch-and-Judy shows and Broadway plays, can produce an emotional participation from the audience, who become the actors in the drama."[42]

The actor as Brando conceives him is a vehicle for the emotions of his audience. He was only sometimes a vehicle of his own, and the audience was not to know when this was or was not the case. Brando was sparing in his use of personal experience for affect in his performances. In this way, among others, he followed Stella Adler. The complexity of Brando's approach to the world, his deep grasp of his own motivations and those of others, makes him a perilous subject for biographers. Many have fallen into the pits he so artfully constructed.

But Brando also left a significant trail with many clues to his thoughts and beliefs. He clearly recognized his own stature, that his work would generate interest for years to come. He seems to have meant his book marginalia to be read: In places where the scrawl is illegible, he rewrites the words above those that are indecipherable. An idiosyncrasy perhaps. One can imagine him playing audience to his own pearls of wisdom, taking himself down a peg for poor penmanship, or for haughty intellectualism, as he listens in on his own dialogue with a book's author.

Yet it is consistent with a larger habit of preservation, the passion for ordering his things, which he was able to realize after moving to Hollywood. Every assistant who worked for him was impressed by his zeal for order, exemplified by the fact that almost every book in Brando's vast library had a number and location.[43] The organization of his music, scripts, papers, and books was undoubtedly a counter to the chaotic personal life, the endless women and romantic affairs, the marriages arranged to legitimate children, and the legal wrangling they precipitated. It also demonstrates a fundamental truth about Brando: Despite his peripatetic life, and appetite for novelty, he was in crucial respects a creature of habit, with a deep center of gravity. He usually knew what he wanted, even if that might change so radically from one moment to the next as to make him appear completely indecisive.

What he had, perhaps in greater supply than any actor of the twentieth century, were extraordinary powers of concentration. When he was on stage or set inhabiting his fiction, absorbed in a book or watching something or someone, he was impossible to disturb. A grandson of Brando's recalled an episode with his grandfather in the late 1990s. Spying a bee by the side of the pool, Brando picked it up by a wing. The bee was unbelievably still, and Brando said, "Watch this." He stuck out his tongue and placed the bee carefully on its surface. Then Brando pulled his tongue back and closed his mouth for ten to fifteen seconds. When he opened his mouth and stuck out his tongue, the bee was there still, not moving. Brando let out a gentle breath and the bee flew away.[44]

HIS LIBRARY AND SCRIPTS

According to Emily Dickinson, one of Brando's favorite poets, "abyss has no biographer."[45] Humility approaching despair is a reliable stance for biographers, given the infinite complexity of human beings, even to themselves. Brando himself observed: "Everyone we know in our lives views us through a slightly different prism.... There is no such thing as being able to judge anything objectively. It is a pose that scientists have foisted upon the world." Others' perceptions of us can't help but be distorted. As a celebrity, Brando was especially subject to such distortion, but his endless curiosity about human nature prevented his believing himself harder to understand than others. As he pointed out to an adoring fan, "I am simply a human being just like you ... nothing more or less than one of some four billion human animals on the earth."[46] When it came to the question of his own distinctiveness, Brando was disarmingly modest.

Still, his penchant for self-contradiction and resistance to pigeonholing, as well as the delight he took in putting people on, has made Brando's life especially prone to myths and clichés. Here, too, he preempted biographers, noting, "I've learned that no matter what I say or do, people mythologize me."[47]

As Brando aged and tragedies marred the apparently charmed life, the regnant myths grew increasingly negative.

- His ambition and materialism drove him to end his promising career on Broadway, which he abandoned prematurely for Hollywood.
- He was coarse, uneducated, and inarticulate and helped to transform those liabilities into 1950s masculine ideals.
- After 1960, he made films just for money and rarely put effort into his roles.
- He was obese and became that way because he despised the idolatry that was generated by his good looks.
- He was prejudiced against Jews.
- He was greedy and exploited the film industry that embraced him.
- He was a fair-weather idealist who supported political causes when they were popular and could bring him publicity.
- He was a miserable man who died alone and virtually penniless.

Each of these myths will be dispelled over the course of this book. Brando's disdain for publicity, which stacked the deck against balanced or admiring perspectives, partly explains their perpetuation. Brando's friends were expected not to speak publicly about him. Breaking that rule resulted in immediate expulsion from his inner circle; so those who did talk (or write) were either already outside the circle or antagonistic toward him. Brando's tendency to compartmentalize his experiences and passions, and his intense secretiveness, also limited people's ability to understand him.

Brando placed a higher value on privacy than on reputation and was willing to be rude or to sell himself short in order to thwart an intrusion. Brando biographies as a whole display more than the usual dependence on gossip, and their facts are subject to more than the usual recycling. The not-infrequent vagueness or omission of references seems a convention of celebrity biographies, as though readers are expected to take them as partially fiction.[48]

When he died on July 1, 2004, Brando left a vast material record of his life and work that has never been explored by biographers. A significant portion of his private property was sold at Christie's in 2005: 328 lots, nearly 60 of which included books, film scripts, research materials, and notes for films. I was fortunate that the private collectors who bought them were willing to share them with me.[49] When the executors of the Brando Estate heard that I had located and digitally photographed the thousands of books and scripts sold at Christie's, they granted me access to their own archives. As the first biographer to have reviewed Brando's archives—those sold to the public as well as those retained by his estate—I can report that Brando's hunger for knowledge was as insatiable as his more legendary appetites for women and food. The library had books from his teenage years; Brando began collecting books in earnest as a young actor in Manhattan and added to the library throughout his life. It reflected his need to know as much as possible about everything that intrigued him.[50] The range and depth of the collection suggests there was very little that did not. Christie's curators, who entered Brando's Los Angeles home on Mulholland Drive in the autumn of 2004, said that the four-thousand-book collection was utterly unexpected and genuinely extraordinary.[51]

What can a library reveal about its owner? Brando seems to have lived among books. Many were in his bedroom, on shelves covered with strong twine to prevent a book avalanche during routine Los Angeles tremors or earthquakes. Intimates remember his bed as littered with them; in countless photographs he is carrying or reading one. The fact that his books have phone numbers scrawled inside and sometimes contain letters, photographs, and other extraneous papers, suggests that they were ready to hand. The list of bedside books alone confirmed his diverse tastes: *1001 Yiddish Proverbs*, *The Pentagon Papers*, Jung's *Man and His Symbols*, Stephen Hawking's *A Brief History of Time*, *King Richard II*, James Gleick's *Chaos: Making a New Science*, *Amnesty International*, *The New Pocket Anthology of American Verse*, *The Great Music of Duke Ellington*, *The International Book of Wood*, Hugh Brody's *Maps and Dreams*.[52] The library validated his gift for language, recalled by close friends and documented in letters and interviews, and his devotion to humor in all its cultural varieties.[53]

Brando's collection also revealed his subversive streak. There were books borrowed from friends, checked out from lending libraries, and stolen from his psychiatrists—all of them catalogued under his system. There were books belonging to his sisters, who were well aware of his habits. Jocelyn scrawled an ultimatum on the front cover of her *Anthology of Islamic Literature* (1966): "This belongs to Jocelyn Brando and it *must* be returned to her or else!" Her brother's library classification number on the facing page, just above the hadith of the Prophet Muhammad, "Trust in God But Tie Your Camel," serves as ironic commentary on her threat.[54]

A significant percentage of Brando's books were gifts. Brando especially admired Lewis Thomas's *Lives of a Cell*, annotating it cover to cover. He sought out the author, who responded with inscribed copies of his other books. Brando owned a copy of Emma Goldman's *Living My Life* with her personal signature ("Emma Goldman, St. Tropez, 1931"), as well as a signed copy of *Jimi Hendrix: Electric Gypsy*—both apparently gifts from friends.[55]

The many women with whom he had affairs gave him books by the dozens, often poetry, sometimes handmade, presented with memories of past dates or pleas for more, and accounts of their relationships. The diversity of his romantic tastes was reflected in the fact that some inscriptions (and books) were in foreign languages with or without translations. Brando made marginal notations in about a quarter of his books; sometimes the marginalia amounted to a line or a check mark. His system of demarcations grew more elaborate over time and included spirited debates with the authors' ideas. The marginalia changed: as a youth he used pencil, which gave way to black or blue pen and lengthy argumentation. By the 1980s, he was highlighting books in red and green, and sometimes yellow or pink. The handwriting, a relatively proper cursive in the 1950s and '60s, shifts to a spidery print as he ages.

He was impatient with pontificating, hedging, and exaggeration. Typical marginal responses include: "were you there?" "did you count?" and "ridiculous." His enthusiasm for subjects is exemplified by "get" next to a book or thinker—his most frequent comment. Invariably, he then added that work or author to his collection. He used another common phrase, "Great God," in the 1950s and '60s to express exasperation with a writer's sentimentality or self-indulgence. "Dio" was perhaps the most common of all; it was the sign of appreciation for something he might use for dialogue in a film. He even annotated footnotes, indexes, and bibliographies, indicating how thorough he could be when exploring a subject that absorbed him.

Books of politics and poetry, well represented in Brando's library, were the most likely to be heavily annotated. This was particularly true of those about India, Japan, the South Pacific, and American Indians. He read widely in American history and legal practice, noting details relevant to civil rights or Indian treaties. He had numerous self-help and psychology books, as well as collections of quotations from major thinkers. And there was science: Brando was an early owner of personal computers when they first became available, and he was drawn to scientific innovation.[56] He loved reading about wildlife, the environment, the seas and planets, and he collected books on topics as small as "the soul of the white ant" and as vast as "infinity."[57]

He had books about every type of pet in his menagerie (dogs, cats, raccoons, pigs) and about insects, whales, porcupines, and bobcats. His interest extended to esoterica: the language of cats, the sex life of wild animals. His commitment to the environment, and to developing sustainable building materials on his Tahitian island, led to exploring the special properties of coconut wood.[58] One garden book contained a detailed plan for a bamboo garden, with instructions on ideal land sloping for the site and its best growing seasons.[59] A photograph of Brando and Jane Goodall discussing primates for a prospective documentary in his lush bamboo garden shows that he managed to implement that plan.

He seems to have had a grammar or vocabulary book for every country he visited, and many of these had annotations. He spoke French, Spanish, and a Tahitian dialect, some Japanese, Yiddish, Italian, and German. The hundreds of books on usage, mostly pertaining to English but sometimes to a foreign tongue, confirm his fascination with the nuances of style, lexicography, and pronunciation.

Many remarked over the years on Brando's acuity for imitation and for picking up foreign tongues, which was enabled by a sensitivity to the rhythms of speech. But his responsibility for

Brando with Jane Goodall on Mulholland Drive. © Thomas D. Mangelsen, www. mangelsen.com.

many of the lines he spoke in his films has been almost completely overlooked. He subscribed to an ideal of brevity; when it came to dialogue, he truly believed that less is more. His script emendations invariably involved cuts: a few forceful sentences substitute for pages of conversation; a lifted eyebrow or grimace replaces lines altogether wherever possible. A final shooting script with Brando's revisions for the oceanside love scene in *One-Eyed Jacks* typifies his method. Crossing out whole paragraphs recounting the suffering of his protagonist, Brando inserts a shrug and one unforgettable statement: "So that's my sad tale."[60] A tireless observer of nature, people, and animals, he recognized the physical poetry of a dancer or the silent empathy of a dog.

Together, Brando's books and scripts reveal the powerful sense of humor that seemed so at odds with the gloomy characters he played. Though he was expert at locating the humor in their darkness, the latter always prevailed. Still, when things couldn't get worse, he recognized that humor was the last stand of human invention. In *The Chase*, Sheriff Calder responds to a hostile townie's hint that he is overpaid ("Taxes in this town, Calder, pay your salary to protect the place"): "Well, if anything happens to ya, Lem, we'll give you a refund." In *Mutiny on the Bounty*, Lieutenant Fletcher Christian turns to a sailor who has just betrayed a mate and asks, "Is there anything else you wished to discuss, early Renaissance sketching, perhaps?"

New access to his annotated scripts and notes on films, to interviews he gave throughout his life, and to the accounts of those who knew him, allow twenty-first-century audiences to appreciate a cultural figure of the twentieth century whose contributions to acting, as well as to public life, can now be illuminated. It is finally possible to recognize the thought behind the performances—whether the subject is acting, political activism, or understanding other cultures.

Brando's Smile describes the powerful "life of the mind" that sustained and goes a long way toward explaining his contributions as an actor and cultural figure.[61] Philosopher Hannah Arendt's phrase is invoked deliberately here: Brando admired her and owned many of her books, annotating them heavily.[62] My purpose is to allow Brando to speak through his films, political activities, interviews, and writings, as an authority on his own experience and beliefs. Despite his lifelong resistance to biographers, Brando offered a steady stream of commentary over the years, including lucid explanations for the major choices he made.

To the end, Brando was bemused by his fame and committed to his own standard of honesty, however adept he was at peddling fictions. In Notes for his Autobiography (NFA), he wrote, "Fifteen books have been written about me. People seem to be interested in those who are puzzling perhaps, a kind of intrest not to far from a cross word puzzle or the hidden answers to the questions to be found on the nightly game show.... I am unconcerned whether people despise the book or find it entrieging. My first concern is that it is true and that it is not boring or simply an exercise in self enthrallment."* Humbled by a lack of education while prone to Midwestern reticence, Brando could be quite guarded about the things that mattered most to him. His ideas about films and his extensive theorizing about culture and human experience is a revelation. And that is the point of this book: to provide insight into the life and mind of an American actor who continues to mesmerize and inspire us for reasons we can now more fully understand.

As he wrote in Notes for his Autobiography, "It's hard to believe that there isn't any acceptable reason for living other than seeing the kids get through before I go—I want to scratch something on the wall of the cave, to leave a grain of something that said I was alive for some pale sliver of a moment in the evening of this species; there has to be something more than just shuffling softly toward the turnstile with our cross-town Transfers to Eternity in our hands."[63]

---

*Brando's original spelling is preserved for all quotations from his own writings (letters, notes, etc.) throughout this book.

BRANDO'S
SMILE

CHAPTER ONE

LESSONS OF THE MIDWEST

FOREBEARS

Marlon Brando's roots were thoroughly American, which may seem surprising because he was so original and unorthodox. Yet Brando's individuality and nonconformity marked him as American in the deepest sense. He was born in Omaha, Nebraska, on April 3, 1924, entering the world feetfirst, a breech delivery that foreshadowed athleticism: the physicality, even acrobatic vigor that he would bring to every role. His parents, Dorothy Pennebaker Brando and Marlon Brando Sr., were Nebraska natives of Irish, English, and German ancestry. His paternal grandfather, Eugene Brando (b. 1857), was from New York state; his grandmother, Marie Holloway (b. 1868), was from Illinois; all four grandparents on his paternal side were American born.

Little is known about Brando Sr.'s mother, Marie, who left Eugene, a harsh, penurious office clerk, in 1900 after seven years of marriage, abandoning their five-year-old son in the process. Raised by paternal aunts and neglected by his father, Marlon Sr. was bitter about his upbringing (though he named his first daughter Jocelyn after one of the aunts). His paternal relatives therefore figured minimally in Marlon Jr.'s childhood, and the actor could only recall his paternal grandfather's Victorian rigidity.[1]

Members of Dorothy ("Dodie" to family and friends) Brando's family, intellectual and eccentric, played a comparatively large role in her son's life with their wide-ranging curiosity, bookishness, and alcohol problems. His maternal great-grandfather, Myles Joseph Gahan (b. 1844), was a renowned Nebraska doctor (chairman of the Nebraska Medical Society and chief surgeon for the Union Pacific Railroad) who transmitted his taste for learning and offbeat spiritualities as well as a predisposition toward alcoholism to the four children he had with Julia Watts Gahan: Dodie's mother Bess (b. 1876), Vine, June, and Myles Jr. A lifelong alcoholic and con man, Myles Jr. seems to have been most susceptible to the paternal weakness, while Bess, the eldest, followed the doctor's idealism and curiosity.[2]

An Irish immigrant who served as a medic in the Civil War, Gahan had graduated from medical school and acquired surgical skills by the time he moved to Grand Island, Nebraska, in 1875. A town of about 900, Grand Island was mostly German and Protestant, with some Catholics and a few Jews by the time Brando's maternal great-aunt, June Beechly, was born in 1881. According to June, the town had been completely Indian prior to white settlement, and a Gahan, "Uncle Jay," was head of the Indian reservation. June recalled an Indian conclave in Grand Island, when she was a teenager. "Tribes from all over the country came.... And mother told me I want you to go up there and see the Indians and watch them dance, because you'll never see anything like this ever again."[3] Healers and idealists, with an appreciation for the native inhabitants displaced by the progressive settlement that benefited their own family, the Gahans had greater awareness than most of their white brethren. This helped to explain why Bess Gahan was so intent on alleviating the plight of the downtrodden, a vision she conveyed to her daughter Dodie, who in

Great-Aunt June in the Midwest, photographed by Marlon Brando Jr.
Reproduced by permission of Brando Enterprises, LP.

turn conveyed it to her son, Marlon Brando Jr. Bess's experience of human weakness through the spectacle of her father's alcoholism probably also contributed to her sensitivity to suffering. The marriage of Myles and Julia was ruined by Dr. Gahan's addiction. According to Brando's Great-Aunt June, her father "tried to kill mother twice," while under the influence of alcohol. At the same time, he was a beloved doctor who "brought all the children into the world in Grand Island and took care of them."

During one of his sojourns in New York City, Dr. Gahan trained with Dr. J. H. Salisbury, an early advocate of the low-carbohydrate diet and inventor of the "Salisbury steak." Dr. Gahan returned to Grand Island and promoted the diet, and some patients boarded at his home to observe the regimen. Among them, according to June, was "a very talented, brilliant attorney named Edelstein who was tubercular, and he lived on that diet in our house for about five years." Edelstein was probably the first Jew hosted by the clan, and his presence signaled a bohemian openness shared by three generations of Gahans, Pennebaker-Myerses, and Brandos. Of all the Gahan tendencies, none was more pronounced than their fascination with non-Western religion and philosophy. Dr. Gahan "dabbled in every ism that was ever known," including Madame Blavatsky's Theosophy, and he believed in reincarnation.

Bess Gahan shared her father's freedom of thought and found a congenial spirit of adventure in the handsome William John Pennebaker, whom she met in a rooming house in Cripple Creek, Colorado, where she was visiting with her sisters in 1896. Bess was twenty and Will was twenty-eight, and her sister June believed that Bess was simply smitten with the idea "that a man that old would fall for her." It was obvious what Bess found appealing in Will, an amateur actor, explorer, and gold prospector who, according to relatives, looked a lot like Marlon Brando Jr.[4] Bess and Will married and their daughter Dodie was born in 1897, like her future husband in the month of January, in Grand Island, where Bess and Will were living. Will soon developed tuberculosis and died in 1899. Bess chose a career instead of settling down as a single mother with her two-year-old daughter. Dodie was sent to live with her grandmother, Julia, and her second husband, O. O. Hefner, in Platte Precinct, Nebraska. Bess moved to Omaha and became secretary to Omaha attorney J. L. Webster, who had famously defended Standing Bear, chief of the Ponca tribe, a case that culminated in US citizenship for Indians. Webster saw the spark in Bess and encouraged her reading and outspokenness on social issues: civil rights for immigrants and blacks, and voting rights for women.

Bess's second marriage, in 1905, to Frank Myers, a staid, taciturn Omaha businessman, facilitated the reunion with her eight-year-old daughter Dodie and allowed her to pursue her own goals, among them continuing work with Webster.[5] Dodie was thrilled to be back with Bess, and Frank Myers intruded little upon the communion of mother and daughter. But the six years of separation from her mother (Dodie spent the last two at a Catholic boarding school) had taken a toll, and her own daughters later speculated that the interlude might have stimulated her genetic predisposition toward alcoholism.[6]

In addition to being "an individual and a renegade" with an outrageous sense of humor, Bess practiced Christian Science's healing touch.[7] While she did not pass this skill on to Dodie, its impact on her grandson is evident. Among the dozens of Bibles in Brando's library, the most heavily annotated—almost every page—was the "Christian Science Bible," Mary Baker Eddy's *Science and Health*. The impact of this tactile healing method on Brando—a man whose lovers often marveled at his touch, and whose silent expressiveness was a mainstay of his career as an actor—appears to have been especially pronounced.[8] (He would later read books on biofeedback and note how the mind can influence the body.)[9] Bess and Dodie were both readers and spent hours discussing books; they also took singing and piano lessons. Dodie also shared Bess's enthusiasm for liberal causes. Even as a mother of small children in the 1920s, when initiatives she cared about were on the state ballot—from improvement of child labor laws and the education of unwed mothers to the reform of health and safety standards, and better conditions for migrant workers—Dodie drove around Nebraska in a dilapidated jalopy giving speeches and handing out pamphlets. Under her mother's guidance, Dorothy Pennebaker Myers grew into a vivacious young woman, considered talented and beautiful by peers, with dark blonde hair, deep-set blue eyes, and a personality as eccentric and independent as Bess's.

Marlon Brando Sr. had also grown up in Omaha. In the fall of 1909, he entered Shattuck Military Academy in Faribault, Minnesota, where he was a model soldier and excelled at sports. Military school was his own choice, motivated perhaps by a desire to remove the taint of a childhood dominated by women. When his money ran out, he transferred to Omaha's public Central High School, where he met Dodie in the fall of 1911. He was seventeen and she was fifteen and it seems to have been an attraction of opposites. Marlon Sr. was tall and handsome, with "a strong masculine presence" but naturally shy.[10] His resolve and desire for acceptance seemed an appropriate counter to Dodie's disordered past, while he was drawn to her joie de vivre and independence. Both harbored overwhelming insecurities that would make their future together so tumultuous: Marlon Sr.'s distrust and resentment toward women stemming from his mother's flight and the coldness of his aunts; Dodie's own experience of how unreliable intimates could be. Their only son would note that neither of his parents knew how to be affectionate toward their offspring.

Dodie and Marlon Sr. (now an army engineer posted on the West Coast) married in Portland, Oregon, on June 22, 1918. When peace was declared five months later, the Brandos settled in San Francisco, where Jocelyn, their first daughter, was born in 1919. By the time their second daughter, Frances, was born in 1922, they were back in Omaha, renting part of a house owned by Dodie's stepfather. In the US Census from 1920, Marlon Sr.'s profession was listed as phone company salesman, and he was doing well enough to afford a servant, though he may have depended on the largesse of his in-laws. Given his ambition, fired by the many slights he believed he had to overcome, it's unlikely that Marlon Sr. could have done anything well enough to satisfy himself. It's also true, however, that while he managed to keep his family housed, clothed, and fed throughout the Depression, he was never particularly successful, which may help to explain why he was so hard on his namesake, who came along two years after Frances.

OMAHA ORIGINS

In 1924, the Brando family was living in a wood-shingled house on Omaha's Mason Street, lined with identical middle-class homes and elm trees. Brando Sr. was working for a limestone products company as a salesman and was often on the road. When Brando was two, the family moved in with Bess on Thirty-Second Street. She had room because Frank had decamped (amicably) to his downtown club, and Dodie's half sister Betty (with whom Dodie was close) was at college. The home of Brando's early years was in some respects vital and nourishing. He was a sunny infant and child, although willful, and liable if thwarted to hold his breath until he turned blue. This only frightened strangers, since Jocelyn and Frances grew accustomed to it.

"Bud," as he was called from the beginning to distinguish him from his father, spent a lot of time outdoors with his sisters—he was closest to Franny—free to roam the neighborhood and adjacent woods. A photograph of the Brando children in the spacious yard at their grandmother's house, ages eight, five, and three, respectively, shows three neatly dressed children remarkably similar in their blond good looks.[11] Brando was always sturdy and athletic, climbing trees, pursuing adventures, and he recalled

Jocelyn, Franny, and Marlon in Bess's yard, Omaha, 1927.
Pictorial Parade/Archive Photos/Getty Images.

those early years as relatively peaceful. The most powerful attribute shared by the Brando children was a sense of humor. This was a quality they identified with their parents, Grandmother Bess, and indeed most of their relatives. Brando's sisters remember his humor as especially infectious, even in a family of wits. The home was filled with pet dogs, chickens, geese, and cats, and the children also spent hours watching the monkeys that were kept by a neighbor in greenhouses down the street. Brando's penchant for protecting and indulging animals was early evident. When his Irish wolfhound named Pat bit an Omaha neighbor and the neighbor beat the dog with a stick, he and Franny retaliated by sneaking into the neighbor's kitchen and pouring salt everywhere. Brando's nephew recalled a story his uncle told about another pet, Toto, an enormous St. Bernard that he had in the 1960s and named ironically after the miniature canine star of *The Wizard of Oz*. Brando was giving a dinner for some Hollywood guests, and his housekeeper had left the main dish on the kitchen counter. When Brando went to get the roast, he found the platter empty, and out of the corner of his eye he saw Toto heading out the back door. Brando ran after him and wrestled the roast away, put it back on the platter, poured gravy over the dents made by the dog's teeth, and served it to his guests.[12]

The Brando children played typical games: rummy, poker, and chess, challenging each other to endless physical contests. Jocelyn remembered a "cowboys and Indians" chess set a family friend had carved for the children, with tepees and ranch houses for pawns and ranch cooks for bishops.[13] One game they played regularly as children was a form of charades called "Essences." A player picked someone and had to describe the person by answering questions from other players, such as, "What kind of a day is this person?" or "What kind of a house?"

Years later, Brando asked his sister Jocelyn for a character sketch to help him write his autobiography, and she followed the "Essence" grid to describe her brother. "What kind of water—a beaver pond"; "What kind of bird—woodpecker with a peacock's tail"; "What kind of instrument—microscope"; "What kind of chemical element—mercury"; "What kind of sport—judo or kickboxing"; "What kind of weapon—boomerang"; What kind of sound—owl or train whistle in the night"; "What kind of playing card—joker"; "What kind of reptile—chameleon"; "What kind of dog—mastiff and bulldog mix"; "What kind of tree—ironwood"; "What kind of store—hardware"; "What kind of nationality—homesick Gypsy."[14]

Dodie was at her best in Omaha. She had apparently inherited the acting bug from her father Will, and here she was able to exercise her talent for theater and other arts. Dodie thrived at the Omaha Community Playhouse, where she helped launch the

Dodie Brando in newspaper photo, Omaha Playhouse, 1925.

career of Henry Fonda by intervening with his father, who was appalled by the prospect of his son becoming an actor. Aware that good acting derives from behavior rather than display, Dodie also knew how to inhabit roles and feel her way into different states of being, impressing Omaha audiences with renditions of Eliza Doolittle in *Pygmalion* (her Cockney accent was reportedly perfect), Ruth Atkins in O'Neill's *Beyond the Horizon*, and Laura Pennington in Pinero's *The Enchanted Cottage*. Jocelyn's one memory of watching her mother act was of sitting on the lap of Fonda, who had hoisted the small child up so she could see Dodie starring in *Pygmalion*. Dodie's immersion in the theater was confirmed by Marlon Sr.'s occasional participation. When he wasn't traveling for work, he sometimes helped build sets, even appearing once or twice in a play. Dodie was multitalented, according to Jocelyn. "She sculpted well, she wrote well. She read everything… she was an excellent actress. We judged from all the parts that she had." Her son, who earned fame in her avocation, had a file of every playbill, notice, and review that mentioned his mother's work in the Omaha Community Playhouse.[15]

Dodie created a festive Bohemian atmosphere at Bess's, which became a gathering place for local artists. Bernard Szold, director of the community playhouse, and his wife Betty were frequent visitors and brought along their friend the artist Edgar Britton; Frances Brando remembers meeting the puppeteer Bil Baird (whose mother and Bess grew up together in Grand Island) with his marionettes on a family vacation in Iowa. Baird and Britton joined their social circle once the Brandos moved to Evanston, Illinois, with radio people and writers added to the mix.

The festive atmosphere also depended on alcohol, and Dodie's growing dependence, which Marlon Sr. shared but handled better, was from her son's birth a significant factor in their lives. Contradictions abounded. This was a family that dosed the children with cod liver oil but throughout Prohibition brewed beer in basement laundry tubs and gin in the bathtub. Marlon Sr. was an upright citizen who believed in discipline, such as putting the children to bed early and feeding them in the kitchen until they

Brando with Grandmother Bess Myers while filming *The Men*. Ed Clark/Time & Life Pictures/Getty Images.

Brando in Evanston with sister Franny. Archive Photos/Getty Images.

acquired proper table manners. He beat his son for misbehavior, yet he drank and consorted with prostitutes when he traveled for work. Dodie hosted Christmas parties where relatives dressed as Santa Claus and taffy pulls for the children and their friends. But she was so unpredictable when on a drinking jag that it became essential for the family to have regular housekeepers. An indifferent mother herself, Bess was not an appropriate substitute, though the children adored her and basked in the attention she was able to give them.

The governess who made the biggest impression on Brando was Ermi. With dark hair and complexion, the attractive eighteen-year-old, of Danish and Indonesian extraction, lived with the family from when he was four until he was seven. Ermi, perhaps because of her personality or her culture, was relaxed about physicality. She bathed and slept with the young boy, both of them nude. While Brando's prodigious sexual appetites came naturally—Marlon Sr. and Dodie were very passionate and each also had adulterous affairs, though his were more frequent—they seem to have had some influence from this early intimacy with Ermi. Throughout his life, he demonstrated a nearly inviolable preference for brunettes, and almost all of his longstanding romances were with women of ancestries different from his own Anglo-Saxon and Irish ethnicity: Asian, East Indian, Hispanic, black, Jewish.

SCHOOLING IN EVANSTON
AND SANTA ANA

Ermi accompanied the family in their move from Omaha to Evanston, when Brando was six, which was critical because of Dodie's difficulty with the transition. Though she surrounded herself in the affluent Chicago suburb with another lively bohemian crowd, and was compensated with summers at theater camps with her children, the loss of the Omaha Playhouse was incalculable. The move was precipitated by a significant promotion for Marlon Sr. to become manager of the Chicago office of the Calcium Carbonate Company, which allowed the family to rent a respectable home at 1044 Judson Street, in the Lincoln Elementary School district. Brando had already shown himself to be a dismal student in his two years at Omaha's Field Elementary School, where he was the only child in the class to fail kindergarten. He was apparently dyslexic, though it must have been mild because he was reading by the time he entered the Evanston school. Indeed, reading was second nature for the Brando children; they went regularly to the public library in Evanston, both sisters were great readers, and books were the most typical of the gifts they exchanged. From a relatively early age, Brando was partly making up for what he missed at school with reading. What he resented most about school was the regimentation and demand for submission to authority. Around this time, Brando's slight stammer was treated in a speech clinic at Northwestern University.

Another passion of the Brando children in Evanston was going to the movies. "Every Saturday we saw the westerns and comedies at the Main [Cinema]; on Sundays we were usually allowed to go to the Varsity, Valencia or Howard theaters," recalled Franny. "We three got to be pretty good at Tarzan yodels. Bud had a complete cowpoke outfit and could become a very authentic little cowboy with a wonderful swagger." One of the actors Brando might have seen during this period was the great British character actor Robert Donat (*The Count of Monte Cristo*, 1934; *The 39 Steps*, 1935), who was already a favorite of his when he arrived in New York at the age of nineteen.[16]

Brando spent six years at Lincoln School, where his fondness for girls and means of expressing interest were already marked

Lincoln Elementary School, Evanston, Sixth Grade, 1935–1936. Brando is in front row, far right. Courtesy of the Lincoln School, Evanston, Illinois.

by a characteristic seductiveness, originality, and tendency to misspell. Signing the back of one girl's sixth-grade class photograph, he wrote: "Yours till the ocaen wears rubber pants to keep its botton dry. Lot's of luck Buddy Brando." He did not fare well academically but made good friends in Jeff Ferguson and Wally Cox, to whom he remained close for life. Cox was like a brother to Brando, and he got to know Jocelyn and Franny well. Sensitive and literate, with maverick intelligences that could not be satisfied at school, Brando and Cox were both from unstable families with severely alcoholic mothers. At Lincoln, Brando defended the diminutive Cox from bullies, while they enjoyed each other's offbeat senses of humor, experimented with words, and invented languages. One of their favorite activities was taking long hikes in the woods, where they examined plants, trees, and insects and often carried their treasures home. When they were both living in Los Angeles as adults, they resumed their childhood

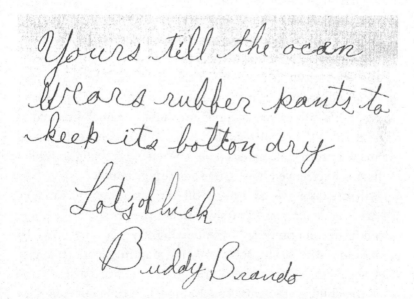

Brando's first mash note, 1936. Reproduced by permission of Brando Enterprises, LP.

pleasure, wandering in the ample woods around Brando's Mulholland Drive home. Brando kept until he died the walking sticks he and Cox collected on their sojourns.[17]

Though the friendship was special, Brando's defense of Cox was typical of a humanitarian courage that became more pronounced over time. Like his intellectual curiosity, Brando's altruism was both encouraged and modeled by his grandmother and mother. He befriended the lone black children at Lincoln School whom many tacitly ignored, and he was upset by his fourth-grade teacher's punitive response. Brando was distressed enough to remember (almost) the teacher's name as Mrs. Miles. It was actually Mrs. Milar, and she was renowned at the school as a disciplinarian.[18] As a boy he regularly brought home sick or starving animals, and even people in distress, among them a woman he found lying on the street. His sister Frances inscribed a copy of the *Tao Te Ching* "For my dear, large-hearted brother," and those who knew him confirmed this attribute.[19]

Brando's extraordinary sensitivity to others' pain was reinforced by Dodie's alcoholism, which became severe in Evanston. Possibly it was his inability to help her that directed his attention to those he felt he could help. At the same time, he was aware of her compassion; when sober, she was devoted to good works. Later in life, after time spent at Alcoholics Anonymous and in 1947 at Yale's Center of Alcohol Studies, she became a dedicated counselor to other alcoholics. Thus she not only taught him about suffering but showed how to do something about it.[20]

Still, the cure was a long way off in those years in Evanston, as the Brando marriage crumbled under the pressure of Dodie's alcoholism and Brando Sr.'s womanizing. They decided on a trial separation in 1936, and the family moved into an apartment at 524 Sheridan Square, where Brando Sr. remained after Dodie took the children to Santa Ana, California.[21] In Santa Ana, they lived with Bess, who had settled there to be near her daughter

Brando and his mother picnicking, 1930s. From Photofest.

Betty and sisters June and Vine. The California respite had little effect on Dodie's drinking, however. She drank even more, disappearing for several days at a time, returning with abject apologies and promises to reform she could not keep. Bess's faith in Christian Science's healing powers apparently faltered in the face of her daughter's devastating addiction. Yet the children seemed to bloom with distance from their father, Marlon Jr. in particular.

Years later, Franny summarized the Brando children's perspective on their parents: "The Terror of Our Father," "The Wound of Our Mother."[22] A punitive man whose response to a chaotic childhood was the overvaluation of order and authority, Brando Sr. was destined to clash with his freedom-loving namesake. Though he could be charming and had a sense of humor, his children mostly experienced him as forbidding and remote. Critical by nature and by the example of his father Eugene, Brando Sr. resented what he couldn't understand or control, which his son, who had inherited his mother's instincts, epitomized. The father focused on the son's inadequacies and the son obliged, failing at school and indulging his wild side. While they shared traits and

Marlon Brando Sr., 1930. Reproduced by permission of Brando Enterprises, LP.

a physical resemblance, their relationship was remarkable for its lack of affinity. Brando disdained salesmanship above all else, and the father's contempt for acting was something the son never quite overcame. At the age of thirty-one, freshly minted Oscar in hand, Brando sat with his father for an interview with Edward R. Murrow. Responding to Murrow's question of whether he was proud of his son, Marlon Sr. replied, "As an actor, not too proud, as a man, well, quite proud."[23] The highly controlled actor, familiar with every muscle in his face, could not conceal a wince when his father denied feeling pride in his son's professional accomplishment.[24]

Nor was there pride in Brando's athletic prowess, no memories of chores shared or skills transmitted. It seems uncanny that the one unmistakable sign of paternal affection was conveyed through a camera lens. Brando Sr. was a devoted amateur photographer who did his own developing and created an extraordinary visual record of his son's childhood.[25] Towheaded in the family garden at three, on his first pony in Evanston at six, outfitted as a cowboy at eight, picnicking with his mother at ten, leaping over fences and swimming in the ocean at eleven, fighting with his sisters at thirteen, the high schooler atop his beloved horse Peavine Frenzy—these images not only picture a boy at home in nature and in love with the power of his body; they also represent a face and physique that was camera-ready from the outset and accustomed to posing for one.

Brando Sr.'s regular photographing of his son becomes all the more relevant to the fact that Brando obliged so many major American and European photographers. There was hardly a significant cameraman, or camerawoman, of the era, it seems, who *failed* to photograph him. The list of those who caught Brando in their lenses reads like a who's who of notables in the field, including Cecil Beaton, Richard Avedon, Margaret Bourke-White, Carl

Brando at age ten. From Photofest.

Brando in Evanston, age eight.
© Bettmann/Corbis.

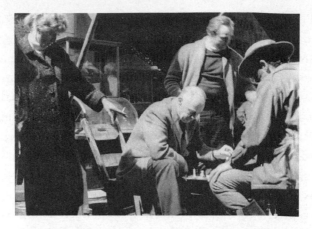

Marlon Brando Sr. playing chess on the set of *One-Eyed Jacks* with Marlon Brando Jr. standing nearby. Photograph and image of Marlon Brando reproduced by permission of Brando Enterprises, LP.

Van Vechten, Philippe Halsman, John Engstead, Ruth Orkin, Edward Clark, Ronny Jaques, Leo Fuchs, and Sid Avery.

One passion father and son shared was chess. A photograph from *One-Eyed Jacks* pictures Brando Sr. engaged in an intense game, his son standing above the board, Brando's longtime friend and fellow actor, Sam Gilman, the opposing player. Chess was a preferred pastime for Brando; he smuggled boards into many film scenes, and there are photographs of him playing on numerous sets. But it seems especially appropriate that this film about fathers and sons, the only film Brando directed, and for which he was so responsible (starring, directing, and writing story and scripts), afforded an image of Brando Sr. playing chess behind the scenes.

Brando turned the bulk of his money over to his father, as soon as he began making it on Broadway, and hired him to work for the film company that he began in the 1950s and named Pennebaker for his mother. Trusting his father with his earnings, and hiring him as an employee, both showed the attachment that accompanied his rage at this father who had beaten him.

He also demonstrated an instinctive awareness that he would never be whole until he worked through his anger. In a long conversation about acting in the early 1980s, Brando told Michael Jackson: "The day Christian [Brando's first son] was born I said to myself my father is never going to come near him. I didn't want my father because of the damage he did to me to get near Christian, and it was a mistake because my father by that time had changed. But *I* hadn't changed. But by the time he died I forgave him and expressed love for him.... I realized I can't live off of hatred, you can't do it, you have to live off of love. It was so hard for me to give that up." Brando's genius was that he learned to make use of that overwhelming rage. "If I have a scene to play and I have to be angry, I can remember my father hitting me...."[26]

As a youth, Brando challenged his father only once. Brando Sr. had retrieved Dodie from a bar where he had found her on a drinking spree; returning home, he had taken her up to their bedroom and begun slapping her. An adolescent at the time, Brando found himself unable to endure the familiar scene and stormed into the room. Filled with adolescent strength and outrage, Brando declared that he would not allow his father to hit his mother again. Unwilling to battle his son, and probably ashamed, his father backed down and left the room.[27] In the one adult confrontation Brando had with his father, a couple of years before Brando Sr. died, the son "took him through our lives" and told him "what he'd done to my sisters, our mother, me." But his empathy for his father was evident in the fact that he spared Brando Sr. one of his deepest convictions: that Brando Sr. was responsible for their mother's early death and the heavy alcoholism that precipitated it. As a young actor in Manhattan, Brando recalled an incident from boyhood when his father had awakened him in the middle of the night to go along to fetch his mother from a bar. The father's obvious aim was to humiliate the mother by exposing her binge publicly to her son. But the father's strategy backfired as usual: Brando sided with his mother's vulnerability; years later, simply recalling what Brando Sr. had done made him furious.[28]

The two years in California away from his father (who stayed in Evanston) during his parents' trial separation (1936–1938) were good ones for Brando. At Santa Ana's Lathrop Junior High School, he excelled as an athlete, winning a school decathlon championship and earning three letters in track and basketball. He also set a school record by doing a thousand consecutive push-ups. He would have done more had the coach not stopped him, afraid that the boy might have a heart attack. Another rare memory of doing something for which he was praised came from Lathrop. After Brando made a screwdriver out of metal, he recalled the satisfaction he felt and the pride because the shop teacher commended his work.[29]

Brando had yet another momentous revelation on the train ride back to the Midwest after his mother reconciled with her husband and they headed to a new family home in Libertyville, Illinois, another Chicago suburb. Now fourteen, Brando was struck by the rhythm of the train and headed to the vestibule between the cars so he could feel the wheels rattling across the steel joints of the track. Spontaneously, he began to pound his hands against the doors and walls in time with the beat of the train. He became an avid drummer as a result. He was probably unfamiliar with the train-simulating rhythm sections of the Cotton Club orchestras headed by Duke Ellington and Count Basie, which mimed locomotives to form a tight rhythmic unit for the rest of the orchestra. But the inspiration he drew from the train was a sign of his musicality, reinforced by his sister Jocelyn's recollection of how impressed she was by a performance of his teenage band, Keg Brando and his Kegliners.

REBELLION: LIBERTYVILLE
AND SHATTUCK

The family's life in Libertyville was as mixed as it had been in Omaha and Evanston. A small farming town, it was a place where people knew one another's business, and Dodie soon became notorious as a drunk, while Marlon Sr. continued to indulge in whiskey and adultery during his travels for work. Fellow students, particularly girls, noted the savoir-faire handsomeness of the new freshman at Libertyville Township High School. Still, Brando was tainted as a lowly farm kid (though they weren't farmers and didn't have antecedents as such) whose truancy and contempt for rules reinforced a general conviction that he was unmanageable.

Some of the reason for his behavior had to do with home. The Brandos rented a house on a horse farm on the outskirts of Libertyville, and Brando would typically trudge home from school to find the place empty. He developed a strategy that he would draw on throughout his life, turning to animals for companionship. He had always had a "St. Francis" quality: sensing a companion spirit, animals were drawn to him. The Brando menagerie in Libertyville included the horse Peavine Frenzy; a Great Dane named Dutchy; a Bantam rooster named Charlie Chaplin; and Betsey, the cow Brando milked twice a day. He recalled that the barn cats would congregate nearby, their mouths hanging open, so he could squirt milk straight from the udder into their mouths.

Brando would often stay home on the farm, cutting classes to read through his mother's library—poetry, Shakespeare, philosophy, religion, and the occasional novel when it proved useful. His 1924 Modern Library edition of Emily Dickinson's *Selected Poems* dates from around this period. The first layer of commentary is in pencil, a second in pen; there is scansion, basic interpretation (beside "The heart asks pleasure first," he writes, "when young"), and a recognition of poetic aspects with which he identified ("About herself," he observes of the line "Much madness is divinest sense," "Non conformest").[30] Having read *Lady Chatterley's Lover*, he would quote from it while pursuing girls, whom he sometimes enlisted to pick up books for him. These seemingly contradictory traits—truant and reader—came naturally and helped to support another deep urge—keeping people off balance and mystified about *who he was*.[31]

Particularly as an adolescent, he liked to do quasi-sociological experiments. One girlfriend he sent on a book errand was Carmelita Pope, whom he met while visiting Jocelyn at a summer-stock theater in Lake Zurich, Illinois. He once arrived at her house for a date with a phonograph record on his head, and he kept it there the whole evening. She wasn't sure whether he was testing the reactions of people to him or his own capacity for withstanding them. It was clear to her that Brando, even at fifteen, was unusual. That's why she believed the story he fabricated to persuade her to buy him books: He told her that he was laid up with a broken leg after falling off a roof trying to retrieve pigeon eggs. Pope remembered his long stays at her Chicago home, where her Italian-Catholic family became a refuge for him. Her mother was welcoming and would feed him; her father had acted in vaudeville with the Orpheum Circuit to pay his way through law school and later helped the FBI pursue organized-crime figures in Chicago. Brando would sit for hours listening to his stories about such Mafiosi as Al Capone and Sam Giancana. Brando never reciprocated with invitations to his house, hinting darkly at his mother's drinking and his father's philandering, but he remembered his debt to the Popes after he became successful on Broadway. When he and Carmelita were acting in New York and her parents came to town, he always insisted on taking them out.

As teenagers, Brando and Carmelita got drunk together for the first time, on a jug of red wine, and she remembers the dogfight he staged for her in the middle of the night, mimicking the barks of different breeds. While her main concern was the sleeping household, the mimicry was superb. But acting was a distant prospect; he would visit Pope backstage when she performed at the Lake Zurich Playhouse and wondered what she saw in it, an indifference she reminded him of when she understudied Kim Hunter opposite him in *Streetcar*. However, reading was something he always took seriously. He once offered her ten dollars to read a book he was keen on, a philosophy tome by Bertrand Russell, which she read uncomprehendingly—and for naught, since he forgot his promise.[32]

The book habit continued at Shattuck Military Academy, the Minnesota military school his father had attended, where he was reading Kant and Schopenhauer and had "more books than even an A student would have in his room." Indeed, when Brando was consigned to detention for misbehavior or failing grades, he spent most of the time reading: about Polynesia in *National Geographic* or Shakespeare's plays, nourishing a fascination with remote cultures and with language.[33]

In sending his seventeen-year-old son to the academy, Marlon Sr. devised a characteristically tough solution that was destined to fail. A great observer with a powerful mind and unlimited curiosity, Marlon Jr. was clearly capable, despite his dyslexia, of learning in the right environment. His aversion to hierarchy made military school the least likely place to unlock his potential. In a sign of how much potential he had, Shattuck turned out to be rather enabling. Yet because he had continuously resisted schooling, there were gaps in his education that embarrassed him and foiled the prospect of his graduation.

When Brando entered Shattuck in September 1941 over Dodie's objections—she recognized military school as the last place where her troubled but sensitive son would flourish—he was a sophomore because he had failed that grade in Libertyville. His letters home identified his favorite subjects as geometry and Latin American history and emphasized his desire to make good academically. They reveal that he greatly misses the animals, as well as his grandmother, Bess, whom he asks after and to whom he writes directly. Brando also worries about his mother, expressing repeated concern when a friend's imminent departure will sadden her. He seems eager to placate his father and also prevent him from visiting—making a strong case for why he should not attend the academy's 1942 graduation ceremonies.

The most striking aspect of the letters from Shattuck is Brando's feeling for language. Even earlier, he had been a bit of a wordsmith, making lists of words he found rare or surprising, a pastime shared with his pal Wally Cox. In a letter to his sister Jocelyn and her husband, Don Hanmer, who was in the army, Brando wrote, "I have some favorite words that I think are beautiful. 'Minnetonka, Fondelayo, lush, golden, soft, Sharon (I might name one of my kids that), yotaomo.' I can't remember any more. I am learning many new and glorious speeches from Shakespeare." The sixteen-year-old Brando offers advice to his older sister and brother-in-law from *Antigone:* "Let be the future, mind the present need, and leave the rest to whom the rest concerns." But he mocks his own literary pretensions, describing himself as "full of fiery enthusiasms, tact, a great amount of knowledge of how life goes for a lad of my years," concluding, "I go now, into the depths of profound thoughts."[34]

Although he would always be a poor speller, over time he acquired a vast vocabulary. One method Brando used is indicated by his copy of *The Brothers Karamazov*, where he underlined, apparently, every unfamiliar word. He also marked, among other things, the translator's description of Dostoevsky: "The shy, unknown youth found himself instantly something of a celebrity. A brilliant and successful career seemed to open before him, but these hopes were soon dashed. In 1849 he was arrested."[35]

His respect for language and conviction of his own limitations in relationship to it was something Brando never lost. He wrote in a notebook sometime in the early sixties: "So here I am, in the middle way having had twenty years largely wasted the years of l'entre des guerres trying to learn to use words and every attempt is a wholly new start and a diffrent kind of failure Because one has only learnt to get the better of words for the thing one no longer has to say or the way in which one is no longer disposed to say it. And so each venture is a new beginning a raid on the inarticulate—with shabby equipment always deteriorating In the general mess of imprecision of feelings, undisciplined squads of emotion. And what there is to conquer by strength and submission has already been discovered once or twice by men who one cannot hope to emulate." Beneath these reflections is a typical selection of titles and phrases separated by tag signs, including: "#Burnt Norton/#and call this day Good friday/#I can't imagine that Christ could have taught you that."[36]

While at Shattuck, Brando sketched a clean profile for his parents and grandmother of the resolute young man struggling to stay afloat amid great challenges, but his profound alienation from the place came through. In one letter from 1942 to his parents, he reports that he had made the Crack Squad, the school's highly prestigious drill team, and he says that it made him "realize more than ever how far from an honor it is too me. I don't give a damn for football teams, swimming teams, and crack squads. . . . I have set my goals and I am hard at them. . . . Duke [the English teacher] has help me a great deal. We have been studying men like Ben Johnson (who at 18 translated Pope's 'Messiah' into Latin verse) and men like Sam Richardson. A study of these men's lives has made me realize what excruciating mental work it takes to get to the sort of development that they did." He writes to his grandmother in February of that year: "I've got lots and lots of questions to ask you about the life stuff. Being up here has given me an opportunity to figure it out for myself, and although I've done well (I think) there are still a lot of answers that I'd like to put the finger on." He writes in an April letter that he has been "busier than a cat on a hot tin roof" (invoking a colloquial expression—Williams's 1955 play was years away) and that "spring is here with all her intoxicating facalties." He wonders whether they have "been to the woods lately" and asks them to "tell me about the animals."[37]

At Shattuck, Brando honed his contempt for arbitrary power, cultivated his skills as a prankster and subversive, and studied drama and poetry with a man he genuinely admired, Duke Wagner, head of the English Department and the drama association. Brando's two-year study of the mentality and customs of a major military academy would prove useful to the many soldiers and veterans he later impersonated in a theater and film era preoccupied with war and its aftermath. Sage McRae (*Truckline Café*), Stanley Kowalski (*Streetcar*), Bud Wilocek (*The Men*), Emiliano Zapata (*Viva Zapata!*), Mark Antony (*Julius Caesar*), Napoleon (*Désirée*), Lloyd Gruver (*Sayonara*), Christian Diestl (*Young Lions*), Fletcher Christian (*Mutiny on the Bounty*), Harrison Carter Mac-White (*The Ugly American*), Freddy Benson (*Bedtime Story*), Weldon Penderton (*Reflections in a Golden Eye*), and Colonel Kurtz (*Apocalypse Now*)—military men all—benefited immensely from Brando's knowledge of Shattuck and its principles.

But in a pattern that would be repeated, the more Brando understood about the place and those who upheld its norms, the more he detested it. By instigating pranks such as setting small fires with Vitalis hair tonic, locking teachers in their quarters so classes had to be delayed or canceled, and stealing the clapper from the bell tower because he was annoyed by its constant clanging, he did his best to disrupt the status quo. Finally, he was expelled in the spring of 1943 for insubordination during an army inspection of the school. Quizzed by an inspecting officer, Brando had confessed that if he found himself on a battlefield without superior officers to direct him, he would "run like hell." This was not the answer the inspectors were looking for. It was a sign of Brando's popularity that the entire student body protested his expulsion and succeeded in gaining a retraction. The group of cadets that argued his case urged Brando in a May 24 letter to return. They spoke for the battalion as a whole, they noted, in their conviction that no one so respected by 230 cadets—for his toughness and spirit on the football team and in general—could be deserving of expulsion.[38]

The letter brought Dodie to tears and highlighted a fundamental truth about Brando's rebellious personality. As he matured and increasingly embraced his eccentricities, his inability to follow rules and fit in tended to arouse admiration and affection rather than the opposite. Unquestionably odd, his oddity nevertheless remained accessible. Some combination of personal magnetism, sensitivity, and the desire to please made him generally appealing. Like other renowned American individualists who created models of independence that their fellows imitated in droves, Brando was destined, it seemed, to democratize his uniqueness.

Among the lasting impacts of Shattuck were the knee injury sustained on the school's football team, which prevented Brando from being drafted in World War II, and the discovery of his talent for acting. Aside from athletics, shop class, and drumming, acting was the only endeavor for which Brando had ever shown aptitude. The mimicry had come early: From a young age he could imitate a person's voice, walk, or accent within minutes of appraising them. His feel for drama seemed innate. Even grade-school friends in Evanston marveled at the realism of his death scenes in games of "cops and robbers" or "cowboys and Indians."[39] Accompanying his mother to summer stock in Wisconsin at the age of ten, his talent for imitation surfaced when he developed a Southern accent simply because he liked the speech rhythms of kids from Tennessee he met there.[40]

On *The Ed Sullivan Show* in 1955, when asked how he had become a drummer, Brando recalled one of his favorite sounds when he lived on the farm: the pulsating donkey engine that powered the water pump. "It just had something to say to me, it had an appeal for me," Brando told Sullivan. "Some people are drawn to tone and others to color, and form." Sullivan pressed him and Brando described the "eccentric, off rhythm," and then, at a loss for words, he reproduced the engine's arrhythmic puffing sound exactly. Yet there was a darker side to this skill. Brando told a friend that, as a small boy, whenever Dodie was drunk and remote, he would do imitations in order to get her attention. Her son's extraordinary renditions of animals, people, and machines were certain to rouse Dodie from an alcoholic stupor and bring her back to him.[41]

Brando's first role at Shattuck was in a one-act play inspired by the King Tut legend, *A Message from Khufu* (1931), by Herman Stuart Cottman. His parents attended. Dodie could see his talent and had a serious talk with Duke Wagner, and then with her son, encouraging him to take acting seriously. Wagner continued to give him starring roles, in such plays as Foster Fitz's *Four on a Heath*, in which he affected an authentic British accent and a memorable death scene, and Moliere's *The Doctor in Spite of Himself.* After he was expelled, Brando went to say good-bye to Wagner, who promised him: "The world is going to hear from you."[42]

MANHATTAN TRANSFER

Jocelyn, twenty-four in the spring of 1943 and living in Manhattan, had already displayed a flair for acting. She had appeared in plays in Libertyville and at the Lake Zurich Playhouse and studied at the American Academy of Dramatic Arts. She had her own stage and film career but would never quite get over the feeling of having been the first sibling in the profession, and then having been overshadowed by the instantaneous success of her younger brother.[43] Franny, also resettled in Manhattan, was a twenty-two-year-old painter attending the Art Students League. No one in the Brando family had graduated from college: Marlon Sr. left the University of Nebraska and Dodie her college of nursing, after a year each. Franny had the most schooling of any of them as an undergraduate at UCLA for two years. In this sense, Brando's choice to pursue the arts rather than formal schooling was consistent with his family. And after a summer of living with his parents and digging ditches for a construction company, Brando readily accepted his parents' offer to support his moving to New York to try out acting school.

But the people central to his childhood, whether he followed them or they followed him, would be part of his life in these new locales. His parents and sisters, his great friend Wally Cox, Carmelita Pope, Grandmother Bess, Great-Aunt June, Aunt Betty: all teachers of these "Midwestern lessons," which, despite his resistance to schooling, had struck deep.

CHAPTER TWO

MANHATTAN SCHOOLING

Arriving in wartime Manhattan during the spring of 1943, the nineteen-year-old found jobs as plentiful as unattached women; he worked as an elevator boy, waiter, and short-order cook. He enrolled at the New School for Social Research in the fall of 1943 because it was "the up and coming place. It was before the Actors Studio, and he went there and he worked with Stella Adler and the rest is history."[1] At first Brando lived with his sister Franny in her Greenwich Village apartment on Patchin Place, but soon he moved in with her neighbor, Celia Webb, a Colombian woman ten years his senior, who was the first of a seemingly endless series of girlfriends in New York. In keeping with a pattern somehow tolerated by numerous women, she would remain his lover long after other women had taken her place as his primary love interest (herself always one among many), and work for him as an assistant. In a different kind of loyalty, he supported Webb and her son over the years and paid the medical bills when she had terminal cancer. Perhaps she spoke for many of his girlfriends in characterizing Brando as "my addiction."[2]

In the winter of 1944, Dodie, who had split up again with Marlon Sr., drove to Manhattan with the family's Great Dane, Dutchy, and rented an apartment on West End Avenue, where Jocelyn (with her one-year-old son Gahan—she had married Don Hanmer in 1942), Franny, and Brando soon joined her. During her New York sojourn, which lasted less than a year, Dodie's drinking was a constant source of anxiety for her children. When she was on an alcoholic binge, Brando and his sisters would spend hours searching for her at bars she frequented in Manhattan.[3] Brando knew that he could never really help his mother, who invariably returned to the source of her grief. It was not long before Dodie reconciled with Marlon Sr. and rejoined him in the Midwest. Her departure sent her son into a severe depression that he overcame at the time through endless walks, reading in the Christian Science Reading Room, and the conviviality of the Adlers.[4]

Brando would eventually symbolize many things to many people, but those who met him in New York during the 1940s, the decade when he became an actor, were struck by his essential Americanness. Practical, down to earth, knowledgeable about how things worked, aroused by injustice and hostile to elitism, outgoing with a prankish sense of humor though somewhat shy, the young Brando was both observer and restless performer, pushing behavior to the edge, ever aware of where the edge was. "He was so powerfully physical, that was the first impression I had of him," Nina Green recalled of meeting him in 1944 as a freshman at Bard College. He was dating her friend Ellen Adler (the daughter of Brando's acting teacher, Stella Adler), and he visited on weekends. "The clowning around and funny animal sounds and backward leaps ... [he] pushed the boundaries of behavior, but always knew where to stop.... What I remember most was the way he looked at people. I remember his eyes, the lids dropping, a way of looking sideways so people wouldn't know he was looking."[5]

As distinctive as he was, Brando could get lost in a crowd, melting into the common humanity to avoid being recognized. If he wanted to project, however, he could appear taller than those with substantial height advantages. Always unpredictable, he struck people as "very human" and "very strange."[6] This would be the appraisal for many years to come, as Brando evolved over the years in Manhattan, Hollywood, Europe, and Tahiti. For many (especially the cognoscenti) who saw him act—and they would eventually number in the millions—another attribute would be added to this list: "genius."[7]

FOR A YOUNG MAN with as many interests as Brando, so physically, intellectually, emotionally open to experience, 1940s Manhattan offered a perpetual feast, catalyzing one lifelong preoccupation after another. His love of music, traced to his mother's encyclopedic knowledge of the international song repertoire, was easy to satisfy there.[8] His adolescent realization of his avocation for drumming was another passion bound to be nurtured in New York. At the Palladium Ballroom on Broadway, the discovery of the Afro-Cuban bands of Tito Puente and Tito Rodriguez, with their conga drummers, would be so galvanizing that Brando bought his own congas and retired his sticks for life.[9]

Brando also was drawn to the athleticism of modern dance, though he claimed to be even more drawn to the female students who studied it. But there was no question of his commitment to the classes he enrolled in with Katherine Dunham, the choreographer, anthropologist, and social activist who so inspired Brando that he briefly considered a career as a dancer. Dunham's teaching appealed to him because of her combined attention to the intellect and the body. She had written a master's thesis on Haitian dance in the anthropology department at the University of Chicago while arousing controversy by introducing a bare torso into dance, making blatant the provocative eroticism of dance. The seeker in Brando who gravitated to big questions and ideas always balanced the athlete who was drawn to the physical arts. His engagement with Latin American musicians and Dunham enhanced a natural agility duly noted by the actor Paul Muni. When they were first getting acquainted, Brando told him about his studies with Dunham. Muni responded, "That accounts for the fact that you move like a panther."[10]

A chance meeting with James Baldwin and Norman Mailer at Hector's Cafeteria in the Village, shortly after his arrival in New York, led to decades of mutual education and camaraderie between the future actor and the future author of *Go Tell It on the Mountain*. Neither Mailer (who was finishing his first novel, *The Naked and the Dead,* 1948) nor Baldwin had published at that point, and Brando, who was always drawn to accents, wondered why Mailer spoke like a Texan after he revealed in their casual conversation that he was from New York. Mailer explained that he had assumed the accent in the army to disguise his Jewishness. Brando and Mailer never clicked, though they encountered each other occasionally in subsequent years, but he and Baldwin quickly recognized their mutual interests—intellectual, political, and psychological. Eventually, Baldwin would give Brando his manuscripts and books to read. Meanwhile, in the 1940s, to cool off in the sweltering heat of Manhattan summers, they rode on the open-air tops of buses and sometimes took the ferry to Staten Island. They discussed race and the value of suffering, and the impact of violent, uncomprehending fathers.[11] When he later began to read Baldwin, Brando highlighted two passages in *The Fire Next Time* that spoke toward their bond. He put a big check beside Baldwin's statement that he defended himself against fear of his father by recognizing "that I already knew how to outwit him," and another check by the sadder revelation, after an encounter with a mentor, that it made Baldwin "think of my father and me as we might have been if we had been friends."[12]

In addition to cultivating new friendships, Brando was also able during this first year in Manhattan to revive old ones. He found that his childhood pal Wally Cox from the Lincoln School in Evanston was living near his sister Franny and her new husband, artist Richard Loving. Their close friendship resumed as if uninterrupted. Cox was supporting himself as a silversmith while pursuing every acting and comedy opportunity he could find. His elaborately patterned silver rings were not only the means of survival but also works of art. Cox influenced the enamel art of Loving, who became an important American painter and taught for years at the Art Institute of Chicago.[13] What he treasured in Brando, Cox wrote Brando in the early sixties, was the instantaneous understanding of ideas impossible to explain to most people.

Cox gained renown for playing the protagonist in *Mr. Peepers*, a 1950s television show about a brilliant but incompetent science teacher, an early nerd, who was "no more like him than . . . Nancy Reagan," according to Brando. Cox also perfected the character type through a mundane humor designed to locate for "serious students of abnormal psychology . . . the exact moment of damage to spiritual tissues that caused my defection from the ranks of heroes to the slippery grease paint and the creaky boards" of the stage.[14]

Brando kept Cox's ashes following his death in 1973, along with Cox's Donaldson Award for Best Supporting Actor in a Musical, the 1949–1950 *Dance Me a Song*. "I'm not sure I will ever forgive Wally for dying," Brando reflected in the 1990s. "More than a friend; he was my brother, closer to me than any human being in my life except my sisters." Knowledgeable about botany, history, physics, chemistry, electronics, and several foreign languages, he "taught me how to speak and to see in words the melodies of life." For his part, Cox considered Brando his greatest friend on this cold planet. Defending his choice, Cox highlighted Brando's profound understanding and affection for human beings in general, and his equally profound ability to comfort Cox in particular.[15] When Brando died in 2004, some of his ashes were mixed with

Cox's before they were scattered in Death Valley. This ultimate disembodied reunion was appropriate. Although in appearance and in their tendencies as actors (the comic straight man versus the dramatic brooder) they could not have been more different, in matters of the heart and mind they could not have been more alike.

THE ADLERS, THE GROUP THEATRE, AND THE NEW SCHOOL

The story of Brando's schooling as an actor begins with Stella Adler, who taught at the New School for Social Research in the 1940s. Erwin Piscator was the director of the New School's Dramatic Workshop, but "Stella Adler was its soul."[16] Stella came from a great stage family, the youngest daughter of Jacob P. Adler, a star of New York's Yiddish Theatre and a leading proponent of Yiddish theater in Europe and America. Jacob Adler's funeral in 1926 was a rare spectacle, as thousands gathered to pay their respects at the Eagle Actors' Club on the Lower East Side, where the body lay in state.[17] Stella's mother Sara (Jacob's third wife) was also a Yiddish Theatre star, and all of his nine children acted, some having extended careers. Stella had her debut in 1906 at the age of four, in her father's production of Zalmon Libin's *Broken Hearts*. For her, acting was the source of being.

In the fall of 1943, when they met in class, Stella was forty-one years old—beautiful, narcissistic, but capable of strong maternal feelings for a remarkably talented and handsome waif like Brando. Adler had everything he could have wanted in an acting teacher: knowledge about the latest methods from Russia, Paris, London, and New York; extensive acting experience in vaudeville and repertory as well as on Broadway and in The Group Theatre; a father who had provided lessons in how to nourish a natural actor's needs and ignore his worst habits; an understanding of the importance of theater and its communal nature; a vibrant Jewish home full of artists and intellectuals into which she welcomed Brando; and a beautiful daughter three years his junior, for him to fall in love with and befriend for life.

Stella had learned how to act from observing her father. In her introduction to her father's memoir, *A Life on the Stage*, Stella describes her first moment of "true consciousness" as being in his dressing room watching him apply his makeup, like a painter choosing his colors. As he changed into another man, she had an almost religious sense of creation. This drama of self-invention was reinforced by her memory of Jacob playing Shakespeare's Shylock. On one side of the stage, the Venetians, their rich arrays reflecting judicial and political power; on the other, Shylock, alone, seated on two low steps, sharpening his knife against the sole of his shoes as he awaited the verdict. When it is read, stripping him of everything including his religion, he crumbles. The performance does not dwell on the injustice done to Shylock but on his grandeur in defeat. "Erect, with a backward glance of burning scorn for this court and its justice," she recalls, "in the full pride of his race, he slowly left the hall. . . . A moment without words, where he summed up, together with his conception of the character, the whole meaning of his life and his theater."[18]

Key elements of Brando's acting glimmer through Stella's account of her father's acting. Both men identified with loners—outsiders isolated from the citizenry—whose dignity is based on their embrace of exclusion and embodiment of suffering. Brando conveys anguish as Terry Malloy in *On the Waterfront*'s bar scene with Edie Doyle by compulsively kneading the chin of his crumpled face. Ellen Adler saw her grandfather's legendary methods at such times in Brando: "The reason why Marlon was so loved by so many is that he would play working class characters in such a way that people recognized themselves, and then he would endow those characters with classical gestures, size and stature."[19] The final moments of Adler's Shylock and Brando's Malloy invoke Christ—one as fallen Jew, the other as resurrected Christian. As Shylock lurches offstage, his eyes darting around, everything he sees becomes a crucifix.[20] Judaism, Christianity's precursor, is doubly violated by the image of Adler's scornful Jew forced to be Christian. At the end of *On the Waterfront*, Malloy, battered and bloody, walks in the savior's footsteps, leading the laborers back to the factory.

Like all great actors, Adler and Brando invite the audience into their thoughts, the action beneath the words, in part by exploiting every prop and piece of scenery. The plainest materials become symbols in Brando's hands. A woolen glove slipped over his hand in *On the Waterfront* signals Malloy's aspiration for empathy, the desire to understand the feelings of Edie, the shy Catholic girl who dropped it. Scenes later, the girl covers her mouth in horror, those same gloves on her hands, as Malloy confesses his role in her brother's death, the tragic threat to their love reinforced by the film viewer's memory of the glove on Malloy's hand. Brando's Malloy is his most Adler-like role, but there would be others that would recall Adler's career.

Adler and Brando both knew that an actor who could not discover his own humanity in the characters he played was unworthy of the name. Acting was not a mere process of imitation or embodiment; it required bringing to it something of the actor's own self, in order to breathe a soul into the character.[21] Jacob Adler's empathy, like Brando's, was bolstered by their shared habit of social observation. Adler loved watching people, especially in the courtroom. He would sit for hours with his then-girlfriend observing trials in his native Odessa, absorbing the drama of witnesses and lawyers, afterward analyzing every detail of what they had seen.[22]

One of Brando's favorite dates as an acting student in New

York was attending court trials in Brooklyn with Jacob's grand-daughter Ellen. (It's not clear whether Brando knew that this had also been one of Jacob Adler's habits.) Cities and stages were substitute classrooms for Adler and Brando, who rebelled against formal education, which each later bemoaned. But each had felt immediate disdain for the institutionalized authority and con-vention they encountered in their respective schools. "The actor does not swim with the stream," Jacob noted around 1917; he "enters a world of gypsies, vagabonds, people of questionable morality. A certain fear surrounds him, as though he had entered a secret order. This has not altogether changed even today."[23]

When Brando entered this "secret order," fate smiled on him in the person of Stella Adler. She would help him find his way into acting. Stella Adler observed, "In acting a person can sit for four months and it's all inside, and then suddenly it will flower. That happened to Marlon Brando. He was not an actor when he came in. He was just a boy."[24]

Adler's methods for helping boys become actors had been honed in The Group Theatre, the most successful of the idealis-tic American acting ventures of the twentieth century. The Group Theatre—usually dubbed The Group—brought together Marxist and early Freudian theory with Stanislavski, who offered the only systematic formulation of the actor's craft. Stanislavski's ideas were inductive, based on the study of great actors.[25] The great intuitive actors themselves drew on a universal fund of knowl-edge about what it meant to assume the experience of another human being and project it outward to an audience. They under-stood the essential loneliness of that procedure, the way it robbed the actor of a self and risked vulnerability in pursuit of power.

There was no director who knew that condition better than Elia Kazan, who joined The Group Theatre in 1932 as an appren-tice fresh out of Yale Drama School and was energized by a the-ater devoted to the poetry of the commonplace. At this point in his life, Kazan's sights were focused on acting, and he "worked like a beaver; every morning," doing his "'sense memory' exercises like prayers at dawn...trying to impress the people of the Group." Despite reservations about his own talent, Kazan had some success with roles in Group Theatre productions: *Waiting for Lefty*, *Paradise Lost*, and *Golden Boy*. He eventually recognized that his true talents lay elsewhere, and he used his firsthand knowledge of the craft to become one of the foremost directors. Respectful, ever open to actors' imaginations and questions, Kazan's antiauthoritarianism (Ellen Adler remembers him as always on the floor during rehearsals) and reliance on intuition gave him extraordinary access to the actors he favored. This is suggested by his sketch of the young Brando, "soft spoken, deeply independent, smiling, gentle, no aggression, subtly humorous, cat-like, lazy, not easy to frighten, or rush; amused at others, secure and confident." Corroborating their mutual understanding, Brando compared Kazan to a Japanese masseuse, who knew just where to touch to reach the vital nerve endings.[26]

The Depression led idealists like Kazan to believe that fundamental change was forthcoming, and Harold Clurman hoped that theater could provide the engine of change. Clurman was an enthusiast who worked for New York's Theatre Guild (a production company promoting high-quality American and foreign plays), and The Group Theatre was his brainchild, the idea launched in the fall of 1930 in a series of weekly lectures outlining a new type of American theater.[27] Clurman's devotion had been kindled at the age of six by a 1907 Yiddish Theatre performance of *Uriel Acosta*, starring Jacob Adler. When he met Stella nineteen years later at the American Laboratory Theatre (he was enrolled with Lee Strasberg in a class for directors, and she was a member of the Lab's acting company), he felt he had met "a living symbol" of everything he treasured, a personification of the old theatrical tradition.[28]

The Lab, begun in 1923, was run by Russian émigrés Richard Boleslavsky and Maria Ouspenskaya, who had worked with Stanislavski at the Moscow Art Theatre (MAT). Their curriculum addressed the *whole* actor, from content classes aimed at intellectual development to training in meditation, movement, and voice. The Lab received valuable publicity from Stanislavski's 1923–1924 tour of America with the MAT, which featured 380 performances in twelve American cities and included a White House meeting with President Calvin Coolidge. Though American audiences could not follow the language of these Russian dramas, they were enormously entertained by the smirks, stares, pauses, and other expressions of thought and feeling.[29]

All three founders of The Group (Clurman, Cheryl Crawford, and Lee Strasberg) were inspired by the realism of the Moscow Art Theatre and disenchanted with the Theatre Guild's commercial ethos and neglect of the actor's craft. Clurman, Crawford (a Smith graduate employed by the Theatre Guild as casting director), and Strasberg, who was renowned for his focus on training "as concentrated as a jeweler over the inner mechanism of a watch"—all appreciated the MAT's democratization of technique. Strasberg was moved by the fact that everyone in MAT productions was equally skilled, even if not equally great. But he recognized that the assimilation of their methods in America required native theorists and teachers.[30] Hence the goal of a permanent company as dedicated to cultivating actors as it was to producing quality plays. The actor Franchot Tone, a success on Broadway before he joined The Group and a success in Hollywood after, advised Margaret Barker, "If you want to be a star, don't come to the Group. If you want to be a good actress, do."[31]

Along with Tone, Adler, and Barker, the initial company included Morris Carnovsky, Robert Lewis, Sanford Meisner, and Clifford Odets. Their first production, Paul Green's *The House of Connelly*, directed by Strasberg and starring Tone, Carnovsky, and

Adler, premiered on September 29, 1931. Most would have agreed with the conclusions of Robert Lewis, who after the demise of The Group became an important teacher of its methods: that the aim of producing contemporary plays reflecting the era's chief dilemmas, while creating a viable group ensemble, had been met. What couldn't be overcome was the fundamental contradiction of an art theater in a commercial system. Still, over a decade, The Group produced twenty-three plays, including the major hits (all by Odets) *Waiting for Lefty*, *Awake and Sing!*, and *Golden Boy*, and in so doing created a model for serious theater in America.

The Group's greatest accomplishment was the legacy it provided actors in the form of technique. Given the strong personalities involved and their profound commitments to acting, it was inevitable that there would be conflict over that legacy. Stella Adler's relationship to the company had always been ambivalent. Drawn in by Clurman, who couldn't imagine The Group without her, Adler felt estranged from most of its members. Its principal focus was on the men of the company, and she was increasingly unhappy with the thin roles she was offered. Yet she remained, because it was one of the few places in America where acting was appropriately revered. For Strasberg, The Group was his life, and some doubted that he had one beyond it. No one denied the effectiveness of his direction, his ability to elicit accomplished work not only from mature actors but also from their fledgling counterparts. Lewis found Strasberg "amusingly talmudic," remembering one of his favorite sayings: "A whole apple is better than half a pear, especially if you want an orange." His primary contribution was showing "us how to have truthful emotions on stage," so that "seeing a Group Theatre production was like witnessing a real accident."[32]

How best to evoke emotions in performance had long been a matter of controversy among dramatists, inciting a divide between adherents of technique and adherents of authenticity who believed that actors had to summon *personal* feelings in order to portray those of their characters convincingly on stage. Strasberg subscribed to the latter view—supported, he trusted, by Stanislavski's theories. He devised "affective memory" exercises for the cast of *House of Connelly*, insisting that they probe their pasts to authenticate the play's climactic scenes. Adler directly challenged the demand that actors draw on their own lives, considering it psychologically destructive. She sought out Stanislavski himself to adjudicate their disagreement, spending a month in Paris working with him.

Returning to The Group in August 1934, Adler relayed Stanislavski's judgment: Affective power inhered in dramatic detail, not in the actor's private history. Comprehensive knowledge of the playwright and play enabled the actor to imagine the character's motivation and to generate truthful emotion on stage.[33] An actor's success depended on how deeply he could penetrate the psychology and environment of his character; the richer the actor's thoughts, the grander his acting. Adler's own exercises thus emphasized intellectual and mental preparation. Emotion, she insisted, evolved from the complexity of the play's plot and the character's motivations within it. Don't *look* for the emotion, she instructed fellow actors, for that would drive it away. She urged them to let it come out of what they were doing.[34]

Since emotional intensity would be Brando's stock-in-trade as an actor, it was a stroke of luck that Adler was teaching the class in which he enrolled at the New School. By avoiding personalization, and emphasizing script analysis, historical research, and action, Adler saved Brando from excavating his past. A childhood of neglect and loneliness provided plenty of Sturm und Drang, but he might have been unable to handle his emotions had he been pushed to reenact them while a vulnerable student. What Brando *did* have was imagination, loads of it, and what Adler called "a sense of truth."[35] That sense of truth afforded a deep and subtle understanding of how emotions were expressed. Adler advised subsequent generations of students to watch Brando if they wanted to learn how to show anger in performance. Brando's explosions were monumental because seven-eighths of their threat was lying underneath them.[36]

Brando believed that Adler's contributions to film acting were unheralded, and that few realized how indebted acting was to her, other Jewish actors of the era, and the Russian theater for most of the performances to which audiences by the 1990s had become accustomed. He never qualified his own debt to Adler, emphasizing her gift for teaching people how to use their emotions: "She could tell you not only *when* you were wrong, but *why*. Her instincts were unerring and extraordinary."[37] Adler herself emphasized the inevitability of Brando's genius. "I taught him nothing. I opened up possibilities of thinking, feeling, experiencing, and as I opened those doors, he walked right through."[38]

Adler taught that the world offered a perpetual feast for those poised to exploit it. There was nothing more important than the actor's eyes, she insisted. His goal is to see specifically, to note the difference between kinds of red—the red of a racing car as distinct from the red of a hibiscus or of blood. "Actors are undercover agents," she declared, describing what it was like to walk down the street with her father, who would never let her rest. He would be calling her attention constantly to details, how this woman walked, how that man used his hands.[39]

In most situations, including class, Brando took her lessons to heart. He stood apart, taking in people, trying to understand their motivations, the workings of the social world. Animals and inanimate things fascinated him just as much; he could imitate a chicken or even a cash register, as he did in class exercises, and it seemed appropriate that his debut on Broadway in 1944 was as a giraffe in *Bobino*, Stanley Kauffmann's play for children.[40] Reading was another way Brando satisfied his need to know and understand, and it was another of the inclinations that Adler appears to have guided. For instance, Kahlil Gibran's *The Prophet* was required reading for her students. Brando had multiple copies of the book in his library, and he gave it frequently as a gift. He was also reading Aristotle in the 1940s, marking, for instance, a Euripides poem quoted in a section of Aristotle's *Rhetoric*: "Since in this world liars may win belief/Be sure of the opposite likewise—that this world/Hears many a true word and believes it not." As a masterful liar, Brando cared deeply about truth, and aphorisms like this were bound to elicit his attention. Equally striking is to see the way the rhetorical emphasis on genuine expression appealed to the young Brando: "Now the reason why sometimes it is not desirable to make the whole narrative continuous is that the case thus expounded is hard to keep in mind," or "say . . . just so much as will make the facts plain, or will lead the hearer to believe that the thing has happened."[41] Brando's reading in this period ranged far and wide, and another acting student at the New School recalled that he sometimes looked "like a nineteenth-century Russian character out of Chekhov or Turgenev, carrying loads of books."[42]

The New School embodied the casual and rebellious ethos of Greenwich Village and suited a nonconformist like Brando, who resisted every institution he entered, from public and military school to Broadway and Hollywood. The courses, faculty, even the architecture were designed to liberate learning, promoting cosmopolitanism and progressive humanism, welcoming everyone into an informal world of inquiry, with few divides between teachers and the mature students the school tended to attract. Begun in 1918 by a group of academic mavericks who sought an alternative to standard higher education, the New School expanded in the 1930s through its embrace of refugee scholars in flight from European fascism, most of them Jews and Socialists. The "University in Exile," which later became "The Graduate

The young acting student, ca. 1944. Lisa Larsen/
Time & Life Pictures/Getty Images.

Faculty of Political and Social Science," opposed fascism and racism, religious intolerance, and nationalism. The school became renowned in particular for its "theory of totalitarianism," which posited basic similarities between fascist and communist regimes and received its most eloquent and systematic articulation in the work of Hannah Arendt, who joined the faculty in the 1960s. It attracted seemingly every major artist and intellectual of the era, from Robert Frost and Aaron Copland to Margaret Mead, Karen Horney, and Erich Fromm, providing not only a gathering place for serious minds but also a platform from which they could reach large popular audiences.[43]

What made the New School unique was its recognition that the aspirations of scholars and artists were interdependent, that academic and artistic expression and freedom were reciprocal. Artists needed learning and scholars needed art. At the same time, the school promoted cultural distinctiveness, featuring international festivals and forums that ensured an incomparable receptivity and access to American, Latin American, and European talent and scholarship. The value of the New School for Brando was its compatibility with instincts or interests that were already established, which is not to deny that it also kindled new ones. He was drawn to what he saw as the strong intellectualism of the school's Jewish faculty. This was not Brando's first exposure to Jews; his mother had been close to Bernard and Betty Szold in Omaha, and artists, entertainers, and intellectuals who frequented the family home in Evanston also were Jewish. As a young actor in Manhattan, having gained confidence from the encouragement he received in classes with Adler, Brando was primed to learn, and he couldn't have been in a more ideal place. He credited a varied group of Jewish mentors at the New School with having "introduced me to a world of books and ideas that I didn't know existed. I stayed up all night with them—asking questions, arguing, probing, discovering how little I knew.... They gave me an appetite to learn everything."

The New School atmosphere was reinforced at the home of Adler and Clurman (by now married), whose apartment on West Fifty-Fourth Street was a gathering place for the Adler acting clan and frequented as well by a Jewish intelligentsia that sometimes included composer Aaron Copland and conductor and composer Leonard Bernstein. Brando compared dinner at the Adlers to "an evening with the Marx Brothers.... Jokes flew around the dinner table like bullets, half in Yiddish and half in English, and I laughed so hard that I nearly got a hernia."[44] Stella's mother, Sara, the star of the Yiddish Theatre, was also living in the apartment from 1944 to 1945, when Brando was most often there. He was especially attentive to her, seeking her out in her room to hear stories about the Yiddish Theatre. She spoke passable English and he spoke some Yiddish, but acting was their common tongue.[45] Despite this bond, Sara initially discouraged Brando's romance with her granddaughter Ellen. Her reluctance would disappear after she saw his breakout performance in the play *Truckline Café*, which convinced Sara that Stella was justified in declaring Brando "the greatest young actor since Papa."[46] Judging from the heartache of her life with Jacob, Sara might have been more resistant to the relationship *after* seeing Brando perform. But, unlike Stella, who deliberately avoided actors as romantic partners, Sara was a fatalist when it came to love, and she probably recognized that Ellen was too far gone to be helped.[47]

In the fall of 1944, a year after enrolling at the New School, Brando landed his first big role as Nels, the fourteen-year-old son of Norwegian immigrants in John Van Druten's *I Remember Mama*, a drama produced by Rodgers and Hammerstein at the Music Box Theatre. The play was a success by Broadway standards, and Brando received good reviews. But apparently regarding it as only a part of his education, he set up a bookcase for himself backstage, where he read between scenes. He describes being approached one evening by Richard Rodgers, who "peered at the book in my hands. It was the *Discourses of Epictetus*." After scanning "the other titles in the bookcase—Kant's *Critique of Pure Reason* and books by Thoreau, Gibbon, and Rousseau . . . he looked at me with a perplexed expression and walked away."[48] For years to come, as his fame grew and he gained control over his time between scenes, especially in the drawn-out downtime of filmmaking, Brando would make sure that he had a private space for reading. As this exchange with Richard Rodgers suggests, he would be an anomaly in the world of theater and film as he had been everywhere else.

Brando was not the only actor who ever read during breaks. What made him exceptional—and the same was true of his

approach to music, women, games, health, and food—was the
energy he devoted to the pursuit. He had learned the lessons of
Stella Adler and the New School in general: An actor's work is
only as good as his mind. So he dedicated himself to intellectual
development. A few trends are conspicuous in his reading from
this period. One was the emphasis on the classics in philosophy,
history, and literature, some of them recommended by teachers or
others he respected. The Gahan family fascination with Eastern
religion and philosophy was also an influence, and his reading
in those fields included works by the Indian spiritualist Krishnamurti. He read the Christian Bible as well, wondering in a letter to his Grandmother Bess, "It is full of beautiful thoughts but
they don't mean much to me. Nana, why do they tell you to fear
God?"[49] Finally, there were works of drama and also dramatic
theory (including some by Stanislavski), a subject he explored
more at this point than at any other time in his life.

Brando reading Krishnamurti in front of a church. © Bettmann/Corbis.

THE EARLY THEATER WORK

Harold Clurman was reluctant to hire Stella's star pupil for a pivotal role in *Truckline Café*, the Maxwell Anderson play he was directing (and producing with Elia Kazan) that was scheduled to open in February 1946. He went to see Brando in *I Remember Mama* and admired the performance, but he remained skeptical because the role of Nels was so different from that of Sage McRae, the depressed and ultimately murderous GI of *Truckline Café*. He finally capitulated, as was his custom when Stella had a strong desire. It turned out to be a good decision. Though *Truckline Café* flopped when it opened on Broadway on February 17 and closed after a nine-day run, Brando won the Donaldson Award for Best Supporting Actor and Clurman was credited with releasing the formidable emotional power of the fledgling actor.[50]

How Clurman did this has become a subject of theater lore. Parts came slowly to Brando; this was as true of him at the end of his career as it was at the beginning. There was no doubt of latent talent, and Clurman recalled Brando's work in the initial rehearsals as arresting. But the young actor seemed unwilling to unleash the deep well of feeling the director believed was there. It was "a volcanic part," Brando remembered, leading to "an explosive, incandescent moment in the play when Sage admits shooting his wife and then breaks down." After Clurman tried everything, including affective-memory exercises that did not help, he followed his instincts. Dismissing the rest of the cast, he commanded Brando to shout his lines. Clurman made Brando do this several times, directing him to increase his volume each time. Brando began to get exhausted and then enraged. Finally Clurman had Brando climb a stage rope while shouting his lines. When he came down, he looked mad enough to hit the director. But something had happened to Brando; in the remaining rehearsals, Brando reached ever deeper into the part. Clurman would remember: "On opening night—and every night thereafter—his performance was greeted by one of the most thunderous ovations I have heard for an actor in the theatre."[51]

Anderson's play was criticized for the size of its cast (reviewers thought it so unwieldy that they commended the director for keeping everyone from colliding) and their long-winded speeches, but Brando made much of his brief time on stage as a haunted, deranged, teeth-chattering fugitive. He prepared for the scene by having himself drenched with cold water and running up and down the stairs backstage. He hollowed himself out, his body gaunt, perfecting a slouch and a withdrawn, almost catatonic mumble that was nevertheless entirely audible when he sat center stage and explained to the waitress why he had killed his wife. When he finally broke down, he was standing again, and Anne Jackson, later an accomplished actress in her own right, recalled how Brando captured the character's pain by crumpling himself into a childlike posture, turning his feet inward and hunching his shoulders as he began to cry.[52] Equally striking was the actor's decision to include a skip in his step as he walked off, handcuffed beside the gun-toting posse, as if McRae were joyously embracing the prospect of death. Though some reviewers overlooked the performance, theater devotees who were there did not forget it.[53]

Brando's success in *Truckline Café* gave him options. He next appeared on Broadway with Katharine Cornell, the prestigious stage actress, in George Bernard Shaw's *Candida*, directed and produced by her husband, Guthrie McClintic. Brando played the young poet Eugene Marchbanks, who falls in love with the beautiful, aging wife of a clergyman. Brando demonstrated range in moving from Anderson's harsh naturalism to Shaw's drawing-room drama, though his distinctive interpretation of Marchbanks was at odds with the rather staid Cornell. Brando described it as two people "dancing to a different beat," constantly struggling to get in step. Contemporary reviewers didn't seem to mind the dissonance and admired both performances. One observed, "If there isn't any Marchbanks, there isn't any play at all, and the latter is one of the toughest roles in the theater. The asinine, 18-year-old introvert can be too effeminate or too loudly positive. " Brando, he concluded, achieves "a balance that makes for a better understanding of the lovesick young nuisance than has been scaled by most of his predecessors."[54]

Brando embraced the unpredictability of the character, breaking the monotony of the stylized farce. He managed to inject conviction and humor into lines like the following: "All the love in the world is longing to speak; only it dare not, because it is shy, shy, shy."[55] But he also found qualities with which he could identify. Marchbanks's neglect and loneliness as a child, and his overwhelming sensitivity to cruelty, spoke to Brando, whose ability to empathize, to invest his "asinine . . . introvert" with a complex humanity was confirmed by the reactions of theatergoers. Despite the fact that the rest of the company consisted of beloved veterans, Brando regularly received the most applause at the end of the play.[56]

Brando's encounter with another leading lady of Broadway, Tallulah Bankhead, was less successful. A connection between Brando's agent, Edith Van Cleve, and Bankhead provided his entrée. Hired to play the part of Stanislas, Bankhead's young lover in Jean Cocteau's *The Eagle Has Two Heads*, Brando found himself in the position of prey, confronting the charged libido of a fragile older actress fearful of losing her beauty. Brando never felt comfortable in the role. He was dissatisfied with the accent he assumed, troubled by Bankhead's strident political conservatism, and most of all troubled by her sexual demands on him. He was relieved to be fired after six weeks of out-of-town trials.

Brando took advantage of other Manhattan opportunities;

perhaps the most enduring was a course on makeup at the New School for Social Research. Given his avowed descent from the Russian and Yiddish theaters, where actors were skilled in makeup techniques, it is not surprising that Brando was engaged with makeup, unlike almost all American-born actors. Russian actors were expert in developing external features, which they believed made their characterizations more vivid. The two Yiddish Theatre actors most adept with makeup, Jacob Adler and Paul Muni, had honed their skills among the Russians. Adler recalled admiringly how they could rebuild themselves, "like sculptors."[57] Brando did his own makeup for years, viewing it as integral to creating a role. Photographs on sets, from *The Teahouse of the August Moon*, *On the Waterfront*, and *The Chase*, for instance, show him fashioning the eyes of his Okinawan interpreter and the bloody faces, in turn, of Terry Malloy and Sheriff Calder. In a letter to the producer of his 1989 movie *The Freshman*, Brando refers to his "complete course in makeup" at the New School, which was enhanced by "the best make-up men at all the studios." Thus, Brando knew just how to "put on the

Applying makeup for *Teahouse* with Glenn Ford looking on. © Underwood & Underwood/Corbis.

Applying bloody makeup in *Waterfront*. Columbia Pictures/Photofest.

scar tissue above my eyes, layer by layer in hot wax in *On the Waterfront*."[58]

Brando's autobiography, *Songs My Mother Taught Me*, features a collection of photographs from a series of films, all displaying the specific characteristics he adapted for each role. They range from the 1950s—Mark Antony, Napoleon, the biker of *Wild One*, the Nazi officer of *Young Lions*—to the later roles of Don Vito Corleone and the South African lawyer of *A Dry White*

The Ugly American with mustache and cigar. © 1963
Universal Pictures, courtesy of Universal Studios Licensing LLC.

Season. Each frame reveals how carefully Brando envisioned the physiognomies, facial musculature, gestures, and accessories of his film personae.[59] He understood the function of a mustache: pencil-thin, it registered tradition and age; more flourishing, it trumpeted sexual energy or sometimes buffoonery.[60] The first mustache he wore for a fictitious character was in the role of Ambassador MacWhite in the 1962 film *The Ugly American*, where he played a man whose authority and self-importance seemed to require both a respectably narrow mustache and a big expensive cigar. Brando knew that people adjusted themselves to the clothes they put on in the morning, to the ways they enhanced themselves with accessories or made up their face with foundation, concealer, and blush.

A FLAG IS BORN

Brando was much too young to have met Jacob Adler, but when the chance arose to appear on stage with Paul Muni, he seized it. Working with Muni meant working with an old Yiddish Theatre master, and Brando did not squander the opportunity. He called Muni's scenes in *A Flag Is Born*—a play by Ben Hecht about the founding of Israel in which Brando played a young Holocaust survivor—the best acting he ever saw. "His performance was magical and affected me deeply. He was the only actor who ever moved me to leave my dressing room to watch him from the wings."[61] When the pair met at rehearsals for *Flag* in the summer of 1946, Muni was fifty-one and had played more than three hundred roles in the Yiddish Theatre before his Broadway debut—a nonspeaking part in *We Americans*. Muni stole the show as an old man in the October 1926 production, and one critic demanded to know how an aged actor of such talent could have been ignored for so long. Over the next decade, Muni kept a Broadway career alive through commercial and critical successes in *Counselor-at-Law* (1932) and *Key Largo* (1939), while starring in a series of well-regarded films, including *Scarface* (1932); *I Am a Fugitive from a Chain Gang* (1932); *Bordertown* (1935); *The Story of Louis Pasteur* (1936), which earned him an Oscar; *The Good Earth* (1937); *The Life of Emile Zola* (1937); and *Juarez* (1939).

Muni's personality and instincts seemed designed to charm a thoughtful individualist like Brando. Muni was committed to the complexity of human nature. "No villain ever thinks of himself as a villain, just as no hero can be all-hero.... Let a small light show through. Remember, he is a human being, and even a monster has a soul!" He teased interviewers, saying he disdained acting. It wasn't a job for a grown man, he insisted, and he would have preferred being a shoe salesman. And he often turned down lucrative offers for roles he considered beneath him because they were tawdry or melodramatic.[62] Muni, like Jacob Adler, regretted missing a formal education, and even though he read voluminously, he feared being exposed as "a blithering idiot." He shied away from Shakespeare, whose work he revered, because he believed mastering the language required a lifetime of study.[63] Like Adler and Brando, Muni was exceptional among actors, in that he had star power but remained throughout his career preoccupied with characterization, challenging himself with every new role, seeking a range of cultural experiences in selecting theater and film projects.

A miserable GI who avenges himself on an adulterous wife in a bleak postwar melodrama, a foppish poet in a comedy of manners, a Holocaust survivor in an unqualified polemic: the scope of Brando's first three major theatrical roles foreshadowed the greatness to come. The magnitude of Brando's acting, and his ability to persuade people that he *was* the persona he had assumed, was nowhere more powerfully evident than in *A Flag Is Born*, because of the play's subject matter and the guilt it inevitably aroused.

Brando's experience in *Flag* provides a fitting culmination to the story of his theatrical apprenticeship, because it brings together so many of its elements. The play was directed by Luther Adler, Stella's brother and the Adler clan member with the most prolonged career on Broadway and in Hollywood. The only project on which Brando worked with Yiddish Theatre actors, it featured Luther's half sister Celia in addition to Muni. *Flag* also featured a former Group Theatre actor in Luther Adler and composer in Kurt Weill, who wrote its original score. The immediacy of *Flag*'s subject matter was consistent with The Group's commitment to drama that addressed the times.

But the most significant aspect of *A Flag Is Born* was that it appealed to Brando's social conscience: his desire to help Jews in particular and the oppressed in general. Brando was one of two non-Jews with leading roles. The other was Quentin Reynolds, a prominent war correspondent who took the role of narrator. The cast and company worked for little or nothing in solidarity with the play's Zionist cause, and playwright Ben Hecht solicited funds for Israel from the audience after every performance. "Give us your money," he declared, "and we will turn it into history."[64] Scheduled for a four-week run at the Alvin Theatre, the play generated so much enthusiasm that it was extended to twelve.

Since 1941, Hecht had been working with a group of Palestinian Zionists to persuade the American government and the American Jewish leadership to help European Jews escape the advancing German army—with money, political asylum, and even weapons. They became known as the Bergson Group after their leading member, Peter Bergson, the Zionist activist, published editorials and advertisements in major papers. Among the most visible was Hecht's sardonic "Ballad of the Doomed Jews," which appeared in the *New York Times* on September 14, 1943, and exposed the world's indifference to the fate of the Jewish people. The Bergson Group also sponsored a 1943 pageant, *We Will Never Die*, celebrating Jewish contributions to civilization over the centuries. Starring Paul Muni and Edward G. Robinson, it opened to a packed Madison Square Garden and filled equally vast venues (including Chicago Stadium and LA's Hollywood Bowl) across the country.

A result of these efforts was President Franklin Roosevelt's 1944 founding of the War Refugee Board, which helped save the lives of 200,000 European Jews. By 1945, the Bergson Group, renamed the American League for a Free Palestine, had turned its attention to Holocaust survivors. And this was where the talents of Ben Hecht became especially useful. Hecht confessed in his autobiography that he had been oblivious to his heritage until the German mass murder raised it to the surface.[65] The son of Russian Jewish immigrants in Chicago, he worked his way up as a muckraking journalist and then turned to playwriting. By 1928, Hecht had won a Pulitzer Prize for a Broadway hit, *The Front Page*, coauthored with Charles MacArthur, which would be turned into the classic film *His Girl Friday* (1940). He became a Hollywood screenwriter in the 1930s, winning two Academy Awards, one for the screenplay of *Scarface*, starring Paul Muni.[66]

A Flag Is Born was the work of a believer: Hecht was determined to stage the facts of the unparalleled horror perpetrated upon European Jewry and hopeful that a play could carry an unambiguous political message while retaining its capacity to enlighten and entertain. Moreover, he felt American Jews needed to mourn the demise of their brethren and atone for their passivity in the face of it. What better forum than theater for this collective expression of grief and atonement? Hecht's confrontational purposes are clear from the prologue: "Of all the things that happened in that time—our time—the slaughter of the Jews of Europe was the only thing that counted forever in the annals of man. The proud orations of heroes and conquerors will be a footnote in history beside the great silence that watched this slaughter."[67]

The play is set in a European graveyard where three survivors of Treblinka gather. Paul Muni played Tevya, an old inhabitant of the shtetl; Celia Adler was his wife, Zelda; and Brando, a cynical youth named David, was convinced that "the dead and the living have the same ears for the Jew—dead ears." The still-devout elderly couple convenes a modest Shabbat ceremony on the cemetery grounds. When Tevya calls upon the kings of ancient Israel for guidance, a cavalcade of Jewish history is brought to life behind him—a splendid synagogue service in Tevya's native village (Berini as cantor is accompanied by an eight-man choir) and biblical scenes of Saul and David in Solomon's temple.

The political heart of Hecht's play, and the key to its successful fundraising, was the analogy between the struggle for a Jewish homeland in Palestine and the American Revolution. This was a mainstay of Bergson Group rhetoric: Their ads and pamphlets characterized the members of the Zionist Irgun militia as "modern-day Nathan Hales" and declared, "It's 1776 in

Original program for *A Flag Is Born*. The Newberry Library, Chicago.

Palestine." Attempting to convince a world court of his people's rights, Muni's Tevya draws on the same analogy. The red, white, and blue theater program reinforced the claim, by picturing a trio of American revolutionary figures above an image of Palestinian Jews with gun, hoe, and flag, as did the play's sponsoring committee, featuring First Lady Eleanor Roosevelt and other prominent Americans.

Hecht's strategy of sanctioning Jewish insurgent violence in Palestine by way of America's original insurgents contained a subtler message for American Jews. Identification with the doomed Jews of Europe had required an admission of vulnerability, even self-imperilment. Identification with the Palestinian freedom fighters meant alignment with American power. The money the play raised through donations and ticket sales, close to a million dollars by some estimates, confirmed Hecht's shrewd appraisal of the postwar Jewish situation.[68]

That situation was of lifelong interest to Marlon Brando, who had grown up identifying with suffering. When he began meeting Jews in the theater world and intelligentsia, he encountered a people that had prevailed over centuries of persecution. Though he would not be loyal to the Jewish—or any—women with whom he slept over the years, his love affair with the Jewish people endured. That attitude has sometimes been misunderstood. He read widely about Jews and their history for much of his life, and sometimes he spoke as if he were "a member of the tribe." Brando's collection of books on Jewish subjects, which ranged from philosophical works by Martin Buber and Gershom Scholem to popular histories and studies of Yiddish humor, was surpassed only by his collection of books on American Indians.[69] While it was acceptable for Jews such as Neal Gabler (Brando owned multiple copies of Gabler's *An Empire of Their Own: How the Jews Invented Hollywood*) to discuss the "power of Jews" in the film industry, such statements were forbidden from a Gentile like Brando. He was roundly criticized for such comments and forced to apologize publicly, though Jewish friends came to his defense.[70]

Anyone who knew Brando, or heard him discourse at length about Jews, was convinced of his sympathy, admiration, and extensive knowledge of Jews and their history. Like a religious convert, he knew more about Jewish history than many born into the faith. Noting the great diversity of Diaspora Jewry, and the high rates of intermarriage, he concluded that Jewish achievements were based in culture rather than genes. In taped conversations for his autobiography, Brando spoke about his early experiences with Jews in Manhattan and his convictions drawn from reading about their history.

> They gave me a sense of education and of the value of education. If anything is Talmudic, it is the regard for learning. And for years and years and years I was puzzled by the

extraordinary accomplishments of Jews. And I thought of all these theories it must be a genetic feature... but then that didn't work because after the Diaspora the Ashkenazi Jews physically were much different, and the Sefardic Jews that didn't joint the Diaspora, that stayed in Palestine, looked different.... The only thing that survived intact from the earliest of times, certainly after the Diaspora, was the Jewish religion and the regards for the Torah and Talmudic thought. It changed from place to place, before you didn't have much variation in Jewish thought, certainly there were sects early on, but they didn't vary as much as the Conservative and Reform groups of Jews do today, but nevertheless there's enough left. If you have to say who were the most intellectual people in the last two hundred years, you'd have to say it was Einstein, Freud, and for better or worse, Marx. In every form, in art, in science, in jurisprudence, in commerce, an extraordinary influence. I think the Jews have been improperly criticized. I think that they should be criticized as every people are criticized.... Because of the suffering, extraordinary, incomprehensible that the Jews have gone through, you forget that the Jews are also human and that they also have done the very things that have been done to them. And this entire business of hanging onto conquered territories at any price, I think is crazy. And you have Jewish fanatics that are all the equal of any Palestinian fanatic groups, and like all people they say they're doing it in defense of this cause. The cause is to ensure the fact that what happened in Germany will never happen again, and you can't blame them for that. If they were going to kill people of Irish extraction and they set about to do it, and I survived, you can be sure I'd be a fanatic, especially if they killed my family.

Brando rejects the notion that "Zionism is equivalent with racism," referring to a 1975 meeting he had with Hollywood producer Dore Schary and others committed to Israel, including Senator

Jacob Javits and Nobel Prize–winning author and Holocaust survivor Elie Wiesel, to discuss the prospects for an Anti-Genocide Bill.[71] Brando confessed: "If I were a Jew in Palestine having lost my family, who knows what I would think. Who knows what I would think if I were a Palestinian who had their house blown up because one of their children had behaved in a militant fashion toward what they believed to be the enemy. . . . It's very hard to explain to the Palestinians that the Jews have the right to be someplace, that this is their homeland. It's just as difficult as it is to explain to Americans that the Indians want their land back. There would be blood in the streets." Still, "there are many Jews who believe that all this conflict should come to an end. There are many Palestinians who are willing to recognize the rights of the Jews to live. And there are many Jews who want, more than we recognize, to give the land back."[72]

In his account of *A Flag Is Born*, Brando calls it the starting point of his "journey to try to understand the human impulse that makes it not only possible but easy for one group of people to single out another and try to destroy it."[73] He could not have had a better vehicle for this initiation than the character of David, nor a better cohort to explore it with than Celia and Luther Adler and Paul Muni. Those present at rehearsals agreed that, in the role of Tevya, Muni was preparing one of the great performances of his career. But Brando's usual restraint worried everyone prior to the opening. In order to reassure the cast, Muni in particular, Luther Adler challenged the young actor. "Marlon uncorked," Adler recalled, and "was incredible: flash, violence, electricity. My sister Celia has owl eyes, but when she opens them in astonishment, they're like saucers. When Marlon started to perform, Celia's eyes became soup bowls. Muni turned scarlet; his lips began to tremble; then he got a kind of foolish grin of approval on his face." Muni retained his admiration for Brando, later marveling, "How the hell can an actor like that come from Omaha, Nebraska?"[74]

A Flag Is Born with Paul Muni and Celia Adler. Eileen Darby/Time & Life Pictures/ Getty Images.

Brando's point of entry was a second-act speech, delivered under glaring spotlights, directly to the audience. "Where were you—Jews? Where were you when the killing was going on? When the six million were burned and buried alive in the lime pits, where were you? Where was your voice crying out against the slaughter? We didn't hear any voice. There was no voice. You,

Jews of America! You, Jews of England! Strong Jews, rich Jews, high-up Jews...you were ashamed to cry as Jews! A curse on your silence! That frightened silence of Jews that made the Germans laugh as they slaughtered. You with your Jewish hearts hidden under your American boots. You with your Jewish hearts hidden behind English accents.... And now, now you speak a little. Your hearts squeak—and you have a dollar for the Jews of Europe. Thank you. Thank you!" With this role, according to a reviewer, "Marlon Brando adds another notch to his performance gun," and the result for those in attendance was explosive.[75] At one performance, a distressed woman shouted back at Brando's David in a heavy Yiddish accent: "Vere ver yu!?"[76]

Both the guilt and the outrage were feelings with which Brando could empathize. He expressed outrage in letters over the British maltreatment of the Jews in displaced-persons camps—barred from entering Palestine and imprisoned behind barbed wire in Cyprus. He expressed guilt in noting the hypocrisy of American racism against blacks he witnessed while helping raise money in DC for the American League for a Free Palestine. Nor, as his remarks above show, was the subsequent Israeli injustice toward Palestinian Arabs lost on him years later. Through all of these experiences, he took his role as a citizen seriously, in the complex terms outlined by Hannah Arendt: active where his conscience demanded but aware that every political action had inadvertent consequences.

For this reason, Brando was never a radical, no matter how independent his thinking. Still, even at this early point in his career, his appetite for good works was palpable—as was, relatedly, his sense of the limits of acting. Of his cross-country fundraising for the American League, he wrote his parents: "It is a tougher and vastly more responsible job than anything the theater could offer.... I'm really stimulated more than I've ever been."[77] For the rest of his life, Brando would strive to balance his devotion to humanitarian causes with the demands of his calling, selecting roles and film projects based on their capacity to reconcile these aims. Such selectivity required a fame that he could never have imagined was so close.

In 1946, all paths led to *Streetcar*, no matter how meandering Brando's steps toward that destiny. Elia Kazan describes how he gave the young actor twenty dollars for bus fare to Province-town, so he could audition for the play's author, Tennessee Wil-liams. It took Brando three days to get there because he used the money to eat and then hitchhiked to Cape Cod. When he finally arrived, Williams's reaction to Brando's reading for the part of Stanley Kowalski was "ecstatic," his "voice near hysteria," as he described it by phone to Kazan. Brando's odyssey of acting fame and fortune had begun.[78] Though he quibbled ever after about how much he had wanted these things, no one who saw his Broadway performance in *Streetcar* could doubt the presence of burning desire.

CHAPTER THREE

BUILDING THE REPERTOIRE

B rando's breakthrough theatrical performance under Elia Kazan in *A Streetcar Named Desire* provided the foundations for the Brando hero of 1950s film: the erotic masculinity qualified by vulnerability; the lyrical brooder whose face and gestures made silence eloquent; and the protagonist who becomes a victim or cultural sacrifice. During that decade, Brando built a body of work that set the standard for acting, while helping to codify a series of cultural transformations that have become commonplace. The sensitive male type, which evolved over the next few decades, originated, at least partly, in Brando's revolutionary portraits of men. Furthermore, Brando advanced a broad humanitarianism: adopting various ethnic identities, pioneering the discussion of racial intermarriage in *Sayonara*, and insisting on humanizing his Nazi character in *The Young Lions*. From the start of his stage and film career, Brando's artistic ambitions and his idealism were inseparable, but it all started with *Streetcar*.

STREETCAR ON BROADWAY

Out for an evening to see Montgomery Clift in a Chekhov play, Marlon Brando treated his date to a lesson in technique. "Look at that," he said, pointing to Clift slouching on stage, hands in his back pockets—a gesture inappropriate for an upper-class Russian of Chekhov's time.[1] It was May 1954 and Brando had already toppled Clift from his predominance as the young star of American theater and film. Brando was probably there more for his friend Maureen Stapleton, who was playing Masha in this Broadway revival of *The Seagull*. Reading the limitations of a rival, however, must have been sweet from his high position in 1954, with two acclaimed movies directed by Kazan behind him (*A Streetcar Named Desire*, 1951, *Viva Zapata!*, 1952), another on the way (*On the Waterfront*, 1954), and two big performances with different directors that showed his dramatic versatility released the previous year (*Julius Caesar* and *The Wild One*, both 1953). Audiences adored Clift, but they saw something fresh in Brando, even though they couldn't have explained what was so right about his acting. Most people, whether or not they knew anything about acting, believed that Brando's gift was his ability to "be himself" on stage. They were convinced that he profited from roles as rough, inarticulate types because they fit his own personality. Many decades after he had memorialized the *Streetcar* character on stage and screen, Brando complained, "Even today I meet people who think of me automatically as a tough, insensitive, coarse guy named Stanley Kowalski."[2]

When Brando arrived in Manhattan in 1944, Montgomery Clift had been on Broadway for more than a decade and had recently established himself as a star through a leading role in Lillian Hellman's 1944 play *The Searching Wind*. Though he was largely untrained, Clift relied on sound intuitions and had done good work under directors as different as Alfred Lunt (*There Shall Be No Night*, 1940) and Elia Kazan (*The Skin of Our Teeth*, 1942). Clift could convey emotions with a naturalness that was rare in conventional male acting. He specialized in vulnerable adolescent men who were boys to their maternal lovers—his romantic interest in *A Place in the Sun* (1951), played by Elizabeth Taylor, refers to herself as "Mama"—troubled men, always longing for more than they could have.

Clift's ease on stage and screen was critical to his appeal, but there was little variation from role to role. Brando's debut in *Streetcar* on December 3, 1947, altered the map, radicalizing prevailing notions of what actors could convey in theater. Recalling his reaction to a preview performance in New Haven, playwright Arthur Miller characterized Brando as "a tiger on the loose, a sexual terrorist. Nobody had seen anything like him before because that kind of freedom on the stage had not existed before."[3]

What such a perspective missed was Brando's knowledge of technique. Combining research and reading with his own powers of imagination, he created his characters—specific accents, gestures, gaits for all of them—from a profound understanding and conceptualization of their environments. He seems to have viewed human beings as vast and heterogeneous. His genius was his ability to *access* so much of this variety, to locate *within himself* the makings for different roles. When he took the stage or entered a film set as Eugene Marchbanks or Terry Malloy, Brando knew his character from infancy to the grave. He knew how the man presented himself to the world, in repose and in anger; how he stood, lounged, walked; whether he touched others when he greeted or spoke to them; whether he arched his brows pompously or apologized for himself with perpetually downcast eyes. Brando understood people's expressions as combining the instinctive and the learned. From childhood, he recognized them as specific to the various stations people occupied even in a democratic society—farmhand, salesman, banker, secretary—inculcated by parents, teachers, religious authorities through apprenticeship, professionalization, and, above all, through imitation. The ways people revealed themselves in the smallest movements fascinated Brando. By the time he had signed on to appear in Tennessee Williams's play *A Streetcar Named Desire* under the direction of Elia Kazan, they had become a staple of his vocation.[4]

Brando's habits of observation gave him a valuable repository of the human theater, which, together with his powerful imagination, proved highly conducive to his work. From Stella Adler's classes he learned a disciplined approach to what he needed for a role, just as his Stanley Kowalski performance would gain immeasurably from Elia Kazan's direction. Kazan was Brando's ideal director, because he, like Stella Adler, sanctioned his instincts. "When you start giving too much direction to an actor like Brando, you are likely to throw him off the track he's instinctively found," Kazan commented. "Sometimes the best direction consists of reading an actor's face and, when you see the right thing there, simply nodding to him.... Then wait for a miracle. With Marlon, it often happened."[5]

Brando was only twenty-three when rehearsals began for *Streetcar* in the fall of 1947, but he was sufficiently well read to recognize Williams's new play as destined for classic status. "We had under us one of the best-written plays ever produced, and we couldn't miss," Brando noted in appreciation of the playwright's sensual poetry and dark humor.[6] The play's modernity was equally hospitable to him, particularly what we would now term its "multiculturalism," which was reflected in the jazz score and the racially mixed cast. "In this part of New Orleans you are practically always just around the corner, or a few doors down the street, from a tinny piano being played with the infatuated fluency of brown fingers," Williams writes, sketching the neighborhood of the Kowalskis. Typical of "a cosmopolitan city," there is "a relatively warm and easy intermingling of races." What made the language of *Streetcar* unique was that it combined Southern gentility and working-class dialects with an up-to-date urban colloquialism. When Blanche DuBois, for instance, inquires of the poker-playing quartet in scene 3, "Could I kibitz?" she may be the first Southerner in American literature to invoke Yiddish slang. Stanley's cold reply, "You could not," demonstrates that he too, like the actor who memorialized him, was familiar with the *"mama loshen."*[7]

While Stanley is undeniably coarse from his first moment on stage, "bellowing" at Stella as he tosses her a "red-stained package" of freshly butchered meat, Williams and Kazan infuse the couple's every word and gesture with joyous passion.[8] This makes the arrival of Stella's sister Blanche, at once needy and censorious (surveying her sister's cramped, dingy living quarters), an unmistakable intrusion. As the visiting relative who overstays her welcome, Blanche is compromised from start to finish, which is true of all the major protagonists. "There are no 'good' or 'bad' people," the playwright explained in the spring of 1947. "Some are a little better or a little worse but all are activated more by misunderstanding than malice. A blindness to what is going on in each other's hearts."[9]

Williams worried that actors might be tempted to interpret Stanley Kowalski as "a black-dyed villain," but with Brando he had little to fear. The actor was preoccupied with human ambiguity. Williams's diagnosis of his play's collective social pathology would have made sense to him: "Nobody sees anybody truly, but only through the flaws of their own ego. That is the way we all see each other in life."[10] Brando was an intriguing case of a leading man with a powerful attraction to villains; he played many of them over a nearly sixty-year career, and always with great complexity. (The only exception was Brando's 1979 television cameo as George Lincoln Rockwell, head of the American Nazi Party, in Alex Haley's *Roots*.)[11] He recognized the charisma of those who wielded power or desired it, and the helpless attraction of audiences to such figures. And because he believed that no one, with the possible exception of a Rockwell, was wholly good or bad, he never accepted the dehumanization of villains. If a character were scripted that way, Brando would complicate him, injecting a transformative humor and nuance.

This had nothing to do with the usual explanation for such revisions: that Brando was a typical star with a need to be heroic and admired by audiences. It was rather that he sought the deepest authenticity of character and insisted on educating his audiences, encouraging them to grapple with a work.[12] He wanted people to come to terms with their own propensities for aggression, their own fascination with power.

Nothing interested Brando more, if his book collection is any indication, than the spectacle of seemingly decent people subscribing to evil systems. (Next to his bed was a copy of Eric Hoffer's 1951 study of the mass psychology of fascism, *The True Believer*.) How did groups become hordes? What made some nations reject totalitarian ideas and others embrace them? "During the McCarthy era, everyone believed the propaganda about the evil of Communism," Brando noted, and "overlooked the evil of Joe McCarthy, and we were very lucky not to have fascism sweep through the country," which might have been the case "had it not been for my particular heroes Ed Murrow [Edward R. Murrow] and then some minor heroes like Izzy [I. F.] Stone [the investigative reporter]."[13] What seems to have disturbed Brando most was mindlessness, and he struggled against the role of the film industry in furthering it. In his favorite quotation book, *The Great Thoughts*, Brando highlights these phrases from Hannah Arendt: "Unthinking men are like sleepwalkers," and "The sad truth is that most evil is done by people who never make up their minds to be either good or evil." He believed that people could not abnegate responsibility toward society. Morality did not allow for opting out, and it necessitated education in a democracy. He also accepted Henry Ward Beecher's warning, highlighted in the same book: "The ignorant classes are the dangerous classes. Ignorance is the womb of monsters."[14]

In drama and in life, Brando was drawn to ethical dilemmas, dramatic situations that prevented effortless affinities and solutions. Thus, some reviewers, including Brando's mother, criticized him for investing Kowalski with a magnetism that made it impossible for audiences to despise the character, as they should.[15] But Brando read the play carefully and recognized Williams's empathy for his male lead. Stanley embodies classic masculine traits: ambition, aggression, and the quest for dominance—of females especially. All are portrayed as signs of health: "Animal joy in his being is implicit in all his movements and attitudes. Since earliest manhood the center of his life has been pleasure with women, the giving and taking of it, not with weak indulgence, dependently, but with the power and pride of a richly feathered male bird among hens."[16]

Stanley is a rooster bursting with phallic pride. Williams's surprise at the advantages of having a more youthful actor than he had expected in the part, noting how "it humanizes the character of Stanley," seems a common instance of an author overlooking a deep strain in his work.[17] Kazan was convinced of Williams's attraction "to the Stanleys of the world," and summarized the ultimate point: "You can't get through life without hurting people. The animal survives—at all costs."[18] The Darwinian foundation of Williams's play was a challenge to author, director, and male star alike. Williams, and Brando in particular, identified with Blanche's pain and abhorred Stanley's violence.

Among the most distinctive aspects of Brando's performance was the character's voice (preserved in contemporary recordings of the play and in the 1951 film version): a low snarl at times, occasionally raised to a frightening pitch, it was for the most part soft and modulated by anxiety. The whine perfected by Brando was critical to his reorientation of maleness, for it pinpointed weakness as a motivating factor in Stanley's need to dominate. Brando's carefully crafted voice suggested a man full of sexual confidence yet perpetually fearing its diminution. This is borne out in the play's famous staircase scene, when Stanley hollers for his wife Stella, who has fled their apartment for the flat above, after he has beaten her while in a drunken rage. Highlighting the disparate aspects of human sexuality, Brando conflates the infant's cry for its mother—"out of which the entire verbal universe is spun"—with the brutal mate's demand that his desire be satisfied.[19] Brando, building on Williams's words and Kazan's direction, felt the play was implying that the most powerful sexual feeling draws on various human impulses, especially the most primal ones.

What Brando achieved in this scene—so erotically charged that the ornate ironwork staircase seemed sexually stimulating in its own right—was the fusion of infant and husband. Kim Hunter, who played Stella on stage and screen, reacted to her pealing spouse with a combination of outrage and helpless trancelike attraction, which fortified the interpretation.

Another distinctive aspect of the performance was the way Brando's physique became central to the play. Williams enables this by giving Stanley frequent onstage changes of dress, inevitably during dialogues with Blanche. He swaps a T-shirt sweaty from bowling for a dry one in the first scene, knots his tie as he threatens her with exposure in scene 5, and removes his shirt before heading to the bathroom with his pajamas in scene 10. Brando milks these moments, linking them to Stanley's drive for control, as he makes clear to Blanche that this is *his* territory and he will undress as he pleases. Brando's Stanley is in perpetual motion—bristling, talking, eating, smoking, pushing people, slamming drawers, compulsively oral, and muscle-bound. Arthur Miller's openness about Brando's sexual magnetism would have offended contemporaries, but reviews of the day acknowledged the actor's physicality, using terms such as *lusty, rough and physical*, and *earthy naturalness* to accompany their unvarying superlatives. "It was awful and it was sublime," one director observed. "Only once in a generation do you see such a thing in the theatre."[20]

What seems to have made the brute so irresistible to

theatergoers was the sensitivity that Brando gave him. The complexities of the characterization are preserved in the Warner Brothers film version of the play, which Brando (and Williams) preferred to the Broadway adaptation. Brando thought Vivien Leigh, who replaced Jessica Tandy for the film, was an ideal Blanche, and the opportunity to power out a single performance, albeit over many takes, suited Brando's talents. Still, there are those who remain partial to Brando's Broadway conceptualization to this day, believing the immediacy of what he accomplished there in the flesh, night after night, to be superior to whatever could be done on film.

Stanley Kowalski's ambiguities as Brando imagined them are stunningly revealed in Carl Van Vechten's posed photographs from the long run of *Streetcar*. He has an image of Stanley, probably during scene 4, where Blanche believes she is privately holding forth to Stella about her husband's "sub-human" traits. In beret, leather jacket over his shoulder, a smock on his arm, lifting a curtain, Stanley stares off at something disturbing, revealed by his wrinkled forehead, mismatched eyebrows, and lips (poised to pout or sneer?). The simple knit sweater, splayed shirt collar, and conventional slacks are those of a schoolboy; Stanley is not quite a man, and this must be factored into any judgments about him. The gesture, with the softest part of Brando's open right hand exposed by the curtain edge, is almost childlike. But Stanley's aggression should not be underestimated: His shoulders, enhanced by the black jacket, blend with the dark curtain behind him, creating the effect of raw power. The flared nostrils, broad chest, beard stubble, and above all the complex array of emotions displayed in this single look—self-pity, anger, and obtuseness—expose the potential danger of this man-boy who has hit his wife and will violate his sister-in-law.

When the rape occurs, Blanche has been so discredited by

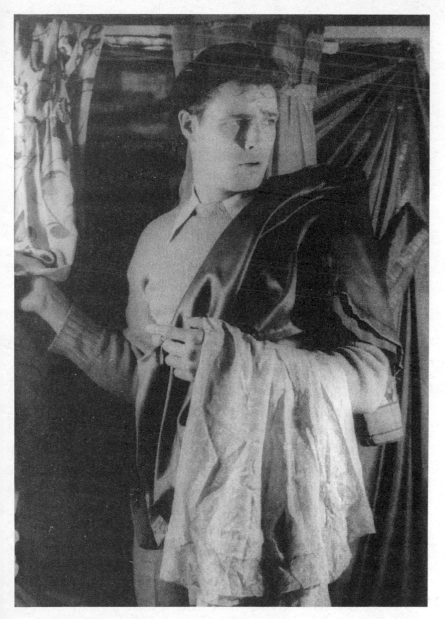

Stanley Kowalski by Carl Van Vechten, 1948. Courtesy of the Van Vechten Trust.

her flirtatiousness and by revelations of promiscuity (with sailors *and* a high-school pupil) that the play's case against him
is hopelessly compromised. There is no American author who
understands more profoundly than Williams the conventional
wisdom that because men and women are socialized *in opposition* to each other, it is to be expected that any given man or
woman will interpret his or her sexual encounter differently.
Williams extends his sympathies to both characters. Blanche is
nervous, on the point of breakdown; Stanley remains the heedless
aggressor whose violation of Blanche is unpremeditated. Stanley
has returned home drunk from celebrating his child's imminent
arrival. Magnanimous, he offers Blanche a drink as he explains
the significance of the silk wedding pajamas he is putting on.
The prospect of sex with his sister-in-law dawns on him gradually as he reads the fearful expectation on her face. "You think
I'll interfere with you?" And then: "Come to think of it—maybe
you wouldn't be bad to—interfere with." The stage direction for
Stanley's speech, "softly," gives the impending violence a hushed
spontaneity, underlined by the following: "What are you putting
on now?...Oh! So you want some roughhouse! All right, let's have
some roughhouse!...We've had this date with each other from
the beginning!"[21] He believes Blanche's resistance is the classic
tease, the not-so-prim schoolteacher playing hard to get. Stanley
(who would have been declared innocent by any court of law in
the land at that time) is the healthy man-boy justified in refusing
to take no for an answer.

Brando and Williams's preference for the film version of *Streetcar* had much to do with the ability of the camera to capture emotion. While Williams considered it "a pity" that Brando didn't
perform more on stage, after watching *Last Tango in Paris* he
declared Brando to be "the greatest living actor...greater than
Olivier."[22] Brando knew that an actor's *belief* in his imaginary
creation was the key to his power, and that awareness transferred

readily from stage to screen. "Through his own intense concentration on what he is thinking or doing at each moment," Harold Clurman observed of Brando's theater performance as Stanley, "all our attention focuses on him."[23] Brando grasped, more expertly than any other actor of his time, the camera's potential to exploit that concentration. On film, he said, "The face becomes the stage," and the eyes were the storytellers. An actor's lines were far less important than what he communicated with his eyes.[24]

Members of the National Theater for the Deaf cited Brando as their favorite actor, noting that they always understood exactly what he was expressing, even though they couldn't hear what he said.[25] He conveyed so much of the character's ideas and emotions, over and above words, aware of how film afforded a vocabulary of image, gesture, and look utterly independent of sound. The majority of Brando's revisions on scripts involved cuts: Directors and screenwriters who worked with him confirm his editing out dialogue more often than adding in new lines, as do copies of his personal film scripts. Moreover, Brando rejected the idea that there was a single way to enunciate. *How* an actor *chose* to enunciate a character's lines was critical to the interpretation. "I played many roles in which I didn't mumble a single syllable, but in others I did it because it is the way people speak in ordinary life," Brando observed. "In ordinary life people seldom know exactly what they're going to say when they open their mouths and start to express a thought. They're still thinking, and the fact that they are looking for words shows on their faces."

The fundamental wisdom of Hamlet's advice to the players, which Brando quoted at length in a chapter on acting in his autobiography, applied to stage and screen: "Suit the action to the word, the word to the action; with this special observance, that you o'erstep not the modesty of nature."[26] Brando's sense of truth in acting was generally unerring, and the only two people he encountered in his career whose discernment he trusted as much as his own were Stella Adler and Elia Kazan. Although Lee Strasberg liked to claim him as a product of his Actors Studio, Strasberg was never Brando's teacher, and Brando could be quite caustic on the subject, probably because no amount of disavowing Strasberg's influence seemed to stick. The term *method* "makes me curdle with irritation," Brando said. "Lee Strasberg is someone I have no respect for. He'd claim credit for *The New York Times* and the Moon if he could."[27] Brando's relationship to the Actors Studio was completely casual; he went there from time to time to meet women, offer tips to other actors, or attend a class taught by Kazan.[28]

On occasion, Brando even gave his own acting lessons, as evidenced by an encounter he had with middleweight boxing champion Rocky Graziano during the Broadway run of *Streetcar*. Graziano tells of seeing a "young bum in blue jeans hanging around" Stillman's Gym, where he trained. One day he asked Brando when he was going to fight. Brando told him that he was an actor, not a fighter, and invited him to his play. When Graziano and his wife went to *Streetcar*, they were amazed to find the unassuming actor in a starring role. A few days later, Brando reappeared at the gym and invited Graziano "to an acting school he's running" in "a crummy old tenement on Ninth Avenue." Brando was preparing for his first (and last until his 1989 cameo in *Roots*) television show, *Come Out Fighting*, in which he played a boxer. Graziano was startled by Brando's performance. "He's playing *me*. Every gesture, every word he says, even the way he fights. . . . It's like looking in the mirror . . . all that time Brando was around the gym he was studying me. And he didn't miss a thing!"[29]

Kazan shared Graziano's admiration for Brando's skills. What made Kazan the best actors' director of the era, a view held by many, was the great respect he had for the craft, an outgrowth of his experience as an actor and with The Group Theatre. He recognized that performances evolve, that several takes are required to get a scene right. He encouraged improvisation, giving his actors freedom and helping them to improve upon their ideas, delighted when their work exceeded his expectations. Like no director Brando worked with before or after, Kazan's "instincts were perfect. Sometimes they were conveyed in just a brief sentence at exactly the right moment, or sometimes he inspired me simply by being there because I trusted his judgment." Kazan included Brando in the list of geniuses he worked with in his lifetime, a group that included Copland and Williams.[30]

In transferring *Streetcar* from stage to screen, Kazan emphasized the prominence of Blanche's subjectivity: "Crawl into her with your camera," he wrote in his notes.[31] By doing so, Kazan put Brando on display as the focus of her anxious, desiring gaze. Blanche, like the gay playwright, in Kazan's interpretation, was helplessly attracted to the person destined to destroy her. In contrast, Stanley and Stella's natural rhythm of desire and satisfaction yields a child, born within a day of Blanche's birthday. Her decayed gentility is replaced by this vigorous new life, identified significantly with his father's Polish-American blood ("maybe... what we need to mix with our blood now that we've lost Belle Reve," Blanche concedes to Stella).[32] Yet sex may be liberating, cleansing even when it's forced, Kazan implies, by juxtaposing Stanley's ravishment of Blanche with an image of a bursting hose, cooling down the street.

The movie version of *Streetcar* allowed Brando to develop nuances from his stage interpretation, enhancing his portrait of Stanley's humor and sensuality. The imitation of a cat screech that Brando improvises in scene 1, and the stroking of Stella's back in scene 7 as he divulges the sordid details of Blanche's past, added depth to a performance that could now be seen in cinemas across the country. Difficulties with the Breen Office, Hollywood's censorship authority, and with the Catholic Church's

Legion of Decency, only whetted the public's appetite. Though
the meddling of censors resulted in cuts and revisions (restored
in the recent director's edition), a wide audience was introduced
to what Stella Adler had seen from the beginning: "a universal
actor" to whom "nothing human was foreign."[33]

THE MEN TO THE WILD ONE

Brando's performance in *Streetcar* was the most famous of his
early work in Hollywood. For his role as Stanley Kowalski,
Brando was nominated for an Academy Award as Best Actor, the
first of four consecutive nominations (for *Viva Zapata!*, *Julius
Caesar*, and *On the Waterfront*). But *Streetcar* was not Brando's
first film, and the one he chose for his introduction to Hollywood
says a great deal about his artistry and individuality.

From the start of his career as a stage actor, Brando disdained
publicity. He exhibited this dislike in various ways, such as in
the tall tales he spun for publicity biographies and interviewers.[34] For someone like Brando, who loved stretching the truth
and testing the gullibility of listeners, the platform granted to
celebrities was initially wondrous, though it quickly grew repug-
nant to him. He could never understand why his opinions were
privileged over those of people with genuine expertise. Brando's critique of publicity, which was catalyzed during his earliest inklings of fame, was never about a sense of superiority, for
he accepted his own cultural commonality. "We are all voyeurs
to one degree or another, including me," Brando conceded, "but
with fame comes the predatory prowl of a carrion press that has
an insatiable appetite for salaciousness and abhors being denied
access to anyone."[35] Brando's efforts to protect his privacy were
often futile, and the more he resisted incursions into his life, the
more avidly, it seemed, he was pursued. The only way to gain

leverage in the exchange with journalists and fans, he decided at a surprisingly young age, was to exploit his fame to publicize causes that concerned him. Similarly, the power he enjoyed in Hollywood from the beginning, as an actor with box-office draw, became a means to promote his values, which were reflected in his choice of film projects. In response to the flood of film offers he received through his New York agent, Edith Van Cleve, after being in *Streetcar*, he instructed her to accept one: Stanley Kramer's *The Men*.[36]

Brando "never had any respect for Hollywood," but he "knew exactly what [he] was doing" when he left the stage for movies. He had no illusions about the Broadway world in which he had triumphed. Though the theater held compensations for actors in the form of sustained rehearsals and camaraderie that arose over months of work, and though there were avenues for the occasional idealistic production like *A Flag Is Born*, commercial considerations reigned as supreme on Broadway as they did in Hollywood. Brando recognized that Hollywood took the impulses of "phoniness" and "greed" to new heights, but it offered much bigger audiences and much higher pay, as well as greater control over his time and choice of vehicles. At the point when Brando arrived in Hollywood, the studio-contract system was breaking down; because of his stature, he could have much greater freedom in selecting roles, enabling him to negotiate one-picture deals instead of long-term commitments.[37]

A careful reader and reviser of scripts, he usually knew what he was getting into when signing onto a picture. The factors that predicted success in most Hollywood ledgers were for him subordinate to other concerns: the subject matter and the challenge and interest of his intended role, the quality of the script, the reputation of the director in handling actors, the setting and what it offered in terms of opportunities for travel or fresh experiences. Brando's first Hollywood film, Stanley Kramer's *The Men*, directed by Fred Zinnemann with a screenplay by Carl Foreman, met all of his criteria. *The Men* was Kramer's third picture, and he was known as a producer willing to address social problems typically avoided in Hollywood. His first, *Champion*, had been an indictment of the violence of boxing; his second, *Home of the Brave*, treated racism in the US Army. *The Men* concerned an even more difficult subject: the plight of paraplegic war veterans, former soldiers with spinal injuries consigned to lifelong paralysis, including sexual dysfunction.

Brando's contractual negotiations with Hollywood proved an accurate forecast of his behavior when he got there; from the outset, he foiled prevailing rituals and expectations. For a community this fresh—only a few decades old—his indifference was more than a slight. Eschewing a hotel, and the grand reception accorded stars, he insisted on living as a guest at his Aunt Betty's modest bungalow in Eagle Rock, California, where his grandmother, Elizabeth Myers, was visiting with her dachshund. He preferred a homelike atmosphere among people he knew and trusted to a posh Beverly Hills hotel the producer had reserved. Theodore Strauss, a *Life* journalist who followed him around on the set of *The Men* reported, "No one has accused him of posing; everyone to whom we've spoken has a sort of confused respect for a man who, up to now, has managed to live as he feels, without caring a hoot what anyone thinks."[38] He was also careless about finances. "Because he rarely looks at money and sometimes pays for a package of cigarettes with a $20 bill, he usually is penniless."[39]

Brando slept every day until noon; when he wasn't working, he "buried himself" in books. According to Strauss, Brando "reads everything, absolutely omnivorous—from Krishnamurti to recent novels." A photograph accompanying Strauss's piece shows Brando searching through a bookcase at his aunt's, where he was likely to have found the religion and philosophy tomes favored by family tastes. Major works of psychology in Brando's collection, by Freud, Jung, and Karen Horney, date from this period. Friends who spent time with Brando in France during the late 1940s and early '50s remember him as extremely interested in psychoanalytic ideas and methods. They recalled too that even then he was talking about the American Indians, possibly from reading up on their history. Brando's close friend Ellen Adler had met Faulkner in Paris around that time, and she may have been responsible for Brando's copy of *Light in August*, though this was not among the books he borrowed, permanently, from her. In his twenties, Brando seems to have read what he believed he needed to know to be educated (Faulkner) or politically responsible (history of the Indians). But he also read with an idealistic resolve to understand himself and others (psychology). He would sometimes confess, in discussing a book, that he saw himself on every page.

Brando brought this same determination to his film work, seeking in-depth knowledge of his subjects. To prepare for *The Men*, he spent a month living among the paraplegics in the Birmingham VA Hospital. Moving into a thirty-two-bed ward, he took up life in a wheelchair, building his upper-body muscles and learning to treat his legs as dead weight. The hospital staff was not informed that Brando was an actor, so this allowed him to blend in with the other patients. He found the community's dark humor—which included using hypodermic needles as water pistols—especially congenial. In one incident, he accompanied a group to a restaurant, the type of outing where the vets endured stares and sometimes overt displays of pity. On this particular evening, a devout Christian serenaded them on the healing powers of Jesus, who could help them walk again if they believed in Him. Brando, seeing a chance to turn the tables, couldn't resist. Hoisting himself slowly to his feet, he took a few stumbling steps and then burst into a jig, shouting, "Hallelujah."[40]

Such antics endeared him to the vets, many of whom, out of

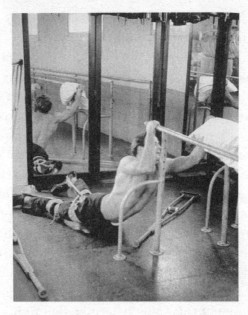

Rehearsing for *The Men*. Ed Clark/Time & Life Pictures/Getty Images.

friendship, agreed to appear in the movie as extras. On his part, Brando was simply overwhelmed by their circumstances. "They were young, virile men," he noted years later, "trapped in inoperative bodies.... Some of the friends I made at Birmingham killed themselves, unable to take it anymore."[41]

All of this intense empathy went into Brando's portrait of Ken Wilocek. A sign of the toll exacted by the film was the lesson it provided in utilizing emotion on screen. Brando had a scene where his character had to admit to himself that his paralysis was permanent and that he would never walk or make love again. He arrived at the studio early, planning to work patiently on creating the right mood, relying on his usual methods, including reading poetry and listening to music. Though the strategies succeeded, Brando's energy crested before the cameras were ready, and he felt drained when he finally played the scene. From that experience, he learned that film actors had to be skilled manipulators of their emotions, protecting them for the cameras, holding the most powerful in check for the close-up. Filmmaking, he understood increasingly, was a highly technical art requiring the utmost in physical and psychological self-control. To succeed in a role, an actor had to know how to keep "simmering all day long, but never boiling over." It was the rare director who was any help to the actor in this regard. The management of emotion was a perilous and lonely enterprise.[42]

Despite Brando's conviction that *The Men* was a learning experience and that he had ruined an important scene, critics responded favorably. This would become a pattern. Brando was his own toughest critic, finding fault in his most celebrated work. Brando's standards, his sense of what might be accomplished in a particular scene, were usually higher than anyone else's. He often believed himself to have fallen short of the possibilities of imagination and communication. It was rare for him to be gratified by his performances or to accept praise from others. Still, he

Brando with Birmingham VA Hospital veterans.
Ed Clark/Time & Life Pictures/Getty Images.

took great interest in their reception: reading letters from fans and often writing thoughtful responses (though this declined over time) and collecting and filing movie reviews, with the help of assistants.[43]

He must have been pleased with the reviews of *The Men*, which, one reviewer asserted, "ranks with the handful of extraordinary movies that do credit not only to their makers but to Hollywood." The review went on to commend the film for resisting miraculous recoveries and keeping its focus on the ordinary courage it took to live with paraplegia. Brando, "in his first movie appearance, does a magnificent job. His halting, mumbled delivery, glowering silences and expert simulation of paraplegia do not suggest acting at all; they look chillingly like the real thing."[44] Brando could never count on critics who recognized inarticulateness as part of his characterization and saw that an actor whose work seemed "like the real thing" had achieved something extraordinary. (That charge would approach absurdity in 1962, when a *Boston Globe* reviewer of *Mutiny on the Bounty* complained about his strained speech in the death scene!)[45]

Viva Zapata! (1952), Brando's third movie, whose production began while *A Streetcar Named Desire* was still in the editing room, was exemplary in this regard. Elia Kazan, the director, and John Steinbeck, who wrote the screenplay, had been discussing for years the idea of a film about the Mexican revolutionary leader Emiliano Zapata. Both had been inspired by the 1934 MGM movie *Viva Villa!* on Pancho Villa, and thought they could interest the producer Darryl Zanuck in the commercial potential of Zapata's storied life. Zanuck had done *The Mark of Zorro* with Tyrone Power and had a fondness for adventure tales with casts of bandits set in exotic places. Zanuck's commitment to *Viva Zapata!* was unsettled by the growing prominence of the House Un-American Activities Committee (HUAC), and Kazan was forced to assuage the producer's worries about its political

Emiliano Zapata. Hulton Archive/Getty Images.

content. The history of a popular Mexican leader who headed a peasant revolt against corporate and imperial usurpers of their land seemed risky in the existing Hollywood atmosphere. Kazan's detailed letter to Zanuck presaged future acts of rationalization and opportunism. Affirming the "strongly, and incontrovertibly anti-Communist" message of this "pro-democratic" film, Kazan enumerated all the reasons why the producer should embrace its subject.[46] The letter accomplished its purpose, securing Zanuck's patronage. While Kazan's case for the "anti-Communist" message was a strident indicator of the lengths to which he would go to promote a project, there was truth in the insistence that Steinbeck's script, and Zapata's ideals in themselves, were compatible with democracy.

At this point in his relationship with Kazan, Brando had no reason to distrust the director's political integrity. That would come later, with his quandary over appearing in *On the Water-front* after Kazan fingered "Communists" at a HUAC hearing. In *Viva Zapata!*, Brando saw an opportunity to work with his favorite director on a screenplay by a major American writer. Among the few subjects Brando had taken to at Shattuck was Latin American history. *Viva Zapata!* gave him the chance to explore Mexico and immerse himself in one of its most dramatic political episodes. He pored over painted and photographic portraits and read every book he could find about the revolutionary hero who so distrusted power.

One of the books Brando bought was *Mexico South: The Isthmus of Tehuantepec* (1947), a classic study of the Indians of Zapata's region by Mexican artist and ethnologist Miguel Covarrubias. Zapata was part Indian himself, as were most Mexicans, and the book detailed every aspect of this world—from music, art, language, courtship rituals, and religious customs to industries, politics, and methods of warfare.[47] Brando would have been intrigued by Covarrubias's portrait of peoples resistant to colonization who were converted to Catholicism "at the point of a sword," their religion displaying "the usual compromise between Indian worship and Catholic superstition." And he would have appreciated the gloomy conclusion about the threat of Fascism throughout Latin America, given "a docile and serviceable lower class of pious, ignorant, and contented peasants ruled by that privileged triumvirate: the Church, the Military, and the Landlord." Had Brando and Covarrubias ever met, their overlapping interests would have yielded stunning conversation. Covarrubias was a jazz devotee who did famous caricatures of the Harlem Jazz scene; he befriended John Huston while the future director was traveling in Mexico and illustrated the play Huston wrote during these travels, *Frankie and Johnny* (1930). Like Brando, Covarrubias was a world traveler whose fascination with Southeast Asia resulted in the book *Island of Bali* (1936); his experience of New

York's modern dance scene and marriage to an American dancer led to the establishment of the first Academy of Dance in Mexico City in 1950. *Mexico South* was hailed as visual ethnography, but it was probably mere coincidence that Brando's character in his own visual ethnography, *One-Eyed Jacks*, was called Chamaco, or "Kid"—Covarrubias's nickname until his death in 1957.[48]

The political and aesthetic features of *Mexico South*, its interest in the peasantry's democratic potential and in the popular arts of indigenous Indian cultures, was compatible with the other book that Brando read in preparation for *Viva Zapata!* As a prelude to the film's screenplay, Steinbeck had written an account of Zapata and the long prehistory of conquest that formed the backdrop to his life. He was a great admirer of Zapata, inspired by his loyalty to common soldiers and fearlessness in battle as well as his exemplary defense of the individual against the opposing forces of Communism and Fascism. While acknowledging Zapata's violence, Steinbeck insisted that he was no crueler than his enemies, and he accepted the myth of his legendary endurance—"He is still alive and still a force." Steinbeck was convinced that Zapata would eventually be recognized as his nation's greatest leader, enjoying "a parallel position to the Virgin of Guadalupe, as the human patron of the freedom of Mexico."

Steinbeck's 359-page narrative gave Brando an early education on the Indians of the Americas. Brando would have noted that the Indians were denied citizenship throughout the period of Spanish conquest and treated as "native animals." This would have explained why the first two popular leaders of Mexico, Benito Juarez and Porfirio Diaz, were "pure Indians," a circumstance that made the growing tyranny and corruption of the Diaz government even more painful for the Indian populations that suffered its worst consequences. Brando, typically, wanted to understand both sides of the conflict, which is why he also read the history of conquest from the perspective of the colonizers, described in William H. Prescott's massive one-volume history, *The Conquest of Mexico and the Conquest of Peru.*[49]

Brando traveled to southern Mexico, Zapata's Anenecuilco region, to explore the legend firsthand. There he studied local accents and gestures and arranged to interview people who had known Zapata. He also met Movita Castaneda, a Hispanic actress with whom he would be involved for decades. Castaneda, who starred in the 1935 version of *Mutiny on the Bounty*, would become Brando's wife in 1960 and raise two of his children, Miko and Rebecca. As in Brando's marriage to Anna Kashfi, the purpose was to legitimate the children, and Brando and Castaneda never lived together as husband and wife. Castaneda had been born in 1916 on a train near Scottsdale, Arizona, to a Mexican mother who was immigrating with her daughters and son to work in the cotton fields. After the family moved to Los Angeles, Castaneda earned money during the Depression by singing on the streets near Paramount Studios. In 1932, during casting calls for that era's *Mutiny on the Bounty*, Castaneda lied about her age and landed a role as the Tahitian love interest of Franchot Tone's character, the ship's gardener and translator. The film was the first of many in which she appeared, including *Apache* with Henry Fonda. By 1951, Castaneda needed a break from Hollywood; while traveling in Mexico, she met Brando when they shared a taxi together in Cuernavaca. What impressed Castaneda most about the youthful American actor was his great affinity for people: his responsiveness to everyone, young and old, beggars, commoners, the distinguished, and the neglected.[50] This deep feeling for humanity seemed especially suited to his subject.

In developing his treatment of Zapata, Brando in his usual way focused on aspects with which he could identify. Despite the historical and cultural distance, Brando, in Kazan's words, was able to find "the man in himself."[51] Zapata was the son of a mestizo, a small class of landowners, part Indian and part Spanish, whose holdings were greatly diminished under Diaz. Emiliano and his brother Eufemio became horsemen, and Steinbeck speculates that Emiliano may have been the greatest Mexican horseman of his time. Zapata was proud of his noble Spanish lineage (the Salazars) on his mother's side, and he was neither a Marxist nor an anarchist. His main concern was protecting the lands of peasants so they could continue to grow their corn and other crops, living as they had for generations. Zapata was driven to politics by the policies of the Diaz government, which sought to consolidate peasant lands in the hands of a few wealthy estate owners, in order to make them more available for lucrative sugar development. Zapata's motto, "It's better to die on your feet than to live on your knees," was a plea for the dignity of ordinary citizens.[52] A visionary who proved immune to the pervasive corruption of Mexican politics, Zapata had an even greater impact as a martyred hero than as a rebel leader.

The film was faithful to the basic outline of Zapata's life. The opening scene portrays a delegation of peasants meeting with President Diaz to protest the usurpation of their lands by sugar developers. The final scene, Kazan's favorite, shows the body of Zapata worshipfully attended by a crowd of women after having been dumped in his hometown square.[53] Building the character from physical details, Brando focused on the eyes as the basis for his interpretation. Slanting his lids, he wore brown contact lenses and emphasized the man's trademark stare, the intense gaze that projected insight and curiosity along with passion for the cause. Zapata's illiteracy, in Brando's portrait, was a consistent source of shame for the proud Mexican leader. It serves as one explanation for his aversion to assuming the presidency and figures prominently in his marriage to a merchant's daughter (Jean Peters), who teaches him to read.

Brando's Zapata anticipates Don Corleone in *The Godfather.* Brando viewed both as traditional men forced into power by the need to defend cherished values. As revolutionary insurgent and Mafia Don, respectively, both resort to extreme violence, yet they exercise authority through a quiet dignity that inspires devotion from their followers as much as fear. Their attitudes toward women, appreciative but dismissive, are similar, as are their loyalties to family and comrades. Both films are bloody. But Kazan knew, as did Francis Ford Coppola later, how to intersperse moments that humanized the protagonist: Zapata playing with puppies just before his assassination anticipates Don Corleone carefully selecting fruit from a street cart before the attempt on his life. Zapata dies and Don Corleone survives to have a peaceful death from old age while in his garden with his grandson. Brando conveys gentleness in both scenes through restraint. In *The Godfather*, the Don doesn't touch the fruit but points so as not to disturb the vendor's display; in *Zapata*, he is at rest on a bed of hay, his hand supporting the puppy perched on his chest. The peacefulness of the protagonists helps audiences forget that they are gunmen and makes the audience recoil from the violence soon visited upon them.

The combative atmospheres of these films ensure that their climactic scenes will center on death. In *Viva Zapata!*, it is the death of Emiliano's brother Eufemio, played by Anthony Quinn. Brando's performance here presages his reaction to the death of his first child, Sonny (James Caan), which is perhaps his greatest moment in *The Godfather*. In both scenes, Brando opts for gestures over words, and they could not be simpler. Confronting his dead brother, Zapata collapses slowly, fussing a bit over the body before bringing his brother's hands up to rest on either side of his own head. Cradled thus by his dead brother, Brando's Zapata demonstrates that the need for consolation applies only to the living. In *The Godfather*, the Don is completely still, his formerly imposing frame shrunken by gun wounds and grief. From his hollowed-out face comes a choked plea to the undertaker:

Brando as Zapata with puppies before his assassination. Hulton Archive/ Getty Images.

"I don't want his mother to see him this way.... Look how they've massacred my boy!" In both scenes, Brando achieves something incomparable through his imagination of how a warrior confronts death—by embodying it and moving on.[54]

Brando's next two pictures, *Julius Caesar* and *The Wild One*, might have seemed antithetical to *Zapata* and to each other. In all three, however, he is cast as a warrior, and the latter two share a fundamental preoccupation with language. *Julius Caesar* is about the power of rhetoric, which it sees as more potent than sabers, while *The Wild One* treats a conflict of generations and social types—older upstanding citizens versus young misfit bikers—as a war of words. From youth, Brando revered Shakespeare, committing to memory many choice speeches as part of his high school work and on his own. Anyone who was taught Shakespearean drama in high school, as he was by Duke Wagner at Shattuck, was expected to memorize long passages. Moreover, Brando had superb recall, especially for poetry, dramatic literature, and foreign languages.[55] He owned a complete collection of the Pelican Shakespeare and many works of criticism on the playwright-poet, which were among the most valuable of the books auctioned after his death.[56] In classes at Shattuck and at the New School, he had opportunities to perform Shakespeare, and he played Sebastian in *Twelfth Night* under Erwin Piscator's direction at the New School's summer institute. As a major actor in 1950s Hollywood, it was likely that he would be asked to do Shakespeare. Brando's care in evaluating proposals was evident in his choice to play Mark Antony in John Houseman's 1953 production of *Julius Caesar*, directed by Joseph M. Mankiewicz.

Both Houseman and Mankiewicz wrote screenplays and directed; Houseman had staged a *Macbeth* set in a Haitian court with black actors for the Federal Theatre Project (1935), and an equally ambitious "fascist" *Julius Caesar* with Orson Welles (1937). Mankiewicz had a reputation for intelligent handling of scripts and actors. The son of German immigrants, the American-born Mankiewicz, who had worked as a journalist in 1930s Berlin, was an idealist and a later participant in the civil rights movement. Mankiewicz was eager to cast Brando but had to overcome resistance from the MGM Studio heads, who were worried that Brando wouldn't be able to manage Shakespeare's language. Mankiewicz recorded Brando delivering Antony's main speeches. The lucidity and resonance of Brando's recordings erased all worries about the actor's diction.

Brando had multiple copies of *Julius Caesar*, as he did for many Shakespeare plays and poetry books in his collection, but his 1935 Hudson Library edition with light pencil marks and comments is probably what he was reading around the time of the film. It has some revealing annotations. He writes "Brooding Irony" above Antony's speech to the conspirators, where he announces his own preparedness to die too ("there is no hour so fit/As Caesar's death's hour"). On Antony's major address to the crowd after Caesar's murder, Brando paraphrases the basic points while adding humorous commentary. Beside Antony's assertion that Caesar did "thrice refuse" the crown, he adds balloon-size exclamation points; beside Antony's rhetorical question to the crowd, "Was this ambition?" he writes, "It can't be." Next to Antony's charge, "Yet Brutus says he was ambitious," he writes, "That blundering old fool." Brando answers Antony's question, "What cause withholds you then to mourn for him?" in the margin: "!!Shame" Throughout Antony's speeches, to pinpoint the rhythm, he adds scansion marks.[57]

Brando was able to make Shakespeare's language authentic by connecting Antony's lines to his actions and motivations and to the larger circumstances of the play. When Brando's Antony shouts at the milling crowd, "Friends, Romans, countrymen, Lend me your ears!" the shrill accent on *lend* gives the demand an urgency nearing desperation. As portrayed by Brando, Antony is a novice bidding for power in the wake of his mentor's bloody death. He has no personal claim on the unruly horde. What he has is plenty of hubris, together with a belief in the supple force of speech, and he makes the most of his opportunity, successfully rousing the mob. Words are tools to Brando's self-serving Antony, hence his slightly sinister smile as he ascends the steps following his eulogy. In *Julius Caesar*, one eulogy begets another. Brutus had allowed Antony to speak, not expecting him to be able to turn the crowd against Caesar's assassins. With Antony

Playing chess on the set of *Julius Caesar*. Ruth Orkin/Hulton Archive/Getty Images.

winning the battle, Brando portrays him as eagerly paying tribute to Brutus's corpse. Antony's self-interest dictates solemnity
as he expertly fits his speech to the demands of the occasion.
Though not as rich a role as Stanley Kowalski or Emiliano
Zapata, the part is one of the most compelling of Brando's early

performances because of his strong interpretation of Shake-speare's hero as a master rhetorician. John Gielgud, a veteran British actor who played Cassius, so admired Brando's work in it that he invited him to join his repertory group in England, an admiration underscored by the British Academy of Film and Television Arts, which awarded Brando a BAFTA for Best Foreign Acting Performance in 1953.

Brando as usual was dissatisfied. "It takes someone of Giel-gud's stature to perform with authority because he has played most of the important Shakespeare roles. But for me to walk onto a movie set and play Mark Antony without more experience was asinine." In a contemporary interview shortly after *Julius Caesar* was released to critical approval and popular success, Brando explained that, despite the film's reception, American audiences lacked the preparation and patience to appreciate Shakespeare's language. American moviegoers, he concluded, "just don't want to have to reach."[58] But Brando was not yet willing to give up on them.

Though some may have believed that *The Wild One*, made in the same year as *Julius Caesar*, was proof that he had given up, Brando approached this next project with high hopes. He would be working again with producer Stanley Kramer on a social-problem film, this one about motorcycle gangs wreaking havoc in a staid town. *The Wild One* was based on an incident in Hollister, California, a small rural community in the center of the state that had been overtaken by a group of bikers. Unexpectedly, the film touched a nerve in the culture, becoming a symbol for the disaffection of American youth and their identification with nonconformists. This was due in great part to Brando's perfor-mance as the alienated Johnny Strabler, head of the Black Rebels.

The Wild One is about communication, or the lack of it. It por-trays intergenerational strife as a problem of misunderstanding. The bikers and the townspeople speak different languages, and their mutual incomprehension results in violence. The motor-cyclists are self-styled opponents of the status quo who take to the road as a way of avoiding responsibility and exhibiting their vaguely defined dissatisfaction with middle-class morality. Their lingo—based on popular tunes and bebop, which involves adding O's to names, as in "Daddy-O," frequent rhythmic tongue twist-ers, and the use of terms such as *crazy* as superlatives—sounds like Greek to the owners of the local café whose corny speech is just as opaque to the bikers. The gang members drag-race to expend their aggressive energy, ultimately finding release in van-dalism. The townspeople range from the innocent or curious to the nervous authoritarians eager to put these young hoodlums in their place.

Brando's Johnny Strabler is rather passive for a gang leader, behaving for the most part as if he has nothing to prove. What arouses him is authority of any kind, especially the police. His motto, "Nobody tells me what to do," is belligerent as well as self-defensive. Never the first to offend, Johnny lashes out when he feels insulted or attacked. Refusing to fight until he is goaded into it (by the head of the opposition gang, Lee Marvin's Chino), he refrains from vandalism or aggression against the townsfolk. Johnny offends by failing to act, ignoring the sheriff's plea to gather his gang and leave town, and never lifting a finger to stop their ravaging. Because he is their head, their destruction reflects his will. Still, Johnny's only definitive act is a display of gallantry. When gang members surround the sheriff's daughter, Kathy, in a dark square, he rides in to foil the impending violation. Johnny and the girl ride off to a blissful union, their bodies merged, the wind in their faces, going nowhere in particular.

Trouble starts when Johnny and Kathy stop to talk, which cre-ates confusion and distrust. Frightened by his anger, the girl runs off, with witnesses misreading her flight and accusing Johnny of rape. His mute hostility, his inability to communicate with anyone, is a direct cause of his victimization. Because he has actually rescued her from assault by his comrades, the beating he receives from the townsmen is all the more unjust. Kathy defends him, explaining to the police that Johnny is innocent of the charges against him. And he is seen redeemed at the end, when he returns briefly to bestow a gift on Kathy in gratitude for her defense. He gives her the trophy he has stolen at the film's outset during a community bike race. The gift, like the giver, is tainted, but the hint that Johnny feels grateful for Kathy's defense of him, that he cares even momentarily what the girl thinks, is sufficient to provide closure to a film that is eager to preserve its protagonist's likability. Brando's rebel is never that threatening—striking out only at another gang member, protecting the honor of the local girl, and parting with a shy smile that implies he is salvageable. This is why Brando's biker could achieve an iconic status that was readily marketable, sending sales of black leather jackets and motorcycles soaring.

Johnny Strabler could be widely emulated because he represented a highly democratic American-style rebellion as a rite of passage that leaves the social order undisturbed. Still, it would be cynical and inaccurate to argue that Johnny's resistance is as superficial as the leather jacket on his back, for the film ends with little hope that Johnny will be incorporated into the social order. And the character and film, like other cultural works of the 1950s, helped to lay the ground for fundamental social change. In an interview discussing Brando's contributions to black civil rights, Black Panther Bobby Seale recalled how liberating it was for him as a boy to hear a major American actor utter such lines as "I don't make no deal with no cops."[59] The performance inspired future participants in subsequent social movements, when their own rebellions were embryonic.

Brando observed years later that no one making *The Wild One* anticipated that it would have such appeal. He also affirmed the affinity he felt for his character's emotional insecurity and rebel-liousness.[60] As with his other major iconic role, *The Godfather*, *The Wild One* touched him profoundly. His access to that emotional depth produced a character who spoke to audiences everywhere, sometimes menacingly. The British Board of Film Censors, for instance, concerned that *The Wild One* might provoke youth to violence, banned the film for fourteen years. Brando was himself a rebel, and he would find rebellion to some degree in practically every character he played. The one exception was Stanley Kowal-ski, whom Brando considered a conformist. Kowalski, Brando observed, "would have voted for Reagan. He was a marine. He would have been a Republican . . . would have thought Joe McCar-thy was one of the heroes of the age."[61] Johnny Strabler is the ultimate rebel in Brando's gallery, but his rebels come from all walks of life and are not confined to the pre-*Godfather* career. Some of his most dangerous rebels are in his later movies: the anarchic assassin Lee Clayton in *The Missouri Breaks* (1976), who invents his own weapons and ends up answerable to no one, which is even truer of Colonel Kurtz in *Apocalypse Now* (1979). For intellectually informed rebellion, there is Ian MacKenzie of *A Dry White Season* (1989), who takes on the South African legal establishment, and the title character of *The Island of Dr. Moreau* (1996), who pursues his experiments with a diabolical disregard for scientific ethics. Hostility toward institutions and their rep-resentatives, no matter the institution or the representative, was the default setting of Brando and his protagonists.

This anti-institutionalism ensured that Brando would never become a bona-fide radical, join a party, or subscribe to a creed. His notes in his copy of Sidney Hook's *Political Power and Per-sonal Freedom* (1959) are a case in point. Brando's disdain for the totalitarianism Hook critiques is clear, but so is his resistance to the critique. He questions Hook's ongoing argument for the superiority of democracy, demanding in a section on the Soviet takeover of Hungary: "Was not the suppression of Hung. what we might do in Cuba if a soviet inspired pure communist revolution had taken place?" Near a passage arguing that well-informed adults are the best judges of their own interests, Brando asks, "What adults, and are they?" and references "The Ford Foundation voting habits." Hook's notion that totalitarian efforts to impose blueprints on history seem monomaniacal to democrats leads Brando to wonder: "and the evangelical spirit in western Christianity, what of that?"[62]

Brando gravitated intellectually and professionally to the flaws and limits of systems. His hunger to know more about everything was motivated in part by dissatisfaction. At the same time, he was idealistic and, though a sharp analyst of human nature, he was usually willing to give individuals the benefit of the doubt. In many ways, then, despite significant idiosyncrasies, his beliefs were compatible with basic American cultural and political ideals whose violation he was quick to denounce. This helps to explain his extraordinary influence. He took on roles that captivated audiences because they expressed common disappointments and aspirations.

ON THE WATERFRONT

Elia Kazan, who directed Brando for the last time in *On the Waterfront* (1954), shared his affinity for American mainstream sentiments, but he and Brando were destined to diverge in matters of politics and personal loyalty. In contrast to Brando, Kazan was an enthusiast, which enabled his commitments for periods of time to Communism, The Group Theatre, Broadway, and then Hollywood. Once he became a member of an organization, Kazan devoted himself to achieving success within it—by seizing opportunities, fending off obstacles, and pursuing and developing talent wherever he found it. When he was summoned before the HUAC hearing investigating Hollywood in 1952, Kazan's main concern was protecting his flourishing career. He had been a member of a Group Theatre Communist cell in the 1930s and knew that his stature as a major Hollywood director would bring HUAC the publicity it had sought by pursuing the entertainment industry. While Kazan hoped to avoid naming fellow members of his Group cell, he knew that refusing to do so could result in jail or, at the very least, the end of his career. From the beginning, Kazan was prepared to act expediently. The political winds, he told himself, would change and he would be vindicated for doing something that was essential to continuing as a director in Hollywood, which he considered essential to his existence.[63]

The House of Representatives investigations of Communism in the entertainment industry had actually begun in the late 1930s, but they were suspended during World War II due to the US alliance with the Soviet Union. The investigations gained steam again during the buildup to the Cold War. By the time Kazan appeared before the committee in the late winter and spring of 1952, all eight of the actors, writers, and directors whose names he gave the committee had been exposed; his testimony was to serve as further proof. It was an illustrious group, including Morris Carnovsky, Clifford Odets, and Paula Strasberg. While Kazan did some of what would be considered his most important work after testifying against his eight former colleagues, his life and career never recovered from it. He became a pariah in an embattled Hollywood, where the HUAC investigation caused irreparable suffering, even suicide. Kazan was not the only Hollywood luminary to cooperate with the committee, but he became a symbol of shameful opportunism in one of the community's gravest episodes, for two reasons. The first was Kazan's relatively quick capitulation to the committee's demands: He was called to testify as a "friendly witness" and had agreed to talk well before appearing on April 10, 1952. Others took longer to capitulate, some serving jail time in the process. The second reason for Kazan's pariah status was the sanctimonious self-defense he published in the *New York Times* (April 12, 1952), rationalizing his testimony as an honest effort to "protect" his country from "a dangerous and alien conspiracy" and affirming the value of "free speech."[64] This was only the beginning. Kazan would spend the rest of his life defending his actions.

Because Brando was known as a fierce individualist and had major box-office appeal, he was relatively protected from the HUAC investigations.[65] He would soon have more firsthand experience with Hollywood blacklisting, though, pulling strings on behalf of his sister Jocelyn, a victim of HUAC, and later having his own films boycotted after he signed petitions against lynching in the South.[66] Like everyone in the entertainment industry in this era, he knew people whose lives had been destroyed by HUAC. That, and his extraordinary level of idealism, ensured that he would take Kazan's betrayal very seriously. A friend who was with Brando in Paris when news of Kazan's testimony became public remembers his anguish. "He is the best director around," Brando lamented, "and I'll never be able to work with him again."[67] The actor eventually accepted the extensive personal rationales he was given and agreed to take the role of Terry Malloy in *On the Waterfront*. Brando later quipped that his decision was sealed by a contract clause negotiated with producer Sam Spiegel, allowing him to end work early when he had psychiatrist appointments in Manhattan. Around this period, Brando had begun to see Dr. Bela Mittelmann, a therapist recommended by Kazan, partly to deal with a host of problems from childhood. These included the distrust of women generated by his mother's unreliability that made it impossible for him to be in a committed relationship, and the rage toward his father that made him hostile toward authority figures. But Brando was also extremely ambitious; he recognized the potential of the script and knew what he and Kazan together could make of it.

Still, many years later, Brando's position on Kazan's testimony remained unequivocal: He greatly admired the man's talent but deplored his actions. In his letter of February 24, 1999, responding to a request that he participate or allow his films to be shown in a segment of the Academy Awards ceremony honoring Kazan, Brando lamented that Kazan had never apologized publicly for the injury and suffering caused by his HUAC testimony. Citing the destructive impact of the HUAC investigations in Hollywood overall, and the deleterious effect on the career of his sister Jocelyn in particular, Brando hoped that perhaps "the years will have allowed [Kazan] to soften his position on these matters" and suggested that, "on the occasion where his name is to be celebrated and honored, that he make a clear acknowledgment of regret" for his actions. Barring Kazan's public apology, Brando concludes, "I think it would be less than appropriate to extend to him any formal meritorious gesture," and "I will withhold my permission to have any part of the motion pictures that I have appeared in . . . displayed on the night of the 71st Academy Awards."[68]

It is sometimes suggested that *On the Waterfront* signaled the passing of an era in filmmaking. Black and white, fact-based, its cast filled with neighborhood extras, the picture's Hoboken, New Jersey, location was integral to the story it told. Darryl Zanuck became notorious for telling Kazan and screenwriter Budd Schulberg, in repudiating their request that he produce it, "It's exactly what audiences don't want to see now. . . . Who gives a shit about longshoremen?"[69] In fact, his presumption was fundamentally correct—that the industry's future was in wide-screen color movies, which displayed what movies could offer. Under siege from television as much as from HUAC, many in the industry believed that pictures like *On the Waterfront* would soon be obsolete. Yet, despite its European neorealist look, the film's nine Oscars at the 1955 Academy Awards ceremony (which tied the record with *Gone with the Wind* and *From Here to Eternity*) proved that it had something to say to American audiences.

The story of the lonely former boxer Terry Malloy; his love interest Edie Doyle (Eva Marie Saint); his brother Charley, the "brains" of the mob (Rod Steiger); parish priest Father Barry (Karl Malden); and mob boss Johnny Friendly (Lee J. Cobb) is one of suffering and hard luck. A congregation on the docks of Hoboken could be the last stop before Abyssinia (Ethiopia) for Father Barry.[70] Johnny Friendly has worked his way up, fatherless, from abject poverty. Edie's father tells her that he has labored so hard on the docks to pay for her teachers' college in Tarrytown, that one arm is longer than the other, and her brother has been killed for violating the longshoremen's code of silence. Terry is an orphan whose loyalty to his older brother Charley is explained by their hardscrabble upbringing. The world of *On the Waterfront* is so unforgiving that a dockworker named Kayo Duggan (Pat Henning), granted his wish for a shipment of Irish whiskey, dies when the load falls on his head. His death is no accident, and the fact that much of this suffering can be traced to identifiable human agents is the source of the plot and character motivation.

Budd Schulberg's screenplay was based on a series of Pulitzer Prize–winning articles by Malcolm Johnson, "Crime on the Waterfront," published in the New York *Sun* from 1948 to 1950. An exposé of union corruption on the New York docks, Johnson's series highlighted the collusion among unions, the mob, shipping companies, and local politicians who were paid to overlook the exploitation of workers and violence against anyone who objected. Schulberg, the son of a producer, had written a respected Hollywood novel, *What Makes Sammy Run* (1941), and another about graft in boxing, *The Harder They Fall* (1947), and was drawn to the brutal world of waterfront crime. Convinced that the subject would make a good script, he met Malcolm Johnson and, through him, a waterfront priest, John Corridan, who became the model for Malden's Father Barry. The result was a script that became the basis for *On the Waterfront*. While the script was the work of many hands, with substantial contributions by Kazan and producer Sam Spiegel, its essential component was Schulberg's passion. Kazan's respect for Schulberg, together with their shared experiences as "friendly witnesses" before HUAC, ensured a positive collaboration between director and screenwriter. Among the most significant of the changes introduced by Kazan was the gradual subordination of Father Barry, the main character in the early scripts, to Terry Malloy.[71]

Terry is a man whose simple goal, survival, is overridden by circumstances that force him to take a stand. Tough but powerless, he has gotten along by giving in. Finally, motivated by love, he defends himself against the mob. In notes to Brando, Kazan emphasized the character's loneliness, as well as his asceticism and inner struggle. His wounds show, despite his swagger; still, his cynicism in conversations with Edie is betrayed by the doubt and sensitivity in his eyes. Brando reconceives Kazan's notes, adding facets that enlarge his uneducated, inarticulate boxer into the ultimate democratic hero. Brando shows the same mastery here that he did in the television show *Come Out Fighting*. There is the ex-boxer's walk—on his toes, but heavy—the arms close to the body, a gait that suggests regret toward the physical power that he never delivered. He evinces the uncalculating charm of a young man discovering a woman—teasing her about her childhood braids and braces, asking her out without trying to mask his desire. In their first passionate kiss against the wall in her bedroom, his hunger for her lips, her smell, reveals feelings as pure as the flowers on the wallpaper.

Though his brother Charley is the talker and Terry Malloy comparatively reticent, he is nevertheless responsible for some of the most renowned lines in movie history. "I'm not gonna hurt nobody. I'm just gonna go down there and get my rights." "From where you stand maybe.... But I'm standing over here now. I was ratting on myself all them years, I didn't even know it." "I'm going to take it out of their skulls!" Brando makes his usual modifications to the words on the page: dropping phrases, adding inflections and emphases. In every instance, what might have been overlooked becomes memorable.

Here, for instance, is the scripted version of Terry on Edie's maturation: "The thought I wanted to get over is that you grew up beauteeful." Now Brando's revision: "I'm just kidding you a little bit.... I just mean to tell you, that you grew up very nice." Brando added the "dink" when he and Edie click glasses during their first drink together. In these scenes with Edie, Brando's changes soften Terry, highlighting his playfulness. They also illuminate a fundamental aspect of Terry and Edie's relationship: It recalls the past, allowing them to experience as adults a childhood wonder they were denied. Brando's changes to the famous taxi scene serve similarly to enhance meaning.

Charley is presumably taking Terry to a sporting event, but we know that Johnny Friendly has enlisted him to ensure that Terry, who has been subpoenaed to testify against the mob, doesn't. The cab ride is Charley's last chance; if he can't persuade his brother, he must deliver him to Friendly at the ride's end. Terry resists, and Charley in frustration draws his gun. Throughout the scene, Brando's alterations call attention to the stark divisions their banter works to suppress. Charley tries to convince Terry to take the better-paying job that the mob is offering to keep him quiet, and Terry responds, according to the script: "A steady job and a few bucks extra, that's all I wanted." Brando's alteration—"a couple extra potatoes" for "a few bucks extra"—forcibly distinguishes Terry from his corrupt brother. As a humble Irish potato-eater, he is content with the simple fare afforded by an honest day's work; *he* doesn't need steak and suits.[72]

Brando's legendary revisions to what follows after Charley pulls his gun on Terry extends this distinction. Schulberg recalled Brando's improvisations: "After a marvelous look that conveys more sadness than anger, Brando sighs, takes an eloquent pause, and says, 'Wow.' That one little syllable is so right that it provides an emotional key to the entire scene." More a gasp than a word, it highlights Terry's shock at his protective older brother becoming momentarily aggressive. By confronting Charley with the enormity of what he has contemplated, it reconciled the scene's ending where Charley frees Terry and continues on to certain death as his brother's sacrificial substitute.[73] Brando's gasp gives way to candor, liberating Terry to express for the first time his grievance over another betrayal by Charley. Again, Brando's revisions are critical. Schulberg's "Final Shooting Script": "I could've been a contender, I could've had class and been somebody. Real class. Instead of a bum, let's face it, which is what I am." Brando's version: "I could a had class, I could a been a contender, I could a been *some*body—instead of a bum, which is what I am, let's face it." The effect of Brando's paring and rearrangement is to build, phrase by phrase, to "*some*body," which reveals the devastating nature of Terry's loss. The victory, so close and inevitable, would have made him someone; coerced by the mob to throw the fight, he is nothing.

"If there is a better performance by a man in the history of film in America, I don't know what it is." Cast, crew, screenwriter—all agreed with Kazan's assessment. Of the high points (the cab conversation; Terry finding Charley's body; the glove in the park), Kazan conceded, "I didn't direct that; Marlon showed me, as he often did, how the scene should be performed. I could never have told him how to do that scene as well as he did it."[74] While there is no denying the power of the script and Brando's delivery of it, what he accomplishes without using words matters even more.

Brando's handling of the gun Charley draws on Terry in the cab transforms a killing device into the saddest instrument on earth, a symbol of lost fraternity. By gently pushing it down, Brando drains the gun of its murderous phallic power and also anticipates the subsequent recuperation of their fraternal bond, in a scene where the same gun figures prominently. After Charley is killed by the mob, his body hung in the alley on a grappling hook, Terry storms into Friendly's bar, Charley's gun drawn, seeking vengeance. Terry is bleeding profusely, having cut his arm while escaping an assault in the alley. Father Barry arrives and tries to defuse Terry's rage, suggesting he avenge Charley's death by testifying against Friendly in court. As Terry considers the priest's advice, he massages his wound absentmindedly with the gun, a gesture that echoes the previous scene, this time by transforming the weapon into a means of comfort. Terry subsequently hurls the gun into a framed portrait of Johnny Friendly, signaling thus his decision to testify. For the moment, at least, Terry opts for his brother's method, words, over his own, punches.

Brando's intimacy with the nonverbal and even inanimate world in the film expands the scope of his performance. The dominant metaphor is the pigeon (Schulberg raised racing pigeons as a boy in California), and Brando's brilliant work makes some of these scenes excruciating. Terry identifies with the pigeons he keeps on the rooftop of the building where he lives; he tends them in a way he was never cared for himself, worrying about their vulnerability to the preying hawks. Then there is the double meaning of *pigeon*. From Terry's unwitting setup of "stool pigeon" Joey Doyle in the opening to the violent close where Terry succeeds through a fierce fistfight with Johnny Friendly in redefining that term, Terry struggles to avoid becoming a snitch. Terry's sham discovery of Joey's racing pigeon catalyzes the plot. It gets Joey to the roof where he is killed, brings Terry to the attention of the crime commission investigating corruption on the docks, and keeps Joey's sister Edie in town. Terry tells Edie that pigeons have gotten a bum rap; contrary to common belief, they are brave and loyal, their marriages ending only in death. Brando holds the birds with tender familiarity, and his reaction to their slaughter is yet another illuminating evocation of grief. He shows in a single scene how loss permeates the one who grieves at that moment and forever.

On the roof after testifying against Friendly at the crime commission hearing, Terry sees Tommy, a boy who had once idolized him but now despises him for "singing to the cops." Tommy tosses Terry's dead prized racer at him, shouting "a pigeon for a pigeon," and runs off. Dead bird in hand, Terry crosses the roof to find that Tommy has killed the entire flock. Brando expresses the fullness of Terry's grief through his body. Partially hidden by the door as he looks into the coop, he responds to Edie, who has followed him, with a silent bid for privacy. In the gentle motion of the hand that waves her away, Brando conveys the enormity of a grief that cannot be shared. There are other such moments: Terry stops beside his dead brother to rest his hand against the wall, before hugging the body to lift it gently off the hook; he grabs the jacket inherited from Joey Doyle and Kayo Duggan as he heads for the docks, pausing to rip a stray thread off the collar (like an act of superstition, to ensure he will survive). These plain gestures make the material world symbolic. Terry puts on the biblical "robe of righteousness" for the first time, the jacket worn by those, Doyle and Duggan, who dared to repudiate "D and D"—deaf and dumb—in the name of justice. After testifying, Terry is able to assume their garment, remembering their suffering and death.[75]

When Terry takes on Johnny Friendly singlehandedly in a fistfight, two things are certain: Terry will get no help from the longshoremen cowering nearby, and Friendly's goons will step in as soon as he calls to them. As the fight begins, the camera sweeps slowly over a small boat labeled "Rebel, New York," an

On roof with dead pigeon after testifying. Photograph by Columbia Pictures/ Getty Images.

identity that raises more questions than it answers. Can *rebel* be attached to a place or is it a state of mind? What does it mean to rebel against forces greater than yourself, to refuse to be pushed around, to stand your ground and speak out? The film's final image of the big man in the expensive coat calling the little men in their tattered jackets to work as the iron door descends, leaves small hope of equity or liberation for the longshoremen in *On the Waterfront*. Terry seems caught in a dynamic of loss and rage that is the plight of the disempowered. The murder of his brother by Friendly's mob spurs his testimony against Friendly; the slaughter of his pigeons drives him into physical combat. Still the film implies that fulfillment for Terry comes in the act of rebellion itself.

There is no evidence that either Kazan or Schulberg was aware of the Albert Camus study *The Rebel* (1951), which caused a sensation in France and the United States for portraying Communism as a destructive creed and initiating a rift between Camus and his friend Jean-Paul Sartre, the existentialist philosopher. *The Rebel* defined rebellion as a type of morality that impelled individuals to act against injustice and tyranny in any form and helped them to adhere to transcendent values, specifically the value of life itself. During extended stays in France in the years before making *On the Waterfront*, Brando was often at Les Deux Magots, a café frequented by Sartre, Simone de Beauvoir, Camus, and other French intellectuals and artists. He was at the café, for instance, in the spring of 1952 when he learned of Elia Kazan's HUAC testimony.[76]

There and at jazz clubs in this Saint-Germain-des-Prés area, where Brando played bongo drums, he found a congenial "stronghold of freedom just after the war," becoming friends with the writer Jean Genet and the singer Juliette Greco, who had famous love affairs with Miles Davis and Brando friend Quincy Jones.[77] We do know that Brando was familiar with *The Rebel* by 1957. He mentions in a 1957 letter to a friend, "I've just finished reading Erich Fromm's *The Art of Loving* and found my own shocking image on every other page. I'm currently reading *The Outsider* [which discussed Camus's *Rebel*] and again finding myself mirrored." Another sign that Brando was thinking carefully about rebellion while characterizing Terry Malloy is that the character came up later in notes he made in preparing for *Mutiny on the Bounty*.[78]

That Brando owned and annotated a later edition of Colin Wilson's book suggests its importance to him. In his 1982 edition of *The Outsider*, Brando marked a passage summarizing a basic principle of Camus's philosophy that is pertinent to Terry Malloy. According to Camus, "Freedom is not simply being allowed to do what you like; it is *intensity of will*, and it appears under any

Golden Globe ceremony, February 24, 1955, when Brando won Best Actor award for *On the Waterfront*. © Leigh Wiener.

circumstances that limit man and arouse his will to more life."[79] As an Irish Catholic, Terry knows that it is not possible to triumph over suffering. It is possible, instead, to decide *how to* suffer and for what purpose, thus asserting one's freedom. Though the protagonist does get the girl and prevail over organized crime at the end, Darryl Zanuck may be forgiven for thinking this would never appeal to Americans in the 1950s era of prosperity and consumption.

Brando believed that audiences identified with the story of a man with the courage to stand up to the mob and to admit his own failure. Kazan was convinced they responded to the theme of redemption: No matter what a man has done, he can atone.[80] Brando's moral had standing up to HUAC as its goal; Kazan's moral had atoning for the past to gain redemption as its goal. The film undoubtedly supported both views. But what persists beyond these explanations is the image of mainstream audiences in the mid-1950s, abandoning the comforts of home entertainment to spend 108 minutes in a grim, colorless world so cold that the actors' breaths were almost visible on the screen. Suffused with an unbearably sad score by Leonard Bernstein, they witnessed violence and death while bonding with characters whose cowardice, occasional courage, and perpetual bad luck demanded empathetic identification. Something powerful was being worked out in the recognition of these brutal working-class lives—many Catholic, culturally and racially diverse—as central to the American experience. The popularity of *On the Waterfront* revealed that Americans were not yet done with suffering, that the traumas of the 1930s and '40s, of Fascism, world war, displacement, and mass death, were not readily set aside. Americans continued to honor a notion of community that was founded in renunciation no matter how often they were told—by advertisers, politicians, and producers—that the times were now different. Leonard Bernstein cites Terry Malloy's "sacrificial gesture at the end of the film," which supplies "the motive of his nobility," to confirm that sacrifice remained a ritual and ideal of national significance.[81]

The unparalleled success of *On the Waterfront* helped to consolidate a quality that had distinguished the Brando hero from the outset—he was one who suffered, and in doing so dignified an essential feature of human existence. Given the brilliance of his performance, there is a temptation to dismiss what comes later in the 1950s as anticlimactic. That would overlook a Napoleon that Laurence Olivier considered the greatest of all renditions of the nineteenth-century emperor; a singing gambler with almost universal romantic appeal; two movies that broke new ground in their depictions of colonialism and race; and a Nazi soldier who provoked some of the first serious discussions by the entertainment industry of the cultural basis for the Holocaust. The roles Brando undertook between 1954 and 1957 represented significant mature work involving experiments with characters from different cultures, challenging norms on interracial romance, testing his abilities as a performer, and extending the boundaries of political debate.

INNOVATION AND IDEALISM, 1954–1958

Brando's idealism has been treated as something of a cliché, a fancy of his to be mentioned but never taken quite seriously. The actor's library, however, reveals his abiding commitment to the political and cultural values portrayed in his movies. Brando's reading in the 1950s appears to have focused on three main areas: comparative philosophy and religion; Asian cultures, including their histories, languages, and arts; and social scientific theory (politics and psychology in particular). What is noteworthy about Brando's collection (and this was as true of his later books as it was of those from the 1940s and '50s) was the preponderance of classics (and influential books that would become classics) and definitive works on subjects that interested him. During this period, he was reading as background for his roles, as well as for his own edification. He was eager to understand the deeper history of Asian countries, to find commonalities among peoples, at the same time as he was fascinated by the otherness of these places and their patterns of thought.

In the years 1954 through 1958, when Brando was earning prizes for being among the top moneymaking stars in Hollywood, he was also winning awards from the US Savings Bond Program and the United Nations for service to the national and international communities.[82] This was a chief motivation for forming his own film company, Pennebaker Productions, named after his mother: Brando's hope of reconciling his good works and his professional aptitude. One of Pennebaker's first goals was to make a film about United States diplomacy and interventionism in Southeast Asia that would bring attention to both the negative and the positive aspects of American foreign policy. Since the early 1950s, Brando had been concerned about the effects of Cold War rhetoric and the indifference on the part of the nation's leaders and representatives abroad to the cultural complexities of the places where America intervened. He recognized, well before many did, the diplomatic missteps that would culminate in the Vietnam War. To this end, he spent a month in the spring of 1956 touring Southeast Asia—researching on behalf of the film that would become *The Ugly American*—an area of the world that had long interested him. The tour was heavily covered in the local press, and though the focus tended to be on trivialities typically aroused by a film star, he did manage to publicize his commitment to cross-cultural understanding.[83]

Brando conveyed his enthusiasm for what he had seen in a

letter to Ellen Adler in August 1956: "Bali is the womb of the earth and as soon as I can manage it, I am going to fluff off this senseless network of nerve ends and go live in a place that was made for living. Oh God Ellen I tell you I have seen some wonder lately in my life and I am going to see more. I've been to the Phillipines, to Hong Kong, and Thiland, Java, Singapore, and Japan. ... Ellen honey try to arrange your life to see some of that before its too late, because the world is swelling with a dreadful effort to standardize so fast that very shortly it will all be gone. Really gone." For Brando, who had chafed under the stresses of fame and fortune in Hollywood almost from the beginning, these relatively untrammeled Eastern countries provided a respite of sorts. Though he was too shrewd an observer of culture to overlook the craving for all things American that threatened the integrity and distinctiveness of places like Bali, he was able to luxuriate in the peace they still offered visitors like him.

Despite their "dreadful effort to standardize," such cultures contrasted starkly with California, described in an earlier letter to Ellen from the summer of 1954. Here he is, "living in Beverly Hills in one of the canyons," with about eight old friends, "in one gay knot...having more fun than a barrel of monkeys that are being used to test a new polio vaccinne." Brando writes from "the sound stage," where

> the horror of this production is full upon me. The director is completely affable and gentle and decent; the fact that he is an intelectual amputee concerns me somewhat since I am contractually oblidged to act this part. The embarrassment of being in this production is equal to that that would be incurd were I oblidged to stand on a table in the Oak room of the plaza and, nude, except for a nosegay of carrots jammed in my puckered ass hole, and attempt to put out my flamming pubic hair with a squirt gun filled with

toothpaste. After I have gained the summit of the heren-
dous pile of manure I am going to Europe for a little while
and commit fornication with dogs in an effort to reduce the
spleen that is being presently generated.[84]

The production to which Brando referred was *Désirée*; the part
was Napoleon. When Brando's mother died on March 31, 1954,
from hypertension precipitated by years of alcoholism, he was
overwhelmed by her loss. During the traumatic period of her ill-
ness, he had signed on to this costume drama directed by Henry
Koster to settle a contract dispute with Darryl Zanuck. Brando's
obvious disenchantment with Koster, and the project in general,
did not prevent his usual serious preparations. He watched the
available screen performances, modeling his soft British accent
on Claude Rains's Napoleon in *Hearts Divided* (1936). From the
biographies of Napoleon, including one he had in his collection,
Napoleon's Victories (1893), a classic memoir by Captain C. Parquin of the Imperial Guard, he picked up attitudes, mannerisms,
and turns of phrase.[85]

Robert M. Johnston's *Napoleon: A Short Biography* (1904), a
historically accurate portrait of the man's life and achievements,
which guided the reader through the 40,000-book maze of Napoleonic bibliography, offers a standard view of Napoleon that Brando's reading would have provided. "What produced the greatest
impression on all who met him was the brilliancy and imperious-
ness of his steel blue eyes" which "revealed the volcanic energy
of the soul beneath." Steely stares were a Brando specialty, and
he used them in abundance. He would have learned too about
Napoleon's passion for prophecy, together with the finickiness
that "was the nightmare of every colonel in the army." Spirited
off to prison by opposition forces, Brando's Napoleon is a stick-
ler for detail and not too distracted to upbraid a soldier for his
untidy uniform. The same obsessiveness informs every civic and

political venture, and Brando makes much of Napoleon as "the modern Justinian," the great codifier of French law, and of his genius for military maneuvers. Among the memorable scenes is Napoleon's return in the middle of the night from Russia, despondent in defeat, shielding his eyes as he recounts the devastation of his armies. The hypnotic recitation reveals Napoleon's remarkable coldness; already strategizing his next move, he shows no remorse for human loss. This foreshadows the ending, where he is angered at mention of the lives extinguished in his conquest of Europe. Brando's Napoleon is an intellectual opportunist continuously hatching plots, confirming the biographic insight that "the field of ambition in which he strove for existence was only bounded by planetary space."[86]

While the script was weak and the picture essentially a drawing-room romance, Brando exploited the chance to play one of history's great men. Bringing alive the leader's singular determination, arrogance, and magnetism, he succeeded in producing a wholly credible Napoleon. The choice of a quiet voice and subdued yet regal bearing suggested a person of inborn authority, devoid of self-doubt. A journalist who interviewed Brando in his dressing room during the filming of *Désirée* described how he physically embodied the role. The five-foot, ten-inch actor had appeared taller in person than on screen, and had come off as sensitive and observant. Just before he went to the set, she "witnessed a startling transformation—he stood up and suddenly he seemed smaller, fatter, completely changed. His soft eyes were now brooding, dark and heavy with pain." Brando made a few adjustments at his makeup table, affixing a nosepiece, arranging his hair, and when he turned to face her, he *was* Napoleon—physiognomy, frame, even the stalking stride.[87] As Laurence Olivier said, Brando's "Napoleon was immeasurably the best Napoleon ever, simply marvelous because of his own particular quality of being so easy, so easily bringing a sense of

On the set as Napoleon. © Dennis Stock/Magnum Photos.

genius to a character who was a genius. He is a very, very remarkable actor. On the movies he learned to be controlled. He wouldn't
like to be called a technician but he was one, a very great one."[88]

Despite misgivings about the picture, Brando managed to find
himself in the role, exemplified by the fact that his Napoleon
had more in common with Emiliano Zapata and Don Corleone
than with other Napoleons. A lonely brooder, Brando's Napoleon treated others as pawns in a perpetual game of chess. There
were elements of this in Brando, of course. Those closest to him
insisted that, however disguised, he was enormously ambitious,
and he was also adept, through his charisma and stratagems, at
bending others to his will. Still, he was no Napoleon, and his ability to convince audiences that he *was* signaled his power as an
actor. As Group Theatre veteran Robert Lewis noted at the time,
Brando's talent was "to work from the inside out," fitting himself
to the character and not the character to himself. An anonymous
theatergoer observed of Brando's acting: "The only other place
I've seen such a terrifying shift of identity is in a schizophrenic
ward. But this man has control of what he's doing."[89]

One actor Brando met in Hollywood during this time was
James Dean, who was seven years younger and idolized him.
Dean had taken up some of Brando's hobbies, including motorcycling and drumming, and was constantly asking director Elia
Kazan during the filming of *East of Eden* about Brando's personal
habits as well as acting techniques. "He dropped his voice to a
cathedral hush when he talked about Marlon. I invited Brando
to come to the set and enjoy some hero worship. Marlon did and
was very gracious to Jimmy, who was so adoring that he seemed
shrunken and twisted in misery. People were to compare them
but they weren't alike. Marlon, well trained by Stella Adler, had
excellent technique. He was proficient in every aspect of acting, including characterization and makeup. He was also a great

mimic. Dean had no technique to speak of."[90] For his part, Brando found the young star appealing and identified with a Midwestern innocence in Dean that made him attractive to Hollywood and also vulnerable to its wiles. Though he felt sympathetic toward Dean, they never became close, but Brando did recommend that Dean see a psychiatrist to deal with his sensitivity and his own "father troubles." People sometimes have to borrow another actor's style when starting out, Brando commented, adding that Dean clearly had developed his own by the time he did *Giant*. He predicted that Dean would have had a major career had he not died so young.[91]

The overt link between Brando as Napoleon and his next role as Sky Masterson was his costar Jean Simmons (the only actress with whom he appeared twice). More fundamental was the conviction he brought to the suave ladies'-man side of both characters. *Désirée* and *Guys and Dolls* were vehicles for Brando's considerable powers of seduction, but, significantly, not of the tough, inarticulate kind he had perfected as Stanley Kowalski and Johnny Strabler. Because Brando knew each character from the inside out, he could imagine and express who they would be when in love. In Sky Masterson, he plays a man who knows women better than they know themselves, captivating them with wit and eloquence. While Brando glows as a romantic lead in white silk gliding through a waltzing lesson with Simmons in *Désirée*, he is almost as bright as the sun in *Guys and Dolls*. As a gambler whose conversance with the Bible surpasses that of the attractive missionary (Simmons), he plies her with rum drowned in milk to help her relax, not to take advantage of her.

In *Guys and Dolls*, Brando fulfills a classic female fantasy: the man who understands virtue as well as vice. Keenly observant, he is a risk-taker who never loses a wager, a commitment-shy maverick who quotes his daddy as often as the Good Book. The greatest source of his allure is a golden tongue, which is matched by a mellow baritone that seems aimed, especially in numbers like "I'll Know When My Love Comes Along," at dazzling women more than music critics. In keeping with Damon Runyon's comic content, Brando's touch was light; he adapted his acting to the musical's task of storytelling through song. As Hollis Alpert wrote in the *Saturday Review*, "Brando can't really sing...but he almost convinces you that he can." His sex appeal, however, was irrefutable, and his abilities in this respect were reflected in the overwhelming reaction of audiences. The mob scene at the November 3, 1955, premiere in Times Square was almost life-threatening for Brando and Simmons. Filmed in Cinemascope and Technicolor, *Guys and Dolls* was the highest-grossing picture of 1955, earning more than $9 million at the box office that year. Nominated for four Academy Awards, the film made many lists of top movie musicals.[92]

Brando gave interviews (probably obligated by the fine print of his contract) to generate publicity, doing his best as usual to subvert the agenda. Conceding some anxiety about the reception of his first singing part, Brando said he believed it "an actor's job to try new things. His voice, facial expressions and body movements, his acting techniques are the tools of his trade...[he] should develop as many uses of them as possible. Mr. [Samuel] Goldwyn was willing to risk more than five million dollars on the picture, so I figured I might as well take a chance with him." Brando's implicit comparison of gambling and movies as big-money risk industries undermined the Hollywood bravado major actors were expected to sustain. Likewise, his emphasis on the unheralded talent behind an extravaganza like *Guys and Dolls* reminded listeners that celebrities do not work alone. Commending his voice coach and the music director, Brando revised the image of the multitalented star. Eager to reaffirm the myth Brando has tarnished, the unctuous interviewer closes with a compliment: "We hear you've developed a fine singing voice. Some compare you to Nat King Cole." Brando's laconic reply punctures the balloon: "Well, I don't think that Nat has very much to worry about."[93]

The success of *Désirée* and *Guys and Dolls* gave Brando the freedom to pursue his next two projects: *The Teahouse of the August Moon* (1956) and *Sayonara* (1957). Brando had enjoyed the Broadway version of *Teahouse* and actively sought the lead role in the movie. "If Marlon had wanted to play Little Eva, I would have let him," producer Dore Schary confessed.[94] Though Sakini in *Teahouse* was not Little Eva, it was an atypical role—not only because Brando was nearly unrecognizable in his makeup as the Okinawan interpreter but also because the character was asexual. A philosophical mediator, he is the first of Brando's comedians, a genre he would try again in *Bedtime Story*, *Candy*, and *Free Money*, with mixed results.

Brando was a puzzling case of an actor with an extraordinary sense of humor and a passion for great comedians—W. C. Fields, Laurel and Hardy, and Charlie Chaplin were favorites—whose own comic work fell well below these standards of greatness. His library had many books on the subject (including anthologies of wit and works analyzing humor in different cultures). Brando's sense of humor was the first thing people noticed about his personality, and it was usually the first thing he noticed about other people. On screen, Brando was most humorous when it was least expected. He used it to relieve tension, or to create empathy for a character who might otherwise seem villainous. The prime example is the unscripted plate-breaking scene in *Streetcar*, where Brando's Stanley, in response to Stella's irritated demand that he help her clear the table, smashes a plate with his fist, sweeps it to the floor, hurls a china cup against the wall, then asks quietly, "My place is all cleared now, do you want me to clear yours?"[95] Brando's German soldier in *The Young Lions* playfully introduces his date to a festive noisemaker with hairlike streamers—"My sister Frieda," he says—for comic effect on the point of a New Year's Eve toast to Adolf Hitler. His buttoned-up ambassador Harrison Carter MacWhite in *The Ugly American* uses his wife's toes as a letter holder in a soothing bedroom interlude, and the sardonic bent of his sheriff in *The Chase* alleviates the general grimness.

But full-blown humor somehow escaped Brando as an actor. Conceding that "I've never been a comic actor and am not very good at it," Brando went on to describe how he was so entertained by his costar David Niven in *Bedtime Story* that he was often laughing too hard to finish a scene.[96] In generic comedies, his surest mode was irony. His direct prologue to the audience as Sakini, where he presents colonialism as a gift—"Okinawa very fortunate. Culture brought to us—not have to leave home for it"—is still amusing, however dated it now seems, as are the scenes where he patiently explains local customs to the dense Captain Frisby (Glenn Ford). The scenes shot on location in Nara, Japan, were its most successful, and an added benefit came from casting Japanese actors in major parts. These aspects, together with the use of Okinawan and Japanese music and musicians, counterbalanced the plot's hackneyed opposition between Asian shrewdness and American military bumbling.

Brando was excited about spending time filming in Japan for *Teahouse*. He immersed himself in books about the country: its language, architecture, plant and animal life, religion, philosophy, geography, and even its art of flower arrangement. The nearly one hundred books on Japan in Brando's library, ranging from the 1940s through 1995 (with the preponderance from the mid-1950s and earlier), suggest that he was motivated by his own interests to visit Japan and make films about the country. But his interest grew with exposure to Japan, and Southeast Asia in general. What concerned him the most in the 1950s was the political situation. He paid close attention to experiences of colonization as well as types of self-government, and the relationship between language and religious customs in Felix Keesing's *Native Peoples of the Pacific World* (1945). On a page about the Buddhist concept of "suchness" (*tathata*), describing how spirituality inheres in the direct experience of the concrete, Brando underlines the statement—"things are separable in words which are inseparable in nature," because words can be rearranged. Moreover, the static terms that we apply to feelings conceal that "our feelings are directions rather than states."[97]

Brando put himself on a starvation diet to achieve the litheness of his Okinawan character, studying Japanese and other Pacific languages and mannerisms to authenticate his gestures and speech inflections. Submitting to two hours of makeup a day, he donned a black wig and wore dark contact lenses, losing himself so completely in the role that many left the theater wondering whether he had even been in the movie. The mere fact of a major actor assuming such a part was significant in 1950s Hollywood. It revealed a sincere lack of vanity and a dedication to furthering cross-cultural awareness that was central to Brando's agenda. Because comedy was not a hospitable genre for him, he accomplished much more on behalf of that agenda in his next two projects *Sayonara* (1957) and *The Young Lions* (1958). Both were big pictures, based on popular novels by James Michener and Irwin Shaw, respectively, concerned with issues central to the culture. As an actor at the height of box-office success, Brando was the obvious choice to star in both films.

Because Brando was conversant with the subjects of both films—Japanese–American relations and the rise of Fascism in Germany, respectively—he played a significant role in articulating their treatment. In *Sayonara*, Brando was concerned about the accuracy of the portrait of Japan and its traditions. He was also intent on enlightening Japanese as well as American audiences on the issue of interracial romance.[98] Having arrived in Tokyo on January 12, 1957, Brando held a press conference arranged by Warner Brothers the next day. It highlighted the importance of friendship and understanding between the United States and Japan and his own knowledge of Japan, including its language.[99] Brando's personal diplomacy, his effort to speak Japanese, and his obvious interest in the culture helped *Sayonara*'s producers gain access to sites such as the Imperial Gardens and the Takarasuka Theatre Company, which had never been filmed.[100]

Brando's high hopes for *Sayonara* were offset by concerns about the director, Joshua Logan; the script, written by Paul Osborn; and the plot of the novel by James Michener on which it was based. "Their interracial romance was doomed by the tradition in both cultures of endogamy, the custom of marrying only within one's own race or caste. In accepting this principle, I thought the story endorsed indirectly a form of racism." Brando insisted that the "Madame Butterfly ending" be replaced with one that portrayed racial intermarriage as a "natural outcome" of love. This allowed *Sayonara* to be "an example of the pictures I wanted to make, films that exerted a positive force."[101] Once these changes were agreed to, Brando accepted the role.

He would have other issues with the *Sayonara* script. Brando was alert to inaccuracies in cultural norms. He questions, for instance, a scene of a Japanese audience eating at a Kabuki theater: "never eat in public," Brando notes in the margin. The comment by his character Major Gruver to a leading Kabuki actor that their all-male theater could have used "a few Marilyn Monroes," inspires a scribbled "gauche." These two false notes remained unchanged in the script, but he did manage to revise another scene he complained about, where Gruver appeared "humorless" and "false" in badgering a dancer to arrange a meeting for him with Hana-Ogi, the dancer he adores. He also altered a scene he found highly inappropriate, where Hana-Ogi is depicted as staring intensely at Gruver in their first meeting: "false that a Japanese girl should be so forward. Doesn't look like candor so much as cheapness." In the actual scene, Hana-Ogi's eyes are averted for most of the encounter, and Gruver behaves more circumspectly, which is far more effective, culturally and dramatically.[102]

Sayonara is in certain respects a fanciful, glossy travel brochure. Yet its detailed appreciation for Japanese art and ritual and its tough political stances—especially its normalization of the cross-cultural affair—enhances its significance. Thus, it exposes the hypocrisy of the US Army for allowing thousands of enlisted men to marry Japanese women and then barring the women from entering the United States, effectively forcing the men to choose divorce or exile. Suggesting that true rapprochement can only occur when traditional and institutional constraints are diminished, the film depicts a journey of self-discovery for Brando's character. The conventional son of a military man, Major Gruver has spent his life conforming; though he is dissatisfied, he has no real access to his feelings. His appreciation of a foreign culture and recognition of the limitations on soldiers in love with Japanese women, as well as the oppressive cultural limitations on Japanese women, sets in relief the compromises he has made. As Gruver becomes more emotionally aware, a development intensified by the double suicide of a soldier friend and his Asian wife, he becomes more appealing. The final scene is a classic romantic affirmation. "We've been wasting two good lives trying to do the right thing, the right thing for Matsubayashi [Girls' Troupe], the right thing for my father, the right thing for the military, the right thing for Japanese tradition, the right thing for the great white race," Gruver pleads, reminding Hana-Ogi of their "obligation" to love. "We live in different worlds, come from different races," she responds. "What will happen to our children, what would they be?" His answer is a prophecy of American multiculturalism: "What would they be? They'd be half Japanese, half American, half yellow, half white, they'd be half you, they'd be half me, that's all they're going to be!" Signaling the new beginning, Hana-Ogi, the Japanese woman who finds it "very difficult to speak in public," announces their marriage to the press. "Major Gruver has asked me to be his wife, he knows there are many people in his country who will be disturbed by this. I know my people will be shocked too. But I hope they will learn to understand."

The movie was nominated for ten Academy Awards, including Best Actor, Best Picture, and Best Director, winning four. Deborah Kerr, who had played Portia in *Julius Caesar*, found herself in the odd position of writing Brando "a 'fan' letter" but "felt absolutely compelled to express my admiration and gratitude for your really exquisite performance.... It was a performance of such skill... for another of the same trade... an unbelievable enjoyment."[103] Veteran actors and ordinary theatergoers commended his Southern military officer, the ace pilot graduate of Princeton and West Point, who embraces an unexpected destiny, marrying a Japanese dancer and taking a moral stand against prejudice.

Brando knew what he was talking about. He had always been attracted to "exotic, dark-skinned" women, a category that ranged over a lifetime from the Jewish women he met as a young actor in New York to the Hispanic, Asian, and Tahitian women he met in Hollywood and on location.[104] Most of his longstanding relationships were with nonwhite women, including the half-Indian Anna Kashfi, whom he married in 1957 (they had met in the fall of 1955 at the Paramount commissary) when she was pregnant with their child. Brando was a visionary who understood that the increasingly global perspectives of average people would help to erode, however gradually, the customs barring cross-cultural romance, challenged in *Sayonara*.

The Young Lions was equally preoccupied with issues of prejudice and justice, but it was focused on the past rather than the future. Here, in attempting to educate audiences about the rise of Fascism, Brando played a role almost antithetical to his previous one. Based on Irwin Shaw's bestselling 1948 novel about the intersecting lives of American and German soldiers during World War II, the original movie script by Edward Anhalt preserved Shaw's basic plot and characterizations. The idealistic Jewish-American soldier Noah Ackerman (Montgomery Clift), the cynical but good-hearted Broadway producer turned unwilling soldier Michael Whiteacre (Dean Martin), and the evil Nazi Christian Diestl (Brando) fight in Europe and Africa, pair off with various women, and eventually meet in a climax that results in the death of Diestl and Ackerman.

Brando had no intention of playing Diestl as a Nazi zealot, bloodthirsty in battle, alternately slavish and violent toward women. He had the contractual right to alter the script, which he exercised, vastly improving the characterization and the movie as a whole.[105] While the bare outlines of character and plot remain in the revised script (though Diestl is now the only one of the three principals to die at the end), Brando's revisions were transformative.[106]

By investing his German officer with humanity and charm, Brando foisted a moral responsibility on audiences, forcing them to reassess presumptions about the inherent evil of those who fought for the Nazis. Convinced that the time had come for Americans to deal honestly with the horrors of World War II, Brando saw real prospects for educating the public. He wanted *The Young Lions* to offer the most complicated perspective possible in a commercial entertainment.

Brando had the first English edition of Wilhelm Reich's *The Mass Psychology of Fascism*, which was published in the United States in 1946. He annotated passages denying that Fascism was the province of a single nation—passages that were directly pertinent to his characterization of Diestl. These included the warning that "One cannot make the Fascist harmless... if one does not look for him *in oneself*"; and again: "Fascism is still being considered a specific national characteristic of the Germans or the

Japanese," because analysts are afraid to acknowledge its "*inter-national*" presence.[107] When he noted that America had been for-tunate to avoid a significant Fascist influence, he probably had the Reich volume in mind.[108]

Brando also read the massive two-volume *History of Philosophy Eastern and Western* (1952, 1953) by Sarvepalli Radhakrishnan, the philosopher-statesman renowned for bridging Eastern and Western thought, and *The Chrysanthemum and the Sword* (1946) by anthropologist Ruth Benedict, which centered on Japan in its general exploration of Eastern versus Western traditions. An argument for tolerance among nations, Benedict's book champi-oned "a world made safe for differences," to which Brando added: "we do not judge nations on the mistakes they have made but how earnestly they try to recognize the ones they have made and correct them."[109] Another book Brando read and annotated carefully during this period was Gardner Murphy's *In the Minds of Men* (1955). Murphy's book focused on India but claimed wide relevance for its applied-psychology approach, which brought individual motivation to bear in analyzing subjects like the rise of Fascism in Germany or the prevalence of caste hostili-ties in India. Taking its title from a sentence in the preamble to the UNESCO constitution—"Since wars begin in the minds of men, it is in the minds of men that the defenses of peace must be constructed"—the book was exemplary as a learned analysis with practical uses (which explained the UNESCO support granted the author), the kind of work Brando especially admired.[110]

When Brando arrived in Paris for on-location shooting of *The Young Lions*, he went to visit Irwin Shaw and was surprised to find that the author had met no one from the production. Explain-ing the changes he had made to his German character, Brando asked Shaw whether he would have portrayed him in the same way that he had ten years earlier. Shaw reaffirmed his belief in the monolithic evil of Germany. The two were sufficiently cordial

Brando greeting Irwin Shaw in Paris, 1957.

in their disagreement to appear jointly on David Schoenbrun's CBS News program from Paris, where they held steadfastly to their opposing views. At a subsequent Berlin press conference, Brando commented, "The picture will try to show that Nazism is a matter of mind, not geography, that there are Nazis—and people of good will—in every country. The world can't keep looking over its shoulder and nursing hatreds. There would be no progress that way."[111]

Christian Diestl is in many ways a classic Brando character: brooding, reticent, erotically charged. Apolitical and idealistic at the film's start, he recognizes Nazism's fanatical elements but hopes that they will be superseded by its democratizing potential. As the son of a shoemaker who has had to sacrifice his ambition to be a doctor, given the dearth of free universities in Germany, he trusts Hitler to abolish the social hierarchy that prevents people from rising above their class. The next time we see him, he is a lieutenant in the army, skillfully guiding his men through an exchange with the French Resistance en route to Paris. He opts for wounding a French fighter in the shooting arm, rather than killing him, and disputes the brutal work of his unit in occupied Paris. Meanwhile, in scenes that enhance his appeal, he romances two beautiful women—a dark-haired Frenchwoman named Françoise (Liliane Montevecchi), who warms up to him after initial hostility, and Gretchen (May Britt), the seductive blonde wife of his commanding officer, Captain Hardenberg (Maximilian Schell). When his company is sent to North Africa with General Rommel's brigade, Diestl continues to be a brilliant strategist who dislikes war. Poised on a hillside to attack a British battalion below, Diestl advises Hardenberg to delay until sunrise, when the sun's rays will blind the enemy, giving the Germans an advantage.[112] The turning point comes after Diestl has rejoined German forces in Europe and chances upon a concentration camp, where his worst fears are realized. After listening wild-eyed to the camp commandant's grousing about the challenges of exterminating sixteen hundred men, women, and children a day, he exits in despair. Diestl's death is a virtual suicide: He smashes his machine gun, walks unarmed into Michael Whiteacre's gunfire, then falls facedown into a puddle.

Brando's acting in *The Young Lions* is full of distinctive moments. He makes superb use of objects: the paper horn in the New Year's Eve scene; the napkin balls he tosses into a wineglass at the sidewalk café while impatiently awaiting the French girls. He locates the latent drama in the smallest actions—shaking the wine Françoise has overturned, in an angry outburst, off his black leather gloves; the martial click he gives his boot heels as he bows in greeting Gretchen Hardenberg; pouring a drink for Gretchen, deciding it is too much, and returning half to the bottle. Brando's evocation of riding a motorcycle in the desert while half asleep is a considerable feat—the rocking motion, the lids drooping as he brushes sand from his eyes. Equally striking is the anguish on his face as he watches a one-legged boy on crutches struggle over a log. So much of what Brando conveys is silent, given his belief in the difficulty of articulating in words the crushing impact of war on soldiers as well as civilians, and of cultivating empathy in American audiences for German suffering.

Diestl's most stirring speech, with Françoise in a Parisian apartment just before he encounters the concentration camp, is among his best ever. Brando later recalled how pivotal this scene was for all his future performances, for it was here that he first recognized that he didn't need to memorize his lines. "I had just written the scene at the dinner table, and instead of memorizing the lines, I put them on my plate and shaded my eyes the whole time so I could read them."[113] Françoise begs Diestl to abandon the now-hopeless fight, and he replies that he has "come too far." It was Brando's decision to put a rotating musical light on the table before him that emits a low, atonal hum as he speaks: "When you are in a *hole*, filled with your own *excrement* for days *on end*, and when you see the faces and the bodies of the men you've killed, you *change*, and when you're out there like that, when you have to live with death *every day, for so long*, you have to keep something in front of you, or you would go *insane*, so I was, I was always afraid that I had just invented you." (Italics indicate words stressed by Brando.) He delivers the whole speech with his hands over his eyes, slowly speaking in the soft German accent he had carefully learned. He looks up only at the end, to check whether she is indeed real. Brando's timing here is critical; he pauses, staring, disbelieving still, finally sighing out, "Yeees." The other actors in the production emphasized how Brando's work affected their own. In the words of Liliane Montevecchi,

"He made me an actress and I was never an actress before, just a puppet."[114]

The Young Lions was a critical and commercial success, nominated for four Academy Awards, despite its controversial subject. While some moviegoers and critics resented Brando's effort to humanize a Nazi soldier, the majority commended his acting and agreed that it was the film's "chief attraction." The praise from other professionals was particularly strong. Brando's Diestl clearly moved the director Otto Preminger. "You seem to have pushed through some sort of an acting sound barrier, and gone far beyond anything I have ever seen before," Preminger commented, adding that he lost "all consciousness" that he was even watching an actor and a movie. Stanley Kauffmann, in his review for the *New Republic*, was even more enthusiastic. *The Young Lions* was "worth seeing because of Brando's performance.... He has caught perfectly the stiff cordiality, the slightly declamatory speech, the somewhat angular movements, the charm and the consciousness of charm that create another man—Diestl—for us." Kauffmann concludes: "He now has the opportunity to be the first American film actor to achieve greatness."[115] Brando saved both Kauffmann's and Preminger's remarks. But the response that seems to have meant most, if careful preservation of the letter and his reply to it are any indication, was from a self-described "average American housewife."

Mary Motley of Detroit, Michigan, thanked Brando for his interpretation of Christian Diestl and confessed that she had often been tempted to indulge feelings of prejudice against the German people. Being a Negro, however, familiar with the pain of prejudice, she had withstood the impulse. She had never quite understood the importance of her resistance until she saw *The Young Lions*. It confirmed what she had known instinctively, that there had to have been decent men in the German army, because every nation or race is composed of good and bad elements.

Brando's characterization gave her confidence in the sentiment that prejudice against a whole people was indefensible. At the same time, she continued, Brando revealed in his expressiveness in the scene at the concentration camp what happens when a good person compromises his beliefs; he becomes responsible for the evil he has enabled. In his letter of May 22, 1958, Brando told Mrs. Motley he was heartened by her grasp of "the most important themes of my part," conceding, "I think that perhaps you have understood the film better than anyone I've talked with." He expressed gratitude for her "understanding and tolerance," adding, "I hardly think you are an average American housewife."[116]

Brando had affirmed the same idea more than a decade earlier in portraying Stanley Kowalski on Broadway: People come in complex shades, never in black and white. He understood that among the greatest horrors of the Holocaust was that those responsible for its worst abuses were human, not monsters. Humans motivated by hatred perpetrated unfathomable cruelty, and other humans out of a sense of duty or indifference permitted it. To claim the humanity of the Germans, even the Nazis, was not to excuse them. By giving American audiences in *The Young Lions* what he believed was a truthful portrait of the human beings behind Nazi atrocities, Brando asked those audiences to contemplate their own propensities for evil. He hoped they would recognize that the potential for brutality was not confined to specific nations or individuals. Intellectual honesty for Brando was synonymous with authentic acting, which could be far-reaching. And touching a person like Mary Motley, making her *think*. *That* was an achievement.

CHAPTER FOUR

THE EPIC MODE, 1960-1963

The more often a critical opinion is repeated, the more it is believed, no matter how tenuous its relationship to truth. This seems the most plausible explanation for the wholesale dismissal of Brando's work from the 1960s. Biographers have claimed that the quality of his acting declined over the decade, and that there is very little worth seeing until his resurrection in *The Godfather* (1972). The fact is, however, that almost all the films released between 1960 and 1972 were profitable and earned the respect of critics. Brando's films from the 1960s feature some of his most accomplished acting. In them he extended the promise of the 1950s by assuming projects that challenged him aesthetically and politically. His notes and script rewrites reveal how seriously he took these roles, and how much he knew about different aspects of moviemaking, from the technical to the philosophical. Brando's extensive reading continued to inform his work and led him to use the Pitcairn Island sequence in *Mutiny on the Bounty* as an opportunity to explore human behavior in Utopia, and to qualify the moral absolutism in his Western *One-Eyed Jacks* by portraying all the characters as corruptible. Brando remained, as he had been from early in his Hollywood career, a magnet for talent. When his name was attached to a project, the prospect of signing other top actors, cinematographers, musicians, and screenwriters, was enhanced.[1] Thus, accomplished composers continued to write scores for the 1960s films: Hugo Friedhofer for *One-Eyed Jacks*, Dave Grusin for *Candy*, and Ennio Morricone for *Burn!* The writers of these years were equally distinguished, including Tennessee Williams (*The Fugitive Kind*), Lillian Hellman (*The Chase*), and Carson McCullers (*Reflections in a Golden Eye*), as were the directors: John Huston, Charlie Chaplin, Gillo Pontecorvo, and Arthur Penn. Brando also appeared with many leading actors: Anna Magnani, Sophia Loren, Elizabeth Taylor, Richard Burton, Robert Redford, Jane Fonda, and Yul Brynner.

More important, his work in the 1960s extended his commitments of the previous decade, reflecting his ideals, enabling him to travel and see the world, and to assume new dramatic challenges. It seems fitting that his two most personal pictures frame the decade: *One-Eyed Jacks* (1961) expressed his sense of what films could be, and *Burn!* (1969) was his favorite. Both were positively reviewed at the time and developed considerable followings over the years, especially among cinema devotees. They typify a range of Brando's performances that are underappreciated.

A number of these films sought to raise the bar for audiences, by repudiating traditional heroism or shedding light on subjects that had been avoided or overlooked. The most significant of them confirmed that aesthetic values and the obligation to entertain were compatible with the goal of enlightenment. While Brando's film company, Pennebaker, was created, like others begun by stars of the era, to provide a tax shelter, Brando was most attracted to the prospect of greater control over moviemaking, which he felt should "address issues like hypocrisy, injustice and the corruptness of government policies."[2] Concern for those who were less fortunate and an eagerness to do something about prejudice and poverty influenced the initial projects the company pursued. *The Ugly American* would explore US diplomatic and military misadventures in Southeast Asia. The Western, *One-Eyed Jacks*, sought to transform the genre by recuperating the cultural diversity of the American West and by exposing the deprivation and violence that so radicalized conventional morality.

Another purpose of Pennebaker Productions was to provide a job for his father. Forced into early retirement, like Arthur Miller's salesman protagonist, Brando Sr. was by the 1950s living off his movie-star son, who bought his parents a ranch in the Nebraska Sandhills. Neither a good business manager nor speculator, Marlon Sr. by this time had lost significant portions of his son's earnings in poor investments.[3] But Brando's decision to continue trusting his father as a financial adviser highlighted a dependency evident in the conclusion to a letter he wrote Marlon Sr. about finances while he was performing in *Candida* with Katharine Cornell: "You're damn swell to always offer your dummy son help when he thinks he does or doesn't need it."[4] This was at least partly acting—the son kowtowing to the father in a manner guaranteed to stroke the paternal ego. But to the extent that the feelings were genuine, they would take time to overcome. During the years Marlon Sr. worked at Pennebaker, Brando could behave affectionately, even hugging his father in greeting. But the few times Marlon Sr. overstepped the bounds of employee—opening his son's mail or firing one of his friends—Brando's ferocious reaction was a reminder that the son controlled the company and that his resentment over his father's verbal and physical abuse remained fresh.[5] *One-Eyed Jacks* would serve as yet another reminder.

BRANDO DIRECTING

There was no project that Brando worked on longer than *One-Eyed Jacks*, especially if the time he spent generating a satisfying plot and script is factored in. The choice of a Western as a vehicle for his new company made sense commercially and was also wise from the perspective of his artistry and acting ambitions. Brando was well versed in the genre and intent on stretching its limits with a more accurate historical approach. The strategies he devised for making the most of the landscape—featuring ocean in addition to desert settings, filming on location at Big Sur, the Monterey coast, and Death Valley—served to distinguish the picture. He created continuity between the desert and ocean scenes by dwelling on dust, which from certain camera angles looked like sea mist. A reminder in Brando's writing on the back page of his 1963 Indian book (he was reading for a prospective Indian film) to use "dust as a characteristic of Indians, one eyed jacks" identifies the deliberateness of the image. Dust symbolized both the life and the death of Indians, as confirmed by a page of "Notes on Indians" he wrote in Tahiti in 1963: "Indian lived dust, slipped on it prayed on it and ate it. Lived it and finally became the dust."[6] Another departure was the representation of the West as a site of cultural and ethnic diversity where Asians, Mexicans, Indians, and Anglo-Americans lived, sharing genes, customs, and diseases and battling over everything else. Brando read numerous books describing this volatile mix of native Indians and Mexicans, black soldiers and white prospectors on the frontier, the dress of citizens and criminals, and details such as how to draw a gun.[7] He also read biographies of Billy the Kid, probably including Pat Garrett's *The Authentic Life of Billy the Kid* (1882), which described the Kid's expressive blue eyes and gentlemanly bearing, concluding: "Those who knew him best will tell you that in his most savage and dangerous moods his face always wore a smile."[8] The region was unrelentingly grim: privileging shrewdness and brute strength, nullifying bourgeois ideals.

An orphan with no surname, of ambiguous parentage and cultural origin, Brando's protagonist is the ultimate marginal man, on the edge in every community—deviant or law-abiding—making him vulnerable to victimization. *One-Eyed Jacks* was also unusual in portraying women as replicating the struggles and norms of men to a degree, but also harboring their own forms of spiritual solace and compassion. "Our early-day heroes were not brave one hundred percent of the time, nor were they good one hundred percent of the time," Brando commented, adding that he had aimed "a frontal assault on the temple of clichés" defining the genre.[9]

As the only movie Brando directed, and also starred in, and did scriptwriting for (on every role), *One-Eyed Jacks* reveals a great deal about his film ambitions. He surrounded himself with experts, from Hugo Friedhofer to cinematographer Charles Lang, who won an Oscar for his painterly portrait of desert and sea. From the point when he began reading and notetaking through the final day of shooting, which stretched into the fall of 1960, the script was unstable. The same was true of the film's sources, for *One-Eyed Jacks* was based on two novels, neither of which had much in common with the ultimate film. Pennebaker had optioned the rights to Louis L'Amour's *To Tame a Land* (1955), the story of a lonely gunman, Rye Tyler, orphaned at twelve after an Indian raid and then adopted by a literate outlaw whose conversance with Plutarch is superseded only by his survival skills.

Drawn to L'Amour's emphasis on California's original inhabitants, their struggles against the Mexicans and Anglo-Americans threatening their land, Brando gives voice here to the "plight and rights of Indians." His character Rye is advised not to hate the Indians, for "he has Indian blood in his veins ... stands on Indian land and breathes Indian air."[10] These elements disappear over multiple revisions. By April 11, 1957, Brando Sr. tells his son in a letter that any lingering details from L'Amour's novel should be stricken to avoid "contractual obligations."[11]

The credited source, *The Authentic Death of Hendry Jones* (1956) by Charles Neider, a Mark Twain scholar who shared

Twain's passion for the West, was similarly more palimpsest than foundation. Neider's novel focuses on the pursuit of the legendary outlaw Hendry Jones, or "the Kid," who is conceived as a greater gunfighter than Billy the Kid. Killed by his former partner, Sheriff Dad Longworth, in the name of the law whose embrace ensures progress, the Kid endures as a folk hero to the Mexican, Asian, and Indian minorities populating California in the late 1880s. His criminality represents resistance to the moderniz-ing tactics of Anglos such as Longworth, defenders of private property and social order. This opposition between a Protestant–capitalist ethos and the heterogeneous figures who threaten it haunts *One-Eyed Jacks*. Yet *The Authentic Death of Hendry Jones* seems to have served primarily as a trigger that spurred writers Calder Willingham, Guy Trosper, and Brando to imagine a story and a collection of voices. The similarities between novel and film are few: a bare outline of main characters Dad Longworth, the Kid, Bob Amory, Lon Dedrick; the protracted scene of the Kid's jailing and subsequent escape; and some phrases ("You bet"; "I'm not hung yet"; "He won't get any older than tomorrow"; "You'll get yours one of these days").[12]

There are shared themes, among them the permeable border between good and bad. As the narrator of Neider's novel observes, "Hell, we never *turned*. Those things just happened. One fel-low went one way and another another and the first thing you knew one of them was called an outlaw and the other was run-ning a faro bank and was protected by the sheriff."[13] Brando's character, Kid Rio, and Karl Malden's Dad Longworth appear in the film's early scenes as bandits who have been together for a decade. Dad has befriended the youthful Rio and tutored him in the outlaw trade, then betrays him and becomes respectable. The father-son relationship is there in L'Amour and Neider, but it takes center stage in *One-Eyed Jacks*, where it is invested with a rare psychodynamic complexity. By enlarging the theme of thwarted succession—the patriarch bent on destroying the heir—acknowledging it as foundational to the Western, Brando reconceives the genre.

One-Eyed Jacks opens through a window framing a busy town square, and a caption, "Sonora, Mexico 1880," which establishes the film as a point of entry into a historical fiction or a fairy tale whose norms, we soon learn, will be slightly fractured. This is confirmed by the immediate image of a bank robber, Rio, eating bananas while guarding the customers as his partner, Dad, collects the money. Tossing the peels on alternate sides of a gold scale, Rio saunters over to a woman who has hidden a precious ring in her handbag, and smilingly takes the spoils, wagging his gun at her. Robbery is a way of life for these men; their playfulness belies the risk. It is also a means for balancing the scales, readjusting the apportionments of fate. The next scene shows a well-groomed Rio courting an aristocratic lady in her home, passing off the stolen ring as his mother's. This scene also concerns getting what he can, giving only what he must. His suit progresses admirably, until Longworth appears with Mexican *Rurales* at his heels. On his way out the door, Rio yanks the ring—an unnecessary expenditure for an aborted seduction—off the lady's finger. Rio and Longworth are chased to a desert mountaintop, Gallon Rim, losing a horse en route, their arrest imminent. A game of chance with a bullet hidden in a hand decides who will seek fresh mounts. Rio considers that staying to protect the Rim is less perilous than riding, so he deceives Dad by hiding a bullet in each hand. This is Rio's betrayal. The next one, Dad's, is far more consequential: Arriving at the horse corral with the gold, he realizes the benefits of going it alone and abandons Rio, who is captured by the Mexican police. As they pass by the corral en route to prison, Rio sees Longworth's horse and the many others that would have saved him.

The story resumes five years later with the escape of Rio and a Mexican prison mate, Modesto. Now bent on vengeance, Rio vows to find Dad and make him pay. Returning to Sonora, he learns from a pair of outlaws about a bank in Monterey, where the town's sheriff is Dad Longworth. Rio and Modesto team up with Bob Amory (Ben Johnson) and Harvey Johnson (Sam Gilman), and head to Monterey. Visiting Dad, Rio convinces him that he was never captured and bears no grudge; he stays for dinner, meeting Dad's Mexican wife, Maria, and stepdaughter, Louisa, and launching a flirtation with Louisa that results in a tryst on the beach and her pregnancy. When Rio shoots a man in self-defense, Dad uses the incident as an excuse for whipping Rio brutally in public and then smashing his gun hand with a rifle butt. Injured in body and soul, Rio rides off to a Chinese Fishing Village with his partners to recuperate. There he broods and is visited by Louisa, to whom he tells the story of Dad's betrayal and his five years in prison. She professes her love but leaves without divulging her pregnancy because he is committed to killing Dad. In the final scenes, Amory and Johnson rob the bank without Rio, shooting Modesto beforehand, and then a child and a teller. Dad blames Rio, who was not there, and jails him, hoping to finish him off. The jail scenes of Rio's dialogues with Dad, fights with Lon, the hostile deputy, and eventual escape, are the only scenes in the film that draw (thinly) on Neider's novel. In a final duel, Rio kills Dad and rides away, promising Louisa to return in the spring when their baby comes. In Brando's original tragic ending, Rio, Dad, and Louisa die, but Paramount producers, mindful of their financial stake, overruled his desire for a somber close to match the film as a whole.

Brando deferred on this but had his way on almost everything else. "It was fitting that Marlon end up directing because this picture was his vision," Karl Malden, who played Dad Longworth, recalled. "He brought the bat and ball so we were all ready to play the game according to his rules."[14] Brando kept multiple annotated copies of the script, handwritten notes on story and dialogue during the development and shooting stages, and instructions for cuts during the editing stage. These scripts and notes reveal his responsibility for most of the conceptualizations, dialogue, and scenes. Many of the film's best details were improvised under his direction during shooting—for instance, Rio eating bananas during the bank robbery, Dad's shoeless escape, Rio fixing Dad's "guess" by hiding bullets in both hands, Rio and Dad's dramatic handshake during their tense reunion, Louisa hiding bullets in her hand to assist Rio's jail escape.

These subtle revisions of plot and characterization created structural parallels and echoes, in keeping with the ongoing substitution of concise and humorous understatement for stiff, long-winded prose. *One-Eyed Jacks* bristles with memorable dialogue Brando introduced in late script revisions or ad-libbed during production. (Italics indicate words stressed by Brando and Malden.) In the early Lon–Rio encounter, Lon blows tobacco on Rio's clothes and then says, "I got a lot of funny things to do today but lippin' with you ain't one *of* 'em." In the Dad–Rio reunion, Rio to Dad: "You're gettin' way ahead of yourself, Dad....*Nothin' happened* to *me*. I just fooled around with them dogfaces till it got dark, and then I went down and stole a *Captain's horse*." Dad: "You sure that's the straight of it Kid?" Kid: "Well you know *me Dad*. If I didn't feel *right about it*, we'd been out there splatterin' each other all over that front yard....A man can't stay angry for five years. *Can he?*" Rio, with Louisa the morning after: "Well that's about it. It ain't gonna help much to say it, but I *shamed you*. And I *wish to God I hadn't*." Their next meeting at the Chinese Fishing Village features the film's best lines. Excising pages of dialogue, he inserts: "*Reasons?* I got *reasons*. I got *seventeen hundred and eight* of 'em. That's how many *days* I spent down in that lead mine in the pen in Sonora. That's how many nights I spent digging the *maggots out of the sores on my ankles*, with the

Scriptwriting on *One-Eyed Jacks*, 1959. Photograph by Sam Shaw, © Sam Shaw Inc., Licensed by Shaw Family Archives, www.shawfamilyarchives.com.

rats running all over me." Louisa asks, "And you think that to kill him will make you a man?" "Well I don't know about that," Rio responds, "but I know that I thought about him every day for five years. And that was the only thing that kept me going." In the argument with Bob Amory, Brando revises "you pig sucker" to the notorious, *"Get up/you/scum-suckin'/pig!"* And he invents the jail dialogue. Rio: "You *dyin* to get me hung, *aint ya!*" Dad: "No Kid. You've been tryin' to get yourself hung for the past ten years, and this time I think you're *gonna make it!*" "You should'a quit when you were ahead." Rio: "Like you huh?" Dad: "Uh hum, like me." Rio: "You're a *one-eyed Jack* around *here* Dad. I seen the other side of your *face....* I *am* gonna get a trial, *ain't I* Dad?" Dad: "Oh sure kid, sure. You'll get a *fair trial*. And then I'm gonna *hang you. Personally!"*

One-Eyed Jacks reflects Brando's ear for colloquial expressions and aptitude for coining memorable epithets. His insistence that language be used with precision and economy is consistent with a respect evident in the many thesauruses, collections of proverbs, and quotation books he owned (and often annotated). He kept lists of words and phrases, and the invention of odd terms and forms was a pastime he always enjoyed with his close friend Wally Cox.[15] At the same time, the film affirms his recognition that most communication is nonverbal, exemplified by his refusal to caption the sorrowful scenes where Louisa divulges her loss of virginity and then pregnancy to her mother in Spanish. Brando was convinced that the actors would give stronger performances in their own language, and that audiences would grasp the essential content. Conveyed by tone and expression to English-speakers, the daughter's repetition of the maternal fate—childbirth out of wedlock—is more intimate. Producer Frank Rosenberg complained about the scene but later admitted that Brando was right.[16] Another trademark of Brando as director was his "enormous patience" in developing the contributions of cast and crew, and his protectiveness toward doubles and extras who are frequently imperiled on film sets.[17]

Brando's talents as a director are particularly evident in a pair of dramatic entrances into saloons and in the dinner at Dad Longworth's when Rio returns. The first saloon scene depicts a group of Mexican police enclosed in a darkened halo; a horizontal display of force, guns drawn, they cut like a razor blade across the saloon melee before them. In the next one, five years later, at the same saloon, Rio enters dressed in black with a red cape, signaling his sacrificial status, or perhaps simply that he is out for blood. Though he is accompanied only by Modesto, their entrance is equally portentous and menacing. At dinner with the Longworths, where a similar blend of ritual and danger prevails, Brando provides a lesson on how to use objects to convey meaning. Turning his fork and knife so they catch the light, he conveys the character's hunger and threatening potential, as well as his penchant for transformation. Orchestrated together with the smile, the charm, the occasional utterance, Brando *demonstrates* one of his central acting principles: It is what the actor communicates *beyond* language that counts most.

Brando's eye for detail and his fascination with history and authentic period speech and customs were everywhere apparent. Rio and Dad shake hands no fewer than three times during their reunion, which calls attention to the gesture's traditional import—a signal between potential enemies that their hands are free of weapons. The Mexican-style hat worn by Rio throughout the film, slightly flattened with leather chinstrap—contrasting with the classic Stetsons worn by Dad, his deputies, Bob Amory, and other Anglo-Americans—confirms the protagonist's cultural marginality. The *Mona Lisa* reproduction looming above Rio at the saloon just before Dad disables him at the whipping post features *La Gioconda* holding a card, an ace of hearts, touching the sleeve of her gown. Rio glowers but misses the warning, walking

Handshake in *One-Eyed Jacks*. AF Archive/Alamy.

straight into Dad's trap, having worn his heart on his sleeve in a
bid for paternal approval once too often.

The film's title was Brando's idea, and he makes good use of the
"Jack" throughout, but his last reference is a peculiar one. Astride
his horse, before their last kiss, Rio tells Louisa to look for him in
the spring: "One of them dark nights you're gonna see a jackass
in the window and that's gonna be me." No screenwriter could
have given the hero that line; this is pure Brando, its meaning
suitably ambiguous. He may be a "jackass" for agreeing to this
Hollywood ending and relenting on his revenge-tragedy massacre of all three principals. He may be a "jackass" for killing the
father, or for waiting so long to do it. Or he may still be a "jackass"
even after accomplishing the ultimate Oedipal feat.

Despite the problems associated with *One-Eyed Jacks*, the
story of directors lost and found (including Stanley Kubrick),
incomplete scripts, ballooning budgets, and foiled shooting
schedules, Brando managed to produce a movie that made money,
won critical approval, and had a lasting influence on the Western

Mona Lisa with card from *One-Eyed Jacks*. Paramount/Getty Images.

genre. The film's quality has been obscured in part because of the expectations the project aroused, a consequence of Brando's success and celebrity. Gossip columnists upped the ante. "I saw the movie and have been thinking about it ever since," wrote

Sheilah Graham. "It will be Paramount's biggest money maker for 1961."[18] It was natural for Brando films to earn huge sums and win awards, and when they earned less or won few, a competitive Hollywood was eager to declare an overrated star in decline. This was especially true of Brando, whose repudiation of the star system had always disturbed Hollywood.

Retrospect can be clarifying. Contemporary reviews were almost uniformly positive. Reviewers acknowledged the film's epic sweep, noting parallels to classics from Jacobean revenge tragedies to Wagnerian operas. *Hollywood Variety* reported: "It is [Brando's] skillful direction and the fine photographic effects that he has achieved that make *One-Eyed Jacks* memorable." In the *New York Times*, Bosley Crowther dubbed it "an extraordinary sort of western," its directing "hard and realistic" as well as "romantic and lush," recalling John Huston and Raoul Walsh. The *New York Daily News* gave it four stars and called it "stunning," and even a rarefied *New Yorker* reviewer, Edith Oliver, conceded in her conclusion that "everyone connected with the picture is good, and if I have made it sound thoroughly unpleasant, then I have misled you. Many of the shocks it administers are refreshing and funny." *The Hollywood Reporter* suggested: "it might be the best western ever made, and surely a classic that will stand with most of the all time great motion pictures; for it has taken the bones of cliché drama and superbly enhanced them with daring innovation.... Brando must, indeed, be honored as the father of this achievement."[19]

One-Eyed Jacks did well commercially, attracting steady audiences worldwide and putting its profits into the millions by the end of the decade.[20] Equally important was its impact on subsequent filmmakers, from Sergio Leone and Clint Eastwood to Martin Scorsese and Quentin Tarantino, who included it on his list of top twenty films. We may never know Brando's full intentions, since he stopped editing after producing a director's cut, whose length has been estimated at three, four-and-a-half, and six hours, respectively.[21] It is likely that the Paramount editors who took over did their best to honor Brando's conception in their two-hour and twenty-one-minute version.

Centering on a charismatic victim, the film highlights victimization as the collective human condition. Yet, as an imperfect victim—specifically, a victim who victimizes—Brando's Rio also modeled a type with special resonance for Americans, at a time when national values were increasingly under challenge at home (the civil rights movement) and abroad (the Cuban missile crisis, Vietnam). The moral and political power of the antihero evolved during the 1960s and '70s: a figure whose claim for protection was based in part on flaws and failings. Brando supplied a classic variation on this in Rio. His loneliness makes him vulnerable to Malden's gregarious Dad Longworth and also provokes his wrath in response to Dad's betrayal. His violation of Dad's stepdaughter expresses his vulnerability and will, as does his subsequent love for her. Moreover, all the characters in *One-Eyed Jacks* are (in Dad's words) "lying faster than a dog can trot." To live is to lie; no one survives without it. Those who can forgive others' deceptions—significantly women (Maria forgives her daughter, Louisa; Louisa forgives her lover, Rio)—are blessed. But this doesn't preclude their suffering. Among men, an uncompromising Darwinism prevails. They respect only the power to kill, deferring to the quickest on the draw. Rio is the dominant male feared by everyone, until Dad flogs him publicly and pulverizes his gun hand. Rio's symbolic castration by his father figure makes him powerless and a liability as far as other men are concerned. He can regain his manhood only by killing Dad.

The psychological implications seem almost too overt. Brando's callous, miserly father, hovering over the film in the role of a Pennebaker executive, is apparently oblivious to his son's talent and effort. Yet the son never stops trying to prove his worth to the father. Brando's West is a dark fantasy where fathers unman their sons. Human bonds are imperiled and cannot grow in man's desultory world. A spark in another person is threatening. The only source of relief is a bitter but enlivening humor. Dad caught in bed by Mexican police, escaping barefoot; Rio snatching the ring off the finger of the woman during the aborted seduction; gunmen who haven't bathed for weeks, complaining about the rank smell of a fishing village: "Phew! What's that?" "*Some*thing dead...."

One-Eyed Jacks is also visually beautiful. The continuous presence of nature—sea, desert, woods, animals—whether mild or tumultuous, affirms the possibility of growth and freedom, which is unavailable to the human characters. *One-Eyed Jacks* pays homage to Dodie Brando's love of nature, which she transmitted to her son along with her dramatic gifts. There is awe in the spectacle of mountains in the desert, woods beside ocean; both exist in tension with human society. The only good happens against this backdrop: Rio and Modesto after their jailbreak, framed by a desert sunset illuminating the land and sky; Rio shivering with pain from Dad's beating, tended gently by Modesto amid sea boulders miraculously enlarged; the lovers' passionate kiss before rolling waves. Each scene elevates the human beings, magnifying their actions. That is the effect of Brando's artistry; he depicts life through a most brutal realism but reveals it in a larger context, the vastness and mystery of nature.

Brando's nephew, Martin Asinof, remembers Brando taking the family to a private screening of *One-Eyed Jacks* after a holiday dinner. Overcome by the violence of the scene where Brando's "Kid" is brutally whipped and mutilated by Karl Malden's "Dad," Martin's mother, Jocelyn, leapt out of her seat, and Franny's teenage daughter, Julie, burst into tears. Brando came over and sat down next to Julie, putting his arm around her and reminding her that Karl was his good friend and would never hurt him, holding up his hand to reassure her that it was perfectly fine, that this was only a movie. But there was no question that "Pop," as Asinof and his cousins called Brando Sr., was a "very hard man," a "nasty man," who left his three children with "a lot of toxic baggage."[22]

Brando's account of how he learned in 1965 on a Navajo Reservation in Arizona of his seventy-year-old father's death is revealing. Brando Sr. had been ill with melanoma, so it couldn't have been entirely unexpected when a clairvoyant old medicine woman pronounced Brando an orphan. Moments later, a phone call for him at the reservation office confirmed the revelation. That night, as he drifted off to sleep, Brando had "a vision of [his father] walking down a sidewalk away from me, then turning around to look at me, a slump-shouldered Willy Loman with a faint smile on his face. When he got to the edge of eternity, he stopped and looked back again, turned halfway toward me and, with his eyes downcast, said: *I did the best I could, kid*. He turned away again, and I knew he was looking for my mother."[23]

The scene captures the sense of ambivalence, resignation, and failure that characterized the relationship of father and son. The smile hints at Marlon Sr.'s triumph as he heads off into eternity with the mother, leaving the son bereft on earth. In his autobiography, Brando also described leaving the hospital in Pasadena on the spring morning of his mother's death at the age of fifty-five: "She was gone, but I felt she had been transformed into everything that was reflective of nature and was going to be all right. Suddenly I had a vision of a great bird climbing into the sky higher and higher...a majestic bird floating on thermals of warm air, gliding higher and higher past a great stone cliff. I keep my mother's ring close to me. For a long while after she died, the stone was vibrant and full of color, pigmented with deeper and deeper shades of blue, but recently I've noticed that the colors have begun to fade....I don't know why."[24] Brando's comments suggest a conviction of maternal vulnerability that overwhelms his own sense of loss. He seems more concerned about his dead mother ("she…was going to be all right") than about his own profound grief, grateful for the death he conceives as a bird's soaring liberation.

Then there is the mother's ring, echoing the metaphor of theft and deception in *One-Eyed Jacks*. Perhaps the real one escaped the complex taint of the one in the movie. Its fading may mean diminishing resentment toward a mother–son relationship that was so conflicted. Time dulls pain, and it dulls brightness. Fading colors also represent the human condition—the son coming to terms with old age.

In making *One-Eyed Jacks*, an experience that summoned to an exceptional degree his talents for acting, dialogue, and cinematography, Brando must have felt at times that he was taking a stab at immortality, for himself and for the mother whose memory it honored. In a letter of April 12, 1960, Brando called *One-Eyed Jacks* "one of the sizeable efforts in my life," to which he had given "two and a half years of worry, anxiety, striving, discouragement, hopes, and work, work, work," a rare confession that he qualifies in the next paragraph: "Of course, you must understand that I realize *One-Eyed Jacks* is simply another Hollywood movie which isn't going to change the face of circumstance for anybody in this world."[25] The negation reinforced the confession and seemed more a reminder to himself than to anyone else. Films are not life; they don't improve things for the suffering multitudes. He chides himself for having thought otherwise.

Brando would never take full pleasure in his successes on stage or screen, a consequence in part of his father's attitude toward acting. According to Brando Sr.'s conventions, acting was self-indulgent, a Bohemian activity that was reserved for women, homosexuals, and outcasts. A man full of pain who lived in terror of his own emotions, he seems to have been threatened by the power of acting to move people. Brando Sr. was even more threatened by the way his son's almost instantaneous and utterly

unexpected success sent the son soaring beyond his own medi-
ocrity and nullified his patriarchal authority.[26] Yet Brando himself was permanently marked by these conventions, and when
they combined with his idealistic appraisal of the corruption of
the reigning production companies on Broadway as well as in
Hollywood—their focus on profit and tendency to indulge rather
than elevate American tastes—he had ample support for his
doubts. To preserve his own integrity, to accomplish something
for which he had respect, he would have to go beyond acting.

THE FUGITIVE KIND

After the expenditure of intellectual and emotional energy in
One-Eyed Jacks, Brando's next project might have seemed ideal.
It fulfilled a tacit promise to appear in a version of Tennessee Williams's play *Orpheus Descending,* written in 1955 with Brando and
the Italian actress Anna Magnani in mind. When it was produced
on Broadway in May 1957, *Orpheus* featured Cliff Robertson and
Maureen Stapleton in the lead roles; it closed after a short run.
Offered the role in 1959 in a film to be titled *The Fugitive Kind,*
Brando accepted. He had reservations about his Orpheus character, the lonely drifter Val Xavier, but he needed the money—a
million-dollar salary—to pay the mounting bills for his divorce
from Anna Kashfi and the ensuing custody battles over their
son Christian (b. 1958). Nor did it make sense for him to refuse
work with a playwright he admired and a good director, Sidney
Lumet. Still he worried about the fundamental vagueness of the
Orpheus figure, Xavier, a guitarist who revered Leadbelly and
Blind Lemon Jefferson but had renounced the life of a musician.
Persisting questions about Xavier's motivations and beliefs were
especially troublesome in light of the powerful characterization
of Anna Magnani's Lady Torrance.

In a letter about *Orpheus* to Williams of March 24, 1955, Brando explained the problem he saw in the two roles. Referring to Magnani, he wrote, "I can't think of an actress I would rather play with providing the potential dynamics of the parts are equal.... When you play with her you either make sure that the PARTS are equally volatile, or plan to carry a fair-sized rock in your hand when you go on stage." Despite Brando's esteem for Magnani as an actress, the pair never jelled on screen, which may have had more to do with the dramatic imbalance he identified than with the actors.

Williams's drama about Orpheus, the musician who sought to spring his beloved Eurydice from hell through song, had gone through several incarnations, beginning with a 1940 Theatre Guild production, *The Battle of Angels*, with none of them succeeding in bringing the Greek myth alive in Williams's archetypal South. Moreover, the weakest link of the screenplay remained the Orpheus character, a vehicle of poetry rather than drama. This was acknowledged implicitly by a sympathetic *New York Times* review that characterized *The Fugitive Kind* as a distinguished film that is "rare today," praising Magnani and Brando as "fine and intelligent performers [who] play upon deep emotional chords. Old feelings of poignancy and longing come through their handling of the words."[27] One of the film's highpoints was Xavier's speech about "the fugitive kind," a scene that also foregrounded cinematographer Boris Kaufman's singular methods of lighting.

There are two kinds of people in the world, Xavier tells Lady, the buyers and the ones that get bought. Then he remembers a third kind: "a kind that don't belong no place at all," typified by a bird that lives its entire life in the sky because it has no legs and cannot land. "I seen one, once . . . its body was light blue colored. And it was just as tiny as your little finger . . . and its wings spread out that *wide*. And you could see right through 'em. That's why the hawks don't catch 'em, because they don't see 'em...these little birds don't have no legs at all, so they have to live their whole lives on the wing. And they sleep on the wind...and they only light on this earth but one time...it's when they die." (Italics indicate words stressed by Brando.) Throughout the speech, Kaufman's camera alternately shades and illuminates, mimicking the mobility of the actor's eyes, mouth, and hands. Brando's gaze shifts constantly, his face a volatile map of wonder and sadness, as he reenacts the bird's soaring rise and fall.

Brando had a gift for commanding attention through storytelling. He could do it by using his whole countenance as an accompanying register, or he could do it through voice alone, as exemplified by his 1954 reading of Hemingway's *The Old Man and the Sea* for a radio program.[28] He respected authors who could create worlds that were complete in themselves. His own access to that world came through imagination and his ability to be in the moment. When he addressed Hemingway's fish in the voice of the old man, Brando was on the sea in his boat, just as he lived temporarily on the wing with Williams's misfit bird. This is what Brando meant when he told writer Irwin Shaw that his character Christian Diestl in *The Young Lions* did not exist until Brando brought him to life.[29]

MUTINY ON THE BOUNTY AND THE DISCOVERY OF TAHITI

After *The Fugitive Kind*, Brando chose to do another historical movie. When he was offered the part of Fletcher Christian in the remake of *Mutiny on the Bounty*, slated for filming in Tahiti, he had been contemplating the role of T. E. Lawrence in David Lean's *Lawrence of Arabia*. Brando was interested in Lawrence (he owned a copy of *T. E. Lawrence, by His Friends*) and knew

Lean to be a congenial director, but the lure of Tahiti drew him to the *Mutiny* project. The Polynesian island had been a focus of his youthful fantasies, modeling a carefree, harmonious existence. In Manhattan, he continued to dream about Tahiti, accumulating books on the subject and searching the Museum of Modern Art for images of the region and its inhabitants.[30]

Brando had written into his contract the promise that the new *Mutiny on the Bounty* would deal substantially with the mutineers' experiences on Pitcairn Island. This, together with the assurance that the film would use locals as extras, convinced Brando to sign on to the film in early 1960. He flew to Tahiti with the producers that spring to help select the cast and shooting sites.[31]

MGM's remake of *Mutiny on the Bounty* was an implicit challenge to the studio's own 1935 version, starring Clark Gable and Charles Laughton, which had won an Oscar for Best Picture. Brando admired Charles Laughton's Captain Bligh but was unimpressed with Clark Gable, who "hadn't even bothered to speak with an English accent.... As always, Clark Gable played Clark Gable."[32] An early script (October 1960) for the remake indicates a screenwriter, Eric Ambler (the first of at least four screenwriters—including William L. Driscoll, Borden Chase, Charles Lederer—of manifold scripts), still dazzled by the original. The Fletcher Christian character is pure Gable, bland and obliging, devoid of Brando's ruminative angst.[33] The mutiny occurs before the arrival in Tahiti and is driven by Christian's concern for the crew rather than by a sense of pride and principle. Christian's behavior on Pitcairn follows this mold, as he strives to create a unified community on the island. Subsequent scripts reveal Brando's handiwork, his annotations steering the story into greater dramatic tension and complexity. By far the most important thematic change he introduces is the emphasis on class.

Brando's Lieutenant Fletcher Christian boards the ship in full aristocratic regalia—gray silk suit, red cape, Puritan-style top hat, and a walking stick—accompanied by French-speaking ladies. His accent is exceedingly refined and he looks down on Captain William Bligh as a vulgar parvenu, questioning Bligh's zeal for the voyage's purpose, transporting breadfruit from Tahiti to Jamaica, which Christian characterizes as "a grocer's errand." In this first appearance, Brando's Christian is an unmistakable womanizer. But his pomposity disturbed critics still devoted to Gable's manly democrat who found Brando's character "oddly foppish," "more a dandy than a formidable ship's officer."[34] Brando's main concerns were intensifying the conflict with Bligh and attempting historical accuracy. The real Christian was a member of the landed gentry, from a distinguished old family with important connections. Well educated, reputed to be a skilled navigator, "he was a gentleman, a brave man." As a *Bounty* sailor who returned to England with Bligh reported, "Every officer and seaman aboard ship would have gone through fire and water to serve [Christian]." Bligh's origins were humbler. The intelligent, ambitious son of a customs officer, he had worked his way up through the naval ranks. Despite a hot temper, Bligh was hardly the sadist immortalized by Charles Laughton. He was closer to the Bligh now played by Trevor Howard, who saw harsh punishment—or what he called "cruelty with purpose"—as a form of efficiency.[35]

Brando was familiar with British classism and could imagine how it might be compounded by a strict naval regime aboard an isolated sailing ship. In multiple scripts of *Mutiny on the Bounty*, he made revisions to emphasize this sensibility. He excised curses from Christian's lines, because gentlemen never swore, and corrected an "Eton expression" (Brando's phrase) given to a common sailor.[36] Elsewhere Brando complained that writers were reneging on promises made to him; chief among them was the promise that the Pitcairn sequences would be complicated by putting Christian directly at odds with the utopian hopes of the common

sailors and having him strategize a return to England. The writers had missed opportunities as well, Brando felt, to represent
the perspectives of Tahitian characters.[37] He was eager that the
clash of cultures be elaborated: "could be more amusing...point-
ing up the idiocy of protocol and our unnatural formality and our
lies." He insisted on authenticity, observing that the Tahitian
translator's English was too "exact he understands too much"...
"every once in a while he uses an extraordinary word."[38] He did
his trademark trimming, substituting a precise word or sentence
for two or more lines of dialogue.[39]

He edited down most of his scenes, among them the argument
between Christian and midshipman Ned Young over a water
cask and the tense discussion, between Bligh and Christian,
about the decision to go around the Horn in (Brando's phrase)
"a ninety-one-foot chamber pot." Brando also wrote the following lines: "I was just thinking that our little errand for groceries
ies might wind up in a page of naval history. If we succeed in
negotiating the horn in the dead of winter."[40] Brando liked his
phrasing enough to reprise it fifteen years later for the part of
Colonel Kurtz in *Apocalypse Now*. In response to Captain Willard's (Martin Sheen) declaration, "I'm a soldier," Brando's Kurtz
says dismissively, "You're an errand boy sent by grocery clerks to
collect the bill."[41] On the *Mutiny* script, Brando's marginalia were
sometimes amusing. Next to an offer by the Tahitian King, Hiti-
hiti, to send his daughter as a gift to King George, Brando quips,
"K Geo too old to do anything about it."[42] More often he provided
instructions for character motivation and plot development. For
example, he recommended that Bligh's character emerge subtly:
"let us discover Bligh's stinginess, ill will gradually, more interesting"; "Bligh must not be gratuitously cruel"; "we should have
Bligh have some conflict about his cruelty."[43] He worried about
integrating story parts and keeping viewers engaged, suggesting
camera shifts to build excitement.[44]

Brando rewrote the scripts for most of his films, before and during production, but *Mutiny on the Bounty* was special because of his emotional and intellectual investment in Tahiti, its traditions and people. From his perspective, the picture was a work-in-progress. It reflected a personal interest in the prospects for happiness in an idyllic setting relatively isolated from modernity. That he believed in the prospect at all was the sign of a persisting romanticism that a decade in Hollywood had not erased. But there was a gap between his intellectual judgment and his hope that experience might prove otherwise. He was thrilled that Tahitians had never heard of Marlon Brando, but he recognized that the very presence of the *Mutiny* production, and the impact of filming there, were already transforming this "island paradise."[45] The judgment comes through as well in Brando's comments on the Pitcairn Island sequence. For instance, "if individuals are not responsible in a democracy it won't work"; "men given freedom is not enough"; "education has little to do with it (cap[acity] to govern)." An idealistic plea scripted for Christian, on behalf of an island where "no King's men ... grow fat while others starve and ... make wars that others have to fight," regaining "the Paradise that was lost," to "live as God and nature intended," earns this acid remark from Brando: "Hardly God's intention." Nor was Brando entirely unsympathetic to Bligh's position. "C. says to Bligh Give the men a sense of creative responsibility B. says no. Bligh is right for wrong reason."[46] Brando believed Bligh's prime offense was blaming everyone but himself when problems arose. Continuing reading about the mutiny even years later, Brando checked and underscored the following in his copy of Richard Hough's *Captain Bligh and Mr. Christian* (1973): "A basic tenet of leadership which Bligh never learned is that you never delegate responsibility. You depute and supervise and it is your responsibility if your subordinates fail you."[47]

The script in various versions ran to more than a thousand

pages. Brando annotated a third of it, in addition to writing a hundred pages of notes on themes, character development, and what he termed "speech characteristics" and "colorful phrases."[48] He translated some of the love scenes into Tahitian, which he began studying before his arrival for filming in the late fall of 1960. Brando's French-Tahitian conversation manual (by this time he was fluent in French), *Cours de Tahitien*, was annotated partly with dead mosquitoes.[49] He understood the film's main conflict to be "political in essence that men who cry for liberty, democracy, humanity if they are not individually equipped to contribute to that idea, cannot make it work and thus a new face of evil is born." Elsewhere he notes, "Man is his own worst enemy." Of Christian he writes, "He allows himself the luxury of vain emotional outburst. Self-love. In retrospect he hates the fact that he allowed himself to be driven. The audience should feel he is justified at time of mutiny. Audience should feel that his guilt is understandable."[50] Brando's observations demonstrate how far he was from idealizing either the hero or the common sailors. The highborn gentleman's regret over what he has lost, together with his anticipation of a future trapped on Pitcairn with the ship's crew, precipitates despair. The sailors, on the other hand, desire a liberty for which they are neither intellectually nor emotionally prepared. These interpretations were consistent with lifelong assumptions—no one was thoroughly good or bad; absolutism was misguided; virtuous aims could have unintended consequences—that Brando had substantiated through reading.

Brando's reading made him as knowledgeable about the mutiny, the South Seas, and Polynesian culture as anyone involved with the film. His library included multiple copies of *The Bounty Trilogy* (1951, 1962) and other titles by Charles Nordhoff and James Norman Hall. In addition, it contained more than a hundred books on Polynesia—its languages, environment, history, and culture. There were scholarly accounts of the region, such as

Reading on the *Bounty*. High-resolution image courtesy of Alexander Khochinskiy.

Douglas Oliver's *The Pacific Islands* (1952, which Brando bought at the American Museum of Natural History in New York), and books on Westerners in the Pacific, such as Frederick O'Brien's *White Shadows in the South Seas* (1920), with accounts of Gauguin and Melville.[51] Books on politics and philosophy directly relevant to the film's conflicts were also in Brando's collection, and he may have been reading them during the time he worked on *Mutiny*. They dealt with race and caste, the nature of community and order, the forces that preserved or threatened them, and what led individuals to rebel. He wrote in Sidney Hook's *Political Power and Personal Freedom* (1959), that "reason is ever subjugated to the contagion of emotion," and he wondered "why there is an incessant belief that men will listen to reason." He underlined the observation that "men must agree on a certain number of fundamental positions—on what is good or evil, true or false—in order not to massacre each other," and a passage on cultural differences that warned against one group imposing its ways upon another.[52]

At the same time, Brando's reading in early 1960 was influenced by the impending execution of Caryl Chessman, a San Quentin convict whose death sentence he had actively opposed. Brando and others who protested (Elizabeth Hardwick listed "the Pope, Albert Schweitzer, Mauriac, Dean Pike, Marlon Brando" in a September 1960 essay on the affair in *The Partisan Review*) considered the death penalty barbaric and especially inappropriate in the case of a man guilty of robbery and sexual assault but not murder. Letters to Brando from UC Berkeley political scientist Eugene Burdick (coauthor of the novel *The Ugly American*) and historian Richard Drinnon confirm that he was among a small group of California luminaries (including scientist Linus Pauling and poets Kenneth Rexroth and Lawrence Ferlinghetti) intent on abolishing capital punishment in the state. The plan was to force a vote in the California legislature through petition, and Brando's participation provided an invaluable means of generating publicity for the cause.[53]

When *Mutiny* director Carol Reed met Brando for the first time that spring, he found him preoccupied with Chessman's recent execution (May 2, 1960). Throughout that summer and fall, Brando explored the possibility of directing a picture based on Chessman's memoir, *Cell 2455, Death Row*. Brando had no delusions about Chessman's innocence, but he considered the punishment extreme, believing the execution to be no better than "an act of vengeance against a man ... suffering from an emotional disease."[54] He was as concerned about the effect of the death penalty on the state and the judicial system that imposed it. He had in his collection *A History of Capital Punishment* (1960) by John Laurence, opening with an epigraph about Abraham and Isaac, and *The Partisan Review* issue with Hardwick's essay characterizing Chessman as a cultural sacrifice. Brando marked and clipped Hardwick's piece, but he may also have read Francis Golffing on the nature of utopia in the same issue.[55]

For Brando, the Pitcairn Islands sequence raised questions about the good society: Under conditions where human needs were satisfied, and people were able to live interdependently on relatively equal terms, how could the eruption of conflict be explained? The failure of such a utopia must stem from factors in human nature. This part of the *Mutiny* story provided an opportunity for exploring the problems that human beings brought to every type of social and political system throughout history.

Of his ambition to focus on the experience of the mutineers on Pitcairn, Brando wrote, "They should have found great happiness. And what happened? Within two years they were dead; they had killed one another. In that bit of tragedy I saw a microcosm of all man's history, his losing battle with the urge to destroy. I saw a vivid and terrifying moral—if an island paradise holds no happiness, creates no love of life, perhaps man can never find it."[56]

The will on the part of some to dominate others, to impose their own culture or eliminate those who think or believe differently—the source of such tendencies was of great interest to Brando. Thus, another contemporary controversy about which he read deeply while he was working on *Mutiny* was the highly publicized arrest and trial of Adolf Eichmann, the Nazi war criminal captured in Argentina in the spring of 1960 and prosecuted in Israel in the spring of 1961. Brando had Henry Zeiger's *The Case Against Adolf Eichmann* (1960) and Roger Manvell and Heinrich Fraenkel's *Dr. Goebbels: His Life and Death* (1961), as well as Hannah Arendt's contemporary coverage of the trial in *The New Yorker*, which became *Eichmann in Jerusalem* (1963), of which he owned multiple copies.

But he could have drawn on any number of books in his library for themes and ideas in *Mutiny*. Among pertinent works with contemporary publication dates were: Freud, *Civilization and Its Discontents* (1962); André Niel, *Krishnamurti: The Man in Revolt*

(1957); Norman O. Brown, *Life Against Death* (1959); and Michael Curtis, *The Great Political Theories: From Plato and Aristotle to Locke and Montesquieu* (1961).[57] Brando was adept at making a theory accessible through physical or verbal means. The omnipresent annotation in his books, "dio," short for "dialogue," was a reminder to himself to draw on the phrase or statement for a film.[58] Brando owned four of Bronislaw Malinowski's anthropology classics on Melanesia. He highlighted a passage in *Sex and Repression in Savage Society* (1953) on the "innumerable forms of courtship and marriage," how "types of wooing and winning vary with each culture," which might have shaped his approach as Fletcher Christian to Tarita Teriipaia's Maimiti.[59]

Brando was himself an anthropologist of sorts, a natural outgrowth of his curiosity and appetite for travel. This ethnographic bent was especially pronounced in his relationships with women. He seems to have had a knack for transforming any romantic occasion into a symbolic interaction. He knew that symbolism was essential to eroticism: how meaningful every sound, look, and touch could be. Fluent in the silent language that ruled sexual encounters, Brando *always* eliminated excess chatter from these scenes.[60] There was no actor who made love on camera more seductively.

The first meeting of Christian and Miamiti (Tarita Teriipaia) becomes a primer on cross-cultural romance that could stand for *any* initial intimacy. It begins with eye contact during the woman's provocative dance, performed in a scant wrapping that exposes much of her body. Her unmistakable advance and his unmistakable interest are followed by her wandering away with backward glances to ensure he marks her course. The embodiment of civilization—naval officer in blue coat with gold buttons, white ruffled shirt, and white knickers—glides slowly toward his prey, his countenance glowing with desire. Miamiti announces

Flirting on the set of *Mutiny.* High-resolution image courtesy of Alexander Khochinskiy.

her whereabouts with a titter; he nears the bush that conceals her. He gently displaces the foliage to reveal the Tahitian woman, her gaze averted. "Hello," he says softly, his British accent caressing the word, as he enters her hiding place. His every move is calibrated. The woman introduces herself in Tahitian. He thumps his chest, pronouncing his name. Her misunderstanding yields a smiling concession to "call me whatever you like." "How *very* sweet," he says, responding to her love custom. He leans in for a kiss that is met with a Tahitian-style brushing of noses; he accepts, amused, before guiding her firmly into his own love game.

Throughout the production, in script revisions, and most of all through his ambivalent gentleman mutineer, Brando sought to invest entertainment with ideas, inviting audiences to confront cultural contrasts and class conflict. Aboard ship, when Christian struggles with sailors to secure water barrels broken loose during a storm, Brando demonstrates how an officer working alongside his men can balance authority with humane concern for their welfare. Critics singled out the scene for its thrilling realism.[61] Convinced that viewers would share his fascination with island rituals, he made certain they were portrayed in detail. "Create beauty of Tahiti, people, customs, life," he urged in his notes, "let's not stop for a travelogue."[62] Hence the ceremonious greeting given Bligh and his entourage, featuring the inhabitants pouring onto the beach and showering officers and crew with flower wreaths, and the extended fishing scene where Tahitian men in boats flog the water, driving their prey into nets held by rows of women.

Brando's best acting comes during the life-changing events for his character—the mutiny and its aftermath. Christian's bold usurpation of power and then retrospective sorrow for all he has lost is made a piece with his previous self-satisfaction. He lashes out against Bligh's kick with aristocratic outrage, uttering his first oath, "You *bloody bastard*! You'll *not* put your foot on

Brando climbing *Bounty*'s rigging. High-resolution
image courtesy of Alexander Khochinskiy.

me *again!*" and seizes command with similar propriety, stabbing
Bligh in the left arm to draw blood and warn Bligh's backers that
his challenge is serious. "You remarkable *pig,*" he declares, glaring at Bligh. "You can thank whatever *pig-god you pray to* that you

haven't quite turned *me* into a *murderer!*" (Italics indicate words stressed by Brando.) He confronts the enormity of his deed with equal dignity, sitting alone in the captain's cabin with his legs taut and his back as straight as a British schoolboy's, as if good posture can restore the order shattered by mutiny. At no point does Christian betray his upbringing; his refinement persists through his last breath, as he dies from burns suffered in an effort to save the flaming ship. This was another of Brando's extraordinary death scenes, which he directed himself (Carol Reed had been fired by the producers early in 1961 and replaced by Lewis Milestone, who soon became disgruntled with the chaotic production), lying on a bed of ice to simulate the shuddering fear aroused by the recognition that death is imminent.

Critics from *Variety* and the Associated Press considered this "the finest performance of [Brando's] career." Though there were reservations (*The New Yorker*: Brando "plays Fletcher Christian as a sort of seagoing Hamlet"), most were favorably impressed.[63] Apart from the *New York Times* and *The New Yorker*, whose writers preferred the 1935 version, reactions to *Mutiny* were almost uniformly positive. A leading box-office grosser for months, the film was nominated for Academy Awards in seven categories, including Best Picture. This was remarkable given the negative publicity surrounding the production. Like another early blockbuster, *Cleopatra* (1963), starring Elizabeth Taylor, tall tales of extravagance and celebrity malfeasance dogged *Mutiny*, centering on its expense, a figure estimated at between $18.5 million and $30 million, depending on the source and its attitude toward Brando.[64] An article in the *Saturday Evening Post*, June 16, 1962, subtitled "The Mutiny of Marlon Brando," blamed delays and cost overruns on "a petulant superstar" who turned "Paradise into a moviemaker's nightmare." The *Post* piece resulted in all-time-high newsstand sales for the magazine, which boasted a circulation of 6,500,000. This was the first time in the *Post*'s

234-year history that a film star had ever appeared on its cover.[65] The article was so scurrilous that Brando not only sued the magazine for libel (settled in his favor out of court) but also accepted magazine and television interviews to tell his side of the story. "If you send a multimillion dollar production to a place when, according to the precipitation records it is the worst time of the year, and when you send it without a script, it seems there is some kind of primitive mistake. The reason for all of the big failures is the same—no script. Then the actor becomes the obvious target of executives trying to cover their own tracks." Brando might have added "no ship," for Canadian shipbuilders were months behind in delivering the *Bounty* replica to Tahiti and fifty percent above estimated construction costs.[66]

Mutiny on the Bounty had two major consequences for Brando: First, it motivated him to respond to critical news coverage. As the ultimate informed citizen, he was a lifelong reader of newspapers. Up until the end, he read the *New York Times* and the *Los Angeles Times* daily.[67] He followed the press on his career religiously, as evidenced by his collection of magazine and newspaper articles dating from the beginning of his time in Hollywood, but he made a habit of not responding. This changed after *Bounty,* which coincided with the births of his first three children (Christian in 1958—mother Anna Kashfi; Miko in 1960—mother Movita Castaneda; Teihotu in 1963—mother Tarita Teriipaia). Recognizing that his image would affect them, he began to respond to distorted or libelous portrayals.[68]

His willingness to talk on live interview shows in the months between the release of *Mutiny on the Bounty* and his work on *The Ugly American* reflected both his new concern for his reputation as well as a longstanding interest in the political role of media. He owned dozens of books on the subject and was a regular reader of the journal published by the Gannett Center for Media Studies. Brando's foiled attempt in 1968 to take a free-speech case to the

Chess on the *Bounty* set. High-resolution image courtesy of Alexander Khochinskiy.

California Supreme Court, after he was charged with defamation by the Los Angeles Police Department for remarks he made on a talk show following the death of Black Panther Bobby Hutton, made clear his conversance with these laws.[69] Interviews Brando gave in the wake of *Mutiny* demonstrated that his early indoctrination into the mixed blessings of an American free press with First Amendment protections had motivated serious study and reflection. They also reveal the growing opposition in his mind between a competitive, publicity-hungry American entertainment world that continually invaded his privacy and the isolated, relatively equable culture of Tahiti, whose inhabitants were mostly unmoved by fame and treated him with a welcome informality.

In an April 19, 1963, interview with Hugh Downs on the *Today Show,* Brando displayed his usual learning and eloquence as he discussed the advantages and disadvantages of a free press and the distinction between print journalism and live-broadcast news. Characterizing "gossip" as "a multimillion dollar industrial complex," he noted that he had been treated as "an enemy of the people" for protecting his private life. Still he vigorously defended the First Amendment. "They don't have it in Russia, they don't have it in France, they have a lot of trouble in Germany with it. There are very few countries in the world where you really can say something, and the press has got an absolute right to make a critical comment about anyone or anything." He goes on to distinguish magazines and newspapers (where interviews can be distorted through misquoting, juxtaposition, and editorializing) from live television (where views can be conveyed uncensored). "I don't think people realize what television has done, what this kind of program does.... Television wins and loses elections for a very special reason, because not only do people see what you say, but they see what you feel." Magazines, in contrast, can have an "official interpretation" that columnists are expected to support. He cited *Time* magazine's prejudice against Tennessee Williams, who he felt had been excoriated in thinly disguised homophobic reviews. Explaining that he no longer was giving interviews to *Time*, he said that the magazine was also responsible, in a prime example of "Ugly Americanism," for deadly riots in Bolivia in 1959.

A few days later, on April 21, on David Susskind's *Open End*, Brando was more direct about his experiences with the press. "I have withstood wrath, hatred, disregard, vulgarity, insults, for years and years and years ... that I've never bothered to say anything about, because libel laws in this country are famously weak, and it's to the advantage of a magazine that you sue it, because they make money in advertising that compensates for what they might lose in the suit." But "there comes a time when you have to pick up a tin can and turn around and fling it with a will, and especially at a time when I have two children growing up in this community." Brando didn't mention the third child, due the following month in Tahiti, the second consequence of *Mutiny*. But his comments about Tahiti on *Open End* suggested high hopes that *this* child might experience his due measure of tranquillity.

Brando's preoccupation with the fate of the mutineers would prove to be somewhat prophetic. Though he would have thirty years of relative contentment on Tetiaroa, the coral-reef atoll he bought in 1967 near Papeete, he would also discover the limits of happiness there. His perspective on the mutineers' experiences in their own utopia shows that he had the wisdom to anticipate this, which did not, of course, enable him to control events.

What Brando found in Tahiti was an absence of all things American: materialism and competitiveness, assimilation and cooptation, preoccupation with mobility and glamour. As he told David Susskind: "To me it's an extremely attractive place because of all the places I've been it's the most democratic. They don't care who you are, they don't care what you do or what you represent, as long as you're decent and generally kind and interested in dancing and the things that they're interested in, then you're completely accepted, and if you're not, it doesn't matter how much money you have or what your influence is, they couldn't care less.... They have a lot of trouble with their teeth, but they don't care. If when they smile they've got five teeth, that's enough." Yet Brando's Tahitian is no jolly native. "Tahitians are tough, they're realistic, absolutely realistic. It's not rare to see a man and a woman fighting.... I've seen five fights break out in a period of three minutes. Break out like matches falling from a building, just flare right up." Above all, he admired Tahitian tenacity, which he illustrated with reference to the fate of Chinese culture there. Throughout the world, "in New York or San Francisco or London or Jakarta, wherever you find it it's intact. You know that these people are Chinese, and they speak Chinese, and they evaluate situations in the way that most Chinese would, and you never see that cracked.... But in Tahiti, it's the only place in Southeast Asia where I've ever been where I've seen the Chinese culture split right down the middle. The Tahitians gave a knuckle sandwich to the Chinese culture that's going to last for the next thousand years. The older Chinese think that the younger Chinese are staying home and taking care of the accounts and...they're out...dancing the tamure...they have Tahitian boyfriends and girlfriends, and it's just riddled with disintegration.... The Tahitians have withstood blackbirding [Polynesian enslavement in the eighteenth and nineteenth centuries for labor on Australian sugar and cotton plantations], they've withstood fifteen different kinds of missionaries, they've withstood the English and the French and the American tourist, the New Zealand tourist and all kinds of exploitation, and...they remain with their unassailable identities."[70]

Brando worried about the impact of modern technology, but his belief in Tahitian resilience lasted to the end of his life. "The Tahitian soul lives, it's extant and vibrant," he said in 1993, adding

Brando on Tetiaroa, 1970s. Reproduced by permission of Brando Enterprises, LP.

that he wanted his island Tetiaroa preserved as a "a place that reminds Tahitians of who they are and what they were years ago."[71] That Brando never lost hope in the potential for a better world was a sign of his own resilience. Such idealism was the motivating force behind his next film, *The Ugly American*, which had been one of the initial projects conceived for Pennebaker Productions.

CHAPTER FIVE

POLITICAL FILMS, 1963-1969

Brando's challenge throughout the 1960s was to find productive avenues for his outsize talents and ambitions. He ended up feeling conflicted about many of his projects, whether because of the scale of the undertaking, his ambivalence toward the project, or the Hollywood system itself. It made sense for him to try directing in *One-Eyed Jacks*, and he might have continued in this vein had he enjoyed the exclusive responsibility for filmmaking and learned to delegate better. But Brando valued loyalty over ability in subordinates, a wrong choice when it comes to making films. Such dilemmas were the rule in Hollywood, but the scope of Brando's success, his peripatetic lifestyle, and the range of his interests exacerbated them.[1]

This didn't prevent him from pursuing his dreams, such as his island Tetiaroa, with its extraordinary natural resources and pristine condition. It became a respite from Hollywood and facilitated a devotion to the Tahitian nation that endured beyond his death.

Brando's most deliberate choice in his films of the 1960s was his selection of projects with substantial political content. The fruits of his conviction that art and idealism could be combined to beneficial effect led to his roles in *The Ugly American* (1963),

The Chase (1966), *Reflections in a Golden Eye* (1967), and *Burn!* (1969). In each of these films, Brando took risks that expanded his repertoire and undermined conventional divisions between aesthetically powerful and politically meaningful cinema. A few of these revolutionary achievements were recognized at the time, others have never been recognized, but their very existence illuminates the possibilities of a considered era.

THE UGLY AMERICAN

The Ugly American (1963) was the product of Brando's travels in the 1950s and the reading and research they spurred. Pennebaker Productions had initiated the film, but Brando sold it to Universal Studios in 1962, just before *The Ugly American* went into production. Brando had never accepted the responsibility of running a film company, and he resented the compromises he had to make as a result of his own failure to take control. Financially strapped by the obligation of supporting two households (Anna Kashfi and Christian, Movita Castaneda and Miko), he was eager to make the deal. Among its components was the promise to make five films for Universal at far less than his established price of $1 million or more. The quality of the films produced under the contract was mixed, ranging from *Bedtime Story* (1964), a farce inhospitable to his talents, to *The Nightcomers* (1972), which earned him a BAFTA nomination. The Universal deal included their financing of *The Ugly American*. The film reflected Brando's increasing activism in response to American foreign policy, which he believed was inconsistent with the nation's founding principles. Significantly, *The Ugly American* and *Bedtime Story* would be boycotted in the South for the same reasons—his civil rights work.[2]

Brando's trips to developing countries for UNICEF, in particular, had complicated his views of American diplomacy and aid programs. Before visiting places such as Guam, the Philippines, Hong Kong, Thailand, and Bali, Brando had been impressed by Western assistance programs. But the more he learned about the ways these programs were implemented, the more convinced he became of their misguidedness. Designed as remedies for Communism, they were often self-serving and ineffective. Worse, he saw American support for anti-Communist dictators in these countries as violating democratic principles while fomenting anti-Americanism. The behavior of Americans abroad, especially members of the diplomatic corps, disturbed him as much as anything else. Their indifference to the customs of the countries, their failure to learn the local languages, and their insularity as they clung to American habits and enclaves countered whatever good intentions they represented.[3]

The Ugly American drew on all of these themes. The film was based on a 1958 novel by William Lederer and Eugene Burdick, which had been on the *New York Times* bestseller list for months and was so admired by then-Senator John F. Kennedy that he sent every member of Congress a copy. In stark contrast, William Fulbright, chair of the Senate Foreign Relations Committee, denounced the novel (as well as the impending film) on the Senate floor.[4] Brando responded with a press conference praising our First Amendment freedoms, which allowed writers and filmmakers to express viewpoints in conflict with powerful officials.

This was typical of Brando's politics. He was quick to criticize the violation of American ideals and would draw on the American right of freedom of the press for support. He made sure to read widely to take in a range of ideology. He read ambassador Charles W. Thayer's *Diplomat* (1959), billed by its publishers as a "corrective" to *The Ugly American*, to understand the opposing position; State Department specialist James Saxon Childers's *The Nation on the Flying Trapeze* (1960), on America's image in the Middle and Far East; and *Community of Fear* (1961) by Harrison Brown and James Real on the nuclear arms race, which was central to foreign-policy concerns. He was also reading Mao Tse-tung at the time (which he mentions in audios of his preproduction ideas for the film): *On Guerrilla Warfare* (1961) and a pamphlet, *Talk with the American Correspondent Anna Louise Strong* (1961).[5]

He drew on what he read to revise the *Ugly American* screenplay, developed themes and storylines, and heavily revised different script drafts. In all of these, Brando focused on three points. First, he insisted that the failures of American strategies in Southeast Asia be exposed.[6] Second, he urged an evenhanded treatment of Communists and Americans: "Dramatic concept of cruel communists is cliché. Why are comm. more cruel... bloody than 50,000 non com. What is Com.? disease that affects the brain and destroys center of kindness, empathy?—concept is dangerously over simplified—John Wayne.... They must be understood, not dispensed with.... If we hold as a national policy that Communists are unworthy of a dignified exchange of views and should be summarily dismissed... we are left with the last refuge of hopeless violence. Talk is all we have." Third, he wanted audiences to recognize how foreign affairs affected them: The film should "make people alert about what is going on in the world." He believed he could only open people's minds by inspiring thought, through well-paced drama, that drew them in at the start and never lagged.[7]

Brando's concern for dramatic authenticity in *The Ugly American* was fused with political purpose. He wanted the film to highlight the impact of American isolationism and smugness. "We do care, but not enough. If we cared enough, things would be done. The Peace Corps [then-President Kennedy's invention] would be seven years old instead of one. There would be fourteen other things like the Peace Corps. There wouldn't be one movie called *The Ugly American*, there would be fifteen movies, and they would have been made a long time ago." Throughout his notes and script commentary, he complains about missed opportunities for dramatic excitement and engaging the audience. "The very beginning speech sounds" like "the United Jewish Appeal," or "an advertisement for SHARE in the New Yorker"; and an ear accustomed to such "speech tunes it out immediately." He finds the opening desperate for a hook, and he spends pages on this point in his critique of the script: "These early moments are precious and should not be spent on smiling children, buffalo butts, and honking jeeps." In its place, he recommends crosscuts between Brando's ambassador at a weekend party—the libertinism of Frederico Fellini's film *La Dolce Vita*—and a politically volatile Sarkhan, the film's fictitious location. "While America has a ball, there's a communist in the jungle by the side of the road in Sarkhan." Such an opening would pinpoint the biggest threat to national interests abroad: indifference, symbolized by the citizen "switch[ing] the television dial from [Ambassador] MacWhite's dramatic report" at the film's end.[8]

Brando worries too about the failure to develop *The Ugly American*'s pivotal friendship between Ambassador MacWhite and the popular Sarkhanese leader, Deong. "The drama hangs," he says, "on their relationship." Its collapse is "the main conflict" of the film, yet "in the end you've only seen the bitterness and the continuous bitterness and then a resolution of the bitterness. But you've never seen something that they had together that they lost." This echoes consistent remarks on the film as a whole. He writes in the margins of his copy of the Lederer–Burdick novel: "Fault in film is drama is in Chinese." Elsewhere he observes: "Plague after plague but we don't know our sin. Story of picture"; "Rambles itself into dramaturgical disrepair"; "Dramatic form wanting, reminded of novel."[9] He warns, "We must be careful not to make the Sarkhanese all smiling and primitive and without anything to reward them as a culture except those elements that were brought in by the Russians and Americans . . . unintentional condescension is what we've gotta avoid. In some way, some of the characters must benefit from these people. They must learn something. They must come away with something—MacWhite, Homer."[10]

The film did suffer as Brando anticipated, from a source that was more political travelogue than novel, and he was right about the opening (the jeep and buffalo remained) and the failure to show Harrison Carter MacWhite and Deong as young men together in the Resistance. None of this prevented *The Ugly American* from being a compelling film, which was partly due to Brando's devotion to the project. His friend George Englund, who produced and directed the film, noted the way Brando's "prodigious creative talent" complemented his "command of the technology of movie production."[11] Screenwriter Stewart Stern's praise was more empathic: "There's no more monumental talent than Marlon's, or a more brilliant mind. It's a mind that comes out of watchfulness. He is the most mistrustful man I've ever met, and the most watchful. He can 'read' anything. He comprehends the subtext of everything, whether it's an animal, a book, or a human being. He has the kind of insight that would paralyze me if I had it."[12] Brando advised on casting and scenes, camera angles and techniques and lens sizes, noticing details as minute as someone in the riot scene not "sweat[ing] enough."

MacWhite was one of Brando's early characters who was an authority figure: a meditative, bookish, but ambitious and prone to quick judgments. He is charming as he weathers a rocky Senate confirmation hearing, teases his wife, reunites with Deong, singing "Annie Laurie" after many glasses of rice wine. Despite injecting him with charisma, Brando carefully builds the case against the ambassador. MacWhite's egotism before the Senate committee is pronounced, and his insistence that "*whomwhey*," a local vegetable, is "a kosher pickle" (Brando's line) introduces an imperialism borne out by his inability to grasp why the road he

sees as utterly beneficial could appear otherwise to the local population. Brando had wanted his ambassador to be even more compromised.[13] With his respect for Sarkhanese customs, knowledge
of the language, and plan to mend divisions between local leaders, MacWhite has the right ideas, but his impatience prevents
their strategic execution. Brando's audio commentary shows that
he preserved an awareness of the situation's political complexity
as well as respect for the character of the ambassador, a man with
sound positions despite his failings and mistakes.

> The enemies in the picture ... [are] MacWhite's rashness, his
> inability to perceive the difference between a proud nation-
> alist and a communist, his incapacity to accept a neutral-
> ist line as an honest one. He was wrong in calling Deong a
> communist and Deong was wrong in trusting the commu-
> nists. Therefore, the naivete of the neutralist also becomes
> an antagonistic, dramatic element of the story.... It's really
> difficult to class MacWhite, even with those qualities that
> he has in the beginning of the picture, as an antagonist,
> because in the end he's proved right. This picture says in
> effect what Dulles always thought, if you're a neutralist,
> you're a goddamn fool, the communists are gonna get ya,
> they're gonna eat ya, and this picture proves it. The neutral-
> ists may be sincere, but they are ignorant and ineffective. It's
> useless to be neutral.[14]

Still, the point of *The Ugly American* was that *any* American strategy would have had poor results. The historical trajectory had
been set well before MacWhite's arrival, which is what Brando
had hoped to dramatize in the opening. Cold War polarization,
together with general disinterest in the distinct aspirations of foreign peoples, had long prevented sustained cultivation of democracy across the world.

On the *Ugly American* script, Brando again proved an expert trimmer, with a sure grasp of speech rhythms, and was responsible for many of the film's best lines. Stewart Stern, who had written the script for *Rebel Without a Cause*, provided some tour de force speeches, including MacWhite's disarming prefatory remarks at the Senate hearing: "I have about fifteen pages here which I wrote last night, an explanation of my qualifications, and as I read them over this morning they sound so much like my own eulogy that I've decided to let my mother publish them privately after I'm dead." But he was always open to Brando's ideas, such as the lines Brando added to the Senate scene to evoke the warmth and intimacy of MacWhite's friendship with Deong: "I think we discussed whatever good friends talk about, personal things. I think we discussed life, the ladies. As a matter of fact I think we spent most of our time laughing." On Deong's character, Brando encapsulated it for MacWhite: "He was a rice farmer, Senator. I think 'ordinary' has very little to do with Deong however." He strengthened the dressing-down MacWhite delivers in his first meeting with embassy staff, breaking in on their squabbling to present "some facts" about the riot at the airport. Noteworthy is that Brando would revise his own revisions, a sign of perfectionism and commitment to verbal vitality. At the scene's end, he enhanced MacWhite's irritable dismissal of Joe Bing, "I don't like bootlicking," adding: "and uh I don't like your coarse manners. Now you get yourself together and you get out," which Stern finished: "uh Bing...*don't call me Mac!*" Stern confirmed Brando's valuable improvisation during filming. According to Stern, Brando contributed a great deal to his part, bringing substance and humor to his reunion with Deong and to the exchanges with his wife.[15]

Brando continuously complained about the scenes between Mac and his wife, Marion (Sandra Church). At the time, he commented: "The love story has no function in this picture. It's dead weight from the point of view of construction, the advance of the plot, which to my mind is absolutely sacrosanct. Sacred as well is the growth of character—the alteration of character anyway. Nothing in the story has any value really except these two considerations. The love story has no bearing on the story at all. It is an interruption." He concludes that the wife "plays the dramaturgical butler who brings the calling card of plot from the front door to the bedroom."[16]

Seeking to remedy this, Brando rewrote almost all of their first romantic encounter in the bedroom of their new home in Sarkhan to deepen an understanding of MacWhite's relationships. He excised what was there and replaced it with dialogue that promoted natural interplay with the ambassador's wife and yielded an appealing scene that also further illuminates the MacWhite–Deong friendship. Brando injected humor and ease, through repartee as well as gestures, like the already noted strategy of using his wife's toes as a letter holder. MacWhite's enthusiastic response to Deong's house gifts and his rush to see him (instead, why not join his wife in bed after a long difficult day worsened by jet lag?) anticipates his overreaction when Deong's views disappoint him. Thus Brando transformed a dispensable interlude into a subtle instrument of plot development.

The ambassador in *The Ugly American* was an intellectual whose maturity and elegance distinguished him from Brando's previous roles. Arrayed in diplomatic white for state occasions, with a pencil-thin mustache, MacWhite's attractiveness was based in sophistication and success, however limited. MacWhite was also the only Brando character to wear glasses throughout the film, and the actor called attention to them: putting on the large horn-rimmed frames to inspect a map of the region or a photograph, for instance, and removing them to stare intently at a dignitary or a reporter. Brando's manipulation of the glasses made them symbolic of American diplomatic efforts to see the situation in Southeast Asia clearly, and American diplomacy's

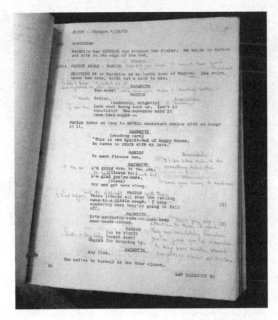

Brando's revised script page from *The Ugly American*.

Revisions reproduced by permission of Brando Enterprises, LP.

ultimate failure to anticipate the consequences of national policy in the region.[17] The film took a complex view of Southeast Asia, eschewing liberal as well as conservative pieties in favor of a position whose prophetic awareness was apparent only after the loss of Vietnam. Reading every sign of independence from Western initiatives as a Communist threat was as misleading as presumptions that developing countries aspired to whatever Americans considered the good life to be.

The parallels to Vietnam were meant to be unmistakable. Vietnam comes up repeatedly in recorded discussions of the film (featuring Brando, George Englund, and executive producer Mel Tucker), and reviewers, like one in the *New York Times*, didn't miss it. The *Times* also praised Brando's performance, his "solidness and vigor," concluding that "Mr. Brando moves through

Using his wife's toes as letter holder. © 1963 Universal Pictures, Courtesy of Universal Studios Licensing LLC.

the whole picture with authority and intelligence, creating an 'ugly American' that provokes dismay but sympathy." The opinion was echoed by others. *Variety* said, "Brando's performance is a towering one," and Brendan Gill in *The New Yorker* called it "dazzling." Gill was mesmerized from the start: "He caused me to see at once that no Senatorial adversary stood a chance against him; at the same time, uncannily, he caused me to see that pipe, brains, and breeding would be insufficient and that all this caged energy wearing the conventional disguise of good will, would lead straight to someone's doom." Then this further note: "I believed in him heart and soul. A well-tailored, pipe-smoking smooth-looking man of nearly forty, the perfect specimen of an upper-middle class White Protestant American—a Brando creation that seemed utterly purged of whoever Brando himself may be."

The Ugly American was the first of two films in which Brando secured parts for his sister Jocelyn in an effort to revive her career after years of blacklisting. Given these circumstances, and their activist family roots, it seemed appropriate that they were together in two of his most political films.[18] Jocelyn, another voracious reader, established her own bookstore, The Book Bin, in Pacific Palisades soon after the opening of *The Ugly American*.[19] Following the inclinations of her mother and grandmother, she would become proficient too in an unorthodox but popular form of psychotherapy: an intensive journal-writing method originated by American psychotherapist Ira Progoff, in which patients were instructed to narrate conflicts from both sides, thus probing the other person's as well as their own perspective. Setting up shop next to her Santa Monica bungalow in a garage remodeled as a studio with her brother's financial help, Jocelyn would run weekend-long sessions in the Progoff method for groups of patients. She also practiced Christian Science, nondogmatically, as Dodie had done, and retained a lifelong curiosity about alternative medicine.

Brando's next major role was in *The Chase* (1966), a suitable counterpart to *The Ugly American*. In conception at least, it was to take as firm a stand on domestic racial politics as the earlier film had taken on global issues.[20] In *The Chase*, as in *The Ugly American*, Brando played a public official, his first sheriff, a good man in impossible circumstances, where any move was bound to go wrong.

THE CHASE

Brando's national and global activism had always been of a piece. During a televised Civil Rights Roundtable with James Baldwin, Harry Belafonte, Sidney Poitier, Charlton Heston, and Joseph Mankiewicz, following Martin Luther King Jr.'s "I Have a Dream" speech, Brando was unique in using the occasion to connect American racism to international events, such as the Nazi genocide of Jews in the 1940s and America's 1962 suspension of aid to Haiti.[21] Brando's reading and travels helped him to recognize the general similarity of racist motivations and violence, while seeing their particular destructive impact. Books he read during or after *The Ugly American* would have been applicable to *The Chase* as well. Taya Zinkin's *Caste Today* (1963) and Ronald Segal's *The Anguish of India* (1965), which offered international accounts of caste and class prejudice, assisted Brando's analysis of American civil rights, just as his reading about Indians in the Americas, inspired by Emiliano Zapata's Mexican-Indian roots, affected his thinking about American diplomacy in Southeast Asia for *The Ugly American* and race relations in Texas for *The Chase*. A reminder to himself on the back cover of Francis Paul Prucha's *American Indian Policy in the Formative Years* (1962)—"cross-check legal obligations of South Africa and U.S. to indigenous people in separate enclosure within their territories and Panama and Cuba—Okinawa, Guam, and Marshall Islands"—foregrounds his habit of thinking globally about local affairs.[22]

Brando's reading around this time was also rich in democratic political philosophy: *The Federalist Papers* by Alexander Hamilton, John Jay, and James Madison (eighty-five essays by Founding Fathers about the American Constitution designed to promote an informed citizenry essential to a healthy democracy), and Mortimer Adler's *The Development of Political Theory and Government* (1959). There was probably no book that meant more to him than Supreme Court Justice William O. Douglas's *America Challenged* (1960). Douglas criticized the reign of conformity since World War II. He believed that the fear of Communism prevented careful study of the USSR, an important new competitor, and that the impact of the media discouraged thoughtful debate and dissent.[23] Brando saw in Douglas a genuinely sympathetic public intellectual and arranged a meeting with him to discuss American

Indian affairs.[24] In *America Challenged*, Douglas put forward the principles of revolutionary freedom and respect for cultural minorities, the foundation of a "great moral tradition." This tradition was the backbone of average citizens like Brando's Sheriff Calder of *The Chase*, who defended the persecuted in the name of national values ignored by the white majority. Brando could have drawn on many of his own public statements for Sheriff Calder's views. As he told an interviewer for *Ebony* in 1963, "One of the amusing things about this country and many of its leaders" is that "they are always talking about the under-educated world and the under-educated Negro; that he is not suited to govern himself because he is under-educated. But to my way of thinking, the Negro is an over-educated person... he knows the meaning of democracy better than most other Americans. He knows the meaning of the Bill of Rights and what civil rights means. He knows what the spirit of this country is as it was constitutionally written, because he has had so little of it extended to him. I think that his knowledge about what is really useful and meaningful about our principles of government is infinitely greater than that of any corresponding white group."[25]

As a man of law, Calder is a departure for Brando, who invests him with his signature ambivalence and charm. He also perfected, in his studied way, a genuine Texas accent. *The Chase's* setting is an uneasy cauldron of cultural groups: oppressed blacks, oil barons and middle-class managers, poor whites, Mexican migrants, and immigrants. Notes and script commentary show that Brando's goal was to amplify this clash of cultures: Sheriff Calder would have a Mexican wife and half-Mexican daughter a class above their migrant brethren, who are servants and seasonal laborers, and the black community would be equally diverse. Recalling his documentation of California's multiculturalism in *One-Eyed Jacks*, he encouraged an emphasis on Texas's regional marginality. "Almost all Texans speak Spanish," Brando

On set, 1965, in *The Chase*. Rex USA.

wrote in notes on the script next to a white Texan's stumbling Spanish encounter with Mexicans, "especially if they live on the border." White society, conceived by Brando, was also internally complex: small-town Texans, whose primary diversion was weekend carousing, versus the more cosmopolitan activities of the urbanites from nearby Houston. This group included the elite, like bank president Val Rogers—whose disapproval of his son Jake's (James Fox) penniless sweetheart has resulted in Jake's loveless marriage to a woman of their own class—as well as the middle-class types who throw their own drunken revels but also socialize with the lower echelons at Sol's Café. At the bottom of the social scale is the Reeves clan: Sol's stepdaughter, Anna (Jane Fonda), who is married to the hard-luck "Bubber" Reeves (Robert Redford), the only town miscreant in prison.

The Chase is more violent than *The Ugly American*, but the violence of both films shares a common source in misguided social policies and the festering injustices they foster. Although Texas in *The Chase* has never outgrown its Wild West origins, it also foreshadows key aspects of the state in the twenty-first century, with its illegal Mexican immigrants (escaped convict Bubber confronting them in a cattle car), *nouveau riche* oil elites (they challenge each other in pledges to the local college), and pervasive weaponry (Calder asserts, "The state of Texas says any man can own a gun, and most of you got two, but deputies you ain't!"). Meanwhile, self-respecting blacks quietly pursue social mobility, while a black underclass remains the perennial scapegoat. Critics found most of the Southern whites caricatures, and Brando, in his "Random Notes on the Script," complained about the vague motivations of Sheriff Calder, whom he called "the old lamplighter" ("in as much as it largely falls to him to meander through the story and illuminate the plot points").[26] Such flaws did not prevent the esteem of serious film critics, nor the picture's immense popularity in Europe, and increasing appeal over time at home.

Brando had an empathetic director in Arthur Penn and a strong supporting cast in Fonda, Redford, E. G. Marshall, Angie Dickinson, James Fox, and Robert Duvall, among others. But he found the script as flawed as that of *The Ugly American*, despite its author, renowned playwright Lillian Hellman. Moreover, the pivotal member of the enterprise, to the film's detriment, was Sam Spiegel, whose editing independent of the director resulted, according to Penn, in the cutting of Brando's best scenes as he improvised around overly expository dialogues.[27] Brando's freedom on Penn's set had to do with the fundamental compatibility of their perspectives. Penn shared the actor's sensual approach to expression, and, like other directors with whom Brando enjoyed working, encouraged his inventive use of props, camera angles, and even recording speeds. Cinema historian Robin Wood saw a preoccupation with physical reality as the essence of Penn's direction, noting how he dwelled on the physicality of people and their surroundings.[28] The parallels to Brando's own instinctive methods were pronounced. Brando's Sheriff Calder, accused of subservience to Val Rogers, is forever polishing—a riding saddle, his shoes—and wiping his hands—he always seems to have a handkerchief—gestures that make manifest his disgust and his eagerness to abandon the unsavory job and town.

Partly because of Spiegel's deleterious editing, Penn never quite considered *The Chase* his own.[29] Moreover, Brando was Brando no matter who directed him, and his Sheriff Calder resonates with some of his most arresting work on film. At Val Rogers's dinner party, Calder sniffs a petal to conceal his irritation, which anticipates the moment in *The Godfather* when Don Corleone sniffs a rose to punctuate the claim that, "after all, we're not murderers." When Calder, brooding, cups a pipe, inspecting the bowl as if seeking wisdom in tobacco leaves, Brando recalls Ambassador MacWhite, who steadies himself, pipe in hand, after his strategy fails. In another parallel to *The Ugly American* where

Brando first appears from behind, bent over a briefcase on the point of his Senate testimony, a semi-moon that foregrounds the risks of the Southeast Asia venture, Brando's sheriff bends over a water cooler in his office, just before outlining to Jane Fonda's Anna Reeves the grave risk he has taken in not summoning trigger-happy backup to hunt her husband. The dangers of enforcing the law alone are realized when townies, enraged by his protection of blacks and criminals, beat him bloody in that same office.

Brando's creative use of film technology in *The Chase*'s beating scene renders symbolic the sacrificial victimization experienced by many of his protagonists. It is widely known that the slow-motion scene where Warren Beatty and Faye Dunaway are gunned down in Arthur Penn's *Bonnie and Clyde* (1967) initiated a new form of cinematic violence.[30] Few, however, are aware that Brando's innovation in *The Chase* the year before is the source of this revolutionary method—a fact confirmed by Brando's notes on the film and that Penn admitted publicly after the actor's death. Recognizing in the beating of the sheriff an extreme reversal of authority requiring distinctive treatment, Brando suggested speeding up the camera to create the effect of slow motion, a method that made the beating, as Brando put it, "the objective correlative of the film as a whole." Penn used the same technique in *Bonnie and Clyde* and made film history.

Disdainful of conventional approaches to violence in movies, choreographed to belie bodily suffering, Brando wanted audiences to feel the sadism and awkwardness of an actual brawl. "Remind me to talk to you about the fight," he wrote to Penn during production. "The beating could be done, possibly—in an interesting, not often used, maybe unprecedented technique." "The idea was his," Penn confessed in an interview. "Marlon said to me, 'If we're going to do this scene, let's really do it until the brutality is boring.'... Instead of throwing movie punches he said,

'How about if we really hit each other but we shoot it at twenty frames instead of twenty-four?' They really are punching him. The action was filmed at slow speed but then projected at regular speed. You see the fists land and the distortion of flesh, just like in real fights. It worked like a dream."[31]

Brando sought realism as well in depicting the courage of Southern blacks in the civil rights movement. "Let's just see once a Negro represented as a stud. These kids face death every day down there," he wrote. A Southern judge would help to dramatize the legal corruption that sustained white supremacy, and Val Rogers could tell Lester, the poor black man he badgers for information, "I'm going to kill you... and there isn't a judge in this county who'll say I can't and you know it." Brando cites the trampling of law in the case of the three civil rights workers whose murders were never prosecuted because "the society magistrate...threw the confession out as not substantial enough." Political honesty and dramatic authenticity were not mutually exclusive, Brando insisted, as he tirelessly prodded Lillian Hellman (in script commentary) to improve the characterization and plotting. "Another essay," he writes on the November 6, 1964, script. "These people are cartoons." How can the whole town fear the return of escaped convict Bubber, when he appears as "a creampuff"? The same goes for Val Rogers—"nobody breathes in that town without a certificate from Val Rogers"—a clout discredited by his "limp wrists and fluttering eyelids." The weakness of these leading catalysts destroys the story's credibility and the purpose of Brando's Sheriff Calder, who "has no conflict, he's just floundering."

Though many of these problems were never resolved, Brando, Penn, and the talented cast produced a respectable film that spoke to some of the most prominent tensions of the era. Once again Brando ad-libbed some of the picture's best lines: (in response to Emily's, "Why don't you stick around and help us protect him")

"With all the *pistols* you *got there* Emily, I don't believe there'd be *room* for *mine*"; (to Ruby) "Some of those people out there are just *nuts*; they're just *nuts* . . . I gotta lock a man up here, who didn't do a *damn thing*, just to keep those *maniacs* from *killin'* him; they're not interested in *doin' nothin'* but gettin' drunk and makin' trouble. I'm *sick* of it. I'm *sick* of *livin'* here, I'm *sick* of this job!"; (to his deputy, inquiring about an assignment) "Forget it! Just keep drivin' around. And turn off that *party hat!*"—the flashing siren. (Italics indicate words stressed by Brando.) Against a backdrop of sexual competition, betrayal, and greed, Brando's sheriff and his wife are decent people who resist excess and the despair that follows. The oasis embodied by the golden-haired Calders is reinforced by their dress, which highlights their affinity to each other and separation from the community. Before the beating, Ruby wears a red sweater over the taupe blouse and skirt that matches her husband's uniform, thus predicting his imminent cloaking in blood. Calder's surrender to violence at the end is an act of self-division, for he must thrust Ruby aside to pummel Bubber's killer, Archie. That momentary suspension of morality signals the necessity of Calder's departure.

"Violence is a subject that an artist who is intuitively and intellectually alive to the world in which he exists can scarcely avoid today; and if there is a more responsible treatment of it anywhere in the cinema, I have yet to see it."[32] Thus, film historian Robin Wood concludes his admiring account of *The Chase*. Wood was thinking of Archie's shooting of Bubber, echoing Jack Ruby's 1963 murder of Lee Harvey Oswald, but he might have had in mind the correspondence between the riots in Watts, a nearby Los Angeles ghetto, and *The Chase*'s final conflagration.[33] *The Chase*'s focus on race problems in the South could only have seemed ironic when Watts erupted on August 11—nine days after *The Chase*'s final scene was shot—and burned for five days. The trigger was a black man's arrest for drunk driving, but the underlying cause was decades of discrimination in housing, schooling, and employment. Brando, Penn, and others working on the film knew that the South was less unique in its institutionalization of racism than many were prepared to admit. Indeed, Brando made this very point at a CORE rally on August 22, 1963, in Gadsden, Alabama, protesting job discrimination.

Violence did not preclude beauty, and *The Chase* was above all visually striking, its Western swamplands and rolling hills providing, as it had in Brando's *One-Eyed Jacks*, a respite from human society. The Calders are identified with nature in their yearning for the paternal farm they hope to recover from oil speculators. A wild horse in their headlights, after an early departure from Val Rogers's party, foreshadows their return to the land at the film's end, in a black car confirming Calder's resignation as sheriff. That Jeffersonian prospect remained an answer of sorts to the corrosive society pictured in the film.

REFLECTIONS IN A GOLDEN EYE

The Ugly American, *The Chase*, and *Reflections in a Golden Eye* offered unique angles on the tumultuous 1960s, and each of Brando's characters had his own relationship to the prevailing violence. Ambassador MacWhite, thoughtful but arrogant, acts precipitously in a setting where the slightest miscalculation ignites a war; Sheriff Calder repudiates action but his town erupts anyway; Major Weldon Penderton in *Reflections in a Golden Eye* internalizes the violence and redirects it against helpless alter egos—a runaway horse and an army private. Violence in *Reflections* is sexual and also unspoken. With the exception of Montgomery Clift in *Suddenly Last Summer* (1959), Brando was the first leading American actor to play a homosexual on film, impotent and closeted, with an aggressively adulterous wife (Elizabeth Taylor). Suffused in a golden hue, the film was set on an army base during peacetime, an environment that made its repressed protagonist exemplary rather than exceptional.

There are obvious differences between Brando's Sheriff Calder and his Major Penderton—realized heterosexuality versus stifled homosexuality, Texas lawman versus Georgia officer, spousal loyalty versus cuckoldry—as well as commonalities. Both are observers alienated from macho models of manhood; instinctively opposed to volatility, they would choose deliberation over violence. Yet both are smoldering and explode when pushed to the edge. *The Chase* and *Reflections in a Golden Eye* share the distinction of having involvement by significant women authors from the South—Lillian Hellman and Carson McCullers, respectively. Hellman wrote *The Chase* screenplay, based on a novel by Horton Foote. McCullers wrote the novella on which *Reflections* was based. Still, the women were largely responsible for shaping the films and Brando's roles in them. Hellman receives exclusive credit for the screenplay of *The Chase*, and McCullers's novella was barely altered from book to film.[34]

Brando's respect for McCullers was evident in the unusually small number of revisions he introduced into the script, and from script to screen. He deleted only one scene, which was in both novel and original screenplay: Major Penderton squeezing a kitten into a mailbox and striding away from its "piteous mews."[35] Stella Adler noted about Brando that "nothing human was foreign to him," but she also recalled his extraordinary sensitivity to animals. "I'd rather die," he told her once, "than hurt anything alive."[36] Brando, apparently, could not find it in himself to play a man who would commit such an act, especially at a time when such scenes could not be faked to prevent harming an animal. The dramatic necessity of the horsewhipping scene was clear, and that was concession enough. Even when he played soldiers and gunfighters, Brando made a point of killing rarely in his films, which makes the blood lust of his late villains—the assassin in *The Missouri Breaks* or the prison warden in *Free Money*—truly distinct.

The most noteworthy aspect of Brando's performance was his embodiment of Major Penderton, the way he transformed himself physically into an instrument of unrequited love and loneliness. Forty-two at the time of the production, he managed to collapse his natural vigor and athleticism into the flaccid awkwardness of a man entirely at odds with himself. The major is not particularly fat, but Brando makes him seem hulking, boneless, to reflect the man's incoherence, the chasm between his buried passions and his public persona as a successful married officer. Brando's Penderton flounders porpoiselike in his uniform, his head and legs and arms flapping extensions of a body that doesn't know its purpose. He walks with a rigid care, as if the ground might open suddenly and swallow him whole. Above all, he seems offended by the surrounding sounds, smells, and sights. His perpetually raised chin displays a resolve to live above the senses. Yet he has small, secretive pleasures. His head hangs seductively over the treasures he keeps locked in his desk drawer in a truss box: a postcard of a male nude and a spoon stolen from Captain Weincheck, another officer, also apparently a closeted homosexual, with a taste for Proust and classical music.

Captain Penderton, predictably, has no sympathy for Captain Weincheck and does his best to oust him from the service. As a veteran of Broadway and Hollywood, Brando was familiar with the self-hatred that made closeted homosexuals the most cunning and punitive regulators of one another. Thus, another probable reason for cutting the scene of flagrant sadism toward the kitten was to further an empathetic portrait of a homosexual whom audiences, straight and gay, might otherwise be inclined to spurn. The Stonewall riots of June 1969 in New York's Greenwich

Out of character with Elizabeth Taylor on the set of *Reflections*. Loomis Dean/ Time & Life Pictures/Getty Images.

Village (violent protests by gay men and women against decades of vilification and abuse) and the first Gay Pride marches were still years away. The entertainment and media industries, in which many homosexuals had careers, were notoriously resistant to overt treatments like *Reflections in a Golden Eye*.

Brando had excoriated *Time* magazine in 1963 on the *Today Show* for its consistently hostile reviews of playwright Tennessee Williams. Brando read aloud from *Time* critiques of Williams, calling attention to the anal rhetoric and physical slurs so obviously misplaced in a reputable journal. The use of terms such as *manure* and *ineffable sashay of self-pity*, as well as the

In character with John Huston on the set of *Reflections*. Warner Bros./Photofest.

review's overall charge that Williams "has hallucinated a vast but specious pageant of depravity in which fantasies of incest, cannibalism, murder, rape, sodomy, and drug addiction constitute the canon of reality," were means both subtle and explicit of dismissing Williams and his work as homosexual and perverse. *Time*'s message was clear: Williams and his ilk have no place in an American dramatic tradition. "All the criticisms are like that," Brando noted, with one stunning exception—a celebration of Williams that somehow penetrated the official "*Time* opinion." Brando closed by reading aloud from the review that called Williams "a consummate master of the theatre...the greatest U.S. playwright since Eugene O'Neill," comparing his monologues to those of Shakespeare.[37]

Well before Stonewall, with typical courage, Brando spoke out against a major magazine's homophobic coverage. It took even more courage to accept the role of Penderton in *Reflections in a Golden Eye*, intended for Elizabeth Taylor's friend Montgomery Clift, whose fragile health had initiated the search for a replacement well before his death on July 23, 1966. Clift's bisexuality was an open secret in Hollywood, his death from heart failure the result of years of alcohol and drug abuse. Brando had always been the first choice to replace Clift, but he was expensive, and during the protracted negotiations, *Reflections* producer Ray Stark reported to Taylor in an August 16, 1966, letter that he had pursued all the plausible alternatives. But no one of the caliber needed to star opposite her in a challenging role was willing to risk playing a closeted homosexual. Indeed, the homosexual content of *Reflections in a Golden Eye* was so disturbing to the Motion Picture Association of America that they avoided it almost completely (or wouldn't admit they noticed it because it might mean they were seeing something that wasn't there) in a 1964 letter about the script, warning only about stand-alone nude scenes of Taylor (Leonora Penderton) in her living room and Robert Forster (Private Williams) in the woods. Stark's letter testified to Brando's persisting stature. Explaining why Taylor had to be prepared to accept a smaller cut of the proceeds, Stark noted that Brando was asking for a million in salary plus seven and a half percent of the film's gross. Stark reminded Taylor that she had promised, once Clift was unavailable, to make almost any monetary sacrifice to get Brando, and also that Brando was at the top of John Huston's list of actors to play Penderton.[38] Huston was the prestigious director of *The Maltese Falcon, The Treasure of the Sierra Madre*, and many other major films.

As Stark and Huston expected, Brando embraced Penderton's pain, making him absorbing, even attractive despite his finickiness and irritability, thus preserving his credibility as a beautiful woman's husband. He is cold but has moments of charm, his Southern accent and manner assisting the flourish of a witticism or smile. In scenes when Penderton watches Private Williams surreptitiously—doing drills with the battalion, riding, or sunbathing nude—his face assumes a childish plushness, gazing in rapt wonder at the young man's physical freedom. Williams's natural power threatens Penderton even as he covets it. He sees the same thing in his wife's precious racehorse, Firebird, which is why he is so determined to thwart the animal. Taking the horse out alone on the sly, knowing his wife will be preoccupied with preparations for her party, he treats it like a live grenade, until he is astride. He lets the horse run free so he can pull it up sadistically, until the animal takes off wildly as he clings to the reins, resulting in Penderton's face being lacerated by tree branches. When the horse finally stops, he beats it viciously with a tree switch—the one time his desire and envy is externalized in aggression. The act is twisted and brutal, painful to watch, as the officer collapses sobbing from self-pity and guilt.

This is among Brando's great moments on film, as he conveys simultaneously the character's infantile narcissism, boyish cruelty, and homoeroticism. The scene culminates with the miraculous appearance of Private Williams, naked, stepping over the major's prone body to lead the traumatized horse away. This is as close as Penderton gets to sexual release, and he luxuriates in his own humiliation. The scene is immediately echoed in the sadomasochistic exchange between wife and husband. Discovering what he has done to Firebird, Leonora lashes her husband across his bandaged face with a riding crop, in front of all the military brass assembled at their house party. Penderton at this moment is a type of Christ, as he stares motionless, his eyes gentle, surrendering to her punishment. The film bears witness to his status as a symbol of collective suffering, in the many reflections of his image: in his bedroom mirror flexing his biceps; in the hallway mirror miming dialogues when he anticipates promotion to general; and, most disturbing, in the bathroom mirror first delicately applying his wife's face cream and then smearing it heavily over his eyelids, distorting his appearance. The scene is a tribute to Brando's bravery and sympathy, as he reveals Penderton reaching feminized depths that he must immediately reject as monstrous.

Penderton never loses his dignity, despite the magnitude of what he represses. A bit of a pedant lecturing to cadets on Clause-witz, the theorist of war whom he worships, he remains a fig-ure of authority. We are reminded here of Brando's conversance with military schools. During his two years at Shattuck, he was exposed to every aspect of officer training and education: drills with firearms, competitive sports, a traditional curriculum heavy in battle tactics as well as history and Shakespeare.[39] At Shattuck, he would have met adults like Penderton, and boys on their way to becoming him, men who luxuriated in the world of men and learned to hide their homoeroticism in order to thrive there.

Penderton comes to life describing the simple pleasures of the enlisted man. "It's rough and it's coarse perhaps but it's also clean, it's clean as a rifle. There's no speck of dust inside or out, and it's immaculate in its hard young fitness.... They're seldom out of one another's sight, they eat and they train and they shower and play jokes and go to the brothel together, and they sleep side by side.... There are friendships formed that are stronger...than the fear of death. And they're...never lonely, never lonely. And sometimes I envy them." By the fireplace, pipe in hand, Pender-ton outlines the ideal of masculinity liberated from female civili-zation and intrigue, symbolized by his wife listening mystified in a provocatively low-cut dress. In making Penderton the spokes-man for the healthy male norm, the film confirms not only the conventionality of his deepest emotions but also the latent homo-eroticism of the norm.

Moreover, it is critical that during a previous speech in the same scene, Penderton has for the first time opposed orthodoxy, paraphrasing his wife's lover, Colonel Morris Langdon (Brian Keith): "Any fulfillment obtained at the expense of normality is wrong, and should not be allowed to bring happiness.... It's better because it's morally honorable for the square peg to keep scraping about in a round hole rather than to discover and use the unorthodox one that would fit it." Asked if he agrees, Penderton replies, "No, I don't." Because it *precedes* his idealization of barracks life, Penderton's implicitly erotic rhetoric of pegs and holes exposes a utopian dimension of *Reflections in a Golden Eye*—the film's recognition of how integral Penderton's impulses are to standard masculinity.

Audiences were unprepared for such insights as Tennessee Williams demonstrated in his introduction to a New Directions reprint of McCullers's novella, published in 1971, four years after the film version's release. Williams takes a brash stand when it comes to aesthetics, declaring McCullers's fiction exemplary modern art, on par with Picasso's *Guernica*, chiding the philistines who marginalize her work as merely "Gothic." But he censors himself on sexuality: he never mentions Huston's film, starring the "greatest living actor" (as Williams categorized Brando in 1975), avoiding the homosexual content of fiction and film.[40] Like so much of Brando's work in the sixties, *Reflections in a Golden Eye* was ahead of its time. As Brando's *Today Show* critique of slurs against Williams confirmed, the playwright's gay identity was common knowledge. But Williams's career would hardly have benefited from saying so outright.

Between his two speeches, Penderton strides to the mantel to grab a pipe and knocks over "Rufus," his wife's favorite figurine, which is of a stereotyped black servant with a big, ingratiating smile. This is no accident. The breaking of this image of black servility is consistent with the major's rejection of moral honor on behalf of the square peg. The world of *Reflections in a Golden Eye* is rife with racism, homophobia, and misogyny, embraced, as the film portrays them, by shuffling black soldiers, "exotic" servants, and awkward homosexuals. Penderton denigrates Weincheck; Langdon torments Anacleto, the Filipino houseboy; and Leonora ridicules homosexuals. The scene in which Leonora and her black servant snicker over a joke about "two little queers," audible to her husband in his nearby study, is typical. Penderton's enlightened challenge to homophobic and racist conventions in the fireplace scene should not be overlooked, despite its qualification by the ending, when Penderton kills Private Williams after discovering him in his wife's bedroom fondling her clothes. The scene anticipates a restoration of normative heterosexuality: Penderton will assume the guise of a husband in his castle defending his wife, reenter the closet, and be promoted to general. Still, what film audiences know matters: that Penderton murders Williams in a rage over the young man's preference for Penderton's wife over him. And this is enough to make *Reflections in a Golden Eye* a film that actually *pointed the way toward* political change rather than *following* in its wake.

From the perspective of the twenty-first century, it is possible to miss the courageousness of Brando's willingness to play a homosexual character with sympathetic understanding in 1966. Brando's acting style would have him pursuing the depths of such a character. Given his respect for the director, script, and costars, he knew they would prompt him to it. Some of the scenes were almost unbearable—Penderton with the horse, Penderton and Leonora home alone engaged in ferocious marital combat, Leonora lashing her husband's face with the riding crop before party guests. The quality of the acting and directing keeps them within the pale of common human feeling. The movie remains compellingly painful for contemporary viewers because the characters are not stereotypes, and their suffering is all too real.

Brando's groundbreaking work in the sixties influenced others in film. Robert De Niro, for instance, was indebted to Brando's mirror scenes in *Reflections in a Golden Eye* for *Taxi Driver*'s (1976) tour-de-force mirror speech ("*You* talkin' to *me*?").[41] Future director Francis Ford Coppola worked briefly as a screenwriter on *Reflections*.[42] Moreover, despite its controversial subject, most contemporary reviews celebrated the acting. Citing Brando beating the horse and lecturing a class of soldiers, film critic Roger Ebert announced: "In this scene and others Brando regains the peak of his magnificent talent," while the *New York Post* proclaimed: "Brando has never been greater. His solitary frenzy of fear, relief and anger, brought about by a horse running away with him, is awesome in its approach to insanity." The *Los Angeles Herald Examiner* added further praise: "Seldom, if ever, has a Hollywood film displayed such fidelity to a literary work of art"; "recalls his early winning days at the start of his career," his speech on "A life among men ... a highlight."[43]

The positive reviews were especially noteworthy, given what seemed the deliberate suppression by distributors of a film with sensitive themes. Roger Ebert found it "fishy" the way the film "crept into town so silently." After all, here was a film "with Elizabeth Taylor and Marlon Brando, no less, and the director was that great man himself, John Huston.... Was the movie so wretchedly bad that Warner Bros. decided to keep it a secret?" Ray Stark wrote to John Huston, reporting brisk sales for the film's first week. Still, Stark expressed suspicion about the timing of the film's release, with minimal publicity and no premiere, during a week that contained both the Jewish High Holidays and the World Series.[44] The same would be true of Brando's next major film, *Burn!* (1969) or *Queimada!*, in Portuguese, his own favorite of the sixties.

REVOLUTIONARY CINEMA, *BURN!*

Burn! was in many ways typical of the sixties for Brando. He had a major director in Gillo Pontecorvo, and experienced film people in cinematographer Marcello Gatti (*The Battle of Algiers*) plus producer Alberto Grimaldi and composer Ennio Morricone, who had worked together on *The Good, the Bad, and the Ugly*. Brando had accepted the project because he admired Pontecorvo's *Battle of Algiers* for its realistic portrait of guerrilla fighters triumphing over an imperial-colonial power. He believed in *Burn!* and its potential for illuminating global problems of slavery, colonialism, and racism. Brando understood the film's history as directly relevant to the American race struggle. He sought out Black Panthers Bobby Seale and Eldridge Cleaver to discuss their revolutionary objectives—partly, he told them, so that he might grasp firsthand contemporary aspirations that recalled those of the black rebels in *Burn!*[45]

Burn! was a highly politicized enterprise from the start. Developed from a story by Pontecorvo and writer Franco Solinas, it was inspired by an incident in the 1520s when the Spanish burned an entire Caribbean island to quell a revolt by indigenous workers. Replacing the workers with African slaves, the Spanish and their descendants spent the next three hundred years exploiting the island's resources. The film explores the nineteenth-century aftermath of these violent beginnings from the perspective of a British agent, Brando's Sir William Walker, hired to instigate a rebellion against Portuguese rule—changed from Spanish to avoid a boycott of the film by Franco's regime—so Britain can secure a foothold in sugar-cane production. Walker sails to the island of Queimada, intending to cultivate a black resistance leader named Santiago, but he arrives just in time to witness his execution. His effort to find a substitute with enough dignity and rage to head a revolt is helped along by Teddy Sanchez (Renato Salvatori), a mulatto businessman eager to foster any opposition to Portuguese rule. The plot of *Burn!* thus comes to center on the transformation of José Dolores (Evaristo Marquez), a simple black porter, into a revolutionary hero.

Burn! is divided into two parts: The first ends when Dolores's militia disarms after triumphing over the Portuguese. An indigenous government headed by Sanchez is installed and controlled by foreign investors, and Walker leaves the country. The story resumes ten years later in the late 1840s, when Walker returns to Queimada as emissary for the Antilles Royal Sugar Company to challenge a native uprising that threatens to topple both the Sanchez government and its neocolonial partners. This time, instead of stirring up a rebellion to establish British commercial interests, Walker's mission is to put one down in order to salvage them. The new 1848 rebellion, which is likened to European popular revolts of the era, is led by Dolores, who has become a revolutionary. Summoned as a kind of Dr. Frankenstein to contain the monster he has created, Walker proceeds to delineate in strategy sessions with Sanchez and his generals what their forces are up against. Dolores is a classic guerrilla fighter: His small bands in the mountainous Sierra depend on destitute villagers and persevere despite being vastly outnumbered. Guerrillas, Walker explains, are formidable opponents because they "have nothing to lose and fight for an idea." Dolores himself says laboring for foreign investors and their local lackeys is equivalent to slavery. He declares that freedom cannot be *given*; it must be *seized*. Subsequent scenes of Dolores's army subjected to every conceivable form of warfare—swords, cannon, guns, fire, and dogs—align Queimada's revolutionaries with freedom fighters across the centuries, including nineteenth-century American slaves. While Dolores dies at the end, his martyrdom foreshadows the inevitable demise of white domination in the Caribbean and elsewhere.

Pontecorvo's decision to film *Burn!* mostly in Cartagena, Colombia, proved advantageous but also produced strife. Intense heat and rough conditions caused illnesses—from ordinary rashes to dysentery—among cast and crew, but Cartagena's Spanish

Playing chess on the set of *Burn!*, Cartagena, Colombia. Courtesy of MGM Media Licensing.

colonial architecture, as well as its Afro-Caribbean population, offered authentic shooting locations and an abundance of extras.[46] Pontecorvo specialized in crowd scenes, and those of *Burn!* are resplendent: a tumultuous carnival that enables the assassination of the Portuguese governor; a hopeful populace pouring onto the beach to welcome Jose Dolores; starving multitudes stampeding for loaves of bread. *Burn!* is "perhaps the least condescending film that has ever dealt with slavery," wrote Pauline Kael, applauding

Pontecorvo's "gift for epic filmmaking" and keeping "masses of people in movement on the screen so that we care about what happens to them."[47]

Brando's nineteenth-century British agent is a learned cynic familiar with ideas that move men and committed to none of them. Cunning and intelligent, he subordinates his needs to his vocation of arch manipulator. He has no attachments, displays no desire for women or men, and is skilled with his fists and multiple kinds of weaponry, but he employs them only when necessary at minimum force. When he shoots a young resistance fighter to prevent flight, he aims precisely, producing a flesh wound before interrogating him. Though he drinks whiskey from an omnipresent flask, it is never to excess, and this too is opportunistic—quelling thirst hygienically in a hot climate. While some critics compared Walker to *Mutiny*'s Fletcher Christian, Brando produced here, as usual, an individual, with unique accent (upper-class Lancashire), carriage, gestures, and walk.[48] Walker's voice lacks Christian's light smoothness; it is deeper, with a craggy, almost barking undertone. While both are upper-class Englishmen, Christian has the upright bearing and elegance of an officer, while Walker works *for* the admiralty but is not *of* it. Moreover, Christian has right on his side, while Walker very clearly from Brando's perspective does not.

Burn! was above all a film about historical change, exploring the combination of forces that lead to seemingly inevitable events. In Walker, Brando embodied a set of interests and theories: progress; Protestant norms of rationality and restraint; racial hierarchy, both across and within civilizations (every culture has an elite, born to rule). With a Marxist director and an idealistic actor working self-consciously in a time of civil rights and independence movements, the film's approach to these nineteenth-century pieties was predictably ironic. Yet Brando discovered Pontecorvo to be a director whose methods were at odds with his talents and politics. Brando charged Pontecorvo with paying black cast members lower wages than whites, and giving them substandard food.[49] Their incompatible approaches to character development exacerbated tensions. For Brando, political values and dramatic authenticity were always delicately balanced, while Pontecorvo saw no separation between them, believing a film's every aspect should validate its overarching theory. "Some of the lines he wanted me to say were straight out of the *Communist Manifesto*, and I refused to utter them," Brando recalled.[50] Brando's methods of shaping a role over time, revising script lines, and feeling his way into the picture's complexities were equally inimical to Pontecorvo's authoritarian style, which brooked no modification of the director's vision.

Yet Brando prevailed, subtly injecting his role as a promoter of commercial interests and evolutionary laws with the human quality of guilt. In the film's concluding scenes, Walker expresses ambivalence and alienation from his mission. He seems moved by the spectacle of violence he has initiated—the clumsy slaughter of the black resistance by British and indigenous troops. Gazing at a dead fighter he recognizes, he says to the British investor Shelton (Norman Hill): "It isn't you who pays, or even Royal Sugar." Then, as he strokes the snout of a horse, "I don't know. I'm just not quite sure what I'm doing here.... Perhaps I'm unable to do anything else." His elevated chin signals a partial restoration of purpose as he takes the reins, "But I do know that whenever I try to do something, I try to do it well." Later, in a lather, he confronts a now silent and captive José Dolores, "It wasn't *I* that invented this war, and furthermore in this case, I—I didn't even *start* it. I arrived here and you were already butchering one another!" His failure at an attempt at rationalization is exposed by his stuttering emotionality and averted eyes. (Italics indicate words stressed by Brando.) These scenes culminate in Walker's vain effort to liberate Dolores before he is hung. True to principle, Dolores refuses the white man's freedom, knowing the threat his martyrdom poses to the colonizers. Walker at first seems unable to fathom a man who is willing to die for an idea. Insight comes slowly—that and his accompanying despair soar to the notes of Bach's Cantata 156, whose tragic solemnity sides with the colonized. Pontecorvo was wise to substitute Bach for a speech to be given by Dolores.[51] Brando's face, a mask of wonderment, conveys all that is needed about the chasm between the two civilizations. Dolores is a man of incomparable nobility whose fierce commitment spells doom for cynics like Walker and the commercial interests he so ruthlessly serves. The end of Walker's control (and the control of those like him) is confirmed when Walker is fatally stabbed en route to his ship by a black man inspired by Dolores. Despite their quarrels, Pontecorvo never doubted his lead actor. "There are many moments when there is no time for dialogue, and then we need the synthesis of Brando's acting and his face. When things are psychological, we trust the face of Brando."

Some reviewers admired Brando but not the film. For instance, Vincent Canby cited Walker's "marvelously complex, rueful intelligence," reminding audiences that "Brando is worth watching under almost any circumstances, and you should enjoy seeing him here." Joan Mellen acclaimed both: "Not since Eisenstein has a film so explicitly and with such artistry sounded a paean to the glory and moral necessity of revolution. Even had United Artists not attempted to sabotage *Burn!*, it would be a film deserving wider viewing and critical attention."[52] *Burn!* suffered from distributors even more indifferent than those for *Reflections in a Golden Eye*. Pauline Kael in *The New Yorker* concurred that "the movie was 'dumped'—opened without the usual publicity," adding that *Burn!* "could have been a hit, because it plays right into the current feelings of the young movie audience."[53] Whatever publicity the film did receive tended to be focused on disputes between Brando and Pontecorvo, avoiding its challenging content. To the end of his life, Brando maintained that in *Burn!*, "I did the best acting I've ever done," expressing pride for the way the picture elaborated "the universal theme of the strong exploiting the weak."[54]

Pontecorvo was a contrast to Brando. He was notoriously inflexible, accounting for why he did so few films. "Like an impotent man, who can make love only to a woman who is completely right," he confessed, unless a film *had to be made,* he passed it up.[55] Brando was different; commitment to a film or a woman made him exceedingly uncomfortable. When he felt attached, as he did with *One-Eyed Jacks* and at times with women, he rarely admitted it. Still, there is evidence—annotated scripts, script notes, research files, letters, and books—that for every film in which he contributed substantially (and this includes most of them), Brando could be passionate for a significant time. Moreover, once he was immersed in a film, Brando's sense of what it needed could be absolute. Whether or not he and Pontecorvo enjoyed the process of making a film together, their mutual respect outlasted it. "If you choose a genius like Brando, you have to give him space for creativity," Pontecorvo told an interviewer in 1991. "He remains for me the very greatest actor ever to play in movies. Also, he's a very deep and nice person."[56]

Brando's admiration for Pontecorvo was displayed in Hollywood's most meaningful way: He wanted the Italian director for the American Indian picture that had preoccupied him for more than a decade—roughly from the early 1960s to the mid-1970s. Brando's work on his American Indian film has been unappreciated, partly because the material record only became available after his death, and biographers routinely ignored Brando's own accounts of his time trying to put the film together. Moreover, process has little relevance in the film industry, which made a magnum opus on the Indians that never reached production an embarrassment.

Yet understanding Brando requires a grasp of the astonishing intellectual and professional energy he devoted to this prospective film. The project shows his perfectionism, ambition, and sense of justice; the difficulties he had delegating responsibility and trusting people; and the sheer pleasure he could experience in the moment when something had truly engaged him, whether it was a book, a person, a problem, or a dramatic situation. Brando's Indian film will be treated at length in chapter 8. Its relevance here is Brando's certainty that the film's director should be Gillo Pontecorvo, which says a great deal about Brando's tolerance for conflict and his vision for the picture. Brando had never been a snob; he was moved by Kevin Costner's movie on American Indians *Dances with Wolves* (1990) and willing to admit it.[57] But he had something different in mind. Pontecorvo's gift for democratic imagery, his ability to humanize a population in his cinematic narratives, and his passion for expressing the plight of the dispossessed were essential to Brando's conception.

CHAPTER SIX

ANNUS MIRABILIS, 1972

For Brando, 1972 was a remarkable year. Three of his films were released, two of which, *The Nightcomers* and *Last Tango in Paris*, represented the culminations of his political films of the 1960s. The most popular of them, *The Godfather*, anticipated his late career as a film icon. Brando's overwhelming cinematic sexuality peaked during the '60s, and its fruits are visible in *Nightcomers*, which he made before *The Godfather*, and *Last Tango*, which he made after it. In these two films, his most erotically explicit ever, Brando extended his political explorations into the area of sexual politics. Both feature graphic sadomasochism in emphasizing the class and cultural politics of male–female relationships. What makes them more significant is the fact that the place of sexuality in Brando's work changed after them. This had nothing to do with his personal life, where his appetites persisted unabated.[1] But in his subsequent work, sexuality was subordinated to the vocations or obsessions of the iconic and demonic characters he played. Brando finished filming for *The Godfather* before beginning work on *Last Tango in Paris*, which explains why he was nominated for an Academy Award for *Godfather* in 1972 and for *Last Tango* in 1973. But *Last Tango*, like *Nightcomers*, is a film with strong ties to Brando's political films of the 1960s, which is why I'll treat it first here.

SEXUAL REVOLUTION:
THE NIGHTCOMERS AND
LAST TANGO IN PARIS

The Nightcomers, filmed at a country house in Cambridgeshire, England, during the fall of 1971, is another Brando film based on a literary classic—in this case, Henry James's *The Turn of the Screw* (1898). The film, however, dramatizes the violent eroticism and mayhem that *precede* James's gothic novel, providing *The Turn of the Screw* with its haunting subtext. Peter Quint, a charismatic Irishman with a seductive brogue (Brando modeled it on landsmen he met at a pub), is one of his great subversives. An anarchic individual consumed with hatred for authority, Quint's danger is subtly camouflaged in a bulky body, uneven gaze, and voice that never rises above a lilt. With a wealth of information about everything from how to tie knots and make a toad smoke until he bursts to knowing where the dead go, Quint controls the governess, Miss Jessel (Stephanie Beacham), and the orphaned aristocratic children, Miles (Christopher Ellis) and Flora (Verna Harvey), on the isolated estate where he is the gardener. Quint (who dons the deceased master's clothes in one scene) is unable to upend the class system, but he exercises his resentment against it through nightly trysts of sadomasochistic sex with the governess (when his knowledge of knot tying comes in handy) and daily corrupting of Miles and Flora. A variation on Stanley Kowalski, Quint is a manipulator whose callousness and brutality don't preclude his affection and need. While Brando considered Quint a "psychopath," he made him enchanting—whether sticking pins in an effigy of the disapproving housekeeper (Thora Hird) or flying kites with the children on the heath.[2]

Brando dominates *The Nightcomers* just as Quint dominates the estate community, an aberrant gardener planting seeds of destruction everywhere. Brando himself challenged the rigid hierarchy of the British set by rejecting the star's dining room in order to have meals with the company, which made everyone so uncomfortable that he ended up eating alone. He drew on personal expertise (he owned the 1944 *Ashley Book of Knots*, which features 3,900 varieties) for the sex scenes and probably on his lifelong hostility toward his father for Quint's tour-de-force tirade against his father.[3] Brando made considerable revisions to the monologue in which Quint tells Miles and Flora about the last time he saw "me Da'." It is Sunday morning and they're in the barn. (The housekeeper has forbidden him to enter the house.) His dark tale, accompanied by background church bells, ends with the incompetent father stripped naked and nearly drowned by irate "Gypos" (Gypsies) he has tried to swindle. Critical here is the father's swaggering effort to teach the son how to make a quid by stealing a decrepit horse, plastering it with glue and rabbit fur to hide its bones, perking it up with a piece of ginger in its anus, and selling it under cover of darkness. The young Quint's lesson in paternal ineptitude illuminates both his contempt for authority and his need to substitute his influence for that of the children's father.

Brando rewrites his part and improvises further in performance, adding ideas and perfecting speech rhythms to reflect Quint's personality and class.[4] A few lines become the following sharper ones: "He spies a big Gypo, comin' down the back, huge man he was... well me dad takes the horse and he walks over to him, oh he was full of himself, you know" [mimes bluster with arrogant expression and puffed chest]. The humor of the scene is all Brando. "Well the Gypo jumps on the horse and he rides the damn thing straight into the water, and no sooner is he in the water he starts turnin and you know buckin and kickin and fartin. I thought the British were comin... and the piece of ginger flew out of the poor animal's ass like it was shot from a cannon. Well by this time me dad, you know, he's trembling and he's turnin white as a fish and prayin, oh God, for the first time in his life." Brando vividly conflates the worthless father and the nag, with nods to politics and religion. References to British cannons; Gypsies, who despite their marginality are better off than Quint's crooked father; and the father's spiritual opportunism highlight Quint's vulnerability: Alone after the events he recounts, he has to face the forces—foreigners, soldiers, the church—threatening a poor Irish boy.

Class proves no barrier to uniting Quint and the aristocratic children. The three are waifs abandoned when young by irresponsible parents. Quint underlines the point, saying, "It's time to go to church" in response to the distant bells, confident that the children will not move while he is talking. More important, the once-helpless boy has become a dangerous man whose hypnotic threat is reinforced by the mysterious smile he flashes at Flora, as he demands a kiss in payment for the toy horse he has carved. His smile is sweet and lascivious; whether or not he has designs on Flora, his promise to fix the toy horse's broken ear is a reminder of her dependence. Such scenes explain how one reviewer could write: "*The Nightcomers* is a much more impressive piece of acting than his highly praised...Don Corleone," noting how his "charming, fascinating man" with "a potential for violence and evil that is never deeply buried...supports the whole film."[5] Even Brando, in touch with screenwriter Michael Hastings years later about a script, reported, "I saw *The Nightcomers* recently and I found myself pleased with it all."[6]

Brando was nominated for a BAFTA Award in 1972 for Best Actor in a Lead Role for *The Nightcomers* (competing against himself in *The Godfather*). Quint's gift of gab makes his world a magical place. Imparting wisdom through story, he transports listeners, a skill that is inseparable from his sexual prowess, both limited only by what he can imagine. Michael Winner, the director of

The Nightcomers, recalled Brando's orchestration of the bedroom scene, all in character, as Quint swiftly subjected the helpless governess to his will.[7] This is the trademark of Brando's screen sexuality: spontaneous, unpredictable, yet always deliberate. He shows his personae knowing what they want and where they are going. The erotic excitement for their partners is that they don't, but they can trust that they will experience passions and satisfy desires they wouldn't believe they had. Lying together afterward, the governess bemoans the wildness of her lust exposed by Quint. Sex, replies the philosophical gardener, echoes and foreshadows our bodily doom; we are born and die in pain. In his copy of William Blake's writings, a section of "The Prophetic Books," Brando marked a description of the imagination pertinent to sexuality in *The Nightcomers* and *Last Tango in Paris*: "The world of Imagination is the world of Eternity; it is the divine bosom into which we shall all go after the death of the Vegetated body. This World of Imagination is Infinite & Eternal, whereas the world of Generation, or Vegetation, is Finite & Temporal."[8] Quint, and Paul in *Last Tango*, use sex to contest that generative dead end, efforts that yield ecstasy for themselves and their partners.

Paul is another of Brando's irreverent sensualists. Nearly maddened by grief over the suicide of his wife, Rosa, at the film's start, he takes solace gradually in an affair with a stranger in a rental apartment. This forty-five-year-old American in Paris despairs about ever really knowing anyone. "Even if a husband lives two hundred fucking years he's never gonna be able to discover his wife's real nature," Paul says in a soliloquy before Rosa's corpse. "I mean, I might be able to comprehend the universe, but I'll never discover the truth about you, never."[9] This is the plight of everyone in the movie, from the most minor—the concierge who laments her unfamiliarity with the tenants—to Jeanne (Maria Schneider), the twenty-year-old Parisian to whom Paul will not divulge any of his personal details, including his name. She is casual, viewing the affair as a fling before marriage; he is in control, forcing her to "put up with" ignorance, one of many submissions. Film audiences, which were almost equally deprived, were not nearly so accepting. They filled the void of Paul with Brando and concluded that he wasn't acting in *Last Tango* but being himself. Recognizing that such fantasies not only enhanced the appeal of an already sensational film but also his status as its director, Bernardo Bertolucci fanned the flames.[10]

Nothing could have been farther from reality, however—not only because, as Brando knew, the truth is more elusive than fiction, but also because of his legendary passion for privacy. Indeed, *Last Tango* deliberately fictionalizes Bertolucci's situation, through its parody of the voyeuristic filmmaker. Jeanne's intended, Tom (Jean-Pierre Léaud), is the director's smug alter ego, always accompanied by a crew as he makes his movie, *Portrait of a Girl*, for television. The obvious irony is that Tom, the proper bourgeois, hasn't a clue about the depths of erotic satisfaction Jeanne is experiencing in the bare apartment. This is the point: how *little we know about others*. Similarly, Paul is not the only one barred from understanding his wife's suicide—so are Rosa's mother (Maria Michi) and her secret lover, Marcel (Massimo Girotti). How little we know others is only surpassed, *Last Tango* suggests, by how little we know ourselves.[11]

That is why asserting that Brando had divulged *who he was*, was presumptuous. Like Jeanne, viewers were asked to surrender to a mystery, the potential for being intimate without the most basic information. Not that knowing someone is necessarily revealing, as Paul's marriage confirms. More comforting and titillating for viewers is accepting Bertolucci's suggestion that they were now accessing memories and fantasies Brando had denied probing journalists for years. Brando was undoubtedly aware of what he was doing. He toys throughout, as does the film, with a dilemma that is foregrounded by cinema: Is anyone what he seems or hopes to be? As well as any film actor, Brando understood what writer Max Picard (*The Human Face* was in his collection) called the "emptiness" of "the cinema face." This is contrasted with the "real" human face, which expresses its divinity in smiling. It was a trap, Brando once said, for an actor to mistake himself for the image projected on screen.[12] *Last Tango* is preoccupied with the fabricating power of film, exposing its own inventions while demanding our belief—a sadomasochistic rhythm replicated in Paul's treatment of Jeanne. For viewers and the Jeanne character alike, arousal demands complete submission to another's fantasy.

More than is typical, *Last Tango* claims its power to create reality. Thus, in the bath, Jeanne says Paul looks like "a pimp," and in the very next scene he becomes one, pursuing, at the behest of a whore, a customer who has abandoned her. The first scene also confirms this cinematic power when the couple has sex beneath Paul's camel-hair coat, as he engulfs Jeanne's vitality to compensate for his brush with death. The filmgoer, like the bourgeois woman, is shocked by his aggressive move to possess her but accepts being transported into a world of fantasy. Because this is *not* pornography, there will be no adherence to convention. The power of Brando's Paul is the power of the actor: inherent in gestures, the more unexpected the better. He shuts the door abruptly, leans against it thinking, walks slowly toward the woman, every step a threat. His face is a mask of determination as he takes her hat, tosses it on the floor, and carries her to the window. They are strangers, but he has no fear she'll scream or run. He has read the situation correctly: youthful profligacy and independence. He knows the spell cast by a man this sure of himself. She will accept the pleasure of his capacity to surprise or shock her; no one has treated her like this before. Hence the significance of the notorious sodomy scene, where Paul pulls Jeanne's pants down, moistens her anus with butter, and climbs on top of her fully clothed, pinning her roughly to the floor. It is like a punishment as he penetrates her against her protests, demanding that she repeat an obscene diatribe against that ultimate bourgeois institution, the family. Yet the exchange is gratifying to both of them. Her tears are an expression of rage over how he has stripped her and revealed her desire for domination through her orgasmic response to it.

Last Tango evokes the ultimate male fantasy in portraying male dominance as the realization of female desire.[13] This is not the place to debate the relative success of feminist challenges to that dominance. But it's worth noting that Brando was familiar with the classic arguments, citing in an interview the array of taboos designed to oppress and exclude women—extending from "so-called primitive" to "modern societies"—which he attributed to men's awareness of their overwhelming dependence on women.[14] Male dominance in *Last Tango* is an ideology—that is, a myth made true by people behaving as though it is.

Paul's effort to keep things risk-free—no names, commitments, past or future—reveals just how risky satisfying sex is. The risk they take comes from gratifying long-buried impulses. Temporary, dilapidated, infested with rats, the apartment is the closest thing in highly cultivated Paris to a state of nature. But *Last Tango* understands how indebted any state of nature is to culture and its rituals. Paul and Jeanne engage in various domestic rites at the apartment, from his shaving and her applying makeup to their arranging furniture and engaging in pillow talk. The tango itself, Paul explains to Jeanne during the contest at the dance hall, is "a rite." Dwelling on doors and doorways, the film highlights the major ritual transitions—mourning and marriage—faced by its protagonists. Like Coleridge's ancient mariner, Paul comes from death to declare his truths to Jeanne on her way to a wedding. In one scene, he carries his young lover in her wet wedding dress over the threshold; in the next, he eulogizes his wife's flower-laden corpse. Paul presides at two ritual occasions, over two white-gowned women he never really possessed. His wife's affair with hotel regular Marcel and Jeanne's violent repudiation of him demonstrate the illusoriness of Paul's mastery.

Because Paul embodies male dominance, his death represents its destruction. But the bleakness of the conclusion confirms our attachment to the myth—and its tenaciousness. Despite a plot that shifts constantly from the rental apartment to the distinct worlds of Paul and Jeanne, there is only one moral when it comes to sexuality. The Parisian home where Jeanne's mother dusts her late husband's Algerian artifacts (he seems to have been studious as well as brave, judging from all the books), like their country estate, is typically bourgeois—from the antiquated furnishings to the self-alienated racist servant proud of the dog that attacked beggars. Neither could be more remote from the expatriate Paul's hotel. But heterosexual relations seem to transcend differences of class and culture: Jeanne's father kept a photograph of an Algerian mistress, and the speeches of Jeanne's fiancé and lover are interchangeable, as are her responses to them. Jeanne's tirade against Tom—"You take advantage of me, you make me do things I've never done.... You make me do whatever you want.... I'm tired of having my mind raped"—obviously could be directed at Paul. Tom's reaction, pounding her with his fists, proves that, however repressed and childlike, he has what it takes to be a man.

This is a challenging role to fill on Jeanne's behalf because she worships the military masculinity of her dashing green-eyed father, the French colonel killed in Algeria in 1958. She repeats the year in telling Paul about it, to counter his ridicule ("all uniforms are bullshit") and to underline its importance. The patriarch's 1958 death aligns him with nationalism in crisis. Initiated by French rebel generals in a 1958 coup against France's colonial government in Algeria, the crisis resulted in a successful challenge of Fourth Republican rule at home. French army rebels in

Algeria surrendered when Charles de Gaulle was installed as president of a new centralized government, presiding over the bloodiest years of the French-Algerian conflict and its end in Algeria's 1962 independence.

Jeanne's father, the colonial officer, haunts *Last Tango in Paris* and can be considered responsible for its plot. His appetite for Algerian mistresses suggests a source for his daughter's sex drive, just as his early death makes her susceptible to the sexual attentions of an older man or father figure. He has taught Jeanne how to shoot his pistol, and she mimics the lessons, dressed in his heavily medaled uniform and cap. At the end, the father provides both the motive and the means for Paul's death, through the same officer's cap and pistol. The motive is Paul's mockery of military convention when he dons the cap askew, salutes, and asks Jeanne whether she prefers her "hero over-easy or sunny-side up?" It seems inevitable that Jeanne will respond with the restoration of bourgeois decorum he has challenged throughout their affair, by inflicting a mortal wound with the paternal weapon. Exposed as the caretaker of a seedy hotel inherited after his wife's suicide, and not the "golden shining ... warrior" his commanding sexuality has led Jeanne to expect, Paul must be dispensed with violently if he will not leave voluntarily. The woman's answer to the man's question, "What the hell difference does it make if I have a flophouse or a hotel or a castle?" is all the difference in the world.

Jeanne's murder of Paul represents the father's posthumous defense of his daughter's honor against the man who has taken her repeatedly out of wedlock as well as the daughter's defense of colonial nationalism against that same man's desecration of its primary symbols. Murder in the name of the father who has given his life to serve French imperial power in Algeria (and trained the family dog to detect "Arabs by their odor") seems the only proper resolution of the daughter's brush with Paul. The significance of *Last Tango*'s Algerian connection is reinforced by the

prominence given in the movie to one of its most important artic-
ulators, Albert Camus, the French-Algerian Nobel Prize–winning
author of *Algerian Chronicles* (1958).

Late in the film, Paul has a drink in Marcel's room, which is
filled with framed photographs: one features Simone Signoret,
whose daughter, Catherine Allegret, plays a maid in *Last Tango*;
the largest photo is of Albert Camus with his perpetual cigarette. Camus is a suitable oracle for this colloquy between men:
Brando owned Camus's last novel, *The Fall* (1957), which he annotated heavily, and it provides an implicit register for *Last Tango*'s
emphatically masculine despair. The existential hero of Camus's
fictional confessions articulates the self-justifications and regrets
of the aging ladies' man. Like Paul, Jean-Baptiste Clamence is
a rolling stone with little to show save for the camel-hair coat
on his back. Clamence has had his own brush with suicide, a
female stranger he's convinced he might have saved from a
plunge into the Seine. For both men, women have been a refuge

Paul in anguish wearing camel-hair coat. © Bettmann/Corbis.

and dominance comes naturally.[15] Essentially actors for whom sex provides the ultimate stage ("I often changed parts but it was always the same play...verifying each time my special powers"), they both end up playing criminals.[16] The human condition in *The Fall* and *Last Tango* is a cycle of pain and guilt, broken occasionally by pleasure, through a romantic possibility or insight invariably foiled. This makes Paul's final role in *Last Tango*, as a rapist killed in a home invasion, especially fitting.

In his collection of paperwork and stills, Brando kept only one *Last Tango* review, which discussed the connection between the film and Camus's novel. Brando's early aspiration to the ministry and ongoing interest in religion may have piqued his curiosity about Kenneth J. Smith's *Sunday Morning Address: The Last Tango to Nowhere*, printed by the Philadelphia Ethical Society. Identifying Paul as "the existential anti-hero par excellence—the loser type, experiencing life in its many facets and finding them all bad," he speculates: "perhaps this is what Albert Camus had in mind...in his novel, *The Fall*: 'A single sentence will suffice for modern man; he fornicated and read the papers.'" The parallel extends to *Last Tango*'s brutally honest appraisal of the secular condition, which, Smith concludes admiringly, is neither pretty nor uplifting, as one might expect from "a serious effort to get down to the very core of human existence."[17]

Camus and Brando provide stylized versions of the exploitative Bohemian male in middle age. Like any fiction, they may resemble but are not to be confused with their creators. Brando invests Paul with traces of his movie history, embellished by personal history related over the years in interviews. It is a canned past served up repeatedly to audiences craving access to the private life of a celebrity. Attaining fame on Broadway in *A Streetcar Named Desire* as a youth of twenty-three, Brando soon became adept at manufacturing pasts for the media. Featured in over a

Paul in dance hall. © Eva Sereny/Redux Pictures.

hundred articles by the age of thirty, he was jaded before arriving in Hollywood.[18]

Indeed, the most intimate aspect of Brando's characterization in *Last Tango* may be Paul's penchant for fabricating personal history. This is echoed in details pieced together by others, such as the police investigating his wife's suicide and Jeanne at the picture's end, rapidly concocting an official explanation of who Paul is while his dead body lies in the background. What do we learn about Paul's past over the course of *Last Tango*? He has been an actor, journalist, bongo player, boxer, and kept husband. He studied "whale fucking" at "the University of Congo," lived in Tahiti and Cuba, is sterile, and married a woman who ran a hotel, which he inherited after she committed suicide. He loves nature, as his mother taught him to, and was traumatized by his parents' alcoholism and his father's harshness. The acting, bongo-playing, Tahitian residence, and references to his parents are facts from Brando's past. The rest are attributes of dramatis personae from his movies or pure inventions. The facts were generally available in features on Brando published in *Life, Time,* and *Newsweek* in the 1950s and '60s; in the 1957 interview he gave Truman Capote in *The New Yorker*; and on talk shows he did during this period. Brando was too good an actor and too careful an individual to divulge on camera what he hadn't divulged often before. Moreover, as chapter 8 will speak about in detail, he never did interviews without a motive, whether it was promoting a cause or defending his reputation. It was rare for him to feel violated by an interview, as he did after Truman Capote's, for he was alert to getting the best of a manipulative proceeding he believed was designed to sell advertising.[19]

The most obvious evidence that we are not watching Brando *himself* on screen in *Last Tango* is that so much of the performance, especially as the film winds down to its tragic close, is about acting. Brando always insisted that everyone was an actor, that life is acting and that no human can survive without utilizing its basic skills. "Lying for a Living," the project he launched in his seventies, was designed to codify the vast range of acting techniques people drew on in public and in private. In his typically democratic way, Brando collected participants from the most humble and ordinary to the highest-paid actors in the world. He wrote the skits, directing and critiquing the performances, which were all recorded.[20]

The characterization of Paul is another variation on the Brando claim that humans spend most of their time, at least socially, acting. Partly because he is determined to disclose nothing to Jeanne, Paul performs and mimes more than usual. While shaving, for instance, he assumes the persona of a French maître d' with a thick accent; he smiles seductively, twitching his eyebrows like

Groucho Marx, before sodomizing her; he shakes water off his wet clothes with a tap dance à la Fred Astaire; he is an avuncular Brit plying her with drinks ("just a sip for Daddy"); a soused romantic ("If music be the food of love, play on"); and a Jimmy Cagney gangster ("Oh you dirty rat!") in the dance hall. His final impersonation, saluting as her father in his French officer's hat, earns the worst review imaginable: a bullet in the gut at close range.

There is much to appreciate in Brando's subtle performance, which was nominated for an Academy Award a year after he won and notoriously turned down the award for *The Godfather.* From the start, when he howls, "Fucking God!" under the subway tracks, to the end, when he attaches the gum from his mouth to the balcony railing before his final breath, Paul is a man who can't understand his fate and responds with outrage. Deeply ineffectual, he tries to conceal this with cool aggression. He mocks Marcel's reading and is more interested in controlling than exploring the world and people around him. He has been a roamer rather than a traveler, moving from boredom, not curiosity. His look of satiety, standing beside Jeanne in front of the apartment taking in the morning air after their first sexual encounter, suggests the predominance of sensuality. However angst-ridden, the fulfillment of physical needs goes a long way toward compensating him. He uses conventional masculine methods with women—silence and withholding balanced by humor and charm. Though these methods have enabled his initial successes, they haven't made up for his deficiencies. Brando never lets us forget that Paul is a cuckold doomed to being mystified by women. While shaving, for example, he seems genuinely put off by Jeanne's playful guess that he is a barber, just as he is disturbed by her account of the man she loves while she is bathing. Even more disturbed when he finds she is talking about *him*, he bites his fingernail and averts his eyes. Brando's acting is masterful, as he substantiates these reactions with a look or a shift of the jaw.

With men, Paul is competitive and equally ineffectual, clumsily assaulting the customer who abandons the whore and refuses to pay, hostile to Marcel, who has hurt his pride. Paul is the kind of depressive who is bad for others because he channels his disappointments outward. Brando creates a persona here that for him is fairly unique. Paul is without redeeming qualities, lacking even negative force (the violent energy of Stanley Kowalski or the pathology of Peter Quint). But Brando makes him so empathetic and charming that we are sorry he is gone at the end. This is not because he is a reflection of Brando but because he is a reflection of us.

Many viewed *Last Tango in Paris* as a work that redefined the possibilities for representing sexuality on film. Some critical responses were ecstatic: Roger Ebert wrote, "*Last Tango in Paris* is one of the great emotional experiences of our time," and Pauline Kael, most famously, wrote, "This must be the most powerfully erotic film ever made," a "landmark" that does for film what Stravinsky's *Rite of Spring* did for music in realigning its methods with a new "primitive force." Others were nonplussed. "Behind the raised consciousness of *Last Tango*," Vincent Canby detected something "old fashioned but . . . topical enough to make a zillion dollars."[21] Canby was right that there was nothing new about the sexual norms represented in *Last Tango,* but their aggressive staging and exploration in a movie that was deliberately not pornographic was a departure in 1972 and long afterward. Still, Brando had been doing this, albeit more subtly, for much of his career, and in this way *Last Tango in Paris* was for him the culmination of decades of portraying male sexuality. In contrast, Brando's other major role of the year, Don Corleone in *The Godfather,* was more indicative of the roles he would explore in the coming decades—men so powerful that they often achieved iconic stature.

THE DON

On January 23, 1970, Mario Puzo sent Brando a copy of his best-selling novel with a note urging that he pursue the lead in the film version: "I think you're the only actor who can play the Godfather with that quiet force and irony the part requires. I hope you'll read the book and like it well enough to use whatever power you can to get the role.... I really think you'd be tremendous. Needless to say I've been an admirer of your art."[22] Brando was not convinced he could play an Italian Mafia head, and he thanked Puzo without reading the book. But Puzo persisted, sending the actor another copy of the book a few months later, along with the screenplay he had adapted from it. Brando read both and decided that he wanted the role.

Hollywood lore has several versions of the famed recording made of Brando's test for studio heads. According to those who were there, director Francis Ford Coppola and producer Al Ruddy arrived at Brando's Mulholland Drive home with camera equipment on a December morning in 1970. When he got up, Brando took out the makeup case he had drawn on for years, blackening his hair, adding a thin mustache, and stuffing Kleenex in his cheeks for jowls. Wordlessly, with an occasional grimace, a cup of espresso in hand, he became the Don.

Henceforth Brando relied on his understanding of the Don and his instincts. "I threw out a lot of what was in the script and created the role as I thought it should be," he said, referring to his reliance on the novel over the screenplay Puzo had adapted with Coppola. "The part of Don Corleone lent itself perfectly to underplaying. Rather than portraying him as a big shot, I thought it would be more effective to play him as a modest quiet man, the way he was in the book." This would be a new take on the gangster: "Because he had so much power and unquestioned authority, I thought it would be an interesting contrast to play him as a gentleman. I saw him as a man of substance, tradition, dignity, refinement... who just happened to live in a violent world and who had to protect himself and his family in this environ-ment."[23] Brando's respect for the character never clouded his perception of the Don's capacity for ruthlessness. It was Brando's choice to give him a raspy, "high voice" that came "through the nose"—"a nose broken early in youth," the actor explained in his notes on the script.[24]

Brando's characterization provides a lesson in dominance. The Godfather, introduced listening to a supplicant's request, is distinguished gradually from the enveloping darkness. A similar emergence would come in *Apocalypse Now.* Only the Don's hand moves, supporting his chin, a slight wave summoning a drink for the weeping undertaker, Amerigo Bonasera. Brando understood that in a world as perilous as *The Godfather*'s, a boss's slightest gesture was consequential. When he points at Bonasera, the undertaker freezes, kissing the hand that he now knows must feed him, just as the Don's godson submits humbly to the booming command (accompanied by a slap and a shaking) that he "*Act like a man!*"

The Don became iconic because he embodied cultural commonplaces, many of them congenial to Brando. The Don was a natural observer, someone whose curiosity about the world and its inhabitants ensured that he was always learning. Uneducated, but with a subtle intelligence, he could be underestimated, which he ably exploited. He was a rebel of the classic American type who insisted on testing those in control. Deeply self-reliant, he dispensed favors and punishment with an unerring faith in his own judgment. He could accept an occasional mistake, and admit his own, but he found "carelessness" intolerable. And he observed, as a traditional patriarch, an absolute divide between the sexes. His faith in reason (which meant accepting the reality of his power), and his resort to violence when reason failed, could appear unobjectionable to Americans accustomed to Western heroes who settled disputes with guns.

Brando empathized greatly with the value of family and kinship that was a central theme of *The Godfather*. It seems somehow appropriate that someone whose own family had been fractured should play a significant role in constructing what would remain a central familial ideal. Brando's was in many ways an ordinary Anglo-Saxon Protestant childhood of the 1920s and '30s, a story of Midwestern middle-class survival in a time of economic hardship. Institutionalized religion exerted little pull, and less orthodox values—Christian Science and alternative spirituality, bohemianism, intellectualism—failed to fill the vacuum created by its absence and by the parental weaknesses of adultery and alcoholism. With the exception of alcohol, which he avoided abusing because of the family propensity, Brando often pursued the bohemian-indulgent paths supported and exaggerated by Hollywood success. But he was drawn to fatherhood, and, his notorious womanizing aside, took seriously the responsibility for his children. His attentions were loving but sporadic, though he devoted most to the most troubled children: son Christian and daughter Cheyenne (b. 1970).

Brando had twelve children—only half of them his biological offspring—whom he supported and whose educations he financed. In some cases, he was deceived into believing that children were his by mothers seeking financial support, but he ended up caring for the children despite this. In others, he assumed financial responsibility for children he became fond of, whether those of assistants or even of ex-wives. He sent his children in Los Angeles to a French school, because he valued the bilingual curriculum and hoped they would be able to converse with their Tahitian siblings. He also made certain that they would be technologically literate. Miko and Rebecca recalled being the first in their school to have personal computers.[25] While none of the children lived with Brando, except for Christian on occasion, they all visited frequently, and he took a keen pleasure in them, especially when they were young. Whatever his intentions, however, Brando was a part-time father at best. His children lived on different continents, and he was always distracted by his work, his causes, and his endless love affairs.

Brando enjoyed some aspects of tradition, such as presiding over a big family dinner. He also prized loyalty and would spurn lovers or friends who breached confidences. But, like many Americans who luxuriated in the tribalism of *The Godfather*, such solidarity eluded him. In adulthood, this was largely for reasons of his own making. Brando was unapologetic about his resistance to bourgeois convention and his profligacy with women, but its deleterious impact on his children grew ever more apparent. Still, performers and filmgoers excluded from domestic unity could take solace in its price. The Corleone Empire was built with blood. The insistence that it was rarely drawn from innocents mattered little, for the film also highlights the interdependence between strong and weak, criminal and spiritual, lawless and law-abiding. Anyone who benefits from crime is implicated in it.

In the world of *The Godfather*, men cook spaghetti sauce from scratch between murders, which can occur in bedrooms, on massage tables, and near yards where children play, as readily as on city streets. Though the Don and his henchmen have offices, they often work at home. While this might appear a means of self-protection or concealment, it also expresses the continuity between business and family. It further highlights the modernity of these Mafiosi: For successful capitalists in the postwar era, the boundaries between labor and leisure were increasingly fluid. These men never relax, even alone, with a drink and a cigarette. The same values and constraints apply everywhere: Sonny

Corleone's (James Caan) compulsive affair with a young woman foreshadows how he mishandles enemies as family head after the Don is shot. Ignoring his father's warning about the inseparability of public and private proves fatal.

Mario Puzo was surprised by charges that he had idealized the Mafia, since he shows the connection between the Mafiosi and those who gain benefit, between the Mafiosi as businessmen and them as family men.[26] The novel condemns those who kill: however seemingly goodhearted, they deserve to be gunned down or garroted by enemies. And it also denies absolution to the wives and children. This is suggested by the conclusion of the novel (and early scripts), where Kay Corleone becomes a Catholic, to the dismay of her husband Michael, the new Don, who would have preferred that she remain Protestant, raising their children in the national religion. Kay's daily prayers for her husband (like her mother-in-law's for Don Vito) require that she be "washed clean of sin." Clearly she feels the need for Catholicism's broad presumption of sin and equally broad rewarding of absolution, which is consistent with Coppola's efforts to collapse distinctions between Mafia and mainstream beliefs.

The novel's epigraph from Honoré de Balzac—"Behind every great fortune there is a crime"—foreshadows a primary theme. When he proposes marriage to Kay Adams (Diane Keaton), Michael Corleone (Al Pacino in black coat and fedora, looking, producers worried, "more like a rabbi than a Mafia Don") explains that his father kills only on principle, from absolute necessity, comparing him to a political leader or "any man who's responsible for other people."[27] She accuses him of being naïve—"Senators and presidents don't have men killed"—to which he deadpans, "Who is being naïve, Kay?" Brando was especially drawn to the film's thesis: that the Mafia is a diabolic mirror for established institutions. "I felt the picture made a useful commentary on corporate thinking in this country," he observed in a *Life* interview.

"If Cosa Nostra had been black or socialist, Corleone would have been dead or in jail. But because the Mafia patterned itself so closely on the corporation, and dealt in a hard-nosed way with money, and with politics, it prospered."[28] Pauline Kael echoed his points in *The New Yorker*, noting that the film portrays "organized crime as an obscene symbolic extension of free enterprise and government policy...not a rejection of Americanism" but "what we fear Americanism to be."[29]

The Godfather was widely admired because it accommodated so many fantasies and fears. For those troubled by the radical challenges of popular movements (civil rights, feminism, Vietnam protests, student activism), it offered an image of women at home with children, supported by successful men. The Italian Corleones (and the concerns about Michael's rabbinical aspect missed the advantage of occasional ambiguity) sanctioned the ethos of American opportunity and confirmed cherished conventions. In the first *Godfather* film, the Corleones were comfortable but not extravagant (despite the big wedding at the film's opening), the family compound on Long Island enabling the domestic proximity of parents and grown children. Their lifestyle evoked a late-1940s setting in which materialism and nationalism were especially harmonious; in the aftermath of a war against Fascism, consumption was patriotic. By depicting its protagonists negotiating threatening transitions—the infiltration of drugs, the changing nature of work in the postwar era—the film affirmed male authority in an era when it was under siege. The aggression of the *Godfather* men was tempered by warmth, their violence a form of passion, their blood rivalry idealistic. In this way, they could not have been less like the sober heroes of Westerns, but their ambition and independence marked them as irrefutably American.

Brando's grasp of these complex tensions was evident in changes he made on the *Godfather* script, and from script to screen. True to habit, his comments were not confined to his own role. He criticized the general use of dialogue to advance plot, recommending, for example, that exchanges between Michael and Kay at the wedding be less "expository... there is no apparent subtext in this scene," and identifying better opportunities for plot and character development. Brando complained too that in the violent scene where hit man Luca Brasi is garroted, Brasi's line here (he'd switch Mafia families "if the money is good enough") is "too bold... too neat." The line was changed in the film to "What's in it for me?"[30]

The bulk of Brando's revisions on his own part are cuts. Portraying power required more than the usual emphasis on "less is more." Thus he reduced the Don's scripted dialogues by half and introduced changes to preserve his authenticity and dignity. He translates *pezzunovanto* as "big shot"; inserts a quietly ironic line at the scene's end (after "Is there anything else?"), "I'd like to go to my daughter's wedding"; deletes a crass reference to Luca's gift ("I'm sure it's the most generous gift today"); delegates—"let Tom say it"—a line of the Don's ("But an act of Congress doesn't come cheap"); and excises (with an "Ugh") a melodramatic phrase ("weeping bitter tears").[31] In the margin of the Don's question to his adviser Tom Hagen (Robert Duvall), "what time do I have to meet this infidel on Friday?" Brando writes: "Where does he learn to say this ['infidel'] and cannot instead of can't?"[32]

Brando's changes in the opening dialogue with the undertaker recall his revisions in *On the Waterfront*, where he shifts and substitutes words, sharpening diction, clarifying ideas, and improving rhythm. Here is the original:

> You never armed yourself with true friends. You thought it
> was enough to be an American. After all, the Police guarded
> you, there were courts of Law. You could come to no harm,
> you had no need for friends like me. But now, you come to
> me and say, "Don Corleone, give me Justice." And you do

not ask with respect; you do not call me Godfather. . . . You come into my house on the wedding day of my daughter and you ask me to do murder and you say "How much shall I pay you.". . . America has ruled; the Judge has ruled! Bring your daughter flowers and a box of candy when you visit her. Forget this madness, it is not American.[33]

Here is Brando's version from the film:

But let's be frank here, you never wanted my friendship. And you were afraid to be in my debt. I understand. You found paradise in America, had a good trade, you made a good living, the police protected you, and there were courts of law. You didn't need a friend like me. But, uh, now you come to me and you say, "Don Corleone, give me justice," but you don't ask with respect. You don't offer friendship. You don't even think to call me Godfather. Instead, you come into my house on the day my daughter is to be married and you ask me to do murder for money.

Discussing the importance of Brando's performance for the accompanying cast and actors in general, James Caan highlighted the effectiveness of Brando's use of the cat. Any other actor, Caan pointed out, would have made a fuss over the creature, but Brando integrated it naturally into the scene with a few notable gestures.[34] The speech is reinforced by his handling of the cat, his anger at the perceived insult controlled through stroking of the animal. The change of tone is obvious when he stands and dumps the cat on the desk, not harshly but with enough vehemence to support an audible thud.

Corleone's subsequent speech to the undertaker similarly benefits from Brando's revisions. Here is the original:

Why are you afraid to give your first allegiance to me? You
go to the law courts and wait for months. You spend money
on lawyers who know you're to be made a fool of. You take
judgment from a Judge who sells himself like the worst
whore on the street. But, if you had come to me as a friend,
those scum who ruined your daughter would be weeping
bitter tears this day. If by some misfortune an honest man
like yourself made enemies, they would become my enemies,
and then . . . believe me, they would fear you.

Here is Brando's revised version:

Bonasera, Bonasera, what have I ever done to make you treat
me so disrespectfully? If you had come to me in friendship,
then the scum that ruined your daughter would be suffering
this very day. And if by chance an honest man like yourself
should make enemies then they would become my enemies,
and then they would fear you.[35]

The speech is cut in half, the language pared to simple eloquence. The face and body do the rest; downcast eyes, shrugging
shoulders, raised eyebrows, and jutting chin show how hard it is
for a proud man to overcome such slights. When the undertaker
leaves, Brando ad-libs one of his most renowned moments on
film. The smile vanishes, he scratches his head, rubs his mouth
and turns to Tom Hagen: "Give this to uh . . . Clemenza. I want
reliable people, people that aren't going to be carried away. We're
not murderers, in spite of what this . . . undertaker says." He drops
his chin as he concludes, lifting the lapel with the red rose pinned
to it, and inhales.

The blood-red rose corresponds to the bloody acts he has spent
his daughter's wedding day authorizing while in his crisp white

The Don in wedding attire. Paramount Pictures/Photofest.

shirt and immaculate tuxedo. Still, this is a man who is drawn to
the sensual and uncompromised, enough to appreciate the scent
of an elegant flower. The gesture unites the film's beginning—in
a chair, a cat on his lap; middle—feeding fish at a meeting in his
office where Michael presides; and end—in the garden with his
grandson. The man who notices flowers will die of a heart attack
among his tomato plants, delighting a child as he did a cat.

One of the few aspects of Brando's performance as Corleone
that is underappreciated is the way he ages. He is introduced
as a relatively vital man in his sixties. Masculine and physically
imposing—"an old bulldog," as Brando conceived him, with a
growling voice—and looking so fine in his wedding "tux that an
inexperienced observer might easily have thought the Don himself was the lucky groom."[36] At his olive-oil company office, just
after the wedding, the Don is forceful as he rejects the proposal

of Sollozzo, the enterprising gangster who wants him to invest in the new drug market, scolding Sonny for divulging his enthusiasm for the deal, giving instructions to Luca Brasi. When he is shot a few scenes later, by thugs sent by Sollozzo, hoping to eliminate a key barrier to his plans, the Don shrewdly anticipates the gunmen's attack, protecting his body as best he can, the muscular frame exposed as he sprawls against his car. In the next major scene, with Bonasera again, before an embalming table, the Don remains a man of consequence. But the skin is gray, the jowls seem looser, the hair thinner. Grieving the death of his firstborn son intensifies an aging process already accelerated by bullets. Here, too, Brando's improvisations are pivotal. The script: "I want you to use all your powers, all your skill, as you love me. I do not want his mother to see him as he is."[37] On screen: "I want you to use all your powers and all your skills. I don't want his mother to see him this way.... [lifting the blanket to reveal Sonny's mutilated frame] Look how they massacred my boy!"

The Don then hosts a boardroom colloquy for Mafiosi from around the country. Here he summons much of his original authority, appearing older than at the wedding but reinvigorated. In the script, the Don is to address them: "Ah well, let's get down to business. We are all honorable men here, we don't have to give assurances as if we were lawyers.... Well, no matter, a lot of foolishness has come to pass." Instead, he does not flatter them as being "honorable," perhaps also recalling Antony's subversion of the word in his speech in *Julius Caesar*. He is far more straightforward when Brando changes the lines to: "How did things ever get so far? I don't know. It was so unfortunate, so unnecessary." Nor does Brando envision the Don as an equivocator or one to dishonor his dead. He cuts: "Perhaps my son was too rash, too headstrong, I don't say no to that," opting for the crisp "Tattaglia lost a son; and I lost a son...." He ignores the script's directive that "he gesture expressively, submissively, with his hands," because the Don is sparing with gestures as well as words and would never behave "submissively." Brando then trims two-thirds of the Don's summarizing speech,[38] keeping and embellishing the plea on behalf of his youngest son: "But I am a superstitious man, and if some unlucky accident should befall him ... then I'm going to *blame some of the people in this room. And that I do not forgive.* But that aside, let me say that I swear, *on the souls* of my grandchildren, *that I will not be the one* to break the peace we've made *here today.*" (Italics indicate words stressed by Brando.)[39]

Brando's part ends with two extraordinary scenes in the Don's garden.[40] Both are set in 1955; it is ten years since Connie's wedding, and the patriarch has aged. Robert Towne wrote the scene with his son Michael after Brando requested that the Don, for once, articulate his feelings. The conversation focuses on business, but the successor, sensing his father's dissatisfaction, provides an opening.[41] The Don rises and sits closer to his favorite son, their heads nearly touching: "I never wanted this for you.... I worked my whole life, I don't apologize, to take care of my family, and I refused to be a fool, dancing on a string held by all those big shots ... but I thought that when it was your time that *you* would be the one to hold the strings.... Senator Corleone, Governor Corleone, Something.... Just wasn't enough time, Michael, wasn't enough time." He sighs, taking his adult son's face in his hands for a kiss. It was this kind of self-possession that endeared audiences to the Don: a man who could be this physically familiar with a grown son and equally prepared to kill on his behalf.

The Godfather is a novelty in Brando's career as the first in which he played a father. Indeed, the Don's death scene was the only time that he ever acted with a child.[42] In contrast to the previous scene with Michael, this one was mostly unscripted. Coppola recalled that the producers considered it unessential, so it was shot while the cast and crew were at lunch.[43] But Brando set aside time to play with four-year-old actor Anthony

The Don's death scene, 1972. Paramount Pictures/Photofest.

Gounaris before the cameras were rolling, a preparation richly rewarded.[44] In the scene, which may be only a day later than the prior one with Michael, the Don seems weaker, the body bulkier, the mouth more sunken, as he wipes sweat from his brow and wearily directs the little boy with the watering can. The Don's fondness for children energizes a moment of invention as he summons the boy for a game. He uses an orange peel to make himself into a jagged-fanged monster, arousing genuine fear in the child actor, who appears to be feeling fear, rather than performing it. The monster-Don placates him with a chuckle and picks up the boy. Then the Don institutes a chase, which results in his heart attack. He falls dying in the tomato patch. The border between movie and reality, unsettled by the child actor's fear, is further shaken by his guffaw at the Don's death throes, which he views as theater. Truly frightened before by the orange-peel monster, the child is now entertained by Brando's acting of the death scene. Whether or not the child is acting, his wisdom is irrefutable: Brando's death scene *is* masterful, and Anthony Vito Corleone's lovable grandfather *is* a scary monster.

Our attachment to the Don makes us conflicted about him, despite what he does for a living. Still, the fear he arouses makes him an even more compelling character. Of all Brando's roles, Don Corleone has most in common with Stanley Kowalski. Both are in significant ways conventional: men among men who take pride in their families. But both are dangerous, and they force audiences to confront their attraction to men who ruthlessly pursue their ambitions and desires. By foregrounding the inseparability of their violence and seductiveness, Brando highlighted the contradictions in American norms of masculinity. While cultural mythology aligned male success with virtue, experience often suggested the opposite—that it signaled a susceptibility to corruption. The Hollywood establishment was so pleased to have Brando back on top that it overlooked what he considered the caustic appraisal of American culture that was *The Godfather*'s message. Cover stories in major magazines about Brando's redemption after years of wandering in the wilderness typically offered a sampling of his opinions and then dwelled on the professional fairy tale.[45] This was not the case with Shana Alexander's profile in *Life*, which linked Brando's ambivalence toward acting and American institutions in general to his understanding of the film's messages. Brando observed, "The Mafia is so... AMERICAN! To me, a key phrase in [*The Godfather*] is that whenever they wanted to kill somebody it was always a matter of policy. Before pulling the trigger, they told him: 'Just business. Nothing personal.' When I read that, McNamara, Johnson and Rusk flashed before my eyes." Alexander's summary of Brando's performance is equally telling: "The picture is as full of life as a Brueghel painting and as full of death as a slaughterhouse. Any actor can die, actorlike, of gunshot or garrote or knife; and in *The Godfather*, dozens do. Amid this wall-to-wall blood, one is stunned by the great power of the actor who can move us by falling dead of natural causes in a vegetable garden, as Brando does.... In dying the way we all expect to die—unexpectedly—he teaches the difference between death as titillation and death as terror."[46]

THE DON'S AFTERLIFE

Brando's characters were believable because Brando believed in them as independent creations. There is no stronger evidence of the autonomy he gave them than the parody he wrote in 1994 about going to heaven and meeting the Godfather. The vignette, which reveals Brando reflecting, quite literally, on Don Corleone's afterlife, arose from a clause in the contract for his autobiography requiring that he promote it. He seems to have sought mastery over this dreaded obligation by inventing parody interviews, including this one with the Don in the other dimension. Brando's portrait is respectful but critical. The Don is in heaven, after all, and resourceful as ever (convening conferences, listening to opera, using computers), but he lacks wings (an offer to earn them by eliminating Saddam Hussein is refused because "there's no violence allowed...up here"). Moreover, his parochialism prevents his appreciation of the rich company ("Ziggy Freud" and "Al Einstein") in the celestial ghetto for agnostics where he resides, "because I didn't really believe in anything."[47] The satire is telling: The Don's pragmatism takes him far, but he will never overcome his murderous impulses or enjoy the fruits of the examined life.

The most notorious result of *The Godfather* was the Academy Award that Brando received for his performance and turned down via a delegate from the Apache tribe. Brando's decision to send Sacheen Littlefeather to the Academy Awards ceremony on March 27, 1973, to refuse a possible Oscar for Best Actor was the most sensational of his efforts over three decades to publicize the grievances of American Indians and to help them gain compensation for injustices of the past and present.[48] It also represented the integration of his acting achievements and his activism.

Brando knew the whole world would be watching, which was why members of the Academy missed the point when they complained that he should have appeared himself to turn down the award on the Indians' behalf. The strategic substitution—American Indian for Hollywood star—was designed to give Indians the worldwide audience he had been struggling to give them for more than a decade. It also supported his longstanding critique of a profit-driven media and the base cravings it fed. The situation was ideally suited to redress Brando's complaint that people ignored the problems of Indians while feasting on every tidbit they could get about Hollywood stars. If he won the Academy Award, he could force them to listen to what he believed they should hear. "I felt it was a tremendous opportunity for an American Indian to be able to voice his opinion to 85 million people," Brando said on *The Dick Cavett Show* on June 12, explaining why he had not appeared himself. One viewer called it "shock treatment" for a global television audience and "one of the most dramatic civil rights protests" ever.[49]

Sacheen Littlefeather hadn't had time to deliver Brando's entire rationale for refusing the award, so on March 30, 1973, the *New York Times* published "That Unfinished Oscar Speech" under Brando's byline. "For 200 years we have said to the Indian people who are fighting for their land, their life, their families and their right to be free: 'Lay down your arms, my friends.'... When they laid down their arms, we murdered them. We lied to them. We cheated them out of their lands.... But there is one thing which is beyond the reach of this perversity and that is the tremendous verdict of history. And history will surely judge us." Brando's speech concluded with the "hope that those who are listening would not look upon this as a rude intrusion, but as an earnest effort to focus attention on an issue that might very well determine whether or not this country has the right to say from this point forward we believe in the inalienable rights of all people...."

Members of the Cheyenne, Paiute, and Lummi tribes accompanied Brando for his June 12 appearance on *The Dick Cavett Show*. In the wide-ranging discussion, which covered, in addition to his recent refusal of the Oscar, the Indian fishing industry and his theory of acting as a human survival mechanism, Brando confirmed that his attitudes toward publicity and the media were unchanged. For every five minutes on himself, he made sure that equal time was spent on the aspirations of the Indian representatives with him. Brando was polite though straightforward about his goals (saying that he found it distasteful to discuss his movies when the audience knew so little about the suffering of Indians), making clear that shows of this sort were worthwhile only to the extent that they illuminated social problems he considered important.

With Dick Cavett in New York City, June 1973. Photograph by Ron Galella/
WireImage/Getty Images.

While biographers sometimes refer to a gap between Brando's emotionally exhausting year of moviemaking in 1972 and the start of filming for *The Missouri Breaks* in 1975, his professional activity continued relatively uninterrupted. The idea that

Brando retreated immediately to Tahiti, where he drowned in the past and ate gluttonously, is unsupported by facts. On *The Dick Cavett Show*, he looked trim and suntanned. Moreover, he typically ate freely between projects, gaining thirty or forty pounds after a film and then dieting like a prizefighter as the demands of production loomed. He spoke candidly about the weight issue in interviews. "I've gone on and off diets for years, usually before starting a new movie. When I have to lose weight, I can do it. It wasn't unusual to drop thirty-five or forty pounds before a picture. I ate less, exercised more and it came off.... Most of my life, I weighed about 170 pounds.... After forty, my metabolism shifted gears, but I kept eating as much as ever while spending more and more time in a sedentary relationship with a good book. There probably isn't a diet I haven't tried."[50]

Eating for Brando was an addiction akin to the alcoholism of his family, and he tried different therapies, including self-hypnotism, to control it. Brando's weight fluctuations can be seen by wardrobe fittings where he weighs in at his usual film weight of 170 pounds; by reports of his dieting on set (turkey and Tab got his weight down for *The Nightcomers*; he lost too much for *The Godfather*, so the Don's paunch required padding); by the hundreds of diet books in his library; by the many photographs of him; and by the logs he kept, when he was dieting rigorously.[51] Nothing was a greater inducement to weight loss than a doctor's suggestion that excess pounds were compromising his health and longevity. Daily logs Brando kept in his last two years to track his weight for medical purposes show that, at his heaviest, Brando was about 260 pounds.[52] Throughout the 1970s and '80s, when Brando was in his fifties and sixties, his weight fluctuated according to the demands of filming and his understanding of its impact on his overall well-being, his sex life especially. The roles that he played as he aged afforded greater indulgence of his tastes and compulsions. Liberated from the image of a sex symbol, his physical condition became a personal choice more than a professional necessity.

Brando's rejuvenated celebrity with *The Godfather* gave him leverage to dictate the terms of subsequent projects and to secure from them significant financial support for his evolving Indian projects and the development of Tetiaroa. "Pictures," as Brando called them, were what he knew and did best; he would never stop making them. For the most part, Brando would be reprising charismatic villains like Vito Corleone, men who had chosen to live by their own laws. And though Brando could sometimes behave like these characters on set, and had major difficulties with directors during this period, his dedication to his characterizations once his energies were focused on the work at hand continued to reward directors and fellow actors alike.

CHAPTER SEVEN

VILLAINS AND SUPERMEN

T*he Godfather* usually is viewed as the end of Brando's serious professional career. Together with *Last Tango in Paris,*
it is seen as a brief, spectacular resurgence of his talent
after which he completely lost interest in acting. Instead, I see
The Godfather as the performance that initiates Brando's late
period: an adventurous casting-out into undiscovered territory
where he dramatizes his own experience of fame, by playing
larger-than-life, anarchic, often demonic figures. Brando once
said that acting was "like blowing up a balloon and then letting
go," thus pinpointing the element of unexpectedness that made
everything he did so distinctive. He invariably repudiated the
method actor label as meaningless, describing his own acting, if
pressed, as instinctive.[1] After he had immersed himself—through
reading, research, and observation—in the world and mind of his
character, he was free to improvise in ways that even he couldn't
anticipate.

When the Academy Award nomination for Best Actor as Don
Vito Corleone was announced, it was pointed out that Brando
had significantly fewer scenes in *The Godfather* than had the
other nominees in their respective pictures. But the logic of
the nomination was obvious: He was the dominant presence

both within the film and beyond it, as the Don became a cultural icon. Don Corleone, whose criminality was reconciled with the highest virtues—dignity, a sense of justice, devotion to family—introduced a signature element of Brando's late roles, a specialization in charismatic villains. Only a few of these films were acclaimed and highly profitable, and some were even ridiculed. But Brando's appearances usually created audiences for them and made them worthwhile.

Moreover, the characters and scenarios Brando devised illuminate his life in ways that his earlier films did not. Brando became more and more self-reflective, whether building on political preoccupations (*Apocalypse Now*; *A Dry White Season; Columbus*), previous characterizations (*The Freshman*), or sometimes drawing, in the nineties, on conflicted areas of his experience (his offspring, *The Island of Dr. Moreau*; his tumultuous affairs with women, *Don Juan DeMarco*; his fears for his son in prison, *Free Money*). The way these films addressed personal events was usually indirect, especially at the outset. He appeared in a remake of H. G. Wells's *Moreau* because of his scientific and political interest in genetic engineering, and in *Don Juan* he played a psychiatrist, not the compulsive romancer of women. But the explorations they sometimes elicited suggest that when he was performing, he could not help but be engaged. Though he claimed to have entered into the films after *The Godfather* and *Last Tango* for money alone, and he earned huge sums in almost all of them for cameos, Brando was invested in some way in each of these late roles, and the particulars of those investments are revealing of his life as an actor and, occasionally, as a man. Above all, the last twenty-five years of Brando's career demonstrate that he was never done with acting. Annotated scripts; notes on characterization, dialogue, and plot; and books he read to develop roles between 1976 and 2001 confirm the energy and intelligence he continued to devote to what he called "the world's oldest profession."

THE MISSOURI BREAKS

Brando's first film after *Last Tango in Paris* was *The Missouri Breaks*, directed by Arthur Penn, who had fostered an environment on *The Chase* that, despite the drawbacks of Hollywood studio production, freed Brando to do serious work.[2] In *The Missouri Breaks*, Arthur Penn once again gave Brando the freedom to create a unique persona. Lee Clayton, the heartless assassin, would be one of Brando's most self-consciously theatrical incarnations of evil. When Penn, Brando, and Jack Nicholson (who played rustler Tom Logan) convened in Montana during the summer of 1975, all agreed they had an intriguing screenplay that was, in the director's words, "not filmable." Brando's character was particularly empty: "There is no Robert E. Lee Clayton," he told Penn, "there just isn't anyone here."[3] But Penn watched as a thinly sketched assassin, with minimal dialogue and human interaction, was transformed into the ultimate eccentric con man.

The best acting, according to Brando, is unpredictable, the actor keeping the audience perpetually expectant. Every scene presents a new possibility for deepening or even reimagining his character.[4] In *The Missouri Breaks*, these assumptions become a theory of survival in the West, as his characterization supplies an otherwise meandering narrative with suspense and purpose. Without Lee Clayton, the film is a mere fight to the death between anarchic rustlers and self-righteous ranchers who value property more than human life. The opening scene confirms the ranchers' perspective: The hanging of a horse thief is so routine that the families attending with picnic baskets barely hush during the swinging man's final moments. The crowd's reaction to the hanging anticipates its failure to deter rustlers, which is why Brando's assassin is already en route. Specializing in innovative killing devices—including a circular spiked weapon that Brando

Robert E. Lee Clayton in *The Missouri Breaks*. Newscom Services.

invented to hurl through the air into the forehead of a rustler (Harry Dean Stanton)—Robert E. Lee Clayton demonstrates that endurance depends on a capacity for surprise worthy of the most skilled actors. Clayton is as literate as he is heartless. Meeting the ranch owner, David Braxton (John McLiam), who has hired him to eliminate the horse thieves threatening his profits, he is quick to admire the man's library, offering a moralistic twist on its value. "I would only claim books," he notes gravely, "that was about right from wrong. Otherwise, how are we to find our Paradise among the stars?"

His Irish brogue and the sinister glint in his eye resemble that of *The Nightcomer*'s Peter Quint, though Clayton prefers his horse "Jess" to women, an unconventionality reinforced by a use of lavender cologne and strange costumes. The issue is not sexual preference so much as unorthodoxy combined with a dramatic ingenuity suited to survival. The ultimate actor, Clayton gets gratification from killing in disguise—once as a preacher, another time as a granny in dress and bonnet. The characterization tells an alternative story about the American West, highlighting the aberrant tendencies accommodated, if not exactly tolerated, by its lawless atmosphere. Until his entrance, when he's hidden behind his beloved horse and pack mule, things seem rudderless. The hefty assassin's arrival catalyzes the drama, and this remains true throughout as viewers await his next move.

Brando gives Clayton one of his loves: bird-watching. As a birder, Clayton traverses the splendid natural setting, book in hand, sounding out long Germanic names for the hawks and other airborne creatures he encounters. Brando had his own classics on the subject: in addition to weighty Audubon Society and *National Geographic* tomes—the 852-page *Field Guide to North American Birds* and *Song and Garden Birds of North America*—he had *Birds of the World* and such esoterica as *The Observer's Book of Birds' Eggs* and a 1947 volume that showed "Field Marks of All Species Found East of the Rockies."[5] Brando's bird books, which date from the 1940s through the 1990s, reflect a genuine preoccupation. Nor are birds a passing fancy of the man-hunting Clayton, who divides people into groundlings and those who can fly. He tells Tom Logan, "I'm not the crawling kind." In one scene, perched birdlike atop his horse, hair wrapped in a white kerchief to give him a bald bird pate, he mutters, "God, God, God," alternately

Singing on the *Missouri Breaks* set with Nicholson, Kathleen Lloyd, and Stanton. Courtesy of MGM Media Licensing.

consulting his manual and peering through binoculars at the sky. Despite a capacity for awe, he is a predator (like the circling scavenger described in another of Brando's books, Thomas Merton's *Zen and the Birds of Appetite*). Clayton's birding binoculars prove handy for tracking the rustlers he is contracted to kill.

All are suspect as he shrewdly appraises people, his eyes and mouth active. He talks constantly (mostly to himself), chuckles, hums, sings, and chews—carrots, tobacco, game—using his teeth to cut leather, or disarming an antagonist with a smile. Complaining of a toothache at the funeral of the foreman whose death he is hired to avenge, he sends shock waves through the gathering by raising the corpse and grabbing ice from the coffin for his throbbing jaw. Brando transforms the obscure figure of the screenplay into a man who quotes Shakespeare to his horse and mule, a performer whose many disguises and accents—from the witty Irishman to the menacing country preacher—bespeak both learning and the malevolent emptiness at his core.[6] The subject of killing inspires his highest pitches of eloquence. Consider this speech, improvised by Brando with an Irish lilt: "Supposing you had a barn full of nasty old bats, you wanted to get rid of them. Well, the worst thing you could do is just get your gun and just start shootin' and bangin' around. What good would it do you? It wouldn't do a damn bit of good. They'd all leave and they'd be back by 7:30 in the morning. Now, if you want to get rid of a whole lot of evil bats, there's only one way. And the way is this: you wait till the dawn comes about 4:30, and you're waiting outside by the barrels there. And then, you close the door real quick, and all the bats are inside. And then while they're sleeping, the lovely little sweethearts, you have every one of the dirty little buggers at your mercy. And that's the only way you can do it." Riding off into a splendid beclouded landscape, his beleaguered mule in tow, he adds to his horse with a flourish, "Come on now, Jess, we know when we're not wanted. Let's go out to the manhunt now."

Clayton adores his horse and guns (his etched silver pistol, he says, is "like a poem"), but humans he can do without.[7] Head rustler Tom Logan cuts his throat ultimately, but that doesn't make Clayton's side any less victorious. The ending anticipates a birth six months hence, for the West is nothing if not regenerative, its inhabitants worn down by the demands of survival but driven to replenish the surrounding wonder. Penn's camera provides equal doses of lyricism and barbarism: the shrunken boy miner desperately serving a stranger for money; the farm wife selling her body to a horse thief so ignorant he'd never heard of Thomas Jefferson; the aging rustler mourning a boyhood dog shot for sticking its tongue on a pat of butter. Painfully particularized, yet full of humor, Penn's West reciprocates Brando's inventions more successfully than some reviewers recognized. For the film was itself heretical in portraying the cruelty of the West with so much sensitivity.

Brando's participation in *The Missouri Breaks* generated the usual media attention, which he obliged with two in-depth interviews. "Brando: The Method of His Madness," by Chris Hodenfield in *Rolling Stone*, exemplifies a skillful writer in pursuit of difficult prey. Despite his elusiveness, or perhaps because of it, Brando looms large here. Everything about him seems inflated: his pay ($1.25 million), his weight, and the way he throws it around. Yet Hodenfield also notes that crew members praised the actor whom prop man Guy Douglas called "their hero."[8] His other quotations are especially revealing. For instance, Bernardo Bertolucci's remarks on how the actor "*dominates* space. Even if Brando is absolutely still, say, sitting on a chair," he has assumed "that privileged space. And Brando's attitude toward life is different from that of other people because of this fact." Or Brando on cinema patrons: "People buy a ticket. That ticket is their transport to a fantasy which you create for them. Fantasyland, that's all, and you make their fantasies live. Fantasies of love or hatred or whatever it is. People want their fantasies over and over. People who masturbate usually masturbate with, at the most, four or five fantasies. . . . And that's all films are. . . . Just an extension of childhood, where everybody wants to be freer, everybody wants to be powerful, everybody wants to be so *overwhelmingly* attractive."[9]

Bruce Cook's *Crawdaddy* piece reads like a continuation of the same conversation. "Brando is one of those figures in whom we invest our fantasies. If you are a woman, you ask yourself what it would be like to be made love to by such a man," men wonder what it would be like "simply to *be* him." The strange disconnect experienced by the object of fantasy is illuminated by Lord Byron's response to a fan request "to know the *real* Lord Byron. 'Madame . . . there is no real Lord Byron.'. . . It's something you can imagine Brando saying, isn't it?" Cook describes the Billings, Montana, natives and the film crew in residence there, reacting to a Hollywood idol. Above all, the reporter watches Brando. "Each time he did a take he managed to get a little something extra into it. This is a man who can act with his eyebrows, who will ad lib something in German—in *German!*—when he thinks the script could use a little spritz."[10] Cook can be forgiven for misidentifying the Hebrew (from the traditional Kaddish prayer for the dead) Brando mutters before bedding down the night he is killed.

A reviewer noted about the same scene that Brando's compliment to his horse—you have "the lips of Salome and the eyes of Cleopatra"—"must be seen to be believed." On the whole, contemporary reviewers found *The Missouri Breaks* bizarre, although the twin billing of Brando and Jack Nicholson attracted audiences. Judith Crist admired the film, which she called "a fascinating tale of complex characters, an engrossing duel between men of multilayered personality against a multidimensional time in history." Brando, Crist wrote, "proves himself master of every nuance of controlled madness, each encounter revealing a new dimension of perverse righteousness and each, peculiarly, serving to expose a further weakness in the other person." "His performance," she concludes, evokes "an almost reflective revelation from others while keeping his own enigmatic persona intact." Brando's most negative review in the *New York Times* called the performance "out-of-control" and set the tone for press of the late period in suggesting that Brando "behaves like an actor in armed revolt." Still, this revisionist Western, with its fine cinematography (by Michael C. Butler) and haunting score by John Williams, has aged well, with critics giving significantly more positive reviews on its DVD release.[11]

SUPERMEN AND NAZIS

The performance confirmed that Brando the actor, whether it was 1946 or 1976, couldn't help but embrace risk. Acting was an imperiling procedure. Living was different. "I would like to conduct my life and be a part of a society that is as good as grass grows. I'd like to be a blade of grass in concert with other blades of grass."[12] A noble but difficult aim, when everyone insists on seeing you as a type of "Superman." This may have been why Brando for his next movie simply threw in the towel and played one: specifically, Jor-El, the father of Kal-El, or Superman. Brando knew something about what awaited the son he sent to Earth; the experience of being "an object of adoration," even idolatry; how "the normal relationships we all require will be denied you." Other aspects of the role were also hospitable—for instance, Jor-El's commitment to knowledge and its transmission to his son. The role was a father's dream, but especially Brando's, given his desire for an intellectual mastery he felt he had missed because of his resistance to formal schooling. His fascination with science was fulfilled by the chance to play a scientist—Jor-El's profession was one Brando had imagined for himself.[13]

But if he was able to appreciate the idealistic aspects of his role in *Superman,* his realism was even more pronounced. Some saw the $2.7 million Brando earned for the film, with more ensured by a contract clause granting him 11.3 percent of the gross, as his capitulation to Hollywood greed. Brando's defense of his right to share in the expansion of a multimillion-dollar industry was at least consistent. He had argued over the years that a star actor was no different from a professional athlete or any other commodity bought or sold in the marketplace. It was only fair that he receive a percentage of the profits his top billing had helped generate. Had Brando's estimation of his own value been exaggerated, he suggested, his demands would have been refused. His participation gave *Superman* a respectability it would have lacked, and it attracted other talent. On set he proved, as usual, a favorite of cast and crew, with neophyte actor Christopher Reeve, in his first major role, especially grateful for the support Brando provided.[14] While his pay distracted critics, they found him credible as the godlike patriarch of the great American superhero, despite his lines, which consisted of solemn oaths, mathematical theorems, philosophical principles, and Shakespearean sonnets. This may have been because Brando carefully pruned his character's pronouncements, an option apparently unavailable to Russell Crowe, whose Jor-El in *Man of Steel* (2013) was chided by reviewers for talking too much.[15]

Brando's British accent in the film distinguished him from the earthlings to whom he sent his child in a spaceship, a lone immigrant young enough that his speech would be as Americanized as that of the natives. Through personal touches, Brando was able to authenticate a role marked by rhetoric as inflated as his character's powers, slipping in a familiar poem—for instance, Joyce Kilmer's "Trees": "'I think I will never see a poem as lovely as a tree . . . ,' a typical ode much loved by the people you will live among, Kal-El."[16] Years later, Brando noted, "Even in *Superman,* a cartoon," "there are universal moments," among them, "Calling from the edge of eternity, giving guidance for his son. It worked because it calls up feelings inside of us."[17] It also helped that he was genuinely interested in the film's futuristic world. As a regular reader of science magazines, and books on popular science and scientific ethics, he was familiar with the problems raised by innovation. He was also sufficiently pragmatic to recognize that technology required capital. A maverick who trusted his own mind, he would not miss an opportunity to make a point because a venture was commercial. What Brando seems to have valued above all was the opportunity for upending traditional authorities afforded by a new scientific age; he saw possibilities that people with enlightened ideas might have more say in social orders to come.

Throughout this late period, Brando sought to balance lucrative projects against those he did for idealistic purposes: the motivations behind *Roots* and *A Dry White Season*. While his late-career earnings were often vast, much of it went to legal fees for his son's murder trial, the special needs of his troubled daughter, and causes he cared about. He lived modestly by Hollywood standards. His home on Mulholland Drive, valued in 1991 at $2.6 million, mostly for the location, was under 4,000 square feet, and his island in Tahiti (which he bought for $142,000 on March 13, 1967) was rustic. His primary concerns there were to preserve the natural beauty of the atoll and promote scientific research.[18] Like many stars, however, he had a long list of dependents, relatives as well as friends, toward whom he could be extremely generous. What he cared about most was the freedom to spend money as he wished, which was enabled by late-twentieth-century filmmaking and his reputation.

Brando followed *Superman* with Alex Haley's *Roots: The Next Generations* (1979), a television series he admired. In keeping with the trend of his roles over the decade, Brando played a villain:

George Lincoln Rockwell, leader of the American Nazi Party. He was familiar with Rockwell, had read about him in his friend James Baldwin's *The Fire Next Time*, bracketing a passage that drew parallels between Rockwell's doctrines and those of the Nation of Islam suggesting that "the glorification of one race and the consequent debasement of another—or others—always has been and always will be a recipe for murder."[19] Brando's ten-minute cameo was awarded an Emmy for Best Supporting Actor (1979). His scene dramatized Haley's April 1976 *Playboy* interview with Rockwell, who was assassinated the following year. Dressed in a black storm-trooper's uniform with red-and-white swastika armband, pipe in hand, Brando's Rockwell is a sardonic figure who keeps a pistol on the desk before him, a precaution (like the hygienic aerosol he sprays, to offset contamination) required, he says matter-of-factly, by Haley's race. Sporting a brown wig, looking plump but handsome, he blows smoke rings as he denies the Holocaust and excoriates the relativism of the "Jew anthropologist" Franz Boas. He refers fondly to the "hate-e-nannies" sponsored by his organization and provides samples of their lyrical bigotry. While he is no monster, despite his evil beliefs, he is a man without empathy. His weariness makes him terrifying—a far-too-believable human being.

APOCALYPSE NOW

Superman and *Roots* were relatively finite undertakings. Brando turned in reliable performances, but neither entailed the research and script revisions of a significant role. His next film, *Apocalypse Now* (1979), was different: an ambitious critique of the Vietnam War based on Joseph Conrad's *Heart of Darkness*, it seemed to combine the commercial potential of *Superman* with the idealism of *Roots*. All evidence suggests that Brando took the role of

Colonel Walter Kurtz seriously, despite negative publicity about his work.[20] In the post-Watergate era, his skepticism about the war and politicians was widely shared. He had high hopes that he and Francis Ford Coppola could do something important with an issue central to American culture and its politics. Somewhere along the way, their relationship soured, primarily over the question of Brando's contributions to the script and story. Brando told his side in a 1978 letter to Coppola: "When I came there, there was no story," Brando writes, referring to his arrival on the Philippine set. "Whatever changes you made, whatever accommodations you made in that week the company was shut down [were] because you were convinced that what I said was true.... You spent a week there with me talking about the film, clarifying it in your own mind but also listening attentively to what I said and reading what I wrote.... It's not really my job to be involved in the overall concept of the script. Most actors really don't discuss that [but] I didn't think at the time I could avoid discussing it."[21]

No one disputes that the film shoot was suspended while actor and director brainstormed on a houseboat. Coppola's collaborative intent was expressed in a letter to Brando from the summer of 1976. The letter described the director's anguish over the unfinished script and the hope that he and the actor would be able to turn it around. Coppola's admiration for Brando's intuitions was clear, as was his conviction that the two of them together would find a way through this complicated and controversial material. If anyone in the business could produce an authentic portrait of the Vietnam War, Coppola suggested, he and Brando could. Coppola's tone here, and the high expectations of what Brando had to offer his film, contrasted sharply with Coppola's June 1979 public critique of an unprepared and overweight actor who figured prominently in the director's difficulties with the production.[22] Perhaps Brando's work on the film after he arrived in the Philippines in the fall of 1976 didn't meet Coppola's expectations. But

Michael Herr, the novelist who received partial credit for the screenplay, recalled, "The actor wrote a stream of brilliant lines for his character," the "part was twice as long in the rough-cut as it was in the released movie." Coppola himself described how he and Brando reconceived the script to increase the suspenseful anticipation of the mythic Kurtz.[23] As Coppola's biographer notes, "This long coda in Kurtz's domain houses the core of the film's meaning, and Kurtz's speeches alight unerringly on the reasons for the American predicament in Vietnam."[24]

Brando was in a position to clarify and enhance this meaning when he arrived on location. His personal files for *Apocalypse Now* include dozens of articles and books, which he annotated, and letters from experts about specific incidents. On the war, Brando was particularly captivated by *Soldier,* the 1973 memoir of Anthony B. Herbert, inspector general of the 173rd Airborne Brigade, one of the highest-rated combat units in Vietnam.[25] A son of Lithuanian immigrants who had devoted his life to the military, Lieutenant Colonel Herbert writes about being shocked by the routine negligence and malfeasance actively concealed by commanders. Herbert filed formal charges, accusing superiors of war crimes after his appeals for investigation were denied. The charges were dismissed and the forty-one-year-old career officer felt forced to leave the US Army.

Brando's copy of the book is full of highlighting that reflects his absorption in *Soldier.* He marked some passages for their authentic dialogue ("Vietnam was the 'unreal world,' they said, 'Brown Disneyland'... Six Flags Over Nothing"; "It was Cover Your Ass time"; "If Carthage had been as dependent on the coconut, there would have been no need for the Roman plow").[26] He marked others for their clear statements of themes ("The generals were has-beens or never-beens of World War II"; "He was applying, whether intentionally or not, the Westmoreland Precept: see no evil, hear no evil, and you will avoid being contaminated by

On set for *Apocalypse Now* in the Philippines. Silver Screen Collection/
Getty Images.

evil").[27] And he read for characterization ("A philosophy of war
is a personal matter, to be dealt with by each individual. It has
to be that way or you go bananas"; "commendations and med-
als just didn't mean very much anymore").[28] Brando also raised
questions and highlighted contradictions, eager for information

beyond Herbert (writing "get" over a reference to Seymour Hersh on the Peers Commission Report in the *New York Times*).[29] In a similar skeptical vein, he revised Lieutenant Colonel Herbert's observation—when you "make your war a war of numbers, you have no trouble sleeping. Most generals and presidents sleep well." Brando added: "and lieutenant colonels."[30]

Both Brando and Coppola were taken by Herbert's book, which came up in tapes of their houseboat conversations, and Herbert's influence on *Apocalypse Now* superseded Brando's part. For example, Brando writes "Possible" across a passage about a deranged chaplain with rosary beads who requests that soldiers be pulled from combat for Mass.[31] The celebrated Lieutenant Colonel Kilgore sequence depicts a priest giving communion to a group of soldiers in the midst of battle, while the manic Kilgore (Robert Duvall) discusses surfboards. Captain Willard's (Martin Sheen) voice-over following his stint with Kilgore's unit could be straight from *Soldier*: "No wonder Kurtz put a weed up Command's ass, the war was being run by a bunch of Four Star Clowns who were gonna end up giving the whole circus away."[32] The most obvious echo of Herbert's book is Kurtz, the stellar officer, groomed for the highest ranks, driven to rebel against the chain of command.[33] But Herbert retained his sanity, while Kurtz becomes a magical figure in the jungle. For his portrait of the individual who transcends the bounds of civilization, Brando drew on a larger and more treasured section of his library.[34]

Religion, spirituality, and myth were among the most heavily represented subjects in Brando's library. He annotated Lao Tzu's *The Way of Life* (1962) cover to cover and had a copy of the 1964 bestseller *Markings*, by Dag Hammarskjold. In the film, Kurtz's bookshelf features volumes—James Frazer's *The Golden Bough*, Jessie Weston's *From Ritual to Romance*, T. S. Eliot's *The Waste Land,* the Bible—that Brando owned sometimes in multiples, on subjects (T. S. Eliot, James Frazer, the Bible) that so absorbed him he read and annotated many secondary works about them.[35] He had books on angels, voodoo, magic, Zen, and the occult, books by and about Krishnamurti. He had Bibles and scriptures from most of the major religions: Judaism, Christianity, Islam, Buddhism, Hinduism, Mormonism, American Indian and Christian Science; books of psalms and Bible interpretation; books on anthropology and myth (by Joseph Campbell, Arnold Toynbee, Kurt Seligmann, and Lord Raglan, among others), including Bronislaw Malinowski's 1948 study, *Magic, Science and Religion and Other Essays.* Brando's collection featured titles such as *Unveiling the Mystery of Creation, How the Great Religions Began, Man and His Gods, Why God Won't Go Away: Brain Science and the Biology of Belief,* which Brando might well have lent to his alter ego, the colonel, or discussed at length with him. But Brando, the ultimate agnostic or seeker (he even owned *The Seeker's Handbook*), was never dogmatic, whereas Kurtz, as Brando told Coppola in their recorded conversations, was "a true believer, in Eric Hoffer's sense."[36]

Brando's conception for *Apocalypse Now* was "to return to the original plot of Conrad's novel, in which a man named Marlow describes his journey up the Congo in search of Walter Kurtz, a once-idealistic young man who has been transformed by his experiences into a mysterious, remote figure involved in what Conrad called 'unspeakable rites.'... What makes Conrad's story so powerful is that people talk about Kurtz for pages and pages, and readers wonder about him. They never see him, but he is part of the atmosphere. It's an odyssey, and he's the *Heart of Darkness.* ... I offered to rewrite the script based on the original structure of the book, and Francis agreed.... Besides restructuring the plot, I wrote Kurtz's speeches, including a monologue at his death.... It was probably the closest I've ever come to getting lost in a part, and one of the best scenes I've ever played."[37] The oft-repeated command that Kurtz be "terminated with extreme prejudice" is a notorious CIA line with which Brando was familiar.[38] Brando also shaved his head to suit Conrad's description of Kurtz as "impressively bald. The wilderness had patted him on the head, and, behold, it was like a ball—an ivory ball."[39] Much of this footage was omitted from the 1979 film, but sections were added onto *Apocalypse Now Redux* (2001), which critics and Coppola himself considered the definitive cut.

Brando's appearances in *Apocalypse Now* amount to about twenty minutes. But Kurtz infuses the whole movie with a sense of doom, as in Conrad's *Heart of Darkness*. Kurtz's spell is cast when Captain Willard first hears his voice, and it deepens as he gets bits of information, drifting up the Nung River toward Cambodia, where Kurtz and his devotees conduct their guerrilla operations. Willard says, "The more I read and began to understand the more I admired him...a tough motherfucker... staged operation Arc Angle...rated a major success....He just thought it up and did it. What balls."[40] Audiences share Willard's obsession with Kurtz, skimming voyeuristically over his shoulder: Kurtz's application for transfer, photographs of Kurtz at an awards ceremony (borrowed from Brando as Major Pendleton in *Reflections in a Golden Eye*). Kurtz is the diabolical catalyst of the journey; his subversive activities initiate it, his sacrificial death completes it. "I made an entrance into the movie with just my bald head," Brando recalled, "without my face, and then I went back out into the shadow, because that was in a sense what had happened to the man's mind, that he was in the darkness...he went back and forth into this netherworld that he had created ...he no longer had any moral reference for anything."[41] If the mad Colonel Kurtz is dispatched, the higher command trusts, his mad reading of Vietnam will also disappear. Yet he is not the only officer who has lost his mind in Vietnam.

Captain Willard is introduced in drunken despair; writhing on the floor of his hotel room, he smashes a mirror, smearing blood over himself. The mission to eliminate Kurtz comes as a salvation for Willard, though it proves fatal to nearly the entire patrol-boat crew. Lieutenant Colonel Kilgore's benightedness is his asset. Kurtz, in contrast, is a seer: He dies with his eyes open, whispering, "The horror, the horror." A type of Christ, he is dangerous not because he is symptomatic of Vietnam but because he understands it. Kurtz knows the impossibility of victory in a war waged to protect American interests, the ineffectiveness of a revolving-door army with sophisticated weaponry against guerrilla forces motivated by belief who are able, Kurtz says, "to utilize their primordial instincts to kill, without feeling, without passion, without judgment." Brando was reading Hannah Arendt's *Crises of the Republic* (1972) around the time of *Apocalypse Now*, and its chapter on the Pentagon Papers (an honest appraisal of the Vietnam War, 1945–1967, commissioned by Secretary of Defense Robert McNamara) is especially relevant to Kurtz. Brando marked, for instance, the assertions that "technical superiority can 'be much more of a liability than an asset' in guerrilla wars," and that after 1965 the prospect of victory receded and the US "objective became 'to convince the enemy that *he* could not win,'" thus avoiding a "humiliating defeat" for the American military. Brando appropriates McNamara's thinking for Kurtz. One can easily imagine him highlighting in full, as Brando did, Arendt's chilling epigraph from Robert S. McNamara: "The picture of the world's greatest superpower killing or seriously injuring a thousand non-combatants a week, while trying to pound a tiny backward nation into submission on an issue whose merits are hotly disputed, is not a pretty one."[42]

Another book by Arendt may have informed Brando's thinking on Kurtz even more—*Eichmann in Jerusalem* (1975). Arendt's portrait of Eichmann helped Brando to extemporize in a way that takes us close to the "heart of darkness." Here is a sample of Kurtz's ravings, completely improvised by Brando, that were not included in the film:

> I, I, I, I had immense plans, threshold of great things.... To look into the abyss without drawing away is everything, the highest the highest honor. To approach the horizon of endurable anguish and to pass it...the unthinkable you must experience the unthinkable. Masses, masses, any any people who go anywhere do anything, as long as the ring of faith is in their nose, yes put the rings in their nose and call it God, country and mother then you can run a slim rope through the rings and herd them all, ten million, a hundred million two hundred million or more. The human animal has no limits, he can...fling himself into outer space and find a new orbit, determined by far greater forces, like that of Jupiter or the Sun....The will to submission is stronger than the will to power, Eichmann, six million Jews....Extremism in defense of liberty is no vice, no vice. This war will never be won by the priests of misery at the Rand Corporation and not in the situation rooms in Washington....This is a time for giants and they send us pygmies armed with chalk, computers, tape recorders, tennis rackets....We are the murderers, we are the monsters that we fear in others. Here we go round the prickly pear, here we go round the prickly pear.[43]

Among the many passages Brando starred in *Eichmann in Jerusalem* was a reflection on why there were not more displays of conscience, of resistance by the Nazis who were slaughtering innocents in the field. Some officers insisted that they had "inwardly opposed" the extermination they dutifully carried out, that, as one officer put it, the crimes committed by his "official soul" were decried by his "private soul."[44] Brando's speeches for Kurtz suggest a different explanation: that perhaps he didn't have a soul. Despite his violence, confirmed by the surrounding corpses, Kurtz is methodical and polite. When he learns Willard is from Ohio, he muses gently about the gardenia plantation he once saw there that made you think "heaven" had fallen "on the earth."[45] Later, reading aloud from T. S. Eliot's "The Hollow Men," *Time* magazine on Vietnam, or Frazer on sacrifice from *The Golden Bough*, Brando makes clear that Kurtz's horror is grounded in principles of civilization.

Reviews of *Apocalypse Now* were mixed. Frank Rich, writing in *Time*, was among the most negative, characterizing the film as "an incongruous, extravagant monument to artistic self-defeat"; Vincent Canby in the *New York Times* called it a "stunning work . . . as technically complex and masterful as any war film I can remember," while highlighting its flaws. Charles Champlin of the *Los Angeles Times* agreed about the flaws but concluded: "As a noble use of the medium and as a tireless expression of national anguish, it towers over everything that has been attempted by an American filmmaker in a very long time." And Dale Pollock in *Variety* warned that this "brilliant and bizarre film . . . complex, demanding, highly intelligent," was entering "a marketplace that does not always embrace those qualities." His predictions proved correct. Many contemporaries were irritated by *Apocalypse Now* and by Coppola's overt parallels in interviews between his subject and his experiences making it ("this isn't a film about Vietnam, the film *is* Vietnam"). Still, it is now widely acknowledged as a major film about Vietnam, a stature assisted by the release of *Apocalypse Now Redux*. This was anticipated by Roger Ebert in the *Chicago Sun-Times*: "Years and years from now, when Coppola's budget and his problems have long been forgotten, *Apocalypse* will still stand, I think, as a grand and grave and insanely inspired gesture of filmmaking."[46]

Apocalypse Now was the most idealistic of Brando's films from the 1970s. His next role as an amoral CEO was the most cynical.

An oil baron, without use for anyone who stands in the way of profit, Adam Steiffel of *The Formula* (1980) worries more about the dead frogs in his chlorinated pool than the humans he has killed. Though a detective played by George C. Scott exposes him, Steiffel triumphs in the end, his "oil shortage business" promising exponential growth in the years ahead. Here too, Brando, in a brief but deft performance, helped to convey prophetic truths. Somewhat camouflaged behind prosthetic teeth, nostril expanders, and thick glasses, Brando earned some positive reviews from Roger Ebert—Brando "appears in three fascinating scenes and leaves us wishing for more"—and Janet Maslin—Brando "plays a captain of industry, and does it with a rakish sense of humor," offering "very memorable" moments with Scott.[47] Like his other projects of the seventies, *The Formula* featured leading actors (Scott, and John Gielgud, with whom Brando had appeared before), had production problems, and paid Brando royally for his limited time—$2.7 million for two weeks. Even though commercially profitable, the film made little impression and reinforced Brando's cynicism about contemporary filmmaking, helping to spur his decision to take a sabbatical of sorts. This was his choice. Scripts continued to come in throughout this period (he turned down a role in *Rambo III*, for instance, because the United States and the Soviet Union were near an accord on missile reduction), but he was determined to pursue his own ends, and the significant income from his recent films made it possible.[48]

During the nine years between *The Formula* and *A Dry White Season*, Brando kept his hand in prospective movies and pursued the usual good works (which included continued time on his Indian projects), read, wrote (a novel, *Fan-Tan*, and a script, *Jericho*, for a movie that got to the production stage but no further), and planned (eco-projects for his island in Tahiti; garden and house renovation for his Mulholland Drive home).

HIATUS AND RENEWAL

Brando had never lacked for things to do when he wasn't filming. He read even more than usual, devoted time and energy to
Tetiaroa and to his children. In 1980, Brando's Tahitian children,
Teihotu and Cheyenne, were seventeen and ten, respectively.
His "other daughters," Miamiti (b. 1977) and Raiatua (b. 1982),
conceived by his Tahitian wife Tarita with other men, and the
daughter of his assistant Caroline Barrett, Petra (b. 1972), whom
Brando also treated as his own (he put Petra through college
and law school), were often on Tetiaroa and occasionally visited
Mulholland Drive. Brando set up a school on the island, with
French-speaking tutors who taught them English in addition to
a variety of subjects, including sociology. His library had books,
workbooks, and textbooks belonging to the island's children.
Brando was also concerned with the educations of his children
in Los Angeles, marking the high school graduation of his son
Miko with a Rolex watch inscribed, "To my beautiful son, from
his very lucky Dad, June 1978," and supporting the college education of Miko's sister Rebecca at the University of Arizona in
the late 1980s.

According to Miko, Brando "loved kids and learned a lot from
them. He picked their brains." And he seemed to them infinitely
knowledgeable. "There was nothing he didn't know something
about," Miko said. "It was like having a walking Internet with you.
You could put him in a room with anyone and he would know about
that person's area or talent." Though Brando was not authoritarian or dictatorial, he did follow his own father's example in sending Miko to military school for a year when he was floundering,
but then he advised him to "find something you love to do, and
you'll never have to work."[49] Brando was especially preoccupied

with his firstborn son, Christian, the product of his brief, tumultuous marriage to Anna Kashfi. Twenty-two in 1980, Christian
was bright but had never graduated from high school, and he had
abused drugs and alcohol since his early teens. Christian was also
idealistic, resistant to Hollywood values, and drawn to nature and
animals. Overwhelmed by his father's fame and talents, and by
the way Brando alternately indulged and neglected him, equally
handicapped by a mother with various addictions, Christian pursued different vocations over the years, including tree surgeon,
welder, and actor, never quite finding his way. Brando tried to help,
financing his endeavors and even those of the women close to him
he believed good for his son (investing $20,000, for instance, in
a new business for Christian's young wife), and encouraging him
to get therapy, but such efforts proved futile.[50]

Brando himself had begun to find peace during these years
through a combination of therapy and meditation techniques.
He had always read widely in psychology and alternative medicine, which were, to begin with, family concerns. His mother,
grandmother, great-grandfather, and aunts were drawn to these
ideas and practices, as well as to more conventional methods—for
example, his mother's work with Alcoholics Anonymous and
Marty Mann in the late 1940s.[51] Though alcoholism ran in the
family, so did the faith that human weaknesses could be corrected. Brando spent years in psychoanalysis but grew increasingly disenchanted with traditional Freudian methods. It was
only in the 1980s that he discovered a clinician, Dr. G. L. Harrington, whose practicality combined with Brando's own relative stability to produce significant results. He expressed his
gratitude by including the doctor in the dedication to his 1994
autobiography.

In Dr. Harrington he seems to have met the right person at the
right time: someone who enabled him to benefit from a lifetime of
reading and introspection. A respected Los Angeles psychiatrist

who had helped to inspire a field called "choice theory," Harrington was rare in his humility toward his expertise: "If all the professionals in our field suddenly disappeared, the world would hardly note their absence."[52] Harrington was also a pragmatist with a good sense of humor, and he encouraged Brando to trust his instincts. For despite a difficult upbringing, and an adulthood marred by fame and the endless conflicts generated by his sexual self-indulgence, he had a talent for living that was as great as his talent for acting.[53] Brando had an extraordinary ability to embrace the moment. As his assistant Avra Douglas remarked, "For Marlon it was about the journey not the destination. That's what we should all aspire to be like. He was always talking about living in the moment, as if right now is all that mattered." This is echoed by Miko, who described a road trip to Death Valley with his father that took "a week from LA, because Dad insisted on stopping to look at every flower and tree on the way. He was never in a hurry to do anything."[54]

Indeed, this is where Brando becomes especially challenging for biographers. It is possible to look at his life beyond film as a record of futility—endless serial romances, many children all needing more attention than he gave them, a major film on Indians foiled, unrealized utopian schemes for Tetiaroa, original film scripts never produced, and films abandoned at the point of production. Some have concluded that America's greatest film star was a failure in life, and occasionally on screen. Brando had his share of disappointment and misery, some of it of his own making. But he never lost his unlimited appetite for experience and knowledge.[55]

What made his intellect unusual was that it was as practical as it was idealistic. He could get as excited about garden tools or ship implements as he could about the causes of evil; he could be as absorbed in books about home building as in books about being at home in the universe.[56] And he could be happy sitting in the doorway of his thatched hut on Tetiaroa, watching the changing colors and clouds drift across the lagoon. "I've sat there in that position, just contemplating life . . . little birds of thought flitting through my mind. I've digested a lot of my philosophy in those times."[57]

It was in this period, too, that Brando consulted an expert on biofeedback, purchasing an instrument for measuring galvanic skin response, a method used by psychoanalysts Carl Jung and Wilhelm Reich. He read a great deal about meditation and befriended swamis well versed in the subject, mastering techniques that allowed him to reduce his blood pressure dramatically, sometimes bringing it as low as 90-over-60. Brando also made his own relaxation tapes, which he used regularly. It was during the 1980s that he began meditating twice daily, even experiencing on multiple occasions satori, the sudden awakening that is the ultimate goal in Zen Buddhism.[58]

Brando's general well-being was reflected in an extended taped conversation (Brando did almost all the talking) with Michael Jackson at his home in August 1983. The topic was developing the famous singer's acting skills. They covered everything from relationships with fathers to racism and hatred, to the wisdom and distortions of the Judeo-Christian Bible, as one of Brando's Tahitian toddlers wandered in and out and secretaries interrupted with messages on the intercom. The candor of Brando's ruminations confirmed his affection for Jackson. He invokes, for instance, his favorite comparison between actors and boxers who both seek to *dominate*. Great actors are like boxers with opponents, sparring with audiences, forcing them to adapt to *their* rhythms, *their* moves. "As soon as they can second-guess you, then they're ahead of you. You got to make 'em wait and get them on your time." He also intuits Jackson's exceptional sensitivities. "You've got more nerve endings than most people. . . . I'll bet you're the kind of person who can get injured by what you're imagining. You can walk into someplace and everyone is chasing around trying to get your autograph and you don't care...what I see in you is not so much loneliness but aloneness." He is just as open about himself. For years, Brando confesses, he nursed a grudge against his country for its racism and violence, but study and travel convinced him that America had no monopoly on cruelty. In Africa, you might be killed for wandering into a territory with the wrong scarification; Cambodians, Russians, the Dutch in Indonesia had slaughtered millions. For prejudicial malevolence, however, nothing could top the caste system of India and the categorical suffering of the Untouchables it perpetrated. The only country that he saw coming close to rivaling India's barbarism toward its own was China.

Brando mentions a novel he is writing on the subject—about piracy on the South Seas during the 1920s.[59] The novel, coauthored with Donald Cammell, was *Fan-Tan*, an adventure tale that recalled maritime romances by Rafael Sabatini and Jack London and featured a hero, Anatole Doultry, with various Brando traits. The novel offers a wealth of information about Brando's favorite subjects, including ships and shipbuilding, Chinese arts and history, and the puzzle of prejudice and hatred. The many boxes in the Brando Estate Archives with Brando's dictation and notes show that he earned his status as lead author.[60] Likewise, for every paragraph in *Fan-Tan*, there are corresponding books in Brando's library. The protagonist, Annie, contemplates the rigorous design of Chinese hulls; the technical capacity of "wireless" radios in the early twentieth century; the formidable appetites of rats, roaches, red ants, and other shipboard vermin; and the fan-tan itself—an elaborate game of chance played with every type of legal tender in the world. The Rabelaisian emphasis on bodily fluids and excess, the distrust that defines the novel's central romantic relationship, the perpetual sense of danger—all provide windows of a kind on Brando's fantasies.

The same was true of another creative project from this period of hiatus, his script for a film entitled *Jericho*. Copyrighted April 7, 1988, "An Original Screenplay by Marlon Brando," *Jericho*, set in Medellin, Colombia, is a spy thriller about the CIA and the Colombian cocaine trade. The opening credits scroll over a scene at a church tower where an altar boy discovers a bell clapper replaced by a maggot-covered human head. Brando's complaints about the dispensable beginning of *The Ugly American* echo in this lesson on how to grip an audience by the throat before the credits end. The immediate image of the well-groomed aristocrat at breakfast, like the Don Corleone fade-in after the horse-head scene in *The Godfather*, reveals who is responsible for the bell's ghoulish silence. The powerful are immune to the grisly violence they authorize. As these echoes demonstrate, Brando the scriptwriter builds on everything he has learned over a lifetime of moviemaking. His prospective role was the jaded CIA agent Billy Harrington, code-named "Jericho," with an unparalleled record and knowledge of Colombia.

"Harrington" is named after Brando's psychiatrist; the character's biofeedback tape reflects a familiar film history (Vietnam, water buffalo, African drumbeats), while his home-surveillance system is the creator's dream. Brando read Robert Sabbag's book about the cocaine trade, *Snowblind* (1978), for details about character types, pricing and smuggling systems, weaponry, and lingo.[61] Harrington's love interest, "Mook," a Colombian singer who divides her time between drug kingpins and Communist guerrillas, is conceived for Rita Moreno, and CIA agent "Smokey Robertson" is for longtime friend Quincy Jones. Jones recalled their long, hilarious discussions about *Jericho*: Brando was to "play a white agent who acted black," while Jones "played a black agent who acted white." Both of them, Brando noted, were "bilingual" in the American languages of race. Every time he walked into a room, the only black among whites, Jones was being read as a representative black man and behaved accordingly. He was also reading the whites. Brando himself drew on similar skills as a dance student in Harlem and a jazz aficionado at all-black clubs in Manhattan during the 1940s and '50s, and later as a civil rights activist. In light of their familiarity with the experience of being the other, it makes sense that Jones and Brando made a habit of studying the language when they traveled to a foreign country. Brando hoped their association on film would dramatize the positive dimensions of life as a constant exercise in translation.[62]

Of all the projects Brando worked on in the eighties, *Jericho* came closest to realization: Elliott Kastner, who had produced three previous Brando films, including *The Missouri Breaks*, signed on as producer. By the end of 1987, *Jericho* was financed and filming locations in Colombia, Mexico, and Washington, DC, were set. But the film was never made, for reasons that remain unclear.[63] Throughout the 1980s and '90s, Brando continued to work on original scripts (*Tim and His Friends*; *Bull Boy*; *A South Sea Story*) and an adaptation, with Nobel Prize–winning author Toni Morrison, of *Cat on a Hot Tin Roof*, entitled "Big Daddy."[64] Brando also kept alive the prospect of a film version of *Fan-Tan*; he had the draft of a screenplay in 1993 and consulted with Michael Hastings, who had done the script for *The Nightcomers*, about another adaptation in 1998.[65] Despite his efforts, Brando never produced a screenplay or fiction that was on par with his standard of performance, which may explain why he didn't pursue them wholeheartedly.

When Brando returned to filmmaking after his hiatus, he was often making movies for the money, but those with whom he worked saw how the process energized him. His assistant Avra Douglas confirms what intimates never doubted: "He cared so much that he needed to pretend he didn't care at all." One of the not-so-well-kept secrets of Brando's life was his dedication to the craft that he revolutionized and complained about—endlessly. His disappointment and occasional outrage when things went wrong on productions—and they did increasingly since his choice of projects predictably shrank as he aged—was precipitated by the high hopes he brought to almost all of them. Still, he continued to demonstrate versatility and inventiveness on film to the very end. This was certainly the case with *A Dry White Season* (1989) and *The Freshman* (1990), in which he delivered two of the best performances of his late career.

THE LAWYER AND THE BOSS: *A DRY WHITE SEASON* AND *THE FRESHMAN*

Brando's trusted Hollywood agent Jay Kanter remained unconvinced by his friend's retirement and proved it in the winter of 1988 by signing him for a cameo in a film about South African apartheid, *A Dry White Season*. It helped that Brando's character, Ian MacKenzie, was a British lawyer—he loved British accents and the drama of the courtroom—and working with Euzhan Palcy, the director from Martinique who had won acclaim for *Sugar Cane Alley* (1983), was attractive. Set in 1976 and based on a novel by distinguished South African author André Brink, the film exposed the vicious police state run by the country's white minority. Because he believed in the cause, Brando donated a portion of his salary to an antiapartheid foundation. It had taken five years for the film to get funded, partly owing to its controversial subject. It ended up being banned in South Africa, and the South African members of the cast feared reprisals from their government.[66] Brando's filming began in London, in the fall of 1988, with a company that included Donald Sutherland, Susan Sarandon, Michael Gambon, and South African actor Zakes Mokae. The film featured songs by Joseph Shabalala performed by Ladysmith Black Mambazo, and a score by jazz composer Dave Grusin, who had done the score for the psychedelic sex farce *Candy* (1967), based on the Terry Southern novel, in which Brando starred under the direction of his old friend Christian Marquand.

A *Dry White Season* was a rare late film for Brando, in that he played a hero rather than a criminal or villain. And though the part was small, he was nominated for multiple Supporting Actor prizes, including an Academy Award. Brando's tweedy barrister was a charming persona with his gravelly voice and wheeze and ponderousness—describing his orchids as "naughty mistresses" that have repaid his loyalty by giving him "a permanent allergy." The proper Brit, he plies his visitor with refreshment and reacts fastidiously to the purpose of Benjamin du Toit's (Donald Sutherland) visit. "Oh, Justice," MacKenzie says, as if suddenly becoming aware of a foul odor, "well I'm afraid that's a trifle more complex to serve you up than a cup of tea.... You see, justice and law, Mr. du Toit, are often just... well, they, I suppose they could be described as distant cousins, and here in South Africa, they're simply not on speaking terms at all." The live chess game on his desk ensures that he'll take the case; that he understands the match is as winnable as it is incremental, with one side having everything to lose, the other everything to gain. In court, the mannerisms of the eccentric barrister distract from his wits. Leaning on his cane, he circles the courtroom, gently ridiculing and then passionately attacking the witnesses called to defend the racist regime. He knows that no amount of evidence will convict the police interrogators who tortured his client to death. Brando's grimace of disgust—brows twitching, lips moving in silent protest as the judge announces the verdict of innocent—conveys the pain of life in the moment. Yet he is equally aware of the regime's eventual defeat. The verdict is no more consequential than a fly landing in his tea; the warrior (who has seen worse) will carry on.

Brando was distressed by the cut of A *Dry White Season* that he was shown before its release. With the exception of his own cameo, and other solid contributions from leading actors, he found the work amateurish, especially the editing. Because he believed in the film's politics, he offered to fund and supervise reediting. When he was rebuffed, Brando was so incensed that he did a television interview on *Saturday Night with Connie Chung* to publicize what he believed to be MGM's indifference to the film. Still, *A Dry White Season* did better than he expected, earning respectful reviews from major critics who uniformly praised Brando's performance.[67]

One of the most successful films of Brando's late career was a comedy, *The Freshman* (1990). Despite Brando's insistence that he lacked aptitude for the genre, he played comic roles throughout his career (*The Teahouse of the August Moon*; *Guys and Dolls*; *Bedtime Story*; *Candy*), and two of his biggest roles in the 1990s, in *The Freshman* and *Free Money*, were comic. He could get along with anyone who had a sense of humor, and his own taste in comedy tended toward the arcane.[68] Among his favorite comedians was a Jewish standup performer named Willie Howard, whose routines Brando saw when he was a young actor in New York. Howard's signature persona, Professor Pierre Ginsbairge, spoke with a French-inflected Yiddish accent. Brando liked to catch Howard's shows between his own matinee and evening performances, finding this an ideal way to relax. He called Howard "the most ridiculous person I ever saw in my life... truly silly," and remembered his own conspicuousness, roaring with laughter among mostly unmoved audiences. On occasion, Howard, noticing the devotee, would play directly to Brando, who never met the comic, afraid that would mar the magic of his humor.[69]

Howard's specialty was double-talk, deliberately unintelligible speech combining actual and nonsensical words, a discourse that Brando perfected—to the dismay, in one instance, of *Young Lions* costar May Britt. Seated beside Brando at the cast dinner, the young Swedish actress, who considered her English adequate, couldn't understand anything he said. He later confessed that he had been doing double-talk.[70] That Britt recalls her embarrassment so fondly suggests his ability to draw people into his irrepressible humor. Brando's sister Fran saw this as "one of his most endearing and exhilarating qualities. Part of it comes from his uncanny ability to observe and mimic. Besides being able to catch and portray people instantly, he is also able to see many hidden or unrecognized qualities in people. Through mimicry and exaggeration and wit and timing... he is able to reduce the mimicked and others to helpless laughter—it is irresistible. And he can make lots of fun of himself as well."[71] Brando was never more fun than when he was doing comedy, which David Niven confirmed just after filming closed on *Bedtime Story* (1964). "I miss you very much and absolutely *loved* working with you," Niven wrote, proposing they appear together in Milos Forman's upcoming *King Rat*.[72]

Brando's passion for Jewish comedians like Howard, Jackie Mason, and Woody Allen made him receptive to Andrew Bergman's script for *The Freshman*, which he read in the spring of 1988. Brando had enjoyed Bergman's *The In-Laws* and was amused by this story of Carmine Sabatini, a mobster with a striking resemblance to Don Corleone, who hires an innocent film student to transport endangered species for an exclusive gourmand club. Full of twists and turns, the movie had an offbeat comic quality that appealed to Brando, who had no qualms about parodying his role in *The Godfather*. While some were offended by what they saw as the desecration of a cultural icon, Brando had never taken himself that seriously. He didn't believe he was, nor did he like being treated as, larger than life. He was not above exploiting the adulation, however.

What he valued was humor, and he would have agreed with Edward (BD Wong), the animal keeper in *The Freshman*, who

asks, "Without humor, what do we have?" In prerelease publicity, Brando explained that "there is no substitute for laughter in
this frightened and endlessly twisting world."[73] Anything, from
Brando's perspective, could be illuminated through the lens of
comedy. His parody of Don Corleone was an expression of affection as well as possession: Only the originator could do justice to
the original. While many had imitated the Don since his immor-
talization in 1972, Brando alone knew his vulnerabilities, and
consequently his comedic potential. Uneducated, resentful of
missed opportunities, domineering, impatient—all this was fair
game for the characterization of Carmine Sabatini.

An incident from June 1989, during the New York filming of
The Freshman, revealed that comedy was no trivial pursuit. One
night in Little Italy, Brando was introduced to John Gotti, the
crime boss, who happened to be playing cards with "an extraordinary group of characters straight out of the Mafia yearbook."
The actor decided to outsmart Gotti with a card trick, using a
shaved deck he often carried. "Suddenly the whole room" was
"quiet as a tomb," as Gotti's companions pondered how to react
to this possible *"disrespect."* Politely and quickly, Brando left.
Gotti called a few days later with an invitation to a fight, which
Brando declined.[74] Where there is humor, Brando recognized,
there is risk. The best comedians followed their instincts fear-
lessly, aware that the greater the danger, the greater the payoff.

From this perspective, *The Freshman* is a work that explores
rather than takes comic risks, with scenarios like the animal-loving
stepfather who shoots wildly at hunters; the German chef who
sings "Deutschland über Alles" while preparing endangered species for wealthy gourmands; the narcissistic banalities of an NYU
film professor. The main theme is a contrast between the imitation and the original, embodied by Carmine Sabatini, whose
likeness to the Godfather is unmentionable because it annoys
him. Sabatini is a childish thug, cracking nuts barehanded while

awaiting an assent to a demand, bullying a broker reporting low stock returns. Like the *Mona Lisa* hanging in Sabatini's living room, which his daughter claims is the original, Sabatini's authenticity is supposed to be equivalent, even superior, to what everyone takes as genuine. Both Sabatini and Corleone are Hollywood fictions, the film insists; if you liked one, you'll like the other. Despite the gimmickry, filmgoers largely complied.

While some remember *The Freshman* for the image of a portly, aged Brando on ice skates, the telling scene features Sabatini and the freshman Clark Kellogg (Matthew Broderick) in his dorm room. With its attention to parents lost and found, a poetry recitation, and allusions to *Curious George*, the scene was determined to be sincere, and there were many ways it could have gone wrong. But Brando kept things light, avoiding sentimentality. He draws attention to their roles, asking Clark with a chuckle whether he wants a bedtime story as he settles into an armchair, invoking a paternal familiarity that remains credible even when the plot's resolution reveals that he has been acting all along. Recordings exist of Brando playing a father for real. An extended 1964 script commentary on *The Chase* (his dictation later typed into transcripts by assistants) is interrupted by Brando impersonating Higgledy-Piggledy for his six-year-old son Christian. "Again, Daddy, again!" the boy commands, as the actor improvises solely for his pleasure.[75] Like all children, and probably Brando's in particular, Christian dreads the ending, which means bedtime and his father's withdrawal—just for the night or maybe for days or months. Still, while the dramatic invention lasts, the child has what he wants, and he at least could care less about the quality of the acting.

Exposing the make-believe dampens neither desire nor the necessity for good acting. It is appropriate that the film's subject is an eating association, for *The Freshman* is also about the appetite for cultural icons, which takes in the Don, *Mona Lisa*,

At home, 1955. Mondadori Portfolio via Getty Images.

and *Curious George*: figures so compelling that people can never get enough of them. Brando appeases these appetites by keeping the copy close to the original and providing pointed echoes. For example, Sabatini's repetition of his favorite image from the poem Clark recites, the reference to the white cat ("the certainty of his fur"), parallels Vito Corleone, repeating Michael Corleone's pride in the little son who "reads the funny papers." The symbolic

white Persian also registers personal history: Brando, according to friends (and photographs), seemed always to have a white
cat among his pets.[76] This moment at the dorm, like others from
Brando's late films, refers to his movie and his personal-but-public
past. (The camera panning the office effects of his psychiatrist in
Don Juan DeMarco passes a framed photograph of Brando and
his father from their joint appearance on *Person to Person*, with
Edward R. Murrow, the only kind of familial scene the actor was
willing to share—one that was already accessible.)

On May 16, 1990, Brando's personal life became scandalously
exposed. Christian Brando fatally shot Dag Drollet, the boyfriend
of his half-sister Cheyenne in his father's Mulholland Drive
home. Drollet and Cheyenne had been together for three years,
and though the relationship was now precarious, she was seven
months pregnant with his child. Brando did everything possible
to help Christian, hiring top Los Angeles lawyers William Kunstler and Robert Shapiro and trying to placate a media to whom he

Marlon Sr. and Marlon Jr., 1955, Edward R. Murrow's
Person to Person show. © Bettmann/Corbis.

had now become easy prey. Brando aged dramatically and vac-
illated between obsessive consultations with the defense team
and withdrawal into his misery. Chief among his worries was
shielding twenty-year-old Cheyenne, whose mental health had
been a growing concern. In August 1989, during filming of *The
Freshman*, Cheyenne had been in a single-car accident in Tahiti,
and Brando had flown back to Los Angeles to oversee her surgery
for a fractured skull and facial injuries. After the shooting, she
was spirited off to Tahiti, and then to Europe, to avoid subpoenas
to testify in California and, later, Tahiti. Reports on Cheyenne's
psychological problems were inconclusive, but it was clear that
drug use catalyzed or exacerbated her fragile mental health.

Brando never entirely recovered from the trauma of the killing
and his son's trial and prison sentence for voluntary manslaugh-
ter. His feelings of guilt were palpable during (televised) trial
testimony, where he confessed that his own unconventional and
erratic lifestyle had led, however inadvertently, to this sordid
violence. He tried to ensure some protection for Christian in jail

Brando with Christian during trial, 1990. AP.

by consulting old friends from the Black Panthers.[77] But he could not help his precious daughter, who committed suicide by hanging at the age of twenty-five, in Tahiti.

Brando did not attend the funeral. A wrongful-death suit filed against Christian and Brando by the family of Dag Drollet was one reason, but it probably also was because he couldn't bear it. He never returned to Tetiaroa. His handwriting became shaky and his taste in poetry bleaker. He had always read poetry for consolation. In his *Pocket Book of Verse*, he underscored stanzas from Thomas Hood's famous "The Bridge of Sighs," about a young woman's suicide, and from Philip Larkin's "Ambulances," about the miseries that stop at every door.

In the aftermath of these events, Brando was often depressed, sometimes irascible. When a film set, like that of *Columbus*, was already troubled, the role suffered. He never took his unhappiness out on subordinates, but directors and producers had long been fair game, and they were especially so during this period. As an actor, he had controlled his private furies, drawing on them for characterizations; *Columbus* was one of the few times where they were reflected in a flat, lifeless performance.

THE TORTURER AND THE HEALER: *COLUMBUS* AND *DON JUAN DeMARCO*

Brando's experience on *Christopher Columbus: The Discovery* was one of the most negative of his late career; he battled with the father-son producers Alexander and Ilya Salkind over the film's content, he disappointed his friends in the Indian community for taking part in it, and his contribution to the film was an embarrassment. What made the whole fiasco even more painful was that the film's subject, the first encounter with the Indians of the Americas, was one about which he cared deeply. Perhaps most important, Brando had already worked with the Salkinds on *Superman* and should have known how unlikely they were to make a film on this subject that was anywhere close to what he had in mind. But Brando needed money to pay bills from Christian's trial, and his multimillion-dollar salary left him in no position to complain about producers seeking to capitalize on the five-hundredth anniversary of Columbus's voyage to the New World. Yet Brando hoped that intellectual honesty could be reconciled with commercial success. He also hoped that the clause in his contract stipulating that the film honor the historical facts would ensure him significant influence, especially given his wealth of knowledge about the Indians. Moreover, he was enthusiastic about playing Tomas de Torquemada. The role of the sadistic fifteenth-century priest and confessor to Queen Isabella of Spain and architect of the Spanish Inquisition was made for Brando, who appreciated the complex possibilities of this learned hypocrite. Like Hitler, Torquemada was rumored to have had Jewish ancestry, which may have fueled his bigotry and fanaticism. Distressed by the stature and influence of Spain's Jews, in 1478 he managed to institutionalize his paranoia in the Holy Office for the Propagation of the Christian Faith. Under his auspices as Grand Inquisitor of Spain, appointed by Pope Sixtus IV, Torquemada effected the expulsion of more than forty thousand Spanish Jews and the death by torture of an additional two thousand.

Brando was able through script revisions to document the cruelty of Torquemada, but he had little success countering the film's suppression of Columbus's violence against the natives. "Instead of a day for celebration, Columbus Day ought to be one of mourning. I wanted to tell the truth about how he and his minions exploited and killed the Indians who greeted them," Brando said, describing how he managed to convince Ilya Salkind of the significance as well as potential profitability of a truthful portrait of Columbus. When Salkind's father, Alexander, arrived on the set, however, Brando's script was tabled. At that point, Brando could have walked out, had he been willing to forgo his salary. Instead, the disconsolate actor responded with "an embarrassingly bad performance," the only time in his career where he was deliberately ineffective in a role.[78] "No one can sue you for a bad performance," he said when it was over.[79] Brando's sabotage was about loyalty—to friends as well as to historical truth. Personal relationships, some of them longstanding, were at stake. But anger and depression probably also played a part.

A January 3, 1992, letter to Brando from Jumping Bull of the Pine Ridge Reservation in South Dakota, written on behalf of American Indian Movement members, begins with the Indian version of Columbus: "For us, Columbus was the first man to commit genocide against the American Indians who welcomed him so warmly and who helped him find his gold.... They were forced to give up their religion or die. They all died anyway." Word has it, the letter continues, that the Salkind film portrays Columbus as a hero. Citing Brando's record of support—questioning by the FBI; arrests; taking fire from the National Guard in Menominee, Wisconsin; smoking the sacred pipe and sweating away sins—the group wonders how Brando, "our brother always," could have been reconciled to this travesty.[80] The truth was, he hadn't been. In the end, the movie failed in every possible way. One reviewer noted that, "to glimpse our greatest actor in this mega-claptrap is a cruelty far worse than anything Torquemada could devise."[81] *Christopher Columbus: The Discovery* was a rare film in which Brando brought his personal travails to the set, where they combined with genuine professional difficulties.

More commonly, even in the 1990s, no matter how reluctant Brando might have been to go to work, once he got there, acting distracted him from his private troubles, providing relief, even pleasure. This was true of the first film he made with Johnny

Depp, who became a good friend. Depp's idealism, their similar senses of humor, their shared love of boxing, and the young actor's promise solidified the bond.

Filming for *Don Juan DeMarco* (1995) began in July 1994. Still uncertain about working on it even as late as January, Brando had sought the opinion of filmmaker Joseph Brutsman, who would later work with him on *Free Money*. Brutsman's predictions proved accurate: that Depp's character, a misunderstood eccentric typical of Depp's dramatic risk-taking, would ensure young fans; that Brando as a psychiatrist whose dimming sexuality is awakened by a depressed youth convinced he is Don Juan would draw mature audiences; that the script, with Depp and Brando in the leads, would yield an appealing film.[82] Women devastated by Brando over the years might have enjoyed watching the aged overweight actor in a toupee taking instruction from a young Don Juan—if they recognized him. Brando plays normalcy so naturally here that he nearly disappears.

After all the years of therapy, Brando seemed to relish modeling his good psychiatrist Mickler on the empathetic G. L. Harrington. The role also allowed him to highlight methods that he had found personally beneficial. One of them, evident in his work with Quincy Jones on *Jericho*, was learning other languages and talking to people in their own. Dr. Mickler rescues Don Juan from suicide in the first scene by embracing his fantasy. Another was a resistance to psychotropic drugs; an exploratory talking cure, Mickler suggests, works best. But when he tells his wife, "No fire, no heat no heat, no life . . . this is a twelve rounder and this is the third round, and you and I are going to go out of here like Halley's comet," he seemed to be speaking for Brando. A few years earlier, at the age of sixty-five, he had written to a producer of *The Freshman* about medical complications from an infected urethra, noting that it was "a blessing" he had ignored the plans of doctors in New York "which would have importantly altered my sexual life."[83] Brando's concerns were sincere: Brando had just fathered a daughter, Ninna, with his housekeeper, Christina Ruiz, with whom he had two more children, in 1992 and 1994. Like his character, he was determined to live out his days to the fullest.

The film reunited Brando with Francis Ford Coppola as producer and drew on Lord Byron's original *Don Juan*. Critics were willing to overlook the clichés.[84] This was a romance, billed as an ideal "date-movie for couples of all ages." The Mickler marriage was solid, just needing cultivation like the garden Marilyn Mickler (Faye Dunaway) tends so carefully. In script revisions, Brando tried to make Mickler more distinctive, but nothing could alter his suburban professionalism.[85] Looking through window blinds upon the Don Juan–influenced transformations of the hospital staff staged daily on the lawn below, Mickler's eyes are remarkable for their blandness, especially when compared with the monstrous chill cast by Don Corleone as he peeks through a different set of blinds. It might have been tempting to equate Brando at this tragic time with the film's characters: the patient who manages to substitute his imagined world for reality and the physician who gradually accepts the substitution, joining his patient on the "Island of Eros." But Brando was too much the realist to mistake celluloid fables, or the celebrity myths they supported, for reality. This may be why he chose to play unqualified villains for his last three films, sometimes probing the characters deeply enough to expose painful aspects of his own life.

VILLAINS REDUX

The last three characters in Brando's late rogues' gallery included an intellectual monomaniac killed by his own creations, Dr. Moreau (*The Island of Dr. Moreau*, 1996); a sadistic, Bible-quoting prison warden, the Swede (*Free Money*, 1998); and a self-pitying, desperate gangster, Max (*The Score*, 2001). Brando found a bit of himself in each of them, as he always did, but he also invested them with current worries, which was rare. While there were sparks of invention in all these performances, they also revealed his exhaustion, and at times he used battles with directors, or the acting process itself, to express contempt toward Hollywood and toward himself for his lifelong participation in its fictions. Brando's performances in these films intensified rather than relieved their grimness. All three were profitable, but *Dr. Moreau* and *Free Money* were critical flops, while *The Score* was a qualified success.

What made the hubristic scientist Dr. Moreau intriguing was the overlap between his interests and Brando's own: the nature of evil; human modification through genetic experimentation; the bonds between humans and animals.[86] A visionary seeking to derail a century of progress, Moreau has retreated to an island where he pursues methods of crossbreeding he hopes will produce a nobler, more altruistic species. The inevitable result, according to the script adapted by Richard Stanley, Michael Herr, and Walon Green from H. G. Wells's classic fantasy, is the creator's death at the hands of his monstrous offspring. Brando held long talks on the film's development with producers and directors, and also improvised freely during filming. A source of his disgruntlement on *Dr. Moreau* was that the film's producers fired Richard Stanley, the original director, who was also the screenwriter before filming began, replacing him with John Frankenheimer. Brando had already spent hours with Stanley discussing the film's themes and script, ground that he had to cover again with Frankenheimer.[87] In keeping with his usual methods, Brando reconceptualized, rewrote, and also improvised much of his scripted part, changes that both directors welcomed. This time, his revisions enabled reflection on historical missteps, including his own. In discussing the film with Frankenheimer and others, he noted that the previous year had been the most difficult of his life. Though he didn't mention details, everyone knew that Brando's daughter Cheyenne had committed suicide in Tahiti five months before he was due on location in Australia for *Dr. Moreau*. The film's account of atom bombs, causing mutations in surviving human populations and untold damage to surrounding ecosystems, paralleled Brando's worry over French nuclear testing near his island of Tetiaroa. Moreau is a self-conceived savior, collecting the forlorn mutants "scattered across the Pacific," their deformations caused by the "French ... exploding their bombs." He explains, "God exists in the very center of the atom past the quark, beyond the nutrinos ... men are animals and I want to make better ones."[88]

Early in the filming, Brando noticed an actor from the Dominican Republic, Nelson de la Rosa, with a genetic mutation, who was two and a half feet tall and weighed twenty-two pounds. De la Rosa had been outfitted in a loincloth with a tail, which Brando found demeaning. So Brando made de la Rosa his sidekick, beside him in nearly every scene, dressed identically.[89] The choice may have represented an ironic recognition of his own needs. Stars typically had entourages, but Brando was especially prone to sidekicks—friends with various forms of expertise in the film industry who became attached to him and benefited from the association. He gave them jobs (as actors, extras, speech coaches, makeup artists, even directors) and they gave him the constancy and loyalty he craved. While the individuals changed over the years, between Manhattan and Hollywood, some remained with him almost to the end of his career. Whatever the rewards, however, the experience of being Brando's sidekick had distinct disadvantages. All of them were diminished by proximity to his stardom, and many, over time, did things to diminish him in return. Through the relationship of Dr. Moreau and Nelson de la Rosa's character of Majai, Brando seems to have imagined an ideal version of the curious interdependence between the

Brando with Nelson de la Rosa on the set of *Dr. Moreau*. (Brando's friend Philip Rhodes stands to his left.) © Avra Douglas/courtesy of Avra Douglas.

dominant, domineering man and the buddy, whose job is to placate, humor, and entertain the stronger partner. Like Lear and his fool, they are as essential to one another as water and air.[90]

The main concern of *The Island of Dr. Moreau* was progeny and inheritance, and Brando's personal life appears also to have found its way into the film here. All of the human animal hybrids on the island bear Moreau's DNA, but the most highly evolved are three sons and a daughter who have been crossed with domestic animals. Literate, formally dressed, Aissa (Fairuza Balk) and M'Ling (Marco Hofschneider) are part feline; Azazello (Temuera Morrison) and Waggdi (Miguel Lopez) are part canine. The doctor has seen to their training and cultivation, the lovely Aissa's in particular. When the leopard man, Lo-Mai (Mark Dacascos), stands trial for slaughtering a rabbit (vegetarianism is compulsory on Moreau's island; killing is a power reserved for the doctor), Azazello, the eldest "son," with an appetite for the hunt, steps in and shoots Lo-Mai after Moreau has granted the creature clemency—a moment that replicates, eerily, Christian Brando's shooting of Dag Drollet. The parallels between Dr. Moreau's daughter, the object of every male eye, and Brando's precious Cheyenne, whose death must have weighed on him, were also striking. Brando rarely played a father on film—his lone previous exception was *The Godfather*—and the decision to assume the role of a diabolical patriarch at a time when his own family life was in such disarray exemplifies an extraordinary confluence of private and public experience.

However affected he was by the overlapping issues, Brando had periods during which he relaxed. He took characteristic pleasure in communing with Australian wildlife. Ever playful, he turned pages of scripted dialogue into paper airplanes and launched them from the balcony of his hotel room. He enjoyed creating Moreau's persona: shaving his head and eyebrows; fashioning buckteeth and the pasty-white coating for Moreau's skin, to protect him from the thinning of the ozone layer; selecting the colorful costumes that were all replicated for de la Rosa's Majai. Brando's Moreau is another mannered Brit who cloaks ambition in affectation. Ice bucket on head, munching on greens, Bach in the background, he tells Aissa, as she massages his shoulders, that he is "simply going to *perish* from the heat." His response to her fears about reversion is similarly quaint. "You're an absolute angel," he says. "You're beautiful inside, you're beautiful outside." His laughter at her wish to look like him produces a full-fanged smile. His techniques of persuasion prove less effective with the bestial offspring that invade his lair. He tells them that their piano banging reminds him of Schoenberg's twelve-tone music, anxious humoring that belabors the distance between the effete scientist and his monsters. Moreau's genteel terror upon discovering that a gruesome death is imminent is marvelously conveyed. While

Conversing with a parrot. © Avra Douglas/courtesy of Avra Douglas.

the film was a mess, Brando still had his moments delivering
what was termed, in an otherwise damning review, "an affectionate caricature of British ham acting."[91] But personal trauma
had aged him, and his sadness was patent. Sheer toughness got
him through the shoot.

Critical reaction to the film was scathing, with the exception
of a few critics who enjoyed watching Brando reprise the role
that Charles Laughton had played in *Island of Lost Souls* (1932).
In the 1990s, when Brando had grown accustomed to ridicule, he
expected that his villains would be misunderstood, even reviled.[92]
Whether or not a film was well received, he almost always had his
pleasures on a set. The invitation for the "Pain No More Party" he
threw at the end of *Dr. Moreau* parodied the rhetoric of novel and
script: "You Must Come To Eat Plenty Flesh—That Is The Law/
You Must Slurp Up Drink—That Is The Law/You Must Dance
Wildly And Laugh Uncontrollably—That Is The Law." And it suggested that his pleasure was shared. It was also reciprocated,
judging from the crew's inscription on the book *Australia: The
Beautiful Land* that they gave him: "You Came To Our Country

As A World Famous 'Actor' You Leave Our Shores As Marlon A 'Mate' Of Ours."[93]

Despite disappointments like *The Island of Dr. Moreau*—some of them initiated or exacerbated by his own irritability or impatience—Brando continued to pursue roles and entertain options for promising projects with major writers and directors (e.g., David Lynch, Baz Luhrmann—he opted out of Lurhmann's invitation to perform in his postmodernized *Romeo and Juliet*, confessing that he couldn't "see my way clear to keeping the characters aright in the circumstances").[94] Though he said his principal motivation was money, the sheer variety of his activity belies this. In April 1997, he traveled to Mexico City to meet with the Nobel Prize–winning Colombian author Gabriel García Márquez about adapting his novel *Autumn of the Patriarch* for film. "When we met, I was very busy trying to convey my ideas in Spanish," Brando writes to "Gabriel" that May, "as the tequila hit home I felt that I was drifting from the points I wanted to make. It was very disconcerting and rare to look into a pair of eyes that moved very little and saw very much." This intriguing project, which involved Sean Penn, Miriam Colon, and Mike Medavoy, in addition to Brando, never materialized.[95]

Of the films he worked on during this decade, *Free Money* (1998) was the most derided and the one he most enjoyed making. A farcical blend of satire and slapstick, directed by the Canadian Yves Simoneau with a screenplay by Anthony Peck and Joseph Brutsman, the film was about Sven Sorenson, a corrupt prison warden called "the Swede" (Brando), in a Minnesota backwater, who freely executes rebellious prisoners. At home, he treats like inmates the unfortunate men—Bud (Charlie Sheen) and Larry (Thomas Haden Church)—coerced into marrying his spoiled twin daughters. Donald Sutherland was Rolf Rausenberger, a judge whose villainy supports Brando's warden, and Mira Sorvino was Karen Polarski, the judge's estranged daughter, who becomes an FBI agent and returns to her hometown to redress the wrongs of her father and the Swede. Despite the solid cast, and Brando's own eagerness to make good on his part, the oddity and excess of the story failed to strike a chord with audiences. Here was another late project where a big paycheck and the pleasures of working with other talented actors were outweighed by the film's harsh reception.

Yet, in *Free Money* Brando played his most unqualified villain ever, and the film is therefore revealing of his views on evil and his comic method. Brando's participation in the film was unstinting: He contributed ideas for characterizations, scenes, and dialogue and drew liberally on his own experience. In the first scene, Brando's Swede is awakened abruptly by his daughters, and he cautions them sternly about the dangers of startling him—a lifelong issue for Brando. It helped that he was familiar with the film's setting from his years at military school in Faribault, Minnesota. Familiar, too, was the mindset of this Bible-thumping enforcer who tattoos "Jesus Saves" on his skull and drapes an American flag over the made-to-order truck he cherishes as much as his daughters. The characterization of a warden known for killing escapees in cold blood would have made sense to Brando, who spent years reading about and protesting capital punishment and unjust sentences.[96] "Think big, be big, like the Swede," one hapless son-in-law (Bud) says to the other (Larry), advice that reinforces the town ethic: Power alone matters.

Free Money's thematic insistence that imprisonment has little to do with being locked up is echoed by cinematography that exposes the dilapidation of this remote forest region, which keeps things gloomy despite the humor. Indeed, Brando was funniest on film when circumstances were grim. And the Swede's prison is as bad as they come; predatory guards give free rein to the worst inmate elements. Here, too, Brando drew on experience; worries over Christian Brando serving time in California energized his critique of the movie's barbaric penal code.[97] The outside is no improvement; everyone lives in fear of the Swede and his cronies.

Whether it's his way of dealing with recent events or simply distracting himself from them, Brando embraces the tradition of Laurel and Hardy and W. C. Fields: his sputtering animal sorrow while gazing on his stolen truck smashed by a railroad car; the deadpan twang as he snaps at a subordinate, "I want you to shut every hole in your body"; and the chuckling, "See you in church," before preparing to grind up Bud and Larry in a garbage truck. The sons-in-law are saved by Sorvino the FBI agent, who is then assaulted by the Swede. Some viewers were appalled to see Brando, looking like Bozo the Clown with reddish tufts of hair, smash Sorvino on the head with her shoe heel, muttering, "This is hurtin' you a lot more than it is me, and that's the way it oughta be." But his reaction when she, blood running down her face, shoots him is as genuine as Paul's in *Last Tango*. Registering the shock of mortal gun wounds was a Brando specialty extending back to childhood, when he often impressed other kids with his dramatic finishes.[98] Because this is farce, the Swede is back to normal in the next scene, an inmate now in the jail he formerly ruled, visited by the new warden (Martin Sheen).

According to scriptwriter Brutsman and director Yves Simoneau, Brando was responsible for the boldest acts of comedy in *Free Money*. He improvised the flag-draped blessing of the Swede's new truck, the Bible-reading scene where he lays down the rules of the household to his "fornicating" sons-in-law; the dinner scene after his truck is stolen where he grouses darkly in Swedish-inflected English; and the notorious moment when he falls facedown into a toilet bowl. He was also responsible for the sterling cast: Donald Sutherland (again), Mira Sorvino, and Charlie Sheen all jumped at the chance to work with him.

Brutsman and Simoneau offer a window into Brando's ideas about comedy, in noting how he liked to be "outside of the plot,"

The Swede with FBI agent Polarski. Newscom.

viewing anything scripted as dated, preferring spontaneity.[99] Brando said in reference to Lily Tomlin that "all of her humor comes from anguish." Then he added, thinking about other comedians he enjoyed—Don Rickles, Richard Pryor, Moms Mabley—that "most humor does."[100] Twenty years later, he seems to have known what that meant from deep within. *Free Money* was politely ignored by major critics and received mostly negative reviews, though it was profitable, as were all of Brando's late films, whatever their drawbacks.

After extravagant performances as Dr. Moreau and the Swede, Brando played a relatively sedate character in his last released film (on July 13, 2001), a businessman-gangster in a crime thriller set in Montreal. *The Score* (2001), starring Robert De Niro (Nick) and Ed Norton (Jack), was a three-generational star vehicle with endless plot twists. As usual, Brando made the genial desperation of his wheeler-dealer persona, Max, look like second nature. Brando's goal, as he told David Page, his costumer, with whom he had extensive conversations about the character, was to play a gay man as the norm. Max is an aesthete who lives in a lavishly decorated mansion with an indoor pool and wears expensive suits, gold rings, and silk dressing gowns with cravats. His engineering of deals has supported his appetite for luxury and kept him a step ahead of the mob...until now.

Critics liked the film. Roger Ebert called it "a classic heist movie," applauding Brando's "dialed-down Sidney Greenstreet." Peter Travers agreed that Brando, "his eyes alive with mischief, is the life of the movie."[101] Despite disgust with Muppets creator Frank Oz, another late director Brando thought incompetent, he enjoyed working with De Niro and Norton and managed to give his character depth. Max is a performer who makes an entrance everywhere he goes, cajoling but never showing his cards. The trouble is, he's not that good: a wanna-be actor-manipulator. Thus, his vulnerabilities are also patent: He's a gay man in a world of thugs, dependent on the skills of others.

He removes his mask only once, in a scene with Nick, his protégé, beside Max's basement pool, its Roman imperial style reminding us that both actors played "the Godfather." In a paisley blue silk robe, with a matching towel, a bottle of champagne, and a glass in his hand, Brando reveals Max's pathos. He and Nick both know he is lying low from the mobsters posted on his

Poolside in *The Score*. Newscom.

doorstep who are ready to pounce if he doesn't produce their money. Max has to plead with Nick to save his life by taking the kind of risk Nick has spent a career avoiding. Max leans in, grasping the pool railing, his voice a raspy whisper: "I'm gonna tell you something. For the first time in my life, I'm scared. I don't know why it is, I was never scared before but I'm scared now, Nick . . . if I don't get him his money . . . don't don't don't. Don't let me slide on this one." His face is anguished, his eyes sad and blue; he is simply an old man in distress. Because Nick is humane, he responds to Max's need.

In the last scene, Max lies in bed watching the news, barely reacting when he learns that Nick has scored, and he is safe. Max doesn't smile because he knows he'll never really be safe. Brando's final image on screen conveys hardness, the realistic acceptance of life's burden.

Max was the last Brando character to appear on screen, but the last one he played was an animated character, Mrs. Sour, founder and head of the "Mrs. Sour Candy Company." *The Big Bug Man* was never completed because the producers could not get financing, but Brando recorded his part. Mrs. Sour was Brando in full feminine regalia: ringlets, wide-set blue-gray eyes, a pair of sagging cheeks to match the sagging breasts, a river of wrinkles flowing from forehead to chest. Brando fashioned a soft falsetto voice and managed to convey wisdom and jadedness in Mrs. Sour's signature stance: one skinny arm provocatively lifting an edge of her dress to reveal ruffled polka-dot panties, the other primping her curls. Sadness and exhaustion prevail in the belligerent, self-involved, still aggressively perceptive Brando eyes.

While supposedly a lark, advertisements promising "a story of how celebrity and success can corrupt even the most good-hearted among us" suggest a deeper meaning that might have appealed to Brando.[102] This animated film, hand-drawn by Peter Shin, also starred Brendan Fraser as Howard Kind, a shy,

Mrs. Sour. Character design by Peter Shin (original in color).

diminutive candy-company employee who is bitten by bugs and transformed into a superhero, the "Big Bug Man." Brando spent a day recording Mrs. Sour's three appearances in the film, and he dressed accordingly. On June 10, 2004 (exactly twenty-one days before his death), he donned a blonde wig, dress, white gloves, and makeup to play the old lady "who sounds like the Godfather."[103] Despite the oxygen tank, which he depended on as death approached, Brando still managed to move the voice directors recording the performance with his acting. As one of them noted, somehow, remarkably, "He *became* her."[104] A corrupt, narcissistic old lady owner of a candy company—who could have predicted this as the Brando character to complete the final decade?[105]

CHAPTER EIGHT

CITIZEN OF THE PLANET

From the beginning of his career to the end, Brando treated his celebrity as a means to public ends. During his theater days, he was engaged in philanthropy, supplementing performances in Ben Hecht's *A Flag Is Born* with cross-country touring where he gave speeches to raise money for a Jewish state. Brando's altruistic uses of fame expressed ambivalence toward work he deemed popular entertainment and dreams of doing something more consequential. He sided instinctively with the vulnerable and the excluded, instincts that became habits at school, on Broadway, in Hollywood, and in his travels.

Now that we have a fuller record of what Brando said, read, and did, it's possible to grasp the consistency of his commitments to learning, self-development, and political causes. There was a reason why he thought of becoming a minister after he achieved fame in *Streetcar*.[1] Brando was a lifelong seeker in pursuit of greater purpose. He was concerned about the world, including its environment, plant and animal life, the interdependencies of ecosystems, and its human cultures. A fan of scientific innovation, he was among the first in Hollywood to own a personal computer.[2] His ambitions transcended acting, with his desire to know *more*, and to *do something* about the injustices and suffering he saw everywhere.

BORN TRAVELER

"I was born in Omaha, Nebraska, and I grew up in America, but I consider myself a citizen of the planet," Brando said in 1978. Patriotism, he continued, postpones acceptance of the inevitable; the earth is "getting smaller all the time . . . pollution doesn't recognize borders. Weather changes that have been brought about by the manipulations of man don't recognize frontiers. Economics certainly doesn't recognize frontiers. Everything is overlapping, whether we like it or not—we are our neighbor's keeper."[3] "Even as a boy, Bud had a great desire to travel, to see far-away places," his mother recalled. "He'd often start on mysterious journeys all by himself."[4] Reading *National Geographic* magazines as a teenager, he was especially drawn to Polynesia. The multicultural world of Manhattan in the 1940s whetted his appetite for human variety, and Broadway success provided the means for travel. As soon as he was able, at the close of *A Streetcar Named Desire* in 1949, Brando went to Europe, spending three months there, mostly in Paris. He studied French (his copy of Berlitz's *Deuxième Livre,* a "natural method" of French conversation, was annotated copiously) and explored, only lured home by the need to earn a living.[5] But the pattern was set: He would be a traveler for life, whether journeying to Egypt and Istanbul for pleasure (February 1967), Australia for work (*The Island of Dr. Moreau*), Southeast Asia for UNICEF, or his Taihitian island Tetiaroa for rest.[6] "I always wanted to go to Tahiti," Brando told a journalist in French in 1997. "And also Japan . . . and to France and to England and especially Ireland . . . my ancestral home. Films have allowed me to travel everywhere in the world."[7]

In 1956, Brando toured the Far East as a prelude to filming in Japan of *The Teahouse of the August Moon*, accompanied by George Englund, Stewart Stern, and the photographer Herman Leonard. Traveling through the Philippines, Thailand, Hong

Brando in Bangkok with Buddha statue. © Herman Leonard Photography, LLC, www
.hermanleonard.com.

Kong, and Indonesia, Brando and Englund were doing research for the Pennebaker Productions film on the UN, which Stern, a scriptwriter, had been hired to develop. By Jakarta, Brando had grown tired of the full entourage. Leaving a note for Englund and Stern, he chartered a plane and flew to Bali with Leonard. "From now on," Brando told the photographer, "you're Mr. Jones and I'm Mr. Smith, *capiche*?" Leonard recalled that the scheme was almost foiled at the outset in Denpasar, when two hundred American tourists suddenly poured through the hotel lobby to register. "Marlon took one look, grabbed me by the collar and leaped over the counter and out the back. With the help of the hotel manager, we escaped in the back of a laundry truck." They ended up at the palace of Prince Tjorkorda Agung Sukawati in Ubud. The "palace" was a series of raised wooden cottages without electricity or running water, but Leonard and Brando felt that they had "found paradise." The prince treated them to daily dances and magic shows, and they were liberated from the modern world: no T-shirts, taxis, or telephones, just rice paddies and bamboo. Leonard's only regret was that the hundreds of photographs he took during this idyllic sojourn were lost. When Brando went on to Japan, Leonard returned to New York, sending all his negatives, as requested, to the Pennebaker files in Hollywood. He never saw them again. All that time "with Marlon in all those exotic places surely must have produced some great classic images," the photographer reflected sadly in December 2004, five months after Brando's death. For the much-photographed actor, it was probably a relief that the record of that respite from fame survived only in memory.[8]

Brando seemed to have his own cache of images to draw on when he chose. Looking at the sky during a conversation on Tetiaroa, Brando noted, "That star next to the moon is always there," which reminded him of a time "in Marrakech on a sparkling, crystalline desert night and I saw the same star. I'd been

talking to this girl a long time—it was four in the morning, and
the muezzin came out in his minaret and started chanting....
It made me feel like I was in Baghdad in the twelfth century."[9]
Sometimes, as in Bali or Marrakech, it was possible to reach a
setting so pure that it felt like a different era. Brando might well
have been a time traveler if he could have been.

The most obvious prospect for travel was on-location filming. All terms being equal—subject, screenplay, director,
pay—Brando's willingness to accept a project was guided by how
keen he was to visit its production site, as in his famous choice of
Polynesian islands (*Mutiny on the Bounty*) over Middle Eastern
desert (*Lawrence of Arabia*). On his first trip abroad for a film,
during the spring of 1951, Brando had traveled to the Morelos
region of Mexican revolutionary leader Emiliano Zapata, met
people who had known Zapata (who died in 1919), and picked up
some Spanish. What he did most of all was watch the men—the
way they walked, sat, ate, rode horses, and treated women, children, and animals. He also fell in love—with Mexican-American
actress Movita Castaneda—and he arranged for her to have a part
as an extra in the upcoming film. This too would become standard practice. For Brando, getting to know a region and culture
would involve language study (he had dozens of conversation
and grammar books from countries he visited), learning local
customs and traditions, while sampling the cuisine and sleeping
with the women.

In his early years as a traveler, Brando was content simply to
savor the atmosphere of Paris, Anenecuilco (Zapata's hometown),
Bali. He preferred anonymity, following the recommendations
of friends for people to look up, locals who might have an extra
bed or their own to offer. He already knew that going anywhere
as a celebrity distorted relationships. This is one reason why foreign travel was appealing to Brando: It offered a better prospect
for freely observing people in their home habitats. The human

zoo was as fascinating to him as the animal kind. Zoologist Desmond Morris, whom Brando sought out in the 1990s after reading his work, noted that they shared "insatiable curiosity" and were both "serious observers of the minutiae of human actions." He was so impressed by the actor that he devoted a chapter to their meeting in *Watching: Encounters with Humans and Other Animals* (2006), which closed with an account of how they were besieged by paparazzi after a London dinner.[10] Morris witnessed how difficult it was for Brando to fulfill his predilection for exploring and looking.[11]

Brando also had an extreme sense of fairness, and he could be fierce if he felt wronged. Lovers, friends, and professional acquaintances recalled his sensitivity to slights, his fear of being cheated or exploited. He externalized this worry as well in his regard for the unfortunate: kids vulnerable to bullies, people he encountered who were poor or neglected, and minorities in the United States and abroad. Brando distrusted power, and he tended to suspect people who had it. Almost as soon as he was famous, he joined efforts to improve things for victims of poverty or prejudice. A telegram he wrote in 1960 shows that he was ever alert to slurs and prepared to use his celebrity to call attention to them. Addressed to the news editor at KNXT, the local Hollywood station, about their coverage of the Olympic Games, the telegram noted that the commentators at the ski-jumping event "consistently referred to the Japanese as Japs. This is a term that is considered by the Japanese as unsavory and derogatory. I am sure that this was an oversight but felt obliged to send this."[12]

Being an actor and a citizen of the planet seems to have merged in Brando. Harold Clurman, while directing the very young performer, was one of the first to see the inseparability of these callings. Clurman thought Brando's genius as an actor was rooted in personal suffering. At the same time, Clurman felt Brando couldn't live up to his own standards of virtue, so he continually sought purification.[13] While Clurman's characterization may strain credibility in light of all the women Brando seduced, those close to him confirmed his idealism. He used his celebrity to spotlight conditions that would otherwise be ignored. He believed in the principle he marked in a passage from Aristotle's *Nicomachean Ethics*: "The life of money-making is one undertaken under compulsion, and wealth is evidently not the good we are seeking; for it is merely useful for the sake of something else."[14] His success and renown obligated him to serve as a public conscience, both at home and abroad.

AMERICAN INDIANS

There was no cause to which Brando was more dedicated than that of the nation's original inhabitants. He felt implicated in events of the previous century that had turned the surviving natives into interlopers in the modern era. Brando's sense of responsibility toward American Indians had roots in the history of his family and the state of Nebraska, where his maternal great-grandfather, Myles Gahan, settled after emigrating from Ireland. Brando grew up hearing about the injustices done to American Indians from his grandmother and mother, and in the late 1940s in Paris, he was already talking about the Indian massacres and his desire to make a film one day that would bring to light the history and their present circumstances.[15] While doing research in 1951 for his role as the part-Indian Emiliano Zapata, he learned more about the larger situation of the Indians in Mexico. The earliest record of his intent to make a film about the American Indians is a March 4, 1958, response to a Mrs. B. R. Hill, who had apparently sent him a script for an Indian movie. I have yet to "read extensively about Indians or their culture, but I have had more than a slight brush with them," Brando wrote, and

"I think that the modern Indian has enormous problems in our society and that an accurate account of the rape and decimation of those people has never been recorded on film. I am anxious to read your script." Thus began his search for the right story.[16]

He hoped to contribute to the recuperation of a history that, along with the native inhabitants themselves, had been expunged. "When I was going to school in the thirties," Brando noted, "most textbooks dismissed the Indians in two or three paragraphs that described them as a race of faceless, ferocious, heathen savages."[17] Knowing the impact of films, and of his own public persona, he saw that educating himself on the subject might be a prelude to educating Americans more generally. Brando had about seven hundred books, many of which he annotated, on American Indians, a collection rivaling those of authorities in the field. Marking "get" in note citations, consulting authors directly for advice on what to read, and collecting catalogs from publishers specializing in Indian subjects were his means to an extraordinary scholarly record. (An Oklahoma University Press catalog on Indian books annotated by Brando, with his personal materials from *The Godfather* set, suggests that he was perpetually searching for books.)[18] To get a sense of how he read, it's almost possible to look over his shoulder as he became engaged with the cause.

Brando marked passages about Indians relevant to both *Zapata* and *One-Eyed Jacks*, for instance, in his *Cowboy Encyclopedia* (1951).[19] We know too that he was reading about the Indians of Mexico during the early 1950s in Miguel Covarrubias's *Mexico South*. One of the first books on the American Indian that Brando recalled reading in the early sixties was *They Came Here First* (1949), by Flathead Indian anthropologist D'Arcy McNickle; Brando annotated it heavily and arranged to meet the author.[20] Yet fascination did not prevent skepticism: questions such as, "What's his source?" and "How often?" beside McNickle's claim that Indian "women often gave as good as they received" in response to harsh treatment from their men.[21] Typically, too, Brando's curiosity overran the book's content. Thus he writes at the start of a chapter on language: "Ask D'Arcy McNickle about Ind. understanding of treaties"; next to a priest's report on the generosity of the Hurons: "get complete report." By an account (from Montaigne) of Indian cruelties, he writes, "Public Executions. Check concurrent European Barbarities."[22]

Brando's marginal comments in the McNickle book display empathy tempered by realism. Brando emphasized the Indians' victimization, but he recognized that they were warring among themselves before the whites arrived.[23] He also discerned their shrewdness; far from being "noble savages," they exploited divisions among the colonizers. Former Indian enemies were capable of uniting to defeat adversaries, as during Pontiac's six-month campaign against the British, about which Brando took note.[24] None of this mitigated the host of official statutes ignored, treaties betrayed, or the ultimate attempts at eradication.[25] But Brando avoided reversing the demonization: "The cavalrymen and settlers who slaughtered the Indians weren't inherently evil" but rather products of a culture that demonized Indians, which doesn't "excuse our country's refusal to settle a debt that is long overdue." How ironic it was, he went on, that, "With the exception of the United States, virtually every colonial power that stole land from its indigenous peoples has at least started to give some of it back," many urged to do so by the US government.[26]

Over and above the ongoing treacheries, what mattered most to Brando was the richness of the Indian way of life: the intricate Apache baskets created "out of the poverty of the desert" and the cultural harmony expressed in their songs.[27] There was some idealization here, obviously, given the prevalence of war songs, but he could be more realistic, crediting Indian leaders with the prescience to distinguish self-inflicted problems, and highlighting passages confirming their skills as ironists.[28] The

Sample of Brando's annotations on his copy of McNickle book.
Annotations reproduced by permission of Brando Enterprises, LP.

most insidious means of destruction, he seemed to think, was the overt assault on Indian languages and ritual practices.[29] But he also saw their history as part of a universal story of oppression, writing in the margin of a book on the Indians of the Southwest: "Hellow tahiti."[30]

Had Brando's concern for the American Indians been limited to his library, it would have represented a unique scholarly side of a leading actor's life. But Brando translated his newfound knowledge into action almost immediately, visiting D'Arcy McNickle in New Mexico to find out what he could do to help. For Brando, the effort to redress these national crimes, masquerading for years as the cost of progress, was a century overdue. While he knew the value of his fame, he was willing to serve as a foot soldier. What pleased him most about being among Indians was their apparent indifference to Hollywood success. From the beginning he noted approvingly, "They didn't give a damn about my movies."[31]

After McNickle directed Brando to the National Indian Youth Council, founded in 1961, he became a regular at council meetings, befriending Clyde Warrior of the Ponca tribe; Hank Adams, a Rosebud Sioux; and Vine Deloria, a Sioux political scientist who, like McNickle, had written extensively about Indians. One of Brando's initial acts of civil disobedience was at an Indian "fish-in" that challenged restrictions on tribal fishing rights at the Puyallup River in Washington. Though officials insisted on releasing Brando two hours after his arrest (keeping Indian offenders longer), he participated the next day in a march in nearby Olympia, Washington, which was followed by a meeting with Governor Albert D. Rosellini. Brando's involvement in the event drew national publicity, helping to lay the groundwork for subsequent campaigns. Fishing entitlements had long been an important Indian civil rights issue, and their successful defense in the 1960s was critical to raising awareness of violated treaties. Brando kept track of the issue, annotating heavily his copy of the *Congressional Record* from the August 5, 1964, Senate hearing on Indian Fishing Rights overseen by Senators Frank Church, Henry Jackson, and Alan Simpson, all of whom he came to know through his advocacy.[32]

At "fish-in" with Robert Satiacum, March 2, 1964. © *Seattle Post-Intelligencer* Collection; Museum of History and Industry/Corbis.

Fish-ins and other initiatives that ordinarily would have been overlooked were blanketed with television cameras when the actor was in attendance. Throughout the 1960s, he appeared in news reports and did interviews on talk shows, all in an effort to publicize how the US government regularly ignored more than four hundred treaties with Indian tribes dating back to the eighteenth century.[33]

Brando often pointed to the lack of distinction between Democrats and Republicans when it came to Indian policy. Indeed, a 1960 ruling by the liberal Warren Court (*Federal Power Commission v. Tuscarora Indian Nation*) had authorized a Democrat, President John F. Kennedy, in 1963 to disregard a treaty with Indians to pursue the Allegheny River Project under the power of eminent domain. When Brando met President Kennedy at a Beverly Hills fundraiser on June 7, 1963, he was already identified as an activist willing to break the law to make a point. "We know what you've been doing with the American Indians," Kennedy told Brando, who replied, "I know what you've *not* been doing with the American Indians." This encounter—in which both Brando and Kennedy were drunk and traded gibes over who had gained the most weight recently—anticipated in its surrealism a later Brando meeting with another powerful figure, Supreme Court Justice William O. Douglas. Brando admired Douglas, who had famously introduced a stay of execution for the Rosenbergs and was a great defender of the environment. Arriving in the judge's chamber with a briefcase full of notes on the Indians, Brando found himself completely inarticulate. He later confessed that he was rendered mute by the spectacle of this man whom he held in such high esteem, sitting there listening so attentively.[34]

Brando's associations evolved with the changing shape of the Indian movement; by the end of the 1960s, he was working with the Survival of American Indians Association (SAIA), the National Congress of American Indians (NCAI), and the newly created American Indian Movement (AIM), headed by Russell Means and Dennis Banks, friends as well as political comrades to whom he gave substantial financial and legal support. Brando named his daughter Cheyenne for the Indians who had been living in Grand Island, Nebraska, prior to the arrival of his great-grandparents. During the 1970s, Brando continued to make television appearances to talk about Indian issues in the United States (*The Dick Cavett Show*) and abroad (the British *Iain Johnstone Show*), to participate with Indian activists on various rights measures, and to develop ideas for television and film.

Brando's decision to send Sacheen Littlefeather to the 1973 Academy Awards ceremony to decline his award for *The Godfather* was the most sensational of his efforts to bring attention to the grievances of Indians. But this was not the last award that he turned down. Later, when the NAACP chose him for the 1975 Spingarn Medal in humanitarianism, he professed embarrassment in light of the far greater sacrifices made by legions of anonymous civil rights workers. In a telegram to the organization, he added, "The question of being honored formally for having contributed in some small measure to the relief of the anguish and humiliation that black people are made to suffer in this country produces a conflict within me and renders me unable to accept such an honor."[35]

For Brando, the Academy Award incident was one of many efforts to publicize Indian affairs; for instance, he gave forty acres of land in Liberty Canyon near Los Angeles to a group representing the Survival of American Indians Association on December 30, 1974.[36] He never stopped resenting that the press preferred him to infinitely more knowledgeable Indian spokespeople such as Clyde Warrior, Hank Adams, and Vine Deloria, or lawyers such as Mark Lane, William Kunstler, and Larry Leventhal, who all had years of experience on the issue. "I don't know how many times I've said, 'Listen, there are perfectly eloquent gentlemen

Donating forty acres in Liberty Canyon to Indians, 1974.
© Bettmann/Corbis.

standing to my left ... they know far better than I do why they're here, don't ask me.'"[37]

Brando took the greatest personal risks on behalf of AIM, adding to an FBI file dating from the late 1940s.[38] In a meeting with Senator Daniel Inouye of Hawaii on December 21, 1976, Brando described his concerns about the surveillance of Indian rights activities, noting his long discussions with Senator Frank Church, whom he had known "for many years," about how the United States "very nearly missed having a police state under the control of the FBI."[39] Church had published in 1975 and 1976 the famous Church Committee Reports from his Senate hearings on the operation and abuses of US intelligence agencies. The largest of the reports was a 1,000-page-volume on the FBI, which focused significantly on the FBI's counterintelligence campaign against domestic dissidents during the antiwar movement and the era of civil rights.[40] Brando's own FBI file featured lengthy documentation of his meetings with AIM members, and the tapping of his phone during the 1970s probably was related to his AIM activism.[41] The American Indian Movement was created in Minneapolis, during the summer of 1968, by a group of two hundred Indian activists determined to redress a century of wrongs against the Indian nations and the miseries of the present—high unemployment, slum housing, prevailing racism—through civil disobedience and even occasionally armed protest, though they only used guns in self-defense. The purposes of AIM were consistent with other political movements of the 1960s that were dedicated to radical social change, from student and Vietnam War protests to feminism and black power. While AIM members did not advocate violence—it would have been self-destructive for them to do so—their revolutionary fervor attracted the attention of the FBI and the CIA, which maintained constant surveillance over its members, subjecting them to arrest and extended court trials.

In 1974, Means and Banks were put on trial for the 1973 occupation of the town of Wounded Knee on the Pine Ridge Reservation in South Dakota. On February 27, 1973, about 250 Sioux Indians and members of AIM had taken over Wounded Knee, calling for the ouster of corrupt tribal leaders and the reopening of treaty negotiations with the US government. Wounded Knee was chosen for what turned into a seventy-one-day siege because of its historical significance as the site in December 1890 of one of the worst massacres of the American Indian wars. The 1973 protest at Wounded Knee had been largely ignored until Brando drew attention to it in the speech that Sacheen Littlefeather delivered on his behalf at the Academy Awards ceremony. Following the speech, a deluge of reporters descended on Wounded Knee. In the ultimate standoff with police, two people were killed, twelve hundred were arrested, and Means and Banks were charged with murder. They were eventually acquitted, and, as was often the case, the incident and their trial helped to publicize their cause but had no tangible legal consequences.

Still, Brando believed in the inspirational impact of these events, which is why in June 1975 he again aided AIM members wanted by the FBI for questioning about the murder of two of their agents. Fearing that the fugitives, including Dennis Banks's pregnant wife, would be killed without a hearing, Brando provided cash and transportation—his motor home. Visited by FBI agents on the set of *The Missouri Breaks* that July, Brando was cooperative, even gracious.[42] He had been more imperiled in Gresham, Wisconsin, earlier that year when caught in gunfire during a Menominee Indian takeover of a Catholic monastery run by the Alexian Brothers on what the Indians considered to be tribal land. Brando ended up serving as an intermediary in their standoff with the National Guard, helping to negotiate a deal that would give the Indians a deed for the property in exchange for their peaceful surrender. "In the end, the Indians went to jail but never got the deed," Brando observed. Five months later, the Menominee tribe was forced, "due to lack of funds and support," to relinquish all ownership of the monastery and its lands.[43] This was typical in American Indian campaigns of the era, though Brando continued to hope that political channels would eventually serve to redress many wrongs.

At the same time, he pursued the prospect of a significant contribution in his area of expertise.[44] That Brando kept the prospect alive through the 1980s is confirmed by his response to actor Sean Penn's inquiry about a film based on Louise Erdrich's *Love Medicine*. In a letter of August 24, 1986, Brando cites his twenty-five-year dedication to the cause and marvels at the general ignorance of the plain truth that, "from the time of our 'founding fathers,' national policy toward the Indians was never anything less than genocidal," that whites simply took "the land away from these aboriginal people." He admires Erdrich's book, he tells Penn, but anticipates difficulties translating it to the screen, paraphrasing H. L. Mencken ("No one ever lost money underestimating the taste of the American public"). He has himself, he noted, been "striving mightily in the past eight years" with "a story about the Sand Creek Massacre." On November 29, 1864, a peaceful village of Cheyenne Indians was invaded by a cavalry regiment of 700 Colorado Volunteers, resulting in the death of about 400 Indians, mostly women and children, many of whom were mutilated. It was to be a part of a television series tentatively entitled "Vision Road," which seems to have run aground for the usual reasons: funding problems, artistic conflicts, studio disinterest. But there is abundant evidence—Brando's handwritten notes, tapes of his ideas for characters and plot, marginalia in books on the subject—of his long-term commitment to it. Brando especially appreciated the hypocrisy of John Chivington, a preacher–colonel who had led the massacre and had notoriously requested a "fighting" commission over a "praying" one.[45]

Brando spent a great deal of time conceptualizing a movie, and from his notes and marginalia we can glean some basic features of what he had in mind. He appears to have been thinking continually about possible directors and screenwriters—he writes in the margin of a Dee Brown book that maybe he "should write the movie." Abby Mann, Vine Deloria, and Leslie Silko were also considered.[46] His direction of One-Eyed Jacks, in which he was drawn to everything from script changes to the historical accuracy of an extra's costume, is recalled in his approach to the Indian film.[47] He highlighted details about soldiers—culling drawings of military uniforms, songs, habits (no bathing at southwestern outposts), language (some immigrant soldiers barely spoke English)—as well as about Indians—clothing of particular tribes, the complex varieties of Indian languages (hundreds in Mexico alone).[48] He identified incidents for movie scenes:

Americans hanging President Washington in effigy after hearing he planned to pay Indians for their lands; a grasshopper plague in Colorado Territory viewed as an evil omen by settlers and Cheyenne Indians alike.[49] Reading *The Camp Grant Massacre*, a novel about the 1871 murders, by US cavalry in Arizona, of Apache Indians who had surrendered, Brando coined phrases from events the book described, writing in the margin: "Bury my leg with me" and "Bad year for smiles" (one character had explained, "It has been a bad year thus far . . . I have not been able to smile").[50]

The prospective film reflected the catholicity of Brando's intellect. There would be a technological component portraying the Indians' 1885 destruction of the overland telegraph line—which cut off the Pacific coast from communication for months—as well as their struggle against the great white weapon of the railroad, the "demonic . . . Iron Horse."[51] There would be scenes of railroad agents appeasing Indians in the United States, set against scenes of deception abroad—peddling Indian lands to unsuspecting immigrants in Europe.[52] One theme would be ubiquitous: the complicity of all nations in the plunder and oppression of indigenous peoples. Though mindful of differences (Canadians and Brazilians behaved best, Americans and Spaniards worst), he planned to confront the painful truth that every colonizer, in the New World and elsewhere, had been ruthless.[53] Some book passages inspired lists of global touchstones. In one book, he scrawled, "Shaka Kahn, Tartars, Boers . . . Arabs in Central Africa"; in another, "German, Japanese, Russians in E. Europe."[54] Three assumptions guided Brando's reading for his Indian picture: The history of the Indians in the Americas was a global issue that had been repeated throughout history; insight depended on grappling with divergent opinions; and knowledge could not be definitive.[55]

Nor did Indian history ever cease. Thus, his developing account of the Indians' past was informed by their present. Brando saw

Indians in the 1960s as immigrants in their own country—forever marked by the fact that they had battled ferociously in the nineteenth century the government they had adopted reluctantly in the twentieth.[56] He was equally alert to the strategic parallels between black and Indian politics, drawn to the paradoxes of their premodern encounters.[57] Some tribes had been slaveholders in the pre-emancipation era, while emancipated blacks had served as "Buffalo Soldiers" (the name was believed to have originated from the Indians who compared their hair to that of buffaloes), filling Western cavalry regiments.[58] Each group, he noted, despised the other for selling out: the Sioux called the black cavalry "Black White Men," and Indians built on the disparaging black sobriquet of Uncle Tom in condemning those Indians they felt submitted to whites as "Uncle Tomahawks."[59] Brando underscored the detail that 25,000 Indians had served in the US Army from World War II through Vietnam along with the grim comment that the Indian "had been feasted, feted, and bemedaled. ... Then he was forgotten."[60]

In all his film preparations, Brando emphasized the deliberateness of American policy and the dignity of Indians in resisting it. The object, he wrote in the margin of McNickle's *Indians and Other Americans*, was "to quickly reduce the Indian to hopelessness so his muffled cries of outrage would not be heard nor reach the conscience of U.S. people."[61] He used the back cover of the same book to outline for the film the Indian struggle against that policy. His protagonist would be a fighter, against "white boys... always in jail always resisting never capitulating, cynical." He would "dream of his forefather as himself." Reparations would be thematized, and comparisons would be made to the Philippines and other countries where indigenous populations were partly repaid in cash for land, resources, and even cultural attributes lost in the colonization process. "Cross check legal obligations of S. Africa and U.S. to indigenous people in separate enclaves within their territories and Panama and Cuba—Okinawa Guam Marshal Isl," he wrote to himself on the back cover of Francis Paul Prucha's *American Indian Policy in the Formative Years* (1962). And finally, the film would pay homage to Indian survival. "The Indian has sung his death chant. He will die before becoming White."[62] What could be a stronger testimony to the power of a civilization?

Brando was still writing "Notes on a Possible Indian Story" in the 1990s, an enduring fascination evident as well in the film he made about the American Indian, *The Brave* (1997), with Johnny Depp.[63] Brando may have cared too much, preventing bringing the movie to fruition. He had spent so many years informing himself about Indian history, doing political work, and trying to counter the indifference of the majority of Americans, that in the end he could not settle on a portrait that satisfied him. For that matter, he even remained unsettled as to whether he would play an Indian or a white man. Next to an image of a great Indian warrior in one book, he wrote, "Maybe Yours Truly," but he seemed equally attracted to the prospect of augmenting his gallery of sinners from the late period with a white villain.[64]

It is also probable that he gave up because he distrusted himself and the industry that had made him so successful. He could not bear another disappointment like *One-Eyed Jacks*—the endless ambition and work, the frustrations, and the inevitable sense of imperfection. Nor could he bear the complex maneuvering and ultimate limits of the alternative—collaborating with a director and producers—for *this* picture. Ultimately, the most important factor in the foiling of Brando's magnum opus on the American Indians was probably that he was overextended. Personal calendars from 1966 through the end of 1975 are filled with references to the film. His calendar features regular meetings about it, which often included Brando's agent Jay Kanter, producers Jack Beck and John Foreman, writer Abby Mann, Hank Adams (trusted friend from the National Indian Youth Council), and, occasionally, his lawyer, Norman Carey. Among the directors considered were Martin Scorsese, William Friedkin, Gillo Pontecorvo, and Bob Rafelson. But Brando is equally involved during the same decade with ecological plans for his new Tahitian island, Tetiaroa, and films to promote them, as well as his commitment to the civil rights movement.

He also vacations and travels routinely. It is a rare month that he doesn't spend on at least two continents, traveling among North America, Europe, and Polynesia. There are the usual romances, particularly with former actress Jill Banner, whom he met while making *Candy* (the only white woman Brando said he loved), who accompanies him on a visit to his childhood home in Omaha, Nebraska. Finally, there are films he's in—the script consultations with directors John Huston, Michael Winner, Francis Ford Coppola, and Bernardo Bertolucci—and the ones he assists—talking with James Baldwin, who was writing a screenplay of *Blues for Mr. Charlie*.[65] If calendars tell truths, they're simple ones: Brando was just too busy during the years he was most engaged with the Indian film to put the necessary time into it.

CIVIL RIGHTS

Brando's race politics, like his concern for the Indians, had family origins: his mother's example as an early proponent of civil rights and the principles of equality she instilled in him. From a relatively young age, he was sensitized to what seemed a patent national wrong. It astounded him that a mere sixty-two years before he was born, it had been possible for one human being to buy another.[66] And he remembered as a boy seeing photographs of lynched blacks surrounded by smiling crowds in the daily newspaper. "When I was a kid, it was very common to read about a black man being dragged through the streets of a town, in the South but also in the North, until he was near dead," Brando told Michael Jackson, recounting also that he was castigated by a teacher in Evanston, Illinois, for befriending a black boy.[67]

Brando admired the resilience of blacks in the movement, the pride they displayed in battling the most vicious oppression. His work against racism developed naturally out of friendships and interests dating back to his earliest days in Manhattan. Through dance lessons at Katherine Dunham's Studio; at clubs in Harlem and on Broadway, where he cultivated passions for jazz and drumming; in dramatic workshops at the New School—all racially mixed worlds despite the prevailing segregation—Brando got to know people (Harry Belafonte, Quincy Jones, Ossie Davis, Ruby Dee) who would figure prominently in the civil rights movement.

Almost immediately upon meeting, Brando and his friend James Baldwin began a process of mutual education. Baldwin was pivotal to Brando's enlightenment. What made the friendship satisfying were all the things they had in common despite antithetical backgrounds: love for humor and language and an independence of thought that made them resist orthodoxies that foiled bonds like theirs. Perhaps their key affinity was abiding awareness of how it felt to be worthless. As the neighborhood truant from the wrong side of the tracks, his mother the town drunk, Brando had been a social outcast.[68] Brando underscored these passages in his copy of Baldwin's The Fire Next Time: "You were born into a society which spelled out with brutal clarity, and in as many ways as possible, that you were a worthless human being"; "this is the crime of which I accuse my country, and my countrymen, and for which neither I nor time nor history will ever forgive them, that they have destroyed, and are destroying hundreds of thousands of lives and do not know it and do not want to know it."[69] Self-scrutiny was essential to confronting injustice. "The questions which one asks oneself"—which

Speaking at civil rights event, with Martin Luther King Jr. looking on at left.
© Bettmann/Corbis.

Baldwin wrote in *Nobody Knows My Name* and which Brando highlighted—"become one's key to the experience of others. One can only face in others what one can face in oneself."[70]

Baldwin admired the way his friend threw himself into civil rights work, noting in the autobiographical account of his own "Baptism," that Brando had always been "in the forefront."[71] Because the movement, in comparison with the Indian rights movement, was more centralized in its organization and tactics, the stakes for Brando were not as high as they were with the Indians. The fluidity of the different Indian organizations, and their comparative neglect in an era of widespread activism, encouraged a hands-on approach among supporters. As Brando told Michael Jackson, "There are twenty-five million Blacks and they have the power, the organization, the money.... There are only a million, a million and a half Indians, they have no money... no support, no organization."

When the movement for black civil rights was reinvigorated during the 1950s under the leadership of the Congress of Racial Equality (CORE), founded in 1954, Brando was one of the first white celebrities to join the cause. The group's ethic of nonviolent protest, and events such as the Montgomery (Alabama) Bus Boycott of 1955, inspired sympathizers nationwide, aware that racism was hardly confined to the South.[72] Brando was incensed by the mistreatment of black performers in Hollywood—Diahann Carroll and Sammy Davis Jr., for instance, were restricted to shabby motels on Sunset Strip, while appearing at palatial venues where they couldn't even order drinks.[73] By 1960, Brando's calendar was filled with civil right activities, especially during the summer of 1963: June 11, he flies to Sacramento to welcome a group of Freedom Walkers; June 25, he strategizes with CORE official Dorothy Gray; July 12, he spends the evening with ACLU and CORE representatives Nate Monaster and Tom Neusom; July 14, he helps Eartha Kitt and others set up a scholarship fund for Medgar Evers's children; July 27, he is picketing against discriminatory housing practices in Torrance, California.[74]

On the historic day of August 28, 1963, Brando is in Washington, standing near the podium as Martin Luther King delivers his "I Have a Dream" speech at the Lincoln Memorial, later participating in a televised Civil Rights Roundtable.[75] Appearing with some of the most prominent activists in the country, his perspective on American racism was exceptional in its globalism.

With Baldwin at the Lincoln Memorial (holding cattle prod). AP Photo/
Los Angeles Times/Larry Davis.

He was the only one to mention the international politics of race,
reflecting on parallels between the situations of blacks in Haiti
and in the United States, and between American racism and the
German genocide against Jews.[76]

Brando later got to know members of the Black Panthers, such
as Bobby Seale and Eldridge Cleaver, and spent hours on different
occasions listening to their analyses of the race situation at home
and abroad and strategies for self-empowerment. These interac-
tions added to Brando's already extensive FBI file and were one
reason why he was refused a chance to screen his film on children's starvation in India for President Lyndon Johnson. Brando's
civil rights activities also led to boycotts of his films in the South,
beginning with *Bedtime Story* (1964).[77] Brando was undeterred.
To quell potential violence, he walked through Harlem with
Mayor John Lindsay in April 1968, following the assassination
of Martin Luther King. Though he later dismissed the incident

as unwitting participation in Lindsay's courting of black votes, Brando's presence in Harlem at that moment of crisis and grief inspired blacks and whites alike. Still, he was alert to the limits of his efforts and their susceptibility to exploitation. And he was aware of the ambivalence felt by many black leaders toward white activists. One of the few times that he experienced such resentment himself was with the Black Panthers after Bobby Hutton was killed; he noticed James Farmer, a founder of CORE, regarding him with what he felt to be absolute hatred.[78] Bobby Hutton was a seventeen-year-old member of the Black Panthers who had been shot by police in Oakland, California, during the turmoil that erupted in the aftermath of King's death. A secretary for the group, Hutton had been a Panther for two years, having joined to help protect blacks from police brutality. On the night of April 7, 1968, he and other Panthers, including the well-known Eldridge Cleaver, were involved in a gun battle with police. After one Panther was killed, Cleaver and Hutton decided to surrender. According to Cleaver, Hutton came out stripped to his underwear to show he was unarmed, while police insisted that he was clad in an overcoat and behaving suspiciously. The police fired more than a dozen bullets into Hutton's body. His funeral was held six days after the death of King.

That the Panthers, notorious for repudiating white liberals, accepted Brando's offer to speak at Hutton's funeral was extraordinary. Their decision was undoubtedly motivated in part by the added publicity Brando's appearance brought to the event, but it also reflected their belief in the sincerity of his sympathies. Brando gained credibility through humility. "That could have been *my* son lying there," he proclaimed, "and I'm going to do as much as I can, I'm going to start right now, to inform White people of what they don't know. The Reverend said, the White man can't cool it because he's never dug it. And I'm here to try to *dig it*. Because I myself as a White man have got a long way to go and a lot to learn. I haven't been in your place. I haven't suffered the way you've suffered. I'm just beginning to learn the nature of that experience. And somehow that has to be translated to the white community, *now!*"[79]

These were no idle words, as Brando demonstrated when he appeared on *The Joey Bishop Show* on April 25, 1968, and spoke his mind about the problem of racism in America and its responsibility for rage among black youth in particular. Making reference to the Bobby Hutton case, Brando, who was well versed in the legalities of public speech, avoided statements that might be construed as defamatory. He referred generally to "the police" as responsible for Hutton's death, rather than to specific officers or a specific department. Still, on June 20, 1968, Brando was sued for defamation by the Oakland police officers involved in the standoff with Hutton and other Panthers. The case churned through the courts, subject to complicated wrangling from both sides. Brando was first acquitted, but then the ruling was reversed on behalf of the individual plaintiffs in the case, though Brando was not required to pay damages, since it was ruled the officers had not suffered financially from his comments. Brando eventually appealed to the Supreme Court of the State of California, seeking first to "secure uniformity of decision," and then "to settle important questions of law," specifically a central legal question highlighted by the case—whether talk shows were protected under free speech. On February 8, 1971, Brando's request for a hearing by the California Supreme Court was officially denied, and the case was closed.[80]

Brando remained active in civil rights issues throughout the 1970s and '80s. In April 1979, he made a rare appearance at a mass rally in LA's Dodger Stadium to aid Reverend Jesse Jackson's Operation PUSH for black high school youth.[81] In August 1983, he went on television with Coretta Scott King to honor the twentieth anniversary of her husband's "March on Washington." Brando's performances in Alex Haley's *Roots* (1979) and the South African film *A Dry White Season* (1989) were efforts to further equality and understanding. Part of Brando's understanding of civil rights issues came from his self-education. James Baldwin's and Toni Morrison's works tutored him on racism. He wrote Morrison in 1991: "It seems somehow improper to close this letter without mentioning the enduring and stabbing beauty of your book *Beloved*. I will remain deeply affected by its poetry, subtlety, strength, and undying conviction that the courage to love in the face of abject horrors offers perhaps the only alternative to madness and mayhem." (His admiration was apparently returned, for Morrison responded, "I would like to end this reply with some suitable language about my regard for your work, but I can't quite handle it.")[82] Brando drew widely on a range of disciplines and genres, popular as well as academic, in attempting to understand the depressing persistence of racial hatred.

Though it was small compared to his collection on Indians, and the books had far fewer annotations, the works on black history and thought reflected similar selectivity. Brando owned a dozen reports from the United States Commission on Civil Rights; classics such as C. Vann Woodward's *The Strange Career of Jim Crow* and Stanley Elkins's *Slavery*; and multiple issues of W. E. B. Du Bois's journal, *Freedomways Quarterly.* There were studies of black living conditions under Southern peonage and in Northern ghettos. There were autobiographies by Huey Newton, Eldridge Cleaver, and Bobby Seale and a manifesto, *Moral Crisis: The Case for Civil Rights* (1964), by John F. Kennedy and Lyndon B. Johnson. There were stories of strategy sessions (Howard Zinn on SNCC, the Student Nonviolent Coordinating Committee) and of famous protests (William McCord on the Freedom Party during one "Long Hot Summer" in Mississippi). Typical of Brando was the collection's globalism, with books about racial struggles in Africa and England as well as in Russia. These included Bloke

Modisane's South African autobiography, *Blame Me on History* (1963) with an inscription from the author on how much the actor's films had meant to him.[83]

Brando's practical approach to racism was evident in his marginalia. From Gordon Allport's *The Nature of Prejudice* (1958), he took the witty definition of being "down on something you're not up on," and also a useful distinction—individuals whose race hatred was a product of custom were ignorant rather than prejudiced. In Frantz Fanon's *Black Skin, White Masks* (1967), he marked discussions of black antiquity, and Jean-Paul Sartre's misunderstanding of the anticolonial Negritude movement.[84] His views on why civil rights legislation finally passed were just as realistic. There had been no radical transformation of the culture; what had changed were America's trading partners in countries rich with resources. He asserted that all over Africa, indigenous rulers were assuming control. He saw that American enlightenment was "purely economic. After the U.S. was confronted with the fact that it would have to go to black Africa with all the colonial countries gone, and they would have to deal with the black man for business," Brando explained. "If the colonial countries had still been in Africa, there wouldn't be any Civil Rights Act today.... How could we possibly get raw materials from black Africa when we were burning black people with gasoline in the South?"[85] Brando's understanding of the economic motivations for the passage of civil rights legislation echoed arguments in works by Du Bois and Fanon as well as in speeches of the Black Panthers and Malcolm X. For a white man of his time and place, however, Brando's views were unusual.

Brando's realism left room for hope, even with the seeming intractability of racism. He had seen too great a change firsthand: worrying about antimiscegenation laws prior to marrying his first wife, Anna Kashfi, who was half-Indian (he married his second wife, Hispanic Movita Castaneda, in Mexico), and hearing racial slurs directed at his children, all of mixed race. But he had witnessed the decline of such sentiments and antici- pated greater openness as the inevitable shrinking of the globe brought peoples together. Still, he marveled at the ubiquity of racism, which he had found almost everywhere he visited. "For a long time I was angry at this country. But then I looked around and saw what the French did in Algeria, what the Dutch did in Indonesia," Brando ruminated. "In Japan they have a class called the Etta, a people which the Japanese can't intermarry with." He had expected a relatively gentle Tahitian society to be an excep- tion, but people were no different there.[86] These problems were basic to human beings over time; no system—political, religious, or otherwise—had ever provided permanent solutions to them. "I'm not a Marxist," he noted, though many of his opinions might have been construed as such. "There have been wonderful mon- archies and horrible monarchies... wonderful democratic peri- ods and bad."[87]

HUMANITARIAN ABROAD: UNICEF AND TETIAROA

Brando reflected on how he had once thought about becoming a minister: "I thought it might give me more of a purpose in life. I flirted with the idea for a while, but in the end it never developed sufficient force to make me want to do it. Or maybe it was because I became interested in the United Nations, which for a while I saw as perhaps our last hope for peace, social justice and a more equitable sharing of the earth's resources."[88] This observation, buried in Brando's autobiography, seems dismissible: another expression of misplaced idealism of the kind found in interviews he did over the years. As the handsome actor whom audiences couldn't get enough of expounded on his concerns beyond films, the obliging journalist recorded every detail.[89] But the fantasy of making a vocation of helping others, the dedication to the UN and to environmental issues, including the more rational distribution of global bounty, were for him interdependent. His interest in the ecology of his Tahitian island, where he planned to develop alternative energy sources, foodstuffs, and designs for housing, grew out of an awareness of worldwide suffering that he had also sought to address actively over decades.

From the mid-1950s, he promoted the UN's technical assistance program, which provided people in third world countries with skills and tools to offset poverty and develop local industries. He spent the most time on the United Nations International Children's Emergency Fund (UNICEF) and became "a roving ambassador for the agency, preaching a different kind of religion"—that all children deserved to have their basic needs met.[90] He traveled to publicize UNICEF initiatives, made television and radio spots, and encouraged other celebrities to participate. He planned a film about the UN, which partly funded his trips during the 1950s to various countries in Southeast Asia.

Despite his growing ambivalence about the underlying purposes of Western assistance, Brando continued to work during the 1960s for UN programs, particularly UNICEF. He visited eleven countries on its behalf, including Greece, Lebanon, Australia, and India, and sponsored fundraising galas in Paris and New York. In March 1967, Brando went to Bihar, India, to help with emergency food relief, making the rounds of villages in a jeep with UNICEF workers.[91] He was so appalled by what he witnessed—thousands of emaciated children, their bodies covered with smallpox sores—that he recorded the suffering on film with a handheld 10mm camera. He was struck by how carefully caste boundaries were maintained at the hospital, with Untouchables separated from other dying children to prevent their ritual pollution. "Some of the trucks had been unloaded by Untouchable

Praying with children in Thailand. Larry Burrows/Time & Life Pictures/Getty Images.

labor," Brando recalled, and a "Hindu, who was absolutely starving himself, and as big as a broomstick, and whose children were
scabrous and on the edge of death, would not allow his children
to have that food."[93] He described scenes of mothers offering
up their babies, hoping that his camera held magic properties
that could relieve their hunger, and he remembered the faces
as corpselike, so taut that "if you touched the cheek of a child, a
hollow spot remained in her flesh."[94] On his last day of filming,
after a child died in front of him, Brando sat down and cried.
Upon his return, he screened the film for UNICEF officials and
media representatives in New York and for various people in Hollywood. In October 1967, he showed the film at a UNICEF event
in Helsinki, Finland, to a group that included renowned Turkish
journalist Altemur Kiliç, and the president of Finland. This was
one instance where a resolution of the misery Brando had seen
was in the offing. The Johnson administration had been working on Emergency Food Assistance to India legislation, which
passed in 1967, to shore up relations with a wavering ally (India
had criticized US policies in Vietnam). In order to receive the
food and stave off famine, however, India had to modernize its
agricultural practices.[94]

Brando continued to show the film to remind people that
some disasters were preventable. He supported the UN World
Food Programme's efforts to develop foodstuffs that might offer
long-term solutions to hunger. The experience informed his
interest in innovative plant and animal proteins (modern versions of breadfruit, the object of the famous *Bounty* voyage), such
as tilapia, a hardy, mass-producible fish farmed increasingly in
the second half of the twentieth century. He familiarized himself
with efforts in Africa, Israel, Japan, and Vietnam to manufac-
ture mashed varieties of this nutritious staple. He was an advocate for alternative energy sources and investigated solar power
and different materials and styles for sturdier homebuilding. His

Screening his film on hunger at UNICEF headquarters, ca. 1967. © UNICEF.

ambition was to create on Tetiaroa, his Tahitian island, an exper-imental site to test sustainable ideas—from new energy sources and forms of nutrition to construction methods. He brought in scientists to study the island's bird sanctuary, reef, and lagoon. Wind- and solar-power specialists assessed its development capacities, and archaeologists from the University of Hawaii excavated the island's *marae* (ceremonial structures).[95]

During filming of *Mutiny on the Bounty* in 1961, Brando had discovered Tetiaroa, a coral reef atoll comprising a dozen islets with a land area of 1,500 acres and a lagoon five miles across. King Pomare V had bequeathed it to an American dentist, Dr. Johnston Walter Williams, in 1904. In 1967, Brando bought it from Williams's daughter, Marjorie Doran, who had lived there for decades, her sole companions a Chinese woman and forty cats and dogs. When Brando visited the island in 1963, he and Mrs. Doran, who was blind, talked for hours. However isolated she was, she knew who he was, having heard him interviewed on her shortwave radio. She found him charming and he found the

Tetiaroa. Courtesy of Te mana o te moana.

beauty of the island overwhelming. "The lagoon was ... infused
with more shades of blue than I thought possible: turquoise, deep
blue, light blue, indigo blue, cobalt blue, royal blue, robin's egg
blue, aquamarine." He visited again, bringing an apple pie, and
told her that if she ever decided to sell Tetiaroa, she should let
him know. He kept his promise to her when he purchased the
island—that he would do everything possible to preserve its natural condition. When he died in 2004, the island had been barely
affected by development.[96]

In 1972, Brando commissioned a field study, directed by Dr.
Yosihiko H. Sinoto of the Bishop Museum in Hawaii. Conducted
over three months (December 1972, January and July of 1973),
Archaeology of Teti'aroa Atoll and Society Islands was part of the
larger program of research Brando had in mind.[97] He was anxious
to kindle interest among Tahitian youth in their national antiq-
uities. He also hoped to establish ties to universities in Tahiti,
France, and the United States, convinced that the island should
benefit Tahitians and that experts in various fields were best
positioned to help him protect it while enhancing its resources.

To that end, students from the University of Hawaii and the École Normale in Papeete participated in the field study, which focused on Tetiaroa's twenty-one *marae*. According to the final report, the island was settled sometime during the sixteenth century. The configuration of the largest and most elaborate ceremonial site, which had a platform suitable for council meetings or dancing, suggested that Tetiaroa played an important role in the nation's political and social system, an assumption further supported by the island's proximity to the Tahitian mainland. King Pomare I, who unified and ruled Tahiti in the late eighteenth century, was believed to have made frequent use of the island, possibly living there. It seemed eerily appropriate that the first European in Tetiaroa was thought to have been William Bligh, who arrived there in 1789 searching for the *Bounty* mutineers.

Brando was not shy about going straight to the source when seeking information, a way of exploiting his celebrity dating back to when he invited Margaret Mead over for dinner to discuss her book. After reading *The Whole Earth Catalog*, he decided that its author, Stewart Brand, would be worth talking to about the ecology and resources of Tetiaroa. Brand brought along an associate, Jay Baldwin, an energy specialist who had worked with Buckminster Fuller, when they met on Mulholland Drive in 1974. Their conversation covered subjects from windmill architecture to Eskimo attitudes toward trash. Brando learned from them that Eskimos had no word for "garbage," since they made use of everything, and Brand and Baldwin learned from him that coconut lumber was as strong as steel.[98]

Brando and Brand conceived of a television series that would introduce environmentally sound techniques for construction and repair, while encouraging self-reliance and holistic values. Brando considered it as a replacement for a thwarted documentary, *Future: Tense*, about "the worldwide crisis of unbridled growth," which was to be filmed partly on Tetiaroa. He had planned to serve as "a partner and narrator" on that film, but in the spring of 1973, Don Widener, the documentary's producer, wrote to say that the networks would not sponsor *Future: Tense* unless they were granted full control.[99]

Brando considered Tetiaroa an ideal TV-series location for demonstrating the potential of aquaculture, wind and solar energy, and eco-friendly architecture. Brando had learned about aquaculture from the Lummi Indians under the direction of marine biologist Wally Heath, who was a consultant on Tetiaroa. Aquaculture represented a point of overlap between Brando's commitments to the Indians and his plans for sustainability on Tetiaroa. On June 12, 1973, he flew from Tahiti to appear on *The Dick Cavett Show*, with a group that included Heath and a representative from the Lummi tribe, who described their aquaculture system and showed a film about it. But Brando insisted that all productive measures on Tetiaroa be accomplished through "simple applications of soft technology," to "improve the lives [of people] without wrecking the environment."[100] He respected Tahitian perspectives on work and pleasure, recognizing the advantages of a slower approach.

The challenge was reconciling the island's commercial potential with the goal of preservation. Brando knew that a successful eco-hotel on Tetiaroa would support research and green development, which was costly. Among the plans he approved with a developer just before he died was for air-conditioning the hotel through deep-ocean water technology. He was equally committed to conservation aimed at protecting local species, while reducing invasive ones (which explains why he was reading *Mosquito: A Natural History of Our Most Persistent and Deadly Foe* around this time).[101]

Brando received criticism from those frustrated by his reluctance to implement their plans, or complaining about the island's primitive state. For the most part, however, he managed to use it for what he wanted—as a retreat and as a haven for friends and family. It was a natural utopia where he could revel in the stars, look at animals and plants, read, think, and also dream—for instance, about a possible gorilla preserve on the island, since he loved watching primates.[102]

What he did manage to do during his twenty-eight years as the proprietor of Tetiaroa was to protect it from plunder—by fishermen, who cleaned out the part of the lagoon that he was forced by his purchase agreement to keep public; and by nature, the cyclone of 1983 that destroyed most of the buildings. He also founded Tetiaroa University in 1981, for his growing children and for researchers from France and the United States. The university never became functional, but researchers were able to obtain recognition for the island as an official bird sanctuary and marine-turtle nesting site. Although he never returned to Tahiti after his daughter Cheyenne's suicide in 1995, he kept his word to Madame Doran, preserving the natural beauty of Tetiaroa. The island was passed on to Brando's heirs, who formalized his dreams with the creation of the Tetiaroa Society. Its goal is a real-world laboratory where theory and practice meet to test technological innovations in a working system. It is especially fitting that development plans for Tetiaroa follow the model set out by the United Nations at the 2002 World Summit on Sustainable Development.

Brando never abandoned hope that the wisdom afforded by science would exert increasing influence in years to come. His faith in such prospects was at the forefront of a television ad he made near the end of his life, in February 2000, for Telecom Italia. Brando took an active role in making the ad, shot at Anza Borrego Springs near San Diego, revising his lines from initial to final script and from final script to performance. Wearing a black fedora and coat, alone on a mountain range, he omitted the name of the company advertised and focused on the technological transformations it harnessed. Comparison of the original script to Brando's revised version reveals his gift for language and understanding of science. He opens with an admission of mortality: "Well... I probably won't live to see the full impact of the wave of change that technology is bringing towards us." Marlon Brando is old, the ad announces, forced to contemplate, like all of us, the world he has known moving on without him. He retains high hopes, nevertheless: "What I'd really like to see is a time when there aren't any boundaries between art, science, religion, philosophy," anticipating the prospective wonders: "the authority of this world become irrelevant as massive quantities of information become available to all of us on this earth" or the word *"impossible* vanish from our dictionaries, or from our ways of thinking." Technology also sanctions the optimistic close. "The way things are changing; I might just hang around. ... Wouldn't that be swell?" Yet the ad makes a paradoxical distinction between the immortality of the film star assured long ago by cinematic technology and the mortality of the man. And Brando's 2004 death confirmed that the technological future he imagined had yet to arrive.[103]

LYING FOR A LIVING

Perhaps because of his ambivalence toward acting, Brando always had plenty to say about it. He could be dismissive: Actors were not artists, films were a business. He'd kept at it because it was a good living, and the hours were unbeatable. These were not the claims of a gnarled cynic; from youth to old age, he maintained that he was an actor because he hadn't found anything better to do, and because he lacked, as he said in *Time* in 1954, "the moral strength to turn down the money." Such remarks, however, seemed disingenuous beside others in the same magazine a year earlier, when he compared European and American filmmaking to the latter's detriment, observing: "The Europeans are businessmen too, but they can handle art because their culture permits it. They're not in such a hurry—people take their time. They examine little things. A director will show you a guy going out his door, down a long hall, down the stairs.... Here, everything has to move fast or people won't like the movie, so it won't make any money.... Why, what happened when you got a picture done with true sensitivity like *The Quiet One* [a 1948 documentary about an emotionally disturbed black child]. That film died."[1] His complaints about the profit motive on Broadway and in Hollywood, and about the aesthetic obliviousness of American audiences, sound like jeremiads denouncing the violation of what he revered.

Observations about acting made throughout his career amount to a set of basic principles. First, the idea that acting was instinct. Everybody acts—from the toddler who quickly learns how to behave to get his mother's attention to husbands and wives engaged in the daily rituals of marriage. Every human activity requires acting of a different sort; none could survive without this inborn skill. Second, the recognition that there was nothing *wrong* with artifice or "lying." We act because we *must*. Third, adept professionals inevitably conceptualized these procedures, holding up a mirror to reveal the dramatic nature of social activity. Fourth, the least important part of any performance is the words. If the acting is effective, the audience should be able to understand most of what is happening from face and gesture alone. (Brando had a habit of watching television without the sound to better apprehend silent expression.)[2] Fifth, an audience's ability to identify with the character mattered more than the quality of the acting or dialogue. This was why Brando told anyone who would listen that he gave stronger performances in *Burn!* and *Last Tango in Paris* than in *On the Waterfront*. Terry Malloy was an everyman whose regret for what might have been was deeply affecting, while the plot and characters of the later two films inhibited empathy.

Many of these ideas were as old as Hamlet's advice to the players. Brando had memorized a lot of Shakespeare, and he considered the Bard's language and dramatic invention unequaled: "One is tempted to believe that he has come from another galaxy. His distance from other writers…has to be measured in light years."[3] Brando frequently drew on Shakespeare's insights, and he clearly knew Stanislavski's work, but he seems not to have benefited from much else in the field of dramatic theory. Given the size and range of Brando's library, his mere hundred books

on theater and film, very few of them annotated, may be surprising.[4] Perhaps he did care more about the language of dolphins,
the subject of a 1989 *Omni* essay, which had Post-its on every page
and was part of a large science collection, or about the history of
religion because he owned and heavily annotated so many books
on it.[5] He did mark up Ingmar Bergman's memoir, *The Magic
Lantern* (1988), which he may have been reading as a model for
his own autobiography, but he seems to have read mainly for discovery, information, and consolation.[6] His range as an actor was
the result of his many varied interests. When it came to acting,
he found inspiration everywhere but in acting books.

People who worked with Brando often marveled at his powers
of concentration. He could immerse himself in scenes, ignoring
cameras and lights as well as directors, like no one else. While
he never "became" a character, extending his role beyond the
set, he felt that an actor had to *commit* to his fiction. He assented
readily when the host on *The Tex and Jinx Show* commented:
"If you aren't convinced of what you're doing, you won't convince anyone else." In that radio interview of December 12, 1955,
which included Marilyn Monroe, Brando also rejected the label
"method actor"; it wasn't the first time nor would it be the last.
Asked to define "the method," Brando answered: "That's what
50 million actors would like to know too. It's an age-old argument and you could spend twelve hours in Walgreen's Drugstore
arguing about it. Stanislavski wrote several long tomes on the
subject." Pressed about his own technique, he characterized it
as "instinctive."

Brando never studied with Lee Strasberg, who in America
had made his name synonymous with method acting. Brando
furthermore disliked the rigidity and elitism associated with a
specific school and prophet. While his mentor Stella Adler was
hardly self-effacing, she presented her techniques as part of a
tradition to which she paid homage through interpretations of

great performances (from the Yiddish Theatre and elsewhere) and redactions of Stanislavski and other theorists. Brando always acknowledged his debt to Adler, but he departed from her teachings by refusing to idealize acting as she did and by downplaying distinctions between those with talent and those without.

His view of acting was essentially democratic: It was a basic human impulse motivated by social necessity. This was a key emphasis in the 1965 interviews he did to promote his movie *Morituri* (made into a 1966 documentary, *Meet Marlon Brando*, by Albert and David Maysles). Questioned about his professional development, Brando said, "We're *all actors* . . . the way that you conduct yourself in this interview is not the way that you conduct yourself at a bar with some of your friends . . . one is able to adjust oneself to a situation." Reporter: "Would you say that your handling of your roles is a reflection of yourself as a person?" Brando: "I think everything we do in life is a reflection of ourselves." In response to a French reporter who wondered whether he thought the status and prestige of actors obligated them to take stands on social issues, Brando said he considered this the responsibility of every citizen.[7]

Brando also saw acting as an evolutionary adaptation. "We couldn't survive a second if we weren't able to act," he said on *The Dick Cavett Show* in 1973. "Acting is a survival mechanism; it's a social unguent, a lubricant and we act to save our lives actually every day. People lie constantly every day, by not saying something that they think or saying something that they don't think or showing something that they don't feel." He gives the example of the underling whose ambition to move up in an agency requires that he celebrate the boss's every harebrained scheme. Such mundane situations call for acting of a very skillful kind. The role is played "day after day after day, in order to survive in your job." And even if the lines change, the motivation doesn't. What makes this acting is the deliberate intention and goal, requiring specific

On *The Dick Cavett Show.* © Bettmann/Corbis.

contrivances. To Cavett's retort that these daily dramas have nothing to do with Brando's performances, Brando insists that he could never play Cavett's role. Then he launches into a review of Cavett as talk-show host. The host's mind is in overdrive as he sizes up each remark, the tone and temper of his guest, the audience reception, deciding when to interrupt with a question, introduce a joke, all the while alert to the station-break schedule. "You're doing this editing at an insane rate," Brando concludes, "and you have this demeanor of levity and lightness and amusement and zest, and it's easy to ascertain that that finally isn't what goes on in your mind, or your feelings at all. . . . That's something that I couldn't do. I couldn't do what you do. And that's a different kind of acting, you're playing a different role." Brando's closing characterization of acting is familiar: "It is a business, it's no more than that, and those who pretend that it's an art I think are misguided. Acting is a craft and it's a profession not unlike being an electrician or plumber or an economist."[8]

He picks up the same point in a 1989 interview on *Saturday Night with Connie Chung,* as if the conversation were ongoing:

"Why did I wind up being an actor rather than a scientist who's studying entomology or an animal trainer? Why did I make that choice?" Chung asks, "Don't you realize that you're thought of as the greatest actor ever?" Brando's mastiff wanders in as if on cue, and Brando exploits the extra. "Tim's the greatest actor ever," he declares, slapping the dog's rump. "He pretends he loves me and he just wants something to eat." During this appearance, Brando gives his most dismissive views on acting, perhaps because he was airing his grievances about *A Dry White Season*. He berated the studio system for overvaluing profit and grimly insisted that he was done with acting and had prioritized other things. Of course, his choice to address the situation on television suggested quite the opposite—how much acting still mattered to him.[9]

His flat denial in response to another obligatory question— whether he regretted playing so few great roles and giving up the stage for film—seemed comparatively sincere. Brando had a strong orientation toward his acting projects to the end, which was evident in two that he worked on with great enthusiasm during 2000 and 2001. Both utilized new technologies to democratize filmmaking techniques and disseminate theories he had been articulating for most of his professional life. The first was a DVD program begun around January 2000 with Scott Billups, an expert in special effects who was considered a leading innovator in new technologies. The idea was a film version of karaoke (empty orchestra) they dubbed "karabuti" (empty stage), which allowed people to insert themselves into movies using camcorders and computers at home. Thus, an admirer of *Casablanca* might don trench coat and fedora, set his video to black and white, and enact a scene, which could then be edited into the film. There would be an option, too, for making original dramas and voice-overs on animated pictures. The technology would be accessible so that anyone with a relatively updated and inexpensive computer could participate.[10]

Brando's belief in the universality of drama provided inspiration for the DVD. Made conscious of their own intuitive theatricality, many could learn to replicate the performances of stars. He also emphasized the power of the most basic stories, again invoking Sidney Meyers's *The Quiet One* for illustration. What resonated especially, he explained to Billups, was the idea of this "traumatized black kid . . . who couldn't relate to people, and finally, through this relationship with this man, he was able to take some mud and make it into an ashtray," which he gave to the man. "That was his passport to freedom . . . he learned to give something."[11] Brando's receptivity to this picture, carried from one century into another (recalled for *Time* in 1953, for Billups in 2000), was informed by "Bud," the neglected child of alcoholics, at Lathrop Junior High School, Santa Ana, California, hammering metal into a functional tool and receiving the rare gift of praise from an authority figure.[12]

There was no greater sign of Brando's enduring interest in his vocation than the classes on acting (mentioned in chapter 6) that he conducted in 2001 and called "Lying for a Living."[13] The idea was to assemble people, eminent and ordinary, from all walks of life, along with professional actors, to participate in a series of lessons on acting fundamentals. Brando had global ambitions for these classes, which he planned to film and distribute worldwide. Among the people he invited was former President Bill Clinton. In a letter to Clinton on December 1, 2001, Brando noted that he would be speaking "French, German, Spanish, and Chinese" in the effort to reach perhaps "a billion people," and he suggested possible roles for Clinton: "Sax player, actor, erudite scholar, experienced political counselor, man-about-town." Clinton was reportedly intrigued until he heard Brando's name for the enterprise.[14] Brando was not only aiming at international audiences but also drawing on a range of cultures for his techniques. His notes, "Research for Acting Lessons Project," from August 28,

2001, for example, begin: "Get Books on Masks," asking, "What is psychological, cultural and social function?" and cites various examples: "The No Theater in Japan. The Chinese Opera.... Africa, Wooden masks.... New Guinea Polynesia the function of tattooing, Decorating the face for war or fun, American Indians." From these traditional forms he goes on to describe "the masks we wear without masks: Japanese subway mask...mask we wear when being criticized by boss."[15]

In "Random Notes on Acting," Brando listed topics and exercises for the classes: "The History of acting—beginning with apes"; "Russian director, Serge Isenstein, who made the experiments with a camera; the 'reality experiences'"; "Acting is not intellectual. It's emotional. The enemy of the actor is the mind." "Make them recite Shakespeare. Bring in costumes and makeup. Do makeup at home." "Jacob P. Adler. Stella Adler's influence on the world; everyone is copying American acting style." "Who acts? Who doesn't? Children act less, one reason why we love children so much."[16]

Under "Students," Brando stipulated: "Some pay—most free. ...Not for actors only." Participants ranged from Jon Voight, Michael Jackson, Sean Penn, Thomas Jane, and Whoopi Goldberg to Brando's lawyer, a used-car salesman, and a fellow named Jim Anderson, whom Brando dubbed "the recycler" after discovering him rifling through the trash and inviting him to join the classes. There were daylong meetings with twenty to thirty students each time, which were planned extensively during the summer of 2001 and then filmed beginning in November.[17] Brando was a sensitive teacher, couching criticism of student improvisations in general principles, alert while lecturing. Noticing a woman daydreaming, he asked what she was thinking. Her spontaneous reply—"about the texture of the floor"—prompted a modest reaction: "You know what that tells me? I've lost the audience. You've got to know when you've lost your audience." But he usually kept things lively, sometimes correcting student grammar, rattling off (a notably esoteric selection of) Yiddish curses, praising Paul Muni, Daniel Day-Lewis, and Meryl Streep as major talents who take risks. For an exercise, he reprised an idea discussed with Quincy Jones for their parts in *Jericho*, instructing the white students to behave black and the black students to behave white.[18] Develop your "inner critic," by suppressing your ego, he recommended, and fill out your characters with details.

One participant, high-wire artist Philippe Petit, was motivated by Brando's classes to begin writing his autobiography, *Man on Wire* (2008). "During the filming of his workshop 'Lying for a Living'—between takes, I was furiously scribbling my first draft in red ink. This terribly talented master of deceit taught me golden rules I had forgotten I knew, which applied as much to the page as to the stage. By practicing the discipline of self-imposed intellectual immobility—akin to the *respect of stillness* Marlon calls for—I was able to apprehend the essence of each chapter before I drafted it. My pen learned to perceive what lurked on the other side of the action it was busy describing until, like him, I could declare, I *can see a smile in the dark*."[19] Perhaps it took another tightrope walker to appreciate Brando's approach: the recourse to instinct, the privileging of controlled emotion, expressive stillness.

Brando was always honing his craft, even more so in life, according to friends and family, than on stage and screen. In the 1950s, his sister Fran commented, "Buddy is really acting all the time. When he came back from France recently, he spoke French all day, and after making that Mexican movie, Zapata, it was Spanish."[20] Those who knew him maintained that his best performances never made it into his movies. Brando said, "You can't act, unless you are what you are and who you are." But he seems to have made a point of keeping others guessing, dissembling, impersonating, fabricating scenes, as if constantly testing his own powers of make-believe.[21] His genius was to be in touch with something more provisional than himself: what he had the potential to be, or felt like being at the moment. This is supported by some of the vignettes Brando solicited (from sisters, longtime friends, former lovers) for his autobiography, memories that he used to jog his own recollections of the past. One of these, from a woman with whom he had a two-year affair, is especially revealing of the dramatic energy he expended in courtship. The woman was Pakistani, a college student of nineteen when they met; her long, detailed account of their romance shows how Brando specialized in reading what women wanted and delivering it in role-playing of the highest order. The woman is traditional, beautiful, naïve, and narcissistic. Brando seems to have transformed himself into what she expected and needed in a lover, and he convinced her that this was his truest self. At the same time, he apparently enjoyed the opportunity his talents afforded of being the man she desired, perhaps even becoming attached to the character he played for her.

So what is this lover's Brando like? He is "at 39 excessively trim and exceptionally handsome," his "splendor and beauty" set off by Toto, the "monstrous" St. Bernard that sometimes accompanied him. He was "born charming...a born romantic and a dreamer." This Brando is relatively solemn; "laughing has never been either your or my nature," his lover notes confidently. They are "both teetotalers" and she adopts his tastes—coffee with cinnamon stick, steak medium-rare, with salad. He gives her gifts of his favorite music: William Kapell playing piano concertos, Miles Davis, *Sketches of Spain.* Once he knocks on her door costumed as a Western Union man with packages. He has a "microscopic memory" and is "a prude...never...vulgar in manner, behavior, or speech." She is convinced of their "soul kinship," that theirs is a "marriage of minds." Through the first four months of 1964, they are "inseparable," he "cannot let go," and she "is like the fruit tree, I bend with every wish of yours." It is clear from this that Brando had shown this lover only a part of his personality, had dramatized a version of his persona to meet her specifications.[22] As the relationship wound down to its inevitable end, he becomes cold, critical, finally withdrawing permanently. But all this is done in character; he never stops playing his designated role.

A male friend from Libertyville, who also sent memories for the autobiography, recalled Brando's teenaged advice on "how to treat women": "Be commanding; do something nice for them; don't let them come around." This studied role—learned from his father or another successful ladies' man—was precocious for a high-schooler; he perfected it over time. He could be callous and cruel, but there was no question that he loved and needed women, and his performances on screen and off ensured that they would love and need him back.[23] On the drama of eroticism, Brando commented, "I always thought that if I wrote something about my sexual knowledge, I'd have something like Krafft-Ebing [a psychiatrist known for his clinical studies of female sexuality] on the peculiarities of women.... There are many roads leading to Rome but they're filled with a lot of strange adventures."[24]

One title Brando considered for his autobiography was *The Actor's Duty*; another that would have been appropriate was *The Actor's Mask*.[25] Brando contributed a body of performances on stage and screen that transformed acting permanently, performances that will inspire global audiences as long as people watch films. That legacy was inseparable from the roles Brando played in the progressive movements of the era, civil rights, justice for the American Indians, the United Nations, UNICEF, and environmentalism. In all of these endeavors, he lent his energies because he believed in the causes and felt obligated to help. Yet it was Brando's fate, on film and in life, to be ahead of his time. Some of the changes he supported—including his global outlook, shown by his insistence that *Sayonara* (1957) end with an interracial marriage (the first in Hollywood film), his challenges to traditional gender roles, his promotion of sustainable ecosystems—are only now, years after his death, becoming more accepted. Some planetary outrages, he realized, would never be redressed. This was clear in his last public appearance at Michael Jackson's 30th Anniversary Concert in Madison Square Garden on September 10, 2001. Brando's participation put him in New York on September 11, making him a witness to yet another major event. His assistant remembers how quiet he was at the hotel, following the news and researching details on his computer, before it became possible a few days later to slip off to the airport. The appearance hadn't gone well either. During his speech, he had spoken about the issue of worldwide hunger among children and was booed by the raucous and youthful crowd.[26]

Brando consistently put forward his beliefs no matter how they were received. That tenacity is illuminated by an anecdote he told about an encounter a decade earlier. He had wandered into an electronics store in midtown Manhattan looking for a part for his camera. The part couldn't have been worth more than two dollars, but Brando recalled that the Hasidic clerk turned the store upside down to find it. It was not because he was star struck; to him, Brando was just an "ordinary fat guy" making a minor purchase. The man's time was far more valuable than the pennies he probably earned on the sale, but he felt a responsibility to his customer. And more than this, Brando said, was the larger principle to which he was committed: the ethic of "leaving the world better than you found it." This was a goal that Brando could understand.[27]

One of Brando's very last projects was doing voice-overs, reciting his favorite poems and Shakespeare soliloquies.[28] Of those he managed to record before his death, there was none he loved

Brando as Brando, 1997. Photograph by Jan Thijs, who recalls (in an e-mail communication) that Brando especially liked this photograph and ordered hundreds of copies. He set up a table in the frigid Canadian air of the *Free Money* set and patiently inscribed a photo for each member of the cast and crew.

more than Elinor Morton Wylie's "Now Let No Charitable Hope,"
which ends:

> *In masks outrageous and austere*
> *The years go by in single file;*
> *But none has merited my fear,*
> *And none has quite escaped my smile.*

ACKNOWLEDGMENTS

This book has depended on the kindness of strangers. Ellen Adler and Tom Oppenheim barely knew me when they shared their memories of Brando and helped me reach out to his other personal friends. Mike Medavoy, executor of the Brando Estate trusted me and gave freely of his wisdom at every stage. Avra Douglas, another executor, shared her wealth of understanding as someone who knew Brando, from years of being his friend, probably better than anyone. David Seeley provided help and advice from the start of the process when he agreed to take a call from a biographer, to the end, when he facilitated my search for permissions. Jeffrey Abrams was the ideal estate lawyer with his expertise and sense of fair play. Austin Wilkin provided audio, high resolution photographs, and everything it seemed I needed just when I needed it. Christian Reed used his research skills to scour the archives when I couldn't get to them myself. Rebecca Brando conveyed her love for her father and guided me to sources I would never have reached without her. Quincy Jones took time from his formidable schedule of global good works to talk to me by phone and in person about his friend "Leroy."

Curators of the Christie's Sale—Helen Hall, Cathy Elkies, and Laura Armstrong, to whom I am especially indebted—protected the privacy of their clients while facilitating my research. Those who bought research materials at the Brando Estate Sale and shared them with me, made my book possible. They include: Cosmo DeNicola; Johnny Depp; Tony Freiburg; Marilyn Gauthier; Bernie Gould; Connie Kaufmann; Alexander Khochinskiy; Melinda Leeka; Charles Mady and Diana Mady Kelly; Richard Marrone; Henry McNeil; Alan Thurston; Noah Wyle; and John Zorn.

My gratitude as well to Brando family and friends who shared their memories with me: Miko Brando; Martin Asinof; Joseph Brutsman; Jay Kanter; Patt

Morrison; Shane Brando; Prudence Brando; Karen Brando; Carmelita Pope Wood; Nina Green Rosenfeld; Harry Dean Stanton; and Alice Marchak. I am grateful too to those who shared their memories of working with Brando on films: Salvo Basile; Bob Bendetson; Stanley Brooks; Angie Dickinson, Paul Doherty; David Page; Peter Shin; Stewart Stern; Jan Thijs; and Marice Tobias.

The process of turning my research into a book was assisted by John Tessitore, who connected me with Joe Tessitore, who provided invaluable counsel as my agent; Anna Mageras; Gene Jarrett, Anne Austin, Francis Antonelli; Kathleen Brandes; Stephen Smith; Devik Weiner; Kevin Murphy; Stephen Deuters; Shaun Lee; Debb Foreman; Radha Ramachandran, Cecile Gaspar, and Yosihiko Sinoto. Fay Torresyap, who helped me with permissions was a true detective. My friend Sylvia Fuks trained her years of editorial experience on my work during walks and through her careful reading. Above all I am grateful to Amy Cherry, vice president and senior editor at Norton, who was the kind of editor writers dream about: tough-minded, thorough, always full of brilliant advice.

I was also fortunate to have family and friends with a seemingly inexhaustible curiosity about Brando. My parents, Ruth and Ephraim Mizruchi, nurtured my teenage obsession, buying me Brando biographies and driving me to Brando film festivals. My mother's open-mindedness was critical. She discouraged my seeing *Last Tango in Paris* at age fourteen, not because she considered the film obscene, but because she worried it would ruin my passion. I am grateful as well to my brothers and sisters-in-law, Mark and Gail Mizruchi; Dave and Anastasia Mizruchi; Sylvia Ary, and my nephew and niece, Josh and Mikayla Mizruchi. My thanks also to: Adrienne Sirken; Chaim Feingold; Chana Feingold; Paul Davidovits; Judith Taplitz; Patricia Herzog; Norman Janis; Dan Aaron; Barry Korobkin; Laura Korobkin; Randy Glassman, Stephanie Byttebier, Nick Forster, and Mike Vignola, and to the Boston University Humanities Foundation for help with the costs of permissions.

There is no group from which I draw more strength and pleasure than my pack. My stepson, Eytan Bercovitch, supported me with his intelligence and insight, and made certain that my computer was completely backed up. My son, Sascha Bercovitch was a constant source of inspiration. With his extraordinary knowledge of Latin America and other cultures, and his experience as a journalist, he prodded me to clarify my aims and neutralize my portrait in ways that improved it immeasurably. No one contributed more to this project from start to finish than my husband Sacvan Bercovitch. He is my soul mate and role model, the person I trust more than anyone in the world and rely on for the best things. I dedicate this book to him with deep gratitude.

APPENDIX: BRANDO'S PLAYS AND FILMS

PLAYS

I Remember Mama (1944–46)
Truckline Café (1946)
A Flag Is Born (1946)
Candida (1946)
Antigone (1946)
A Streetcar Named Desire (1947–49)

FILMS

The Men (1950)
A Streetcar Named Desire (1951)
Viva Zapata! (1952)
Julius Caesar (1953)
The Wild One (1953)
On the Waterfront (1954)
Désirée (1954)
Guys and Dolls (1955)
The Teahouse of the August Moon (1956)
Sayonara (1957)
The Young Lions (1958)
The Fugitive Kind (1960)
One-Eyed Jacks (1961)
Mutiny on the Bounty (1962)

The Ugly American (1963)
Bedtime Story (1964)
Morituri (1965)
The Chase (1966)
The Appaloosa (1966)
A Countess from Hong Kong (1967)
Reflections in a Golden Eye (1967)
Candy (1968)
The Night of the Following Day (1968)
Burn! (1969)
The Nightcomers (1972)
The Godfather (1972)
Last Tango in Paris (1972)
The Missouri Breaks (1976)
Roots: The Next Generations (1977)
Superman (1978)
Apocalypse Now (1979)
The Formula (1980)
A Dry White Season (1989)
The Freshman (1990)
Christopher Columbus: The Discovery (1992)
Don Juan DeMarco (1995)
The Island of Dr. Moreau (1996)
The Brave (1997)
Free Money (1998)
The Score (2001)

NOTES

INTRODUCTION

1 Marlon Brando, with Robert Lindsey, *Brando: Songs My Mother Taught Me* (New York: Random House, 1994), p. 84. Brando had in his library Max Picard's *The Human Face*, a meditation that begins, "He who looks upon a human face is moved to the very core of his being," and he turned down a page with a passage describing "the cinema-face." "The cinema-face has no sound. It is dumb. The air about the cinema-face is dumb. There is altogether no space surrounding it. Only an emptiness into which some other cinema-face must at once cast itself...." (New York: Farrar and Rinehart, 1930), pp. 3, 131.

2 Marlon Brando, quoted in Helen Dudar, with Peter J. McElroy and Joseph Kahn, "Marlon Brando: Hollywood's Bad Boy?" *New York Post*, 1955, p. 48. According to Dudar, Brando's comment dates from "when he was making his fourth film," *Julius Caesar*, in 1953. Article in Brando Estate Archives.

3 Martin Asinof, interview with the author, June 5, 2013, with follow-ups July and August 2013.

4 Recounted by Ellen Adler, interview with the author, February 15, April 22, May 7, December 17, 2010.

5 Brando's remarkable library confirms a comment made in a documentary interview by his son Teihotu, who lives in Tahiti: "If he hadn't been an actor, he might have been a professor . . . of something." *Imagine . . . Brando*, Stella Adler's Studio, December 2, 2008.

6 Merkin's *New York Times Magazine* obituary of Brando, December 26, 2004, whose title, "Wild One," says it all, reinstates the usual clichés

despite the qualifications ("of course," "in some ways," "quite"). "Brando was more than a male pinup, of course, but in some ways his complex emotional articulation—his eloquently tongue-tied mixture of truculence and sensitivity—was icing on the beefcake." He was, she concludes, "a man who never quite escaped his own raw presence." The same is true of Camille Paglia's "Sullen Hero," *New York Times Book Review*, July 21, 1991, p. 10.

7 Peter Manso, *Brando: The Biography* (New York: Hyperion, 1994), p. 308.

8 Arendt explained in a letter to Gershom Scholem about the Eichmann controversy: "What confuses you is that my arguments and my approach are different from what you are used to; in other words, the trouble is that I am independent. By this I mean, on the one hand, that I do not belong to any organisation and always speak only for myself, and on the other hand, that I have great confidence in Lessing's *selbstdenken*, for which, I think, no ideology, no public opinion, and no 'convictions' can ever be a substitute." Hannah Arendt, *The Jewish Writings*, edited by Jerome Kohn and Ron H. Feldman (New York: Schocken, 2007), p. xlv.

9 This has been attributed to Reb Nahman, but an exact reference is not available. See Arthur Green, *Tormented Master: A Life of Rabbi Nahman of Bratslav* (Tuscaloosa: University of Alabama Press, 1979).

10 Brando in *Songs*, p. 146.

11 Recalled by Tom Oppenheim, interview with the author, May 7, 2010.

12 Ellen Adler, interviews with the author.

13 Quoted in Manso, p. 505.

14 Truman Capote, "The Duke in His Domain," *The New Yorker*, November 9, 1957, p. 79.

15 The Maysles film on the Beatles tour of the United States was called *What's Happening: The Beatles in the U.S.A.*; Ellen Adler, interviews with the author.

16 Albert and David Maysles, *Meet Marlon Brando*, 1966.

17 This was how Brando signed himself or was addressed in letters, respectively, from Johnny Depp, May 5, 1997; and to Sean Penn, August 24, 1986; and to President Bill Clinton, December 1, 2001, in the 1990s and later. Letters in Brando Estate Archives and in a private collection.

18 The playbills from *I Remember Mama* (1944), *Candida* (1946), and *A Flag Is Born* (1946) are reproduced in the Christie's catalogue, *The Personal Property of Marlon Brando: Thursday 30 June 2005*, p. 193. The parody interviews, featuring some of Brando's famous characters, including Don Corleone, are in the Brando Estate Archives. They are discussed in chapter 6.

19   Jocelyn Brando, July 5, 2004.

20   Brando, quoted in Manso, p. 685.

21   Quincy Jones recalled going to jazz clubs with Brando in Manhattan and LA, as well as Brando's favorite phrase, interviews with the author, July 23, 2012, and June 17, 2013.

22   The note, dated July 6, 1965, was not signed but was in his materials under "Annotated Scripts from *The Chase*," in a private collection.

23   This list of composers for Brando theater and film scores includes Kurt Weill, Leonard Bernstein, Alex North, Hugo Friedhofer, Dave Grusin, Nino Rota, and Gato Barbieri. Brando regularly gave *Sketches of Spain* as a gift to girlfriends and had many copies. Ellen Adler interviews, and the sixty-page "memoir" by the Pakistani college student Brando dated for two years, written at his request for his autobiography, Brando Estate Archives. There are also logs in the archives of Brando's music collection. Many friends recall his love for Miles Davis's *Sketches of Spain*, including Quincy Jones. Quincy Jones, interviews with the author.

24   D'Arcy McNickle, *The Indian Tribes of the United States: Ethnic and Cultural Survival* (New York: Oxford University Press, under the auspices of the Institute of Race Relations, London, 1962), p. 5. Brando's annotated copy of McNickle's book is in a private collection. Other Brando marginalia, his annotations on Marilyn Ferguson's discussions of uniquely powerful minds and perceptual states in her *The Brain Revolution* (notes on chapter 20, "The Anatomy of Creativity"), and the "self-tests" he took in selected psychology books (Khochinskiy Brando Library [hereafter, KBL], Boxes 32 and 22), suggest a healthy regard for his own abilities, despite messages (from others) and testimonies (on his part) to the contrary. Ferguson books, private collection. Additional psychology books are in KBL, Boxes 22 and 32.

25   Ellen Adler recalled a small dinner at Brando's Fifty-Seventh Street apartment in New York, where she, her mother Stella, and Margaret Mead were the guests, Ellen Adler, interviews with the author.

26   October 14, 1996, interview on the set of *The Brave* (1997), conducted in French and translated into English. The French and English versions of the interview, apparently never published, are in a private collection.

27   According to Christie's curators, these were organized according to Brando's films. Helen Hall, interview with the author, June 16, 2011. His materials from *Apocalypse Now*, for example, included the books and articles Brando was reading for the film, photographs from the set, film stills, additional reading materials, telegrams and letters about the film

and received during filming, etc. For instance, a telegram of September 23, 1976, from Brando's assistant informs him that "LA animal health services" had come to the house that day because his dog "Rufus...bit a jogger on Mulholland." There was also a detailed letter of September 24, 1976, to Brando about fish-farming equipment, presumably for his Tahiti island development. These materials are in a private collection.

28 Curators and auctioneers at the Christie's sale on June 30, 2005, remarked that they had never seen a sale of an actor's property that was attended by so many fellow actors. Helen Hall, interview with the author; Cathy Elkies, interview with the author, May 17, 2011.

29 "Obama: *Godfather*, McCain: *Viva Zapata*," "For all that divides them, it seems, Brando unites them," according to the *Chicago Tribune*, September 23, 2008, in an article citing the favorite actors and films of the 2008 presidential candidates.

30 These quoted lines are spoken, respectively, by Brando characters Sky Masterson in *Guys and Dolls* (1955) and Sheriff Calder in *The Chase* (1966).

31 According to Jay Kanter, who was Brando's agent for most of his career, the actor was drawn to characters with English accents, and he especially loved to play lawyers. Jay Kanter, interview with the author, April 21, 2011.

32 See Wallace's wonderful riff on Brando in *Infinite Jest* (New York: Little, Brown, 1996), pp. 157–58.

33 Murphy quoted in Manso, p. 341.

34 From Stella Adler, *The Art of Acting* (New York: Applause, 2000), pp. 78, 79.

35 See interviews with Robert Duvall and Arthur Penn in *Brando*, TCM Documentary, 2007.

36 Robert Duvall interview in *Brando*, TCM Documentary, 2007.

37 Constantin Stanislavski, *An Actor Prepares*, translated by Elizabeth Reynolds Hapgood (New York: Routledge, 1948), pp. 149–50.

38 Gitta Parker, a journalist who wrote "A thousand talents, A thousand faces, A thousand moods...This is Brando," noticed Stanislavski's *My Life in Art* and *The Collected Works of William Faulkner* in Brando's dressing room during filming of *Désirée*, summer 1954.

39 Capote, "Duke in His Domain," p. 60. It's also worth noting that Brando himself liked to confuse people, sometimes listing his eyes as "hazel" on licenses. Mostly, however, he confirmed their blue-gray color, as did friends and family.

40 *The Diaries of Paul Klee, 1898–1918*, translation authorized by Felix Klee (Berkeley: University of California Press, 1964), p. 173.

41 Notes, "Research for Acting Lessons Project, August 28, 2001," for the

acting classes Brando called "Lying for a Living," Brando Estate Archives (hereafter, "Lying for a Living" Transcripts). The classes are discussed in the Epilogue.

42 Brando: in *Songs*, p. 212; in Lindsey Interviews; and in "Lying for a Living" Transcripts, Brando Estate Archives. (Robert Lindsey's interviews with Brando for *Songs My Mother Taught Me* are in the Brando Estate Archives and listed hereafter as Lindsey Interviews.)

43 Christie's curators Cathy Elkies and Helen Hall, who prepared Brando's papers and scripts for public sale, recounted in interviews with the author how carefully they were organized. Brando's assistants noted his passion for ordering his books and papers. This was confirmed by his assistant, Avra Douglas, who is now a Brando Estate executor, in interviews with the author, February 29–March 4, June 18 and 19, 2012, and June 23 and 24, 2013.

44 Shane Brando, interview with the author, March 6, 2012.

45 *The Letters of Emily Dickinson*, vols. I–III, edited by Thomas H. Johnson and Theodora Ward (Cambridge: Harvard University Press, 1958), p. 899.

46 Brando in *Songs*, pp. 144, 145.

47 Ibid., p. 145.

48 See, for example, Manso, *Brando*; Richard Schickel, *Brando: A Life in Our Times* (London: Pavilion, 1991); and Stefan Kanfer, *Somebody: The Reckless Life and Remarkable Career of Marlon Brando* (New York: Knopf, 2008).

49 It was fortunate, too, that the Brando Estate chose Christie's for its estate sale, for the auction house keeps records worthy of a research archive. When I told curators about my project in the spring of 2010, they allowed me to draft individual letters to anonymous buyers of lots with valuable research material, which curators forwarded on my behalf. Fifty-three out of fifty-seven of these buyers responded and provided access to their materials.

50 His book buying began in New York, if not sooner. A fellow acting student from this time recalls his purchases of Modern Library editions of Freud, Krafft-Ebing, and Dostoevsky (Manso, *Brando*, p. 113).

51 Cathy Elkies was the first to enter the house, and Helen Hall worked extensively on the collection. Related in interviews with the author.

52 The List of Books around Marlon's Bed included thirty-five books, Brando Estate Archives.

53 Harold Clurman, who directed Brando in *Truckline Café*, was hardly an unqualified fan of the actor's. But he noted in his memoir that "Brando is not only acutely perceptive, but articulate as well. He has a good ear,

a feeling for language....Abroad he quickly picks up foreign tongues and intonations. He 'assimilates' people with his whole body. His verbal reactions to people are brief, cryptic, and astonishingly perspicacious." Clurman, *All People Are Famous: Instead of an Autobiography* (New York: Harcourt Brace, 1974), pp. 259–60.

54 James Kritzeck, *Anthology of Islamic Literature: From the Rise of Islam to Modern Times* (New York: Mentor Books, 1966), KBL, Box 85.

55 Brando told Lawrence Grobel in their interview how much he enjoyed Thomas's *Lives of a Cell*. Grobel Interview Transcripts, Brando Estate Archives (hereafter, Grobel Interviews). Thomas's books are in KBL, Boxes 49, 24, and 71.

56 Jay Kanter recalled that Brando was the first person he knew in Hollywood with a personal computer, that he owned two or three of the unwieldy machines and updated constantly as the quality of computers progressed. Jay Kanter, interview with the author.

57 KBL, Boxes 36, 47, and 48. The collection looks like that of a college professor, though identifying the academic specialization would be challenging. Typical of his holdings is the Columbia University Press anthropology catalog, 1982–1983, addressed to "Marlon Brando, 12900 Mulholland Dr...."

58 KBL, Box 88. The atoll was a veritable coconut plantation, and Brando was keen to make use of this bountiful resource. Brando heavily annotated a book about coconut wood, including details on the best types of chain saws for cutting it ("tungsten carbide tipped circular saws"), the products made from it (from boards to chess sets), and the types of insects and animals to which it was vulnerable.

59 KBL, Box 25.

60 Brando's scripts for *One-Eyed Jacks*, Herrick Library, Beverly Hills, and in a private collection.

61 Manso, for example, reports that Brando was reading and visiting libraries by the age of six, and that he would cut high school and spend the day reading classics (Eliot, Shakespeare, books on religion) in his mother's library. At Shattuck Military Academy, which he entered at sixteen, Brando was reading Schopenhauer, Kant, and Freud, among others. Acquaintances in Paris from 1949 recall the young Brando as "a voracious reader," Manso, *Brando*, pp. 19, 40, 74–75, 273. But Manso loses interest in Brando's reading after 1949 and does not connect the habit to the performances.

62 Hannah Arendt, *The Life of the Mind*, vol. 1: *Thinking* (New York: Harcourt Brace, 1978).

63 Notes for MB Autobiography, Brando Estate Archives. Brando wrote his own notes for his autobiography, *Songs My Mother Taught Me*, but he also solicited notes from close friends and family. These materials are in the Brando Estate Archives. (They are cited hereafter as [author's name], Notes for MB Autobiography.)

CHAPTER ONE. LESSONS OF THE MIDWEST

1 Brando recalls his paternal grandfather once in *Songs*, p. 8. Details on Marlon Brando Sr.'s family are from a Census quoted in a private genealogy done for Brando in 1995 by Marsha S. Dennis, a self-described "fan" of the actor's and professional genealogist at the Genealogical and General Research Records Office in New York City. Letter of July 12, 1995, and Genealogy in Brando Estate Archives.

2 Brando's two youngest sons, born in 1992 and 1994, respectively, were named Myles Jonathan Brando and Timothy Gahan Brando.

3 Brando taped an interview with his great-aunt June Beechly in 1957 when she visited him in Japan during filming of *Sayonara*. All subsequent quotations from Beechly in the paragraphs that follow are from this interview, audiotape in Brando Estate Archives.

4 Frances Brando Loving refers to "our mother's handsome amateur actor father, Will Pennebaker, [who] died of tuberculosis when she was two. We have some wonderful pictures of him looking very like Bud as a young man." Notes for MB Autobiography, Brando Estate Archives.

5 This history is recounted in the interview Brando taped with his great-aunt June Beechly in Japan. It is detailed as well by Brando's sisters Jocelyn (RG1755: AM *Nebraskans in Film Project*, Series 4 Interviews, Folder 1, Jocelyn Brando, May 4, 1981) and Frances (RG1755: AM *Nebraskans in Film Project*, Series 4 Interviews, Folder 2, Frances Brando Loving, May 4, 1981), and in the 1995 Genealogy by Marsha Dennis. Additional details in a *History of Nebraska* entry on Myles Gahan, Brando Estate Archives, as well as Manso, *Brando*, pp. 1–5.

6 Frances Brando Loving refers to this conviction, which she shared with her sister Jocelyn, Notes for MB Autobiography, Brando Estate Archives.

7 This is Brando's characterization, *Songs*, p. 21.

8 Details on Brando's tactile sense were recounted in Ellen Adler, interviews with the author, February 15, April 22, May 7, and December 17, 2010; and Carmelita Pope, interview with the author, February 3, 2012. For books on religion, see especially KBL, Boxes 78, 10, and 17.

9 He marks, for instance, a paragraph in Barbara Brown's *Stress and the Art of Biofeedback*, challenging the medical orthodoxy that "the body's vital functions" are "beyond the control of mind" (New York: Bantam, 1977), p. 5 (KBL, Box 10), and in Elmer and Alyce Green's *Beyond Biofeedback*, a dictum familiar to Christian Science: "Our bodies tend to do what they are told *if we know how to tell them*" (New York: Delacorte Press, 1977), p. 2 (KBL, Box 17). Brando read deeply on these issues of autogenic training, biofeedback, and mental telepathy.

10 Frances Brando Loving, Notes for MB Autobiography, Brando Estate Archives.

11 Jocelyn Brando, Frances Brando Loving, Notes for MB Autobiography, Brando Estate Archives.

12 Brando recalled this incident with Pat in Lindsey Interviews, Brando Estate Archives. Martin Asinof related the story about Toto and the roast in interview with the author, June 5, 2013, with follow-ups in July and August 2013.

13 Jocelyn Brando, *Nebraskans in Film Project*.

14 Jocelyn Brando, Notes for MB Autobiography.

15 See reviews in *Omaha World-Herald*, October 26, 1926, and May 11, 1927. These carefully preserved materials from Dodie Brando's acting career are in the Brando Estate Archives. Jocelyn Brando, quoted in RG1755: AM *Nebraskans in Film Project* Series 4 Interviews, Folder 1, Jocelyn Brando, May 4, 1981.

16 "Brandos Put Life in the Old Block," Frances Brando Loving, *North Shore*, July 1979. Ellen Adler recalled Donat as a favorite of Brando's from the start of his time in Manhattan, interviews with the author.

17 The walking sticks were sold as part of the Christie's sale in 2005 and pictured in the Christie's catalogue, *The Personal Property of Marlon Brando: Thursday 30 June 2005*, pp. 24–25.

18 Mildred Milar recalled being "Brando's 4th grade teacher at Lincoln School," in "Evanston trivia: Did you know that Marlon Brando once lived on Judson Avenue?" by Bob Seidenberg, *Evanston Review* (March/April 1979).

19 See *Songs*, pp. 5–12, 19, for these details on childhood. Frances's inscription was on Stephen Mitchell's translation of the *Tao Te Ching*, KBL, Box 93.

20 The record of Dodie's participation at the Yale Summer School is in the Marty Mann Papers, Special Collections Research Center, Syracuse University Library, Syracuse, NY.

21 These details on Evanston are from two pieces from local papers:

"Evanston Trivia," by Bob Seidenberg, and Frances Brando Loving, "Brandos Put Life in the Old Block."

22 Frances Brando Loving, Notes for MB Autobiography, Brando Estate Archives.

23 Interview with Edward R. Murrow, *Person to Person*, April 1, 1955.

24 Ibid.

25 This was confirmed by Martin Asinof, interviews with the author.

26 Brando taped this August 1983 conversation with Michael Jackson, which took place in his Mulholland Drive home. Their main subject was developing Jackson's acting skills.

27 Lindsey Interviews.

28 Brando interview with Michael Jackson, August 1983, Brando Estate Archives. Ellen Adler, interviews with the author, February 15, April 22, May 7, December 17, 2010.

29 Brando described making the screwdriver to Robert Lindsey (Lindsey Interviews), even remembering the high school teacher's name as Mr. Wilkensen. He kept the three letters he earned from Lathrop Junior High School in track and basketball, and they were sold at the 2005 Christie's sale as Lot 327.

30 *Selected Poems of Emily Dickinson*, with an introduction by Conrad Aiken (New York: Modern Library, 1924), pp. 6, 8. The scansion appears periodically throughout the book, which is in a private collection.

31 See Manso, *Brando*, pp. 9, 19, 40, 57, 59, 74–75; and *Songs*, pp. 52–53, for recollections of Brando's reading growing up.

32 Carmelita Pope, interview with the author, February 3, 2012.

33 Manso, *Brando*, p. 74; and *Songs*, pp. 52–53.

34 This letter to his sister Jocelyn and her husband was written sometime between 1940 and 1942.

35 Fyodor Dostoevsky, *The Brothers Karamazov*, translated from the Russian by Constance Garnett (London: William Heinemann, 1951), p. v. Brando's copy is in a private collection.

36 Brando's notes in a stenographer's notebook, Brando Estate Archives.

37 These letters written by Brando to his parents and Grandmother Bess from Shattuck are dated February 1942 (exact date not available), February 5 and April 2, 1942, respectively, Brando Estate Archives.

38 The letter was signed by Harry Webster, Larry Branley, Joe Bill Hall, Dave Bronson, and Dave Claypool, a self-described "committee of five," envelope dated May 24, 1943, Brando Estate Archives.

39 Frances Brando Loving, "Brandos Put Life in the Old Block."

40 Manso, *Brando*, p. 27.

41 *The Ed Sullivan Show* 1955 interview with Brando and George Englund's account of Brando doing imitations for his mother are both included in *Brando*, TCM Documentary, 2007.

42 Brando's answer to the inspecting officer, the Shattuck play, and Wagner's statement are recounted in *Songs*, pp. 58, 54, 59. Jocelyn Brando describes her parents' reaction in her interview for *Nebraskans in Film Project*.

43 Martin Asinof described a persisting competitiveness on Jocelyn's part, interviews with the author.

CHAPTER TWO. MANHATTAN SCHOOLING

1 Jocelyn Brando, *Nebraskans in Film Project*.

2 Quoted by Ellen Adler, interviews with the author, February 15, April 22, May 7, and December 17, 2010.

3 Ellen Adler recalled accompanying Brando on his searches, interviews with the author.

4 Brando: *Songs*, pp. 97–98.

5 Nina Green, interview with the author, November 30, 2011.

6 Sam Shaw, *Brando in the Camera Eye* (New York: Exeter, 1979), p. 20.

7 Tennessee Williams and Elia Kazan were the first to use this term to describe Brando, but not the last. Williams is quoted in Elia Kazan, *A Life* (New York: Knopf, 1988), p. 346. Kazan himself makes this assertion on p. 659.

8 She "knew every song that was ever written," he commented in his autobiography, and also admired classical music, especially powerful modernists like Stravinsky. See *Songs*, p. 9. Also see Brando's collection of song and music books, KBL, Box 45.

9 Jocelyn Brando was interviewed for the Adler Studio documentary *Imagine Brando* (Madoff Productions, 2008). Brando describes the experience in Lindsey Interviews and in *Songs*, pp. 22–23 and 66–67.

10 Muni quoted in Jerome Lawrence, *Actor: The Life and Times of Paul Muni* (London: W. H. Allen, 1975), p. 293. For Brando's response to Manhattan jazz clubs, see Lindsey Interviews and *Songs*, pp. 66–67.

11 Baldwin was open in most of his writings about his father's harsh treatment of him. See, in particular, his candidly autobiographical first novel, *Go Tell It on the Mountain* (New York: Knopf, 1952). Brando never admitted publicly that his father beat him, but he confided it to friends such as Michael Jackson, in their taped conversation from August 1983.

12 The marked pages, 42 and 89, are in Brando's copy of *The Fire Next Time*, in KBL, Box 45. Account of meeting Baldwin and Mailer: Lindsey Interviews and *Songs*, p. 63. Memories of riding on the open-top buses with Brando and Baldwin to cool off during Manhattan summers in the 1940s, Ellen Adler, interviews with the author.

13 Loving built two large kilns at the Brando family farm in Mundelein, Illinois, when he and Franny moved there in 1953. These allowed him to expand the scale of his work as well as his reputation. When he was hired in 1961 at the Chicago Art Institute, he taught enameling as well as drawing and painting. "Richard Loving," The Enamel Arts Foundation, www.enamelarts.org.

14 Wally Cox, *My Life as a Small Boy* (New York: Avon, 1961), p. 124.

15 Wally Cox's letters to Brando and Cox's Donaldson Award certificate, Brando Estate Archives. Brando's comments about Cox appear in the Lindsey Interviews and in *Songs*, pp. 95–96. Ellen Adler also spoke at length about the friendship in her interviews with the author.

16 *Songs*, p. 78.

17 *New York Times*, April 3, 1926.

18 Stella Adler, Introduction to Jacob Adler, *A Life on the Stage*, translated from the Yiddish with commentary by Lulla Rosenfeld (New York: Applause Theatre Books, 2001, first excerpted in *Die Varheit*, Prologue April 16, 1916, and subsequent chapters, April 30, 1916–February 28, 1919, and *Die Neie Varheit*, April 1–July 30, 1926), pp. xiii–xiv. In Joseph Rumshinsky's music for the play, Shylock's movements were accompanied by, a "somber Hebraic cello line" that reinforced the Jew's enclosure in a world of his own. See Lulla Adler Rosenfeld, *The Yiddish Theatre and Jacob P. Adler* (New York: Shapolsky Books, 1988), p. 305.

19 Quoted by Tom Oppenheim, Lecture on Jacob Adler (available on the Adler Studio website), delivered February 22, 2009, at "Jews/Theatre/Performance in an Intercultural World," a conference at the Jewish Theological Seminary in Manhattan. In the same lecture, Oppenheim quotes Stella Adler's characterization of her "mission from my parents" to "make it better for them. Otherwise, why are they here?" "Unless you give the audience something that makes them bigger—better—do not act. Do not go into theater. Unless you can create something bigger—better... there is no use climbing around chattering on a stage." www.stellaadler.com/cultural-center/jacob-adler-center.

20 Tom Oppenheim, director of the Stella Adler Studio of Acting, describes this in detail, interview with the author, May 7, 2010.

21 Adler, *Life on the Stage*, p. 93.

22 Ibid., p. 30.

23 Ibid., p. 82. The parallels between Adler and Brando are almost uncannily abundant. They were subversive pranksters in childhood. They were extraordinarily competitive with other actors. They were exceedingly fortunate in their career breaks. They were "a cause of grief to every woman who loved [them]" and shared the distinction of making two different women, almost simultaneously, pregnant. They were inept in business. They were indifferent to materialism. Adler at home could easily be Brando: "He filled the house with dogs, cats, canaries, and plants, told humorous stories, and played tricks that made his children laugh. But he was not talkative, and kept many things to himself." Indeed, the impressions of Harold Clurman, one of the few who knew them both, are strikingly complementary. Of Adler he noted, "Everything about him breathed a masculine fullness which commanded the admiration of both sexes. With this there dwelled within him a sensibility which one might (even today!) call 'feminine.'" Clurman characterized Brando's Stanley Kowalski in *Streetcar* as a "roughneck, gross, bluff, and brutal." But he also observed that "none of the brutishness of his part is native to him," and, given Brando's "acute sensitivity," he could easily have played Stanley's female antagonist, Blanche Du Bois. All the points above about Adler can be found, in order, in *The Yiddish Theatre and Jacob P. Adler*, pp. 7, 85, 138, 250, 193, 249, 286, 321, xiv. The points about Brando are from Ellen Adler interviews; Clurman, *All People Are Famous*, p. 259; and *The Collected Works of Harold Clurman*, edited by Marjorie Loggia and Glenn Young (New York: Applause, 1994), p. 134. See *Collected Works*, p. 895, for Clurman quote on Adler's "masculine fullness."

24 Adler interview in Helen Krich Chinoy, *Reunion: A Self-Portrait of the Group Theatre* (reprint of *Educational Theatre Journal*, vol. 28, no. 4, [December 1976]), p. 512.

25 Harold Clurman makes this point in *On Directing* (New York: Macmillan, 1972), p. 145.

26 Quotes in this paragraph are from, respectively, Elia Kazan, *A Life* (New York: Knopf, 1988), p. 64, and Elia Kazan, *Kazan on Directing* (New York: Vintage, 2009), p. 198. Brando's comment from a 1963 interview on *The Tonight Show with Johnny Carson* is in *Brando*, TCM Documentary, 2007.

27 See Wendy Smith, *Real Life Drama: The Group Theatre and America, 1931–1940* (New York: Grove Weidenfeld, 1990).

28 Harold Clurman, *The Fervent Years: The Group Theatre and the 30's* (New York: Da Capo, 1983, reprint of 1945 edition), p. 28.

29 Mel Gordon, *Stanislavsky in America: An Actor's Workbook* (New York: Routledge, 2010), pp. xii–xiii.

30 Strasberg and Clurman quoted in *Reunion*, pp. 544–45.

31 Tone quoted in Smith, *Real Life Drama*, p. 29.

32 Lewis quoted in *Reunion*, p. 485. The final observation, about "witnessing a real accident," is Lewis quoting the Theatre Guild character actress Helen Westley.

33 Gordon, *Stanislavsky in America*, pp. 154–55; Smith, *Real Life Drama*, pp. 179–82; and *Reunion*, pp. 508–9, provide complementary accounts of the Strasberg–Adler disagreement.

34 *Stella Adler on Ibsen, Strindberg, and Chekhov*, edited by Barry Parks (New York: Vintage, 1999), pp. 87, 300, 303. While Brando owned a number of books on acting, he seemed much more interested, if annotations are any indication, in books on biofeedback and autogenic training, which offered similar advice in more scientifically nuanced terms.

35 Stella Adler emphasizes her differences from Strasberg in *Reunion*, p. 508, and Ellen Adler makes the point about Brando's vulnerability as a young student in her interviews with the author.

36 Adler, *The Art of Acting*, p. 165.

37 *Songs*, p. 81.

38 Stella Adler, quoted in Paul D. Zimmerman, "*The Godfather*: Triumph for Brando," *Newsweek*, March 13, 1972, p. 59.

39 Adler, *The Art of Acting*, pp. 180, 52.

40 After being told this by Brando, Paul Muni replied, "Ahhh, that's a difficult part. *I've* never done it. Tell me—you got a Method neck?" Paul Muni Collection, Houghton Library, Harvard University, Box 5.

41 Brando had a copy of the 1941 one-volume Random House edition of *The Basic Works of Aristotle*, translated by Richard McKeon, which is marked throughout with light pencil lines, the annotating style he used in his youth. These quotations from the section on "Rhetoric" are, respectively, from Book II: Ch. 23, p. 1420, and Book III: Ch. 16, p. 1443. Brando's copy of Aristotle is in KBL, Box 64. He also owned every book I have drawn on above in my account of the Yiddish Theatre and The Group Theatre, including: *The Fervent Years*; *Real Life Drama*; *Stella Adler on Ibsen, Strindberg, and Chekhov*; *A Life on the Stage*; *The Yiddish Theatre and Jacob P. Adler*, etc. KBL, Boxes 86 and 92.

42 Quoted in Manso, *Brando*, p. 113.

43 I have drawn on Peter M. Rutkoff and William B. Scott, *New School: A History of the New School for Social Research* (New York: The Free Press, 1986), for this and subsequent paragraphs. See pp. 37, 12, xii, and xiii for quotations.

44 Quotes in last two paragraphs are from Lindsey Interviews and from *Songs*, pp. 72, 98.

45 How much Yiddish Brando knew has been a point of controversy. Alan King was convinced of Brando's fluency, as was Stanley Brooks. But Ellen Adler thinks his gift for imitation helped him to exaggerate his actual knowledge of the language. Ellen Adler interviews; Stanley Brooks, interview with the author, April 18, 2011; Alan King with Chris Chase, *Name-Dropping: The Life and Lies of Alan King* (New York: Scribner, 1996).

46 Ellen Adler interviews.

47 Ibid. See also Rosenfeld's account of the Jacob and Sara Adler marriage in *The Yiddish Theatre*.

48 *Songs*, pp. 92–93.

49 Brando letter to parents and grandmother, fall 1943, quoted in *Songs*, p. 76.

50 When *Truckline Café* closed after nine performances on Broadway, Clurman and Kazan took out one-page advertisements in the New York papers excoriating the reigning theater critics as a "group of men who are hired to report the events of our stage and who more and more are acquiring powers which, as a group, they are not qualified to exercise—either by their training or by their taste." Quoted by Wolcott Gibbs in *The New Yorker*, "The Theatre," March 9, 1946, p. 43.

51 See Christie's catalogue, *The Personal Property of Marlon Brando: Thursday 30 June 2005*, p. 191, for a photograph and details about the Donaldson Award. For quotations from Clurman, see *On Directing*, p. 117; for quotations from Brando, see *Songs*, p. 101.

52 Anne Jackson described Brando's performance in an interview she gave with her husband, Eli Wallach, for *Brando*, TCM Documentary, 2007.

53 The theater and film critic Pauline Kael, for example, offered recollections of being in the audience at *Truckline*. See Karl Malden, *When Do I Start?* (New York: Simon and Schuster, 1997), p. 159, and Carlo Fiore, *Bud: the Brando I Knew* (New York: Delacorte Press, 1974), p. 52, for accounts of the reception and the preparations backstage.

54 Brando's comment on *Candida* is from the Lindsey Interviews and *Songs*, p. 103. The review is from *Billboard*, April 13, 1946, pp. 50–51.

55 *Candida*, Act II, p. 2.

NOTES TO PAGES 53-60

56 See Fiore, *Bud*, pp. 63–65.

57 Adler noted that they could make themselves shorter, taller, fatter, thinner. *The Yiddish Theatre*, p. 171. Stanislavski provided a window into such methods in his autobiography, with a series of photographs that revealed the distinct faces he crafted for various roles. The director Edward Dmytryk described Brando as "one of those actors, rare today, particularly in Hollywood, who uses makeup freely to help establish or enhance a character." *It's a Hell of a Life But Not a Bad Living* (New York: Times Books, 1978), p. 225.

58 Brando letter to Mike Lobell, July 10, 1989, Brando Estate Archives.

59 These photographs appear between pages 348 and 349 in *Songs*. Materials from *The Island of Dr. Moreau* include the memos and images Brando selected so carefully for *Songs*, in a private collection. He might have been familiar with Stanislavski's autobiography, *My Life in Art* (Boston: Little Brown, 1924), translated by J. J. Robbins, which features a similar collection of photographs revealing Stanislavski's makeup and dress for various roles.

60 That is perhaps why Brando used them rarely (unless, as in *Viva Zapata!*, he was playing a historical character who had one). Aside from the full-bearded look Brando wore in *Burn!* (1969), and the trim mustache he adopted to support the patriarchal authority of Don Corleone (and his own sendup of the role in *The Freshman*, 1990), his only other facial hair was the walruslike mustache he assumed for the farce *Free Money* (1998).

61 *Songs*, p. 108.

62 Quote from Lawrence, *Actor*, p. 56; see p. 119 for Muni on shoe salesman. It was probably just a coincidence that Brando, according to his nephew Martin Asinof (interview with the author, June 5, 2013, with follow-ups July and August 2013), also claimed he would have made a very successful shoe salesman and enjoyed it.

63 Lawrence, *Actor*, pp. 219, 247. Brando said something similar about playing Mark Antony. See chapter 3.

64 Hecht quoted in David S. Wyman, "Ben Hecht's 'A Flag Is Born': A Play That Changed History," www.wymaninstitute.org/articles/2004, p. 4.

65 Ben Hecht, *A Child of the Century* (New York: Simon and Schuster, 1954), p. 517.

66 I have drawn on Robert Francis, "Ben Hecht's 'A Flag Is Born': Propaganda Plus Top Drama," *Billboard*, vol. 58, no. 37 (September 14, 1946), pp. 3, 45; Wyman, "Ben Hecht's 'A Flag Is Born'"; Edna Nahshon, "From

Geopathology to Redemption: 'A Flag Is Born' on the Broadway Stage,"
Kurt Weill Newsletter, vol. 20, no. 1 (2002), pp. 5–8; and Steven Whitfield,
"The Politics of Pageantry, 1936–1946," *American Jewish History*, 84.3
(1996), pp. 221–51, for factual details above.

67 "A Flag Is Born," quoted in Nahshon, "From Geopathology to Redemption," p. 7. See *A Child of the Century*, pp. 550–87, for Hecht's firsthand account of the Roosevelt administration's persistent refusal to rescue European Jews. He concludes: "With all our mass meetings and stinging propaganda we had managed to rouse no protest against the Jewish Massacre from Roosevelt, Churchill, Stalin, or their official governments. The war for the rescue of humanity from German defilement ended 'triumphantly' with all the Jews of Europe exterminated and the great victors still indifferent to that amazing fact," p. 587. These events were foremost in Hecht's mind as he set out to write *A Flag Is Born*.

68 See Wyman, "Ben Hecht's 'A Flag Is Born,'" p. 5, on play's earnings.

69 Brando owned hundreds of books on Jewish history and culture. They are difficult to isolate among his library holdings since books on Jewish subjects were distributed throughout the collection when it was sold by Christie's to various buyers.

70 Brando's comments on *Larry King Live* during an extended interview in 1996 became notorious. King himself defended Brando's devotion to Jews and Jewish causes and insisted the comments had been exaggerated. Brando remained enraged at King to the end of his life, believing that King had set him up to generate publicity for his show. In a letter to King, responding to an invitation to King's birthday party, Brando charged, "That discussion . . . produced the reaction you clearly anticipated, you made me out to be Anti-Semitic." Letter in Brando Estate Archives, not clear that it was ever sent.

71 The meeting with Javits, Schary, and Wiesel on February 16, 1975, in New York City is cited in a detailed calendar from 1975, kept by Alice Marchak, Brando's secretary from 1958 through the late 1980s, in the Brando Estate Archives.

72 Brando's extended remarks here are from his taped interviews with Robert Lindsey. Only a few of his observations appeared in *Songs My Mother Taught Me* as Brando stated them, and Lindsey understandably avoided potentially inflammatory subjects such as the Israeli–Palestinian conflict, genocide across the world, and comparative suffering. *Songs*, pp. 73–74. Chapter 15 of *Songs* focuses on *A Flag Is Born*.

73 Lindsey Interviews and *Songs*, p. 107.

74 Luther Adler and Paul Muni are quoted in Lawrence, *Actor*, pp. 292–93.

75 "A Flag Is Born," quoted in Nahshon, "From Geopathology to Redemption," pp. 7–8; Francis, "Ben Hecht's 'A Flag Is Born,'" p. 45.

76 Recounted by Ellen Adler, interviews with the author.

77 *Songs*, p. 110.

78 Kazan, *A Life*, pp. 341–42.

CHAPTER THREE. BUILDING THE REPERTOIRE

1 Ellen Adler, interviews with the author, February 15, April 22, May 7, December 17, 2010.

2 *Songs*, p. 143.

3 Miller, introduction to the 2004 edition of *A Streetcar Named Desire* (New York: New Directions), quoted in Kazan, *Kazan on Directing* (New York: Vintage, 2009), p. 65.

4 Brando discusses such details with Robert Lindsey in interviews for his autobiography, and also with Michael Jackson in their taped conversation from August 1983.

5 *Kazan on Directing*, pp. 166–67.

6 *Songs*, p. 124.

7 Tennessee Williams, *A Streetcar Named Desire* (New York: Signet, 1951), with an Introduction by the author, "On a Streetcar Named Success," p. 48. According to the *OED*, the term *kibitz*, as Williams uses it here, meaning "to look on and offer unwelcome advice, esp. at a card game," came into wide usage around 1920.

8 *Streetcar Named Desire*, scene 1, p. 13.

9 Williams's letter to Kazan, April 19, 1947, quoted by Kazan in *Kazan on Directing*, p. 62.

10 Williams, April 19, 1947, quoted in Kazan, *Kazan on Directing*, p. 62.

11 Even here, Brando invested his villain with a certain charm, and it's likely that the characterization would have been complicated over time. He won an Emmy for Best Supporting Actor for the performance.

12 In his interview with Edward R. Murrow, *Person to Person*, April 1, 1955, Brando noted that he considered it the responsibility of films to raise the level of audiences, as opposed to pandering to them.

13 List of Books around Marlon's Bed, Brando Estate Archives. He offered these observations about McCarthy, Murrow, and Stone in the Lindsey Interviews, Brando Estate Archives.

14 George Seldes, ed., with a foreword by Henry Steele Commager, *The Great*

Thoughts (New York: Ballantine, 1985). This heavily annotated book is in KBL, Box 95.

15 Dodie Brando, interviewed in *Omaha World-Herald*, 1948. Brando's mother may well have resisted her son's bully because he recalled aspects of her husband.

16 *A Streetcar Named Desire*, p. 29.

17 Williams's letter to his agent is quoted in Kazan, *Kazan on Directing*, p. 63.

18 Kazan, *A Life*, pp. 350, 351.

19 Barbara Johnson, quoting Jacques Lacan in "Apostrophe and Abortion," in *A World of Difference* (Baltimore: Johns Hopkins University Press, 1987), p. 198.

20 Quoted in "Cinema: A Tiger in the Reeds," *Time*, October 11, 1954, p. 6. See also Philip C. Kolin "The First Critical Assessments of *A Streetcar Named Desire*: The *Streetcar* Tryouts and the Reviewers," *Journal of Drama Theory and Criticism* (fall 1991), pp. 45–67.

21 *A Streetcar Named Desire*, pp. 129–30.

22 *Memoirs/Tennessee Williams*, introduction by John Waters (New York: New Directions, 2006), pp. 83, 131.

23 Clurman, quoted in Kazan, *Kazan on Directing*, p. 67.

24 Brando made this point about the actor's "face" on film as his "stage" many times. He is quoted making this point to an actor he was directing in *One-Eyed Jacks* by Shaw, *Brando in the Camera Eye*, pp. 50–59; and by Tom Oppenheim, interview with the author, May 7, 2010. He also made the point in Lindsey Interviews and in his ten-day acting class, "Lying for a Living," in 2001, both in the Brando Estate Archives.

25 Patricia Bosworth, *Brando* (New York: Penguin Lives, 2001), pp. 212–13.

26 See *Songs*, pp. 202, 204.

27 Lindsey Interviews.

28 See *Songs*, p. 85; Lindsey Interviews; and "Lying for a Living" Transcripts.

29 The middleweight champion told the story on *The Martha Raye Show*. The show, during which he relates this anecdote about Brando, was covered in a newspaper piece, "Brando and the Rock." Clipping in the Brando Estate Archives, n.d.

30 Brando: Lindsey Interviews; *Songs*, pp. 170–71; Kazan, *A Life*, p. 659.

31 Kazan, *Kazan on Directing*, p. 156.

32 *A Streetcar Named Desire*, p. 44. In the theater version of *Streetcar*, Stanley got his boy. But the Hollywood censors insisted that Stanley be punished for his ravishment of Blanche, rendering the film infant's gender ambiguous by having the baby wrapped in a white blanket, rather than a blue one, as in the play.

33 Adler quoted in "Cinema: A Tiger in the Reeds," *Time*, p. 6.

34 Lot 323 in Christie's catalogue for the New York estate sale of *The Personal Property of Marlon Brando: Thursday 30 June 2005*, p. 193.

35 Brando: Lindsey Interviews and *Songs*, p. 143.

36 Jay Kanter, interview with the author, April 21, 2011.

37 Lindsey Interviews and *Songs*, pp. 152–54.

38 Theodore Strauss, *Life* Archives. Notes for Article on Marlon Brando in *The Men*, 1950: see life.time.com/culture/marlon-brando-rare-early -photos-of-the-hollywood-legend-in-1949/.

39 Strauss, *Life* Archives.

40 Ibid.

41 Lindsey Interviews and *Songs*, pp. 149–50.

42 Brando describes this experience in his conversation with Michael Jackson, August 1983, and also in "Lying for a Living" Transcripts.

43 Brando's autobiography and personal files include numerous letters from fans as well as his responses to them. Brando's script files, in private collections, invariably contain stacks of contemporary reviews. Hundreds of miscellaneous contemporary reviews and fan letters, also in Brando Estate Archives.

44 "The New Pictures, July 24, 1950," *Time*, pp. 1–2.

45 "Once more I must caution Brando against mumbling," Marjory Adams wrote in her otherwise positive review of the film, which she called "magnificent in scope, heart-tuggingly beautiful" (with the exception of Brando, whom she found inferior to Gable). "I made next to nothing out of his final words as he lay on the sandy beach after fighting through a disastrous fire on the *Bounty*." *Boston Globe*, November 16, 1962, p. 20.

46 Kazan's letter to Zanuck is reproduced in Kazan, *Kazan on Directing*, pp. 170–71.

47 Brando would note this years later in the margins of the script of *The Brave* (1997), a film about Indians he made with Johnny Depp.

48 Quotations from Miguel Covarrubias, *Mexico South: The Isthmus of Tehuantepec* (New York: Knopf, 1947), pp. 355, 68–69, 406–7.

49 Brando's copies of Covarrubias and Prescott's 1,288-page history are in KBL, Box 97, and KBL, Box 54. Steinbeck's bound volume of notes is in the Kazan Collection at Wesleyan University's Cinema Archives. The quotations in these two paragraphs are from John Steinbeck, *Zapata: A Newly Discovered Narrative by John Steinbeck, with His Screenplay of Viva Zapata!*, edited by Robert E. Morsberger (New York: Penguin, 1975), pp. 46, 47, 20, 22.

50 Rebecca Brando interview, March 2, 2012.

51 Kazan, *Kazan on Directing*, p. 166.

52 The line was used as a rallying cry for the Spanish Republicans in the Spanish Civil War. Albert Camus was probably drawing on a different source when he quoted the line in *L'Homme Révolté* (1951; first English translation, *The Rebel*, published in 1954).

53 Kazan, *Kazan on Directing*, p. 167.

54 Kazan uses the apt word *fussed* to describe what Brando does with Quinn's body. He recalls in *Kazan on Directing* that he gave no direction in that scene: "If you start giving directions to any actor like Brando in a scene like that you're very liable to hurt yourself," p. 168. And Brando, in a letter to Coppola (in Brando Estate Archives), confirms what fellow actors observed, that he "directed himself" in *The Godfather*, 1980, pp. 1–2.

55 Those who knew him corroborate Brando's extraordinary memory for literature and language. Ellen Adler, Jay Kanter (April 21, 2011), Rebecca Brando (March 2, 2012), Avra Douglas (February 29–March 4, June 18 and 19, 2012, and June 23 and 24, 2013), Tom Oppenheim (May 7, 2010), and Patt Morrison (April 22, 2011) all recalled, in interviews with the author, Brando reciting from memory extended passages from Shakespeare, as well as Shakespeare's sonnets and other poetry.

56 Brando's 152-book collection of Shakespeare and other literary classics, Lot 316 at the Christie's sale, was expected to sell for $600 to $800. It sold for $21,600. See Christie's, sale 1600, June 30, 2005, www.christies.com. These books are in a private collection.

57 Brando's annotated copy of *The New Hudson Shakespeare* edition of *Julius Caesar* (Agnes Knox Black, 1935) is in a private collection. These annotations are on pp. 91, 97, 104, 105, respectively.

58 Lindsey Interviews; *Songs*, p. 174; and *Time*, "Cinema: New Picture, June 1, 1953," p. 2.

59 Bobby Seale's interview is in *Brando*, TCM Documentary, 2007.

60 Lindsey Interviews and *Songs*, p. 178.

61 Lindsey Interviews.

62 Brando's copy of Sidney Hook's *Personal Power and Political Freedom: Critical Studies in Democracy, Communism, and Civil Rights* (New York: Criterion, 1959), with these annotations, which appear on pp. 114, 109, and 110, respectively, in KBL, Box 64.

63 For Kazan's thinking during this period, see Kazan, *A Life*, pp. 448–66.

64 Account of Kazan and HUAC in previous paragraphs, Victor Navasky, *Naming Names* (New York: Viking, 1980), pp. 199–222; Kazan, *Kazan on Directing*, pp. xix, 94, 169, 181, 206, 221, 254, 296–98 and Kazan, *A Life*,

pp. 420, 432, 440–71 and passim, 630, 818; Dmytryk, *It's A Hell of a Life But Not a Bad Living*, pp. 93–103, 145, 146–47; Malden, *When Do I Start?*, pp. 217–18, 236–38; and *Songs*, pp. 193–97.

65 According to Brando family lore, an attempt had been made to blacklist Brando just before the release of *Julius Caesar*. When studio heads at MGM were approached with the news that Brando was going to be added to the roster of "Communist"-leaning stars, and picketers were enlisted at theater sites across the country, the studio responded in the expected way by paying hush money to protect their box office. Martin Asinof, Jocelyn Brando's son, referred to this in an interview with the author, June 5, 2013, with follow-ups July and August 2013.

66 Lindsey Interviews. The correspondence between Brando and various agents discussing Jocelyn's blacklisting and her brother's successful efforts to secure work for her in the early 1960s, which also includes an exchange between Brando Jr. and Sr. and some notes by Jocelyn herself, is in the Jocelyn Brando File, Brando Estate Archives.

67 Ellen Adler interviews.

68 Letter to Richard Schickel, Brando Estate Archives.

69 Quoted in Kazan, *A Life*, p. 508.

70 "Don't blame me when they pack you off to Abyssinia," Father Vincent tells Father Barry after the raucous anti-Teamster meeting he runs in the church where a church window is shattered by a rock. See Budd Schulberg, *On the Waterfront: Original Story and Screenplay, Final Shooting Script* (Carbondale: Southern Illinois University Press, 1980), p. 42.

71 Schulberg appeared on May 23, 1951. *On the Waterfront*, edited by Joanna Rapf (Cambridge: Cambridge University Press, 2003), p. 4. For Kazan's account of Sam Spiegel's contributions, see Kazan, *A Life*, pp. 517–18. Kazan's own annotated version of the script is in the Kazan Collection, Wesleyan University Cinema Archives.

72 Schulberg, *Final Shooting Script*, p. 100.

73 Ibid., p. 49, and Budd Schulberg, "The King Who Would Be Man," *Vanity Fair* (March 2005), p. 10, on the force of Brando's "wow."

74 Schulberg, *Final Shooting Script*, p. 104. Kazan, *A Life*, p. 517; p. 521 (on the crew's great admiration for Brando's "professionalism"); pp. 525–26 (on the "small miracles" "Marlon was always presenting me with"). There are, for instance, differing accounts of whether Eva Marie Saint's dropped glove was an accident or was suggested to her by Brando. See Malden, *When Do I Start?*, pp. 245–46.

75 *King James Bible*, Book of Isaiah, 61:10.

76 Ellen Adler, interviews with the author.

77 Brando mentioned Genet, Greco, and the Saint-Germain-des-Prés scene in his October 14, 1996, interview on the set of *The Brave* (1997), conducted in French and translated into English. Apparently it was never published, and is in a private collection.

78 "It is essentially the same," Brando noted of the situations of Malloy and Christian. Christie's catalogue, *The Personal Property of Marlon Brando: Thursday 30 June 2005*, p. 153.

79 George Englund reproduces Brando's letter from the spring of 1957, in Japan during the filming of *Sayonara*. *The Way It's Never Been Done Before: My Friendship with Marlon Brando* (New York: Harper Collins, 2004), pp. 83–84. For the summary of Camus's ideas, see Colin Wilson, *The Outsider: On the Alienation of Modern Man* (New York: Putnam, 1982), p. 30. This is the rare book of literary criticism annotated by Brando. The markings, with some caricatures, run throughout Wilson's discussion of Hemingway, Sartre, and Camus and include a section on *"L'Homme Révolté,"* which Brando might have read in French at some point. Brando's photocopy of Wilson's book is in KBL, Box 50.

80 Lindsey Interviews; *Songs*, p. 199; Kazan, *A Life*, p. 528. For criticism on the film, see, in particular, Leo Braudy, *On the Waterfront* (London: British Film Institute, 2005); *On the Waterfront*, ed. Joanna Rapf (Cambridge: Cambridge University Press, 2003); and David Bromwich, "Brando and *On the Waterfront,*" *Threepenny Review*, no. 65 (Spring 1996), pp. 19–21.

81 Quoted by John Burlingame, "Leonard Bernstein and *On the Waterfront,*" in Rapf, *On the Waterfront*, p. 139.

82 The Christie's catalogue, *The Personal Property of Marlon Brando: Thursday 30 June 2005*, features photographs of these various awards, pp. 176–79.

83 In the Brando Estate Archives is a file of 200 news items from various places where Brando, George Englund, and Stewart Stern toured while researching their film on American diplomacy and the United Nations programs.

84 Brando letters in possession of Ellen Adler.

85 *Napoleonic Victories* is in Brando's Book Inventory, Brando Estate Archives. Women mention going on dates with Brando to the public library. In *Songs*, he describes reading in various Manhattan libraries. For borrowed books, never returned, see, for instance, Burke Davis, *Gray Fox: Robert E. Lee and the Civil War*, checked out of the American Library in Paris, March 31, 1973, KBL, Box 1; Sartre, *On Genocide*, checked out

January 6, 1970, from LA Public Library, KBL, Box 82; Ibsen, *Hedda Gabler*, checked out January 6, 1951, from New York Public Library, KBL, Box 86.

86 See Robert Matteson Johnston, *Napoleon: A Short Biography* (New York: A. S. Barnes, 1904), pp. vii, 5–6, 93, 126, and 143 for quotes and other details brought out in Brando's performance.

87 Gitta Parker, "A thousand talents, A thousand faces, A thousand moods …This is Brando," n.d., clipping in Brando Estate Archives. The article was written during the filming of *Désirée*, summer 1954. Parker was a journalist who sometimes wrote for *Collier's Magazine*.

88 Laurence Olivier on *The Dick Cavett Show*, January 24, 1973.

89 Quoted in "Cinema: A Tiger in the Reeds," *Time*, pp. 6, 2.

90 Kazan, *A Life*, p. 538.

91 Brando discussed Dean in Lindsey Interviews and in *Songs*, pp. 220–22.

92 AFI Catalog of Feature Films: http://www.afi.com/members/catalog/DetailView.aspx?s=&Movie=51518.

93 The recording of this radio interview is in the Herrick Library, Beverly Hills, California.

94 Quoted in Bob Thomas, *Brando* (New York: Random House, 1973), p. 117.

95 Williams liked Brando's spontaneous improvisation in rehearsals on Broadway so much that it was added to subsequent editions of the play.

96 Lindsey Interviews and *Songs*, p. 305.

97 Felix Keesing, *Native Peoples of the Pacific World* (New York: Macmillan, 1945), p. 34, KBL, Box 6.

98 Brando describes editing the *Sayonara* script in *Songs*, pp. 244–45, and the actual script, in a private collection, contains his revisions. Brando's work on *The Young Lions* script was reported in *Variety*, September 26, 1957, and confirmed by his handwritten revisions on "First Draft" of *The Young Lions* script, April 25, 1957, in a private collection as well as in the film.

99 In the 1990s, when he met the parents of his long-term Japanese lover and impressed them with his command of Japanese, his knowledge had grown considerably. Avra Douglas, interview with the author.

100 See Manso, *Brando*, pp. 422–23, for an account of the episode.

101 Lindsey Interviews and *Songs*, p. 244.

102 Brando's annotated script for *Sayonara*, private collection.

103 January 9, 1958, letter reproduced in Christie's catalogue, *The Personal Property of Marlon Brando: Thursday 30 June 2005*, p. 174.

104 Lindsey Interviews and *Songs*, p. 347.

105 Brando mentions this contractual right to change the script in *Songs*, p. 249.

106 Brando, "First Draft," *Young Lions* script, private collection.

107 Brando's annotations in his copy of Wilhelm Reich, *The Mass Psychology of Fascism* (New York: Orgone Institute Press, 1946), pp. xii, ix, respectively, KBL, Box 57. Brando's interests in these questions never abated. Another book he annotated a few years later was Gudrun Tempel, *The Germans: An Indictment of My People* (New York: Random House, 1963), KBL, Box 65.

108 Lindsey Interviews.

109 Brando's comments in his copy of Ruth Benedict, *The Chrysanthemum and the Sword* (New York: Houghton Mifflin, 1946), p. 15, KBL, Box 6.

110 Gardner Murphy, *In the Minds of Men* (New York: Basic Books, 1955), frontispiece, KBL, Box 64. Brando's annotations run throughout.

111 Press conference quoted in Tony Thomas, *The Films of Marlon Brando* (Secaucus, NJ: Citadel, 1973), p. 113. Brando had a copy of David Schoenbrun's 1957 book, *As France Goes*, in his library with the inscription, "To Marlon Brando, in grateful memory of a most intelligent interview, David Schoenbrun, Paris, July 15, 1957." KBL, Box 27.

112 Brando emended this scene in the "First Draft," *Young Lions* script, suggesting that his character recommend delaying the attack until sunrise. "Christian says this and is complimented by Hard," he writes, p. 84.

113 Brando discusses his work on *The Young Lions* in Lindsey Interviews.

114 See quotes from Liliane Montevecchi and Parley Baer in Manso, *Brando*, pp. 455–56.

115 Letter from Otto Preminger to Marlon Brando, February 1958, quoted in Christie's catalogue, *The Personal Property of Marlon Brando: Thursday 30 June 2005*, p. 172. Stanley Kauffman, "A Young Lion," *The New Republic*, April 28, 1958, pp. 21–22.

116 Correspondence between Brando and Mary Motley, Brando Estate Archives.

CHAPTER FOUR. THE EPIC MODE, 1960-1963

1 See, for example, Sam Spiegel's argument for signing Brando for *On the Waterfront*, quoted by Kazan, *A Life*, pp. 515–16. See also the Paramount executive who said, "We feel that anything is worthwhile so long as we get a Marlon Brando picture. This young man . . . is one of the few actors left people want to see. . . . Look at how much money he brought in with

Sayonara and *The Young Lions*," "Brando's Bargain Beauty," *Ottawa Citizen*, October 4, 1960. Brando's costar, Pina Pellicer, claimed she'd "be happy to *pay* Brando for the experience" of working with him.

2 Brando's efforts to align filmmaking with idealism are discussed in chapter 8. Brando discusses aims of Pennebaker Productions in Lindsay Interviews, Brando Estate Archives.

3 *Songs*, p. 233. Brando Sr.'s ill-fated investment in a cattle ranch is documented extensively, Brando Estate Archives.

4 Letter quoted in *Songs*, p. 114.

5 George Englund, the friend, describes the incident in *The Way It's Never Been Done Before*.

6 Brando's extensive notes are on the back cover of *Indians and Other Americans* by Harold E. Fey and D'Arcy McNickle (New York: Harper, 1959). Brando's heavily annotated book, which includes an inscription by D'Arcy McNickle, is in a private collection. Brando's "Notes on Indians Sept. 3, 1963 Tahiti," Brando Estate Archives.

7 Brando's copies of James D. Horan's *The Great American West* (1959); John Collier's *The Indians of the Americas* (1948); *The Indian in Modern America* (1956), edited by David Baerreis; Don Russell's *The Lives and Legends of Buffalo Bill* (1960); and Bruce Grant's *The Cowboy Encyclopedia* (1951) would all have aided his work on *One-Eyed Jacks*.

8 Pat F. Garrett, *The Authentic Life of Billy the Kid* (New York: Macmillan, 1927), p. 21; Manso, *Brando*, p. 484, on Brando's reading of biographies.

9 Brando, quoted in *One-Eyed Jacks* Information Guide, Paramount Pictures, 1961.

10 Notes on Manila Hotel stationery are in the *One-Eyed Jacks* collection, Herrick Library, Beverly Hills.

11 Marlon Brando Sr., in letter to Marlon Brando Jr., April 11, 1957, Paramount Inter-Office Communication.

12 Charles Neider, *The Authentic Death of Hendry Jones* (New York: Harper and Row, 1972), pp. 23, 34, 180, 205, 64, 86, 3, 225.

13 Neider, *Hendry Jones*, p. 11.

14 Malden, *When Do I Start?*, p. 275.

15 Brando's papers reveal a passion for lists of all kinds, but especially lists of favorite phrases, sentences, aphorisms.

16 "One scene was played between a Mexican mother and daughter. Because he believed it would enhance their performances Mr. Brando let them play it in Spanish. The stunned producer waited until the scene was completed and then suggested to Mr. Brando: 'How about doing it in English

now for the Spanish-speaking countries.' The section remained in Spanish and Mr. Rosenberg now concedes he was wrong on this point." Murray Schumach, "'One-Eyed Jacks' Wasn't All Work," *New York Times*, February 20, 1961.

17 Malden, *When Do I Start?*, pp. 274–75, and "'One-Eyed Jacks' Wasn't All Work."

18 "Kubrick Resigns Brando Film," *New York Times*, November 20, 1958, p. 43. The *Miami News* (March 28, 1960, p. 122), for instance, reported on the costs of making the fiesta scene. Sheilah Graham made her predictions in the *Deseret News*, February 3, 1961, p. 6.

19 *Hollywood Reporter* and *New York Daily News*, quoted in Manso, *Brando*, p. 496. For other reviews, see, for example, *The Sun*, June 13, 1961; *Los Angeles Times*, July 2, 1961; *Washington Reporter*, April 15, 1961; *Ottawa Citizen*, May 23, 1961; *Vancouver Sun*, June 13, 1961. See also more recent academic treatments: Jonathan Bignell, "The Method Western: The Left-Handed Gun and *One-Eyed Jacks*," in *The Book of Westerns*, edited by Ian Cameron and Douglas Pye (New York: Continuum, 1996), pp. 99–110, and Simon Petch and Roslyn Joly, "The Radical Vision of *One-Eyed Jacks*," *Film Criticism* 29 (fall 2004), pp. 38–64.

20 *Hollywood Variety* reported, on August 23, 1961, "Another big money maker abroad is Paramount's *One-Eyed Jacks*."

21 Carlo Fiore recalled a six-hour director's cut: *Bud: The Brando I Knew*, pp. 267–68. Frank P. Rosenberg referred to a four-hour and forty-five-minute version, "Eyeing 'Jacks': A Producer Scans a Hectic Three-Year Stint with Star-Director Brando," *New York Times*, March 26, 1961. Manso cites a three-hour version in *Brando*, p. 494.

22 Martin Asinof, interview with the author, June 5, 2013, with follow-ups July and August 2013.

23 *Songs*, p. 265.

24 Lindsey Interviews and *Songs*, p. 229.

25 *One-Eyed Jacks* collection, Herrick Library, Beverly Hills.

26 Observations about Marlon Brando Sr. in Frances Brando Loving, Notes for MB Autobiography, and in Lindsey Interviews, Brando Estate Archives.

27 Bosley Crowther, *New York Times*, April 15, 1960; Marjory Adams, *Boston Globe*, November 16, 1962; Brendan Gill, *The New Yorker*, November 16, 1962.

28 "Meet Ernest Hemingway," hosted by Leon Pearson on NBC Radio, December 19, 1954.

29 Hemingway's *The Old Man and the Sea,* KBL, Box 85.

30 Brando talks at length in both the Robert Lindsey and the Lawrence Grobel interviews, as well as in Grobel, *Conversations with Brando* (New York: Hyperion, 1991), about the importance of Tahiti in his life. His commitment to Tahiti and his island is discussed in chapter 6.

31 These details were written into the contract between Arcola Picture Corp. and Marlon Brando, dated October 3, 1960, Brando Estate Archives.

32 Lindsey Interviews; "Lying for a Living" Transcripts; *Songs,* p. 270.

33 *Mutiny on the Bounty* scripts from September 24, 1960, in private collection.

34 Crowther, *Mutiny on the Bounty,* movie review, November 9, 1962.

35 Brando had an enormous file of research materials for the film, including a set of research notes prepared by Robert E. Lewis, a magazine editor with a passion for the *Bounty* story. These twenty-five pages of notes conclude with a section on writings by Samuel T. Coleridge, including a comparison between the *Bounty* story and *The Rime of the Ancient Mariner,* Brando Estate Archives. See also: Pitcairn Island Study Center, Pacific Union College, http://library.puc.edu/pitcairn/bounty/encyclopedia.shtml; *Australian Dictionary of Biography,* http://adb.anu.edu.au/biography/bligh-william-1797.

36 Excisions of curses from *Mutiny on the Bounty* scripts of the following dates: 1/21/61, p. 134A1; 1/17/61, p. 134E; 7/27/61, pp. 153A/154. Other revisions appear in *Mutiny on the Bounty* scripts: 11/21/60, pp. 52, 64B, in private collections. *Mutiny on the Bounty* was notorious for its multiple scripts, most of which were sold at the 2005 Christie's sale.

37 Brando wrote: "Christian's attitude not what was agreed to," and "there is absolutely no point of view of the Tahitians," *Mutiny on the Bounty* script, 7/10/61, pp. 147, 156, 164, 165, in a private collection.

38 *Mutiny on the Bounty* script, 11/21/60, pp. 58, 64A, in a private collection.

39 *Mutiny on the Bounty* scripts: 1/21/61, pp. 134F–134G, 136, 142, 148; 10/18/61, pp. 189B, 189D, 189E, 189F, 189H, 189I, in a private collection.

40 Brando's excisions for the water-cask scene from script 5/30/61, p. 104; 5/21/61, p. 104A; and 5/30/61, p. 104B. His handwritten note of the dialogue between Bligh and Christian over the Cape Horn route, entitled "Vegetable Cart," is in a private collection.

41 Brando's lines in *Apocalypse Now* in the second revised, second draft script, 6/25/79, are consistent with his speeches in the film, which were all credited to Brando by those who worked on the film. See chapter 8 for more on *Apocalypse Now.*

42 *Mutiny on the Bounty* script, 11/21/60, p. 70, in a private collection.

43 *Mutiny on the Bounty* Script, 7/5/60, pp. 10, 80, 82. Reproduced in Christie's catalogue, *The Personal Property of Marlon Brando: Thursday 30 June 2005*, p. 156. "Tips it," Brando wrote at another point, "surprise is more effective"; "in scene below decks let Christian be afraid of isolation and state his determination fully"; "lets have a little something of a conflict" "save this for a glorious announcement. Important fact" "build gag." *Mutiny on the Bounty* scripts, 7/10/61, pp. 145, 146, 147, 155, 156; 11/22/60, pp. 63, 64A, 66, 84B, in a private collection.

44 "In general there is nothing to keep story alive," Brando wrote, "cuts to warriors with spears could build tension to contrast with gaiety"; "maybe he should disappear and then come back making his entrance dramatic and build to shots of him walking alone, cut back to men waiting, waiting." *Mutiny on the Bounty* script, 11/21/60, pp. 51, 57, 65, in a private collection.

45 "Leading Woman Never Heard of Brando!" "No Dating or Dressing-Up Problems for Tahitian Teen-agers"; *Mutiny on the Bounty* (1962), Pressbook, pp. 6, 7, http://www.tcm.com/tcmdb/title/12737/Mutiny-on-the-Bounty/tcm-archives.

46 *Mutiny on the Bounty*, script from 8/26/60, p. 118. Reproduced in Christie's catalogue, *The Personal Property of Marlon Brando: Thursday 30 June 2005*, p. 157.

47 Richard Hough, *Captain Bligh and Mr. Christian: The Men and the Mutiny* (New York: Dutton, 1973), p. 128, KBL, Box 47.

48 *Mutiny on the Bounty*, Notes handwritten by Brando prior to and during filming. Reproduced in Christie's catalogue, *The Personal Property of Marlon Brando: Thursday 30 June 2005*, p. 151.

49 *Cours de Tahitien*, B. de Bermingham, KBL, Box 87.

50 *Mutiny on the Bounty*, Notes handwritten by Brando prior to and during filming. Reproduced in Christie's catalogue, *The Personal Property of Marlon Brando: Thursday 30 June 2005*, p. 151.

51 KBL, Box 87.

52 Hook, *Political Power and Personal Freedom*, pp. x–xi, 15, KBL, Box 64.

53 These letters, some addressed to Brando, some copied to Eugene Burdick, May 16, 1960; from Eugene Burdick to Brando, May 11, 1960; from Richard Drinnon to Brando, May 19, 1960, files on capital punishment, Brando Estate Archives. Three hundred thousand signatures were required to force a vote in the state legislature.

54 Chessman Case Files, Brando Estate Archives. Files include dozens of contemporary magazines, political pamphlets on abolishing the death

penalty, and pages of Brando's handwritten notes. Reed is quoted in Manso, *Brando*, pp. 518–19.

55 Elizabeth Hardwick, "The Chessman Case," *Partisan Review* (June 1960), pp. 503–13. (List of famous protesters on p. 504; Kierkegaard epigraph on p. 503.) KBL, Box 64.

56 Brando's notes for his lawsuit against the *Saturday Evening Post*, Brando Estate Archives.

57 He was also reading various books on religion, including Alfred Metraux's *Voodoo in Haiti* (1959), Ross and Hills, *The Great Religions* (1959), and Joseph Gaer's *How the Great Religions Began* (1962). Evidence of this comes from photographs used as bookmarks, women's names and phone numbers scribbled on frontispieces, front and back covers, etc. KBL, Box 78, has the books on religion: Metraux; Ross and Hills; Gaer. For other contemporary books, Brando's annotation style helps date his reading. Those familiar with his reading habits confirm that he usually bought books new and read them around the time he bought them. Avra Douglas, interviews with the author, February 29–March 4, June 18 and 19, 2012, and June 23 and 24, 2013, and Patt Morrison, interview with the author, April 22, 2011.

58 Avra Douglas confirmed "dio" meant "dialogue," Avra Douglas interviews.

59 Brando also owned and annotated Malinowski's *Magic, Science and Religion and Other Essays* (1948), KBL, Box 78; *Sex and Repression in Savage Society* (1953), KBL, Box 79; and *Crime and Custom in Savage Society* (1951), KBL, Box 87.

60 Brando's annotations on *Mutiny on the Bounty* script, 3/5/61, pp. 71, 71A, 71B; 3/6/61, pp. 91F, 91G; 5/11/61, p. 86B; 6/6/61, p. 86C. Editing of the love scenes between Christian and Miamiti, both in a private collection.

61 *Variety* review of *Mutiny on the Bounty*, December 31, 1961; *The New Yorker*, November 16, 1962.

62 Brando's handwritten notes for *Mutiny on the Bounty*. Reproduced in Christie's catalogue, *The Personal Property of Marlon Brando: Thursday 30 June 2005*, p. 151.

63 "Brilliant—That's the Word for Brando," *Sunday Express* (London); "Superb Film, New 'Mutiny' Bounty for Brando Fans," *Fort Worth* (Texas) *Star Telegram*; "Mutiny Sails in Triumph with Brando," *Chicago Tribune*; "One of the great screen spectacles," "Brando is still the most fascinating actor around," and "knows what he's doing," AP wire, November 9, 1962. See other reviews in *Mutiny on the Bounty* Pressbook, http://www.tcm.com/tcmdb/title/12737/Mutiny-on-the-Bounty/tcm-archives.html.

64 Peter Manso gives the highest figure—$30 million—in *Brando*, p. 554; *Life*, December 14, 1962, p. 113, reported $20 million; *Variety*, January 17, 1962, reported $18 million "or thereabouts," while also providing weekly numbers on box office grosses: 12/26/62; 1/16/63; 1/30/63; 2/6/63, etc.

65 "'Mutiny on the Bounty' Causes Sellout for *Saturday Evening Post*," Metro-Goldwyn-Mayer press release, June 15, 1962, Brando Estate Archives.

66 The files from Brando's defamation suit from *Mutiny on the Bounty* in the Brando Estate Archives are voluminous. They include all the interviews given by cast and crew from the production during Brando's legal case. Among the statements in the press that are contradicted by this record of interviews is that Brando was on bad terms with costars Trevor Howard and Richard Harris. Both defended Brando's point of view and remained friends with the actor long after the production. Howard appeared with Brando in *Morituri* and in *Superman*. Dave Jampel's *Variety* interview with Brando, from January 1963, is quoted in Thomas, *The Films of Marlon Brando*, p. 163. Brando also appeared on the *Today Show* and made the same point. Brando was subsequently quoted in *Variety* on January 16, 1963, praising the accuracy of the printed interview with Jampel.

67 Avra Douglas, Brando's assistant, and Rebecca Brando, his daughter, confirmed this in interviews with the author.

68 Collections of newspaper articles about his life and career are in the Brando Estate Archives. Brando explained a new dedication to countering distorted, libelous accounts following the births of his children, in an interview with David Susskind on *Open End*, April 21, 1963.

69 The Bobby Hutton incident is discussed in chapter 8. Brando's books on the media and free speech were scattered among his larger collection and included in books on political science and language. See KBL, Boxes 5, 11, 12, 41, 46, 75, 82.

70 Brando on the *Today Show*, April 19, and on *Open End*, April 21, 1963. Tapes in Brando Estate Archives.

71 Lindsey Interviews. Chapter 8 describes Brando's discovery and purchase of his Tahitian island and plans for its development.

CHAPTER FIVE. POLITICAL FILMS, 1963-1969

1 In a frank letter of April 17, 1964, a friend named Gene Frenke, who never worked for Brando, spelled out the actor's dilemmas as he saw them. Noting that Brando was "one of the great personalities in the picture

business today," he pointed out that he was in a position to select the best projects, producers, and directors. Instead, he suggested, Brando was being "moved, used and mis-used, mostly by second and third rate talent." Frenke's examples were Brando's two most recent films, *Mutiny on the Bounty* and *The Ugly American*, Brando Estate Archives.

2 Lindsey Interviews; *Songs,* p. 194; Manso, *Brando,* p. 573.

3 Brando articulated these points in audiotaped discussions on the film typed up as transcripts, in notes, and in marginalia in *The Ugly American* by Lederer and Burdick, as well as in Lindsey Interviews and in *Songs,* pp. 232, 234–35, 288–89. See also Englund, *The Way It's Never Been Done Before,* pp. 69–71, 99–101.

4 "Remarks on *The Ugly American,*" May 19, 1959, United States Senate, J. William Fulbright Papers, Series 71, Box 16, File 5, University of Arkansas Libraries. Fulbright's remarks on the film quoted in *Indiana Evening Gazette,* March 23, 1962, p. 16.

5 These books were in Brando's personal collection. KBL, Boxes 29, 82, 36, and 68. He annotated *The Nation on the Flying Trapeze* and *Community of Fear* extensively, and *On Guerrilla Warfare* slightly. Brando mentioned Mao in audio commentary that he recorded at the time of the making of *The Ugly American* in which he discussed the plot, dialogue, and storyline, Brando Estate Archives.

6 "We must present in full the criticism that is leveled against us. We dare not minimize it," he wrote. "It has great shock value, the ramifications of our failure in Cuba, which lost us the economic conference which followed, or severely damaged it."

7 All quotations are from typed and handwritten notes on the film, variously entitled "Criticism for *Ugly American*" (typed), "Notes *Ugly American Outline*" (handwritten), in private collections. Page numbers are cited when available.

8 Brando notes for *The Ugly American* script, typed, untitled, in a private collection.

9 Brando's annotated copy of *The Ugly American* by William Lederer and Eugene Burdick (New York: Norton, 1958), in a private collection. Comment on "drama in Chinese," p. 87.

10 Brando, audio commentary on *Ugly American,* Brando Estate Archives.

11 Englund, *The Way It's Never Been Done Before,* p. 113.

12 Stern quoted in William Baer, "On Rebel Without a Cause: A Conversation with Stewart Stern," *Michigan Quarterly Review,* vol. 38, no. 4 (fall 1999).

13 In the scene where Homer Atkins, the good American character

supervising the road, reports the death of his young native engineer, Punjit, for example, Brando recommends: "Callousness to life on part of [Ambassador] should be equal to that of com.—Atkins should tell him off strongly, say he sounds like communist official." In the film, MacWhite softens his callousness with a dose of sympathy. Brando's recommendation in handwritten notes, in a private collection.

14 Brando, audio commentary on *The Ugly American*, Brando Estate Archives.

15 Brando's heavily annotated script from *The Ugly American*—some of it in Brando's hand, some in the hand of an assistant who trusted Brando for spelling (hence the errors)—in a private collection. Stewart Stern, interviews with the author, July 21, July 26, and September 20, 2013.

16 Brando, audio commentary on *The Ugly American*, Brando Estate Archives.

17 Brando's Fletcher Christian (*Mutiny on the Bounty*) and Dr. Moreau (*The Island of Dr. Moreau*) wear glasses briefly; Adam Steiffel of *The Formula* wears them; and Ian MacKenzie, the lawyer in *A Dry White Season*, keeps a pair of reading glasses perched on his nose, but the glasses become a centerpiece of characterization only in *The Ugly American*.

18 Brando archive materials include correspondence between MB Sr. and MB Jr. regarding Jocelyn Brando's blacklisting, letters to producers, and contracts with agents and producers, all engineered by Brando and his agent, Jay Kanter, under Brando's direction. Brando's Papers, Jocelyn Brando File, include: letter from MB Sr. to MB Jr., December 30, 1963; letter to MB from Jocelyn's agent Ronald Leif, December 6, 1963; Jocelyn's 3-Year Contract with Revue Studios "commencing January 1, 1961"; letter to Jocelyn from Ronald Leif, January 16, 1961; a contract between Jocelyn and Revue Studios, October 21, 1960; and MCA Artist's "Notice," October 21, 1960; as well as pages of handwritten notes on Jocelyn's experiences of blacklisting.

19 Marlon Sr. letter to Marlon Jr., November 8, 1963, reports at the end that Jocelyn "is really operating under full steam at the book bin and enjoying it 'hugely.'"

20 As evidenced here, too, by Brando's exhaustive notes and script revisions.

21 This event and Brando's work in civil rights and other political activism is discussed at length in chapter 8.

22 Brando's copy of Francis Paul Prucha, *American Indian Policy in the Formative Years* (Cambridge: Harvard University Press, 1962), was thoroughly annotated. On his copy of Fey and McNickle's *Indians and Other*

Americans, he writes on the back cover: "Phillipines and other countries got war reparations, why not Indian?" For more on Brando's reading on the Indians, starting in the late 1950s, see chapter 8.

23 Most of Brando's copies are annotated, KBL, Boxes 34, 52, 82. William O. Douglas, *America Challenged* (New York: Avon), pp. 24, 31, KBL, Box 29.

24 Brando's admission that he froze at the sight of Douglas, so that he could barely converse, signaled his esteem for the justice. He mentions this in Lindsey Interviews, and in *Songs*, p. 379.

25 "Marlon Brando Fights for Civil Rights," *Ebony*, October 1963, pp. 60–67.

26 All quotations are from typed and handwritten notes on the film, variously entitled "*The Chase*, Notes," and "*The Chase*, Random Notes on the Script," February 9, 1965, some untitled without dates. They are also from notes written onto the scripts themselves, including the original script by Lillian Hellman, November 6, 1964; "The Final Shooting Script," March 30, 1965; and revised scripts May 14 and 20, 1965, in private collections.

27 *Arthur Penn Interviews*, edited by Michael Chaiken and Paul Cronin (Jackson: University of Mississippi Press, 2008), p. 164. This interview took place in 1982. According to Angie Dickinson, who played Ruby Calder, the wife of Sheriff Calder, Brando encouraged his fellow actors to improvise with him. "I'm not the only one who's allowed to improvise, you are too," he told her. Angie Dickinson, interview with the author, September 25, 2013.

28 Robin Wood, *Arthur Penn* (New York: Frederick Praeger, 1969), pp. 6–7.

29 "Between us, it's not really my film," Penn told an interviewer in October 1965 about *The Chase*. *Arthur Penn Interviews*, p. 11.

30 Film historian Robin Wood offers a key articulation of this claim in *Arthur Penn*, p. 12 and passim. The claim is repeated in *Arthur Penn Interviews*, pp. xi–xii.

31 *Arthur Penn Interviews*, p. 198. This interview was not published until 2008. See also the Arthur Penn Interview in *Brando*, TCM Documentary, 2007, in which the director again credits Brando with this innovation.

32 Wood, *Arthur Penn*, p. 70.

33 Shooting Schedule and Temporary Index Breakdown for *The Chase*, in a private collection.

34 While Hellman distanced herself from the film to some extent when it appeared, Brando's film notes and script annotations suggest her engagement with some of the revision process. He often addressed his commentary to Hellman in these notes and script marginalia.

35 *Reflections in a Golden Eye*, script, revised September 21, 1966, pp. 135–36.

36 *Stella Adler on Ibsen, Strindberg, and Chekhov,* ed. Barry Parks, p. 201.

37 Brando on the *Today Show,* April 19, 1963. Brando was drawing on a recent short piece, "No Time Like the Present (excerpts from *Time*)," in *Esquire,* vol. 59 (April 1963), pp. 58–59, that had treated *Time*'s portrayal of Williams, providing excerpts of reviews *Time* had done of Williams's plays over the years. The short piece had been published anonymously.

38 The Motion Picture Association of America, letter of September 15, 1964, and Ray Stark's letter to Elizabeth Taylor, August 1966, *Reflections in a Golden Eye* Folder, Herrick Library, Beverly Hills. Angie Dickinson confirmed that Brando's star remained high in the 1960s. She recalls that her agent tracked her down in London to tell her about the prospective part in *The Chase.* She asked him whether the script was good, and her agent shrieked: "Angie, it's Marlon Brando's wife! Take the part!" Angie Dickinson, interview with the author, September 25, 2013.

39 Brando Estate Archives.

40 Tennessee Williams's "Afterword," 1971, is reproduced in the 2000 Houghton Mifflin edition of *Reflections in a Golden Eye,* p. 134. Williams made the comment about Brando as "the greatest living actor...greater than Olivier" in *Memoirs,* 1975. See *Memoirs/Tennessee Williams,* p. 83.

41 Martin Scorsese mentions his debt to Brando's talking mirror scene in *Reflections,* for the scene in *Taxi Driver,* in *Brando,* TCM Documentary, 2007.

42 John Huston materials on *Reflections in a Golden Eye,* Herrick Library.

43 *Chicago Sun-Times,* October 17, 1967; *New York Post,* October 12, 1967; *Los Angeles Examiner,* October 12, 1967.

44 Stark's letter in *Reflections in a Golden Eye* Folder, Herrick Library.

45 Bobby Seale describes an all-night vigil with Brando in an interview for *Brando,* TCM Documentary, 2007.

46 Roger Ebert traveled to Cartagena to interview Pontecorvo in April 1969, just before the filming there ended, and met a hot and forlorn director with an ill son and star (Brando was away being treated for some sort of skin rash), and numerous problems. See "We Trust the Face of Brando," *New York Times,* April 13, 1969.

47 Pauline Kael, "Mythmaking," *The New Yorker,* November 7, 1970, p. 159.

48 See Vincent Canby's admiring review, "The Screen: Marlon Brando and Black Revolution," *New York Times,* October 22, 1970, for the Fletcher Christian comparison.

49 Pontecorvo's crew thought Brando overlooked these cast members' preferences for a simpler cuisine. *Songs,* pp. 325–26; author interview with Salvo Basile, cameraman for *Burn!*

50 Lindsey Interviews and *Songs*, p. 324.

51 Pontecorvo describes this decision and Brando's approval of it, as well as the inspired response to Brando's clipped performance: "He did the scene in a marvelous way. When he finished the scene, the whole crew applauded," quoted in Joan Mellen, "A Reassessment of Pontecorvo's *Burn!*" *Cinema* 32 (winter 1972–1973), pp. 38–46.

52 Ibid.

53 Kael, "Mythmaking," p. 159.

54 Lindsey Interviews and *Songs*, p. 320.

55 As Pontecorvo put it, "I make one film every eight or nine years.... If you had the list of films I've refused, 'The Mission,' 'Bethune,' etc., you'd have a telephone book," Gerald Peary, "Film Reviews, Interviews, and Sundry Miscellany," geraldpeary.com, "Talking with Gillo Pontecorvo," at the Berlin Film Festival, 1991.

56 Peary, "Talking with Gillo Pontecorvo."

57 *Songs*, p. 467.

CHAPTER SIX. ANNUS MIRABILIS, 1972

1 Through his sixties and seventies, when Brando fathered three children with Christina Ruiz (in 1989, 1992, 1994), he pursued women with incomparable energy, as confirmed by letters from his many conquests in Brando Estate Archives. This is also confirmed by his assistants.

2 Grobel Interviews, Brando Estate Archives.

3 Michael Winner's director's commentary in the DVD of *The Nightcomers* provides details about Brando's behavior on the set. The commentary includes descriptions of his extensive knowledge of ropes and knots, which is evident as well in the *Burn!* scene where he ties the noose for José Dolores's execution. The *Ashley Book of Knots* and Des Pawson's *Handbook of Knots* (1998) are in the KBL.

4 See Christie's catalogue, *The Personal Property of Marlon Brando: Thursday 30 June 2005*, p. 119, for page from *The Nightcomers* script, with Brando's handwritten revisions. See the film for changes from script to performance.

5 *Pittsburgh Post-Gazette*, May 5, 1972.

6 Fax to Mr. Michael Hastings, United Kingdom, from Marlon Brando, Los Angeles, California, June 18, 1998, Brando Estate Archives.

7 Director's commentary in DVD of *The Nightcomers*.

8 *The Portable Blake* (New York: Viking, 1946), p. 655. Brando's copy of the book is in a private collection.

9 *Last Tango in Paris: The Screenplay*, p. 163.

10 "I didn't ask him to become anything but himself," Bertolucci told *Time*. "It wasn't like doing a film. It was a kind of psychoanalytic adventure," February 12, 1973. Brando rewarded the director's comments with a cold shoulder.

11 As Brando told Shana Alexander in an interview he gave for *Life* after the making of *The Godfather*, "The biggest gap is not expressing what you feel but knowing what you feel. Most people don't know." "The grandfather of all cool actors becomes the Godfather," *Life*, March 10, 1972.

12 Picard, *The Human Face*, pp. 131, 100–101. Brando seems to have borrowed the book permanently from his friend Anita Kong Wylie. Brando's copy (KBL, Box 78) had two marked passages: those above on the cinema face and the smiling face reflecting the divine. See Lindsey Interviews and *Songs*, p. 146.

13 E. Ann Kaplan's, "Importance and Ultimate Failure of *Last Tango in Paris*," *Jump Cut*, no. 4 (1974), pp. 1, 9–10, rehearses the usual platitudes, including: "One often feels that Brando is not really acting, but that he is rather expressing a real hostility toward society.... The result, however, of Brando's using the film in this way is that he absolutely dominates the film and thus sends the whole thing off balance." Kaplan's claim that Paul in the first scene "virtually rapes" Jeanne is exemplary.

14 Brando mentions this in Grobel, *Conversations with Brando*, p. 89. He also had many books of anthropology and psychology, far too numerous to mention (Karen Horney's *Feminine Psychology*, for instance; Deborah Tannen's *You Just Don't Understand: Women and Men in Conversation*; Margaret Mead's *Sex and Temperament*), on sexual customs in different cultures, and on masculine and feminine psychology, that covered such issues.

15 "I possess nothing," he says, though he "has seen everything, in a way." "Nature favored me as to my physique," Clamence exults. "I was made to have a body." "One can't get along without domineering or being served. ...I wanted to dominate in all things." These quotations are from Brando's copy of Albert Camus, *The Fall*, translated by Justin O'Brien (New York: Knopf, 1957), pp. 8–10, 44, 54, 17, 28, respectively. Brando marked all of these passages, in a private collection.

16 Quotes are from *The Fall*, pp. 60, 62. For more on acting, see pp. 60–62; and women as a refuge, guilt, see pp. 98, 108–9.

17 *Sunday Morning Address: The Last Tango to Nowhere*, Kenneth J. Smith, Philadelphia Ethical Society, September 16, 1973. This review was in

Brando's materials on *Last Tango*, in a private collection. For more on Brando's interest in the ministry, see chapter 8.

18 Brando followed this press, carefully, out of curiosity and also wariness, keeping, apparently, most articles written about him from the early days on Broadway through his old age, Brando Estate Archives.

19 Capote and Brando continued to do battle until the end. Capote paid winking tribute in his famous novel *In Cold Blood* by putting Brando's 1955 acceptance speech for his Academy Award for *On the Waterfront* in the mouth of Perry Smith, one of the murderers, who plans to use it if ever "called upon to make a speech." *In Cold Blood* (New York: Vintage, 1965), p. 146. Brando consigned Capote to hell in the parodic post-life celebrity interviews he wrote (and never published) for his Random House auto biography, Brando Estate Archives.

20 These acting lessons are discussed at greater length in the Epilogue.

21 Roger Ebert, *Chicago Sun-Times*, October 14, 1972; Pauline Kael, *The New Yorker*, October 28, 1972; Vincent Canby, *New York Times*, February 2, 1973.

22 Mario Puzo's letter is reproduced in Christie's catalogue, *The Personal Property of Marlon Brando: Thursday 30 June 2005*, p. 123.

23 Brando discusses this in Lindsey Interviews; in "Lying for a Living" Transcripts; and in *Songs*, p. 411.

24 These quotations are from Brando's personal script of *The Godfather*, in a private collection. These quotations appear on the back of the last page of the bound script. Coppola and Ruddy's visit is recounted by Brando in Lindsey Interviews and in *Songs*, p. 407. Ruddy is quoted in Thomas, *The Films of Marlon Brando*, pp. 229–30, and also in a feature of the 2001 DVD version of *The Godfather*, "A Look Inside."

25 Rebecca Brando, interview with the author, March 2, 2012; Miko Brando, interviews with the author, September 21 and 23, 2012, and June 16, 2013.

26 Puzo lamented the failure to appreciate "the irony in my books," as quoted in Mario Puzo, *The Godfather: The Original Classic* (New York: NAL, 2002, first published 1969), p. 431.

27 Coppola recalls producer Robert Evans's complaint in the director's commentary for *The Godfather* DVD.

28 Shana Alexander, "Brando Plays a Mafia Chieftain," *Life*, March 10, 1972 (cover story).

29 Pauline Kael, "Alchemy," *The New Yorker*, March 18, 1972, p. 138.

30 These quotations are from Brando's annotated personal script of *The Godfather*, in a private collection, and from an additional copy of Brando's

annotated personal script, in another private collection. The complete personal script is dated March 16, 1971; the loose script pages, dated May 3, 6, and 7, 1971, represent revisions of the complete personal script.

31 These quotations are from Brando's loose script pages. The quotations appear, respectively, on p. 1; p. 7, Scene 1C; p. 4, Scene 1A.

32 Brando's *Godfather* script, p. 30, in a private collection.

33 Brando's loose script pages, Scene 1A, p. 3, in a private collection.

34 James Caan on *Brando*, TCM Documentary, 2007.

35 Brando's loose script pages, Scene 1A, p. 4.

36 Puzo, *The Godfather* (novel), p. 12.

37 Brando's loose script pages, Scene 55D.

38 This includes the following: "What manner of men are we, if we do not have our reason? To what purpose would I start all these troubles again, the violence and the turmoil? My son is dead, and that is a misfortune and I must bear it.... We are all men who have refused to be puppets dancing on a string pulled by the men on high.... We have to be cunning like the business people, there's more money in it.... Who is to say we should obey the laws they make for their own interest and to our hurt?" Brando's personal script for *The Godfather*, pp. 115–16, in a private collection.

39 Brando's *Godfather* script, in a private collection. They appear, respectively, on pp. 112–13 and 115–16.

40 *The Godfather* was filmed in the spring and early summer of 1971, shooting schedule, in a private collection.

41 Brando respected Pacino's acting abilities and encouraged Coppola to hire him for the role of Michael.

42 Brando as Napoleon appeared briefly at a New Year's celebration in *Désirée* (1954) carrying his heir, whom he hands off distastefully, describing the infant as "damp." He also acted with a pair of youth in *The Nightcomers* (1972), but the girl was nineteen and the boy around fourteen when the film was made. And he played, after *The Godfather*, the father of Superman, holding another infant son, again briefly (1979).

43 Director's commentary, *Godfather* DVD.

44 Michael Corleone refers to his son as "three years old" in the previous scene; the cast list gives Anthony Gounaris's age as four. Notes by Brando's secretary, Alice Marchak, from *The Godfather* production confirm the time Brando spent "with child playing and getting to know him," Brando Estate Archives.

45 See, for example, *Life*, March 10, 1972; *Newsweek*, March 13, 1972; *Rolling Stone*, January 20, 1972.

46 *Life*, March 10, 1972, p. 44.

47 Brando taped these interviews, which were then transcribed by his assistants. The one featuring the Godfather is entitled as "Random House TV Interview, August 27, 1994," Brando Estate Archives.

48 Brando's work on behalf of Indians is discussed at length in chapter 8.

49 Brando made these comments in his appearance on *The Dick Cavett Show*, June 1973. The viewer, David R. Convis, responded in a letter of June 8, 1973, to Sacheen Littlefeather, Sacheen Littlefeather file, Brando Estate Archives. The file also contains about a dozen letters from Littlefeather to Brando that reveal their relationship as formal and always cordial.

50 Lindsey Interviews and *Songs*, p. 345.

51 Wardrobe fittings for assorted films, Brando Estate Archives. KBL includes diet books in Boxes 7, 9, 18, 20, 21, 22, 32, and 40. See Peter Cowie, *Coppola: A Biography* (New York: Capo, 1994), p. 67, on the "padded false paunch" Brando used.

52 These logs, entitled "Progress Report," from 2003 and 2004, record Brando's daily weight, pulse, and blood pressure. His weight, predictably, is highest during the Thanksgiving Christmas holiday period, from late November through December. The highest weight recorded is 258 on December 2 and 3, 2003, but the pulse rate is 67 and the blood pressure 110/75. The lowest recorded is 228 on May 22, 2003. That log page includes the following note: "May 15, 2003 MB had his Breathing Test (improved a lot better) and check-up with Dr. Strieter. He was given another set of menus and low fat/No Sodium diet. They asked for a copy of MBs Progress report, Nutritional intake and Medicine chart." Brando Estate Archives.

CHAPTER SEVEN. VILLAINS AND SUPERMEN

1 Tom Oppenheim recalled the balloon image, interview with the author, May 7, 2010. In a radio interview, for instance, on *The Tex and Jinx Show*, December 12, 1955, with Marilyn Monroe, Brando quipped in response to the question "Can you define method acting?" "That's something a million actors would like to know," and then went on to eschew the label referring to himself as "an instinctive actor." See the Epilogue for more on Brando and theories about acting.

2 *Arthur Penn Interviews*, pp. 158–59.

3 Ibid., pp. 104–5, 143.

4 Brando mentions this in many places: his autobiography; his classes in

"Lying for a Living"; and in his recorded conversation about acting in August 1983 with Michael Jackson, Brando Estate Archives.

5 The full title of this last book is *A Field Guide to the Birds: Giving Field Marks of All Species Found East of the Rockies*, by Roger Tory Peterson. These books and others on birds, including *Birds, Beasts, Blossoms and Bugs: The Nature of Japan*, are in the KBL, Boxes 28, 43, 77, 78, 84, 90, 94. Brando also bookmarked a section on Vanishing Species—Cuckoos, Woodpeckers, and Whooping Cranes, with a handwritten note (writer not evident) on Bird Calls in Roger Tory Peterson's *How to Know the Birds* (New York: Signet, 1957), pp. 96–97, KBL, Box 77.

6 See Thomas McGuane, *The Missouri Breaks: An Original Screenplay* (New York: Ballantine, 1976), for pre-Brando version of Robert E. Lee Clayton and his dialogue.

7 All of these quoted lines, as well as the details of character such as cross-dressing and multiple disguises, are Brando's additions. According to Arthur Penn, Brando did most of the work developing his character during filming, when McGuane was barely present. See *Arthur Penn Interviews*, pp. 105, 117, 143.

8 Chris Hodenfield, "Brando: The Method of His Madness," *Rolling Stone*, May 20, 1976, pp. 34–39, 75, and Bruce Cook, "Candid Conversations with the Leading Man," *Crawdaddy*, December 1975. Cook's article was reproduced in the 1976 Ballantine Books edition of Thomas McGuane's script, *The Missouri Breaks: An Original Screenplay*, pp. vii–xv.

9 Hodenfield, "Brando," pp. 38, 39.

10 The young actor Frederic Forrest: "the guy's incredible ... he builds character from everything"; and makeup man Robert Dawn: Brando is "doing his own stunts: I saw him take a twenty-five foot jump out of a tree," are both quoted by Cook in *The Missouri Breaks*, pp. viii–ix, xii, xiii, xxi.

11 Judith Crist, "A Duel of Giants," *Saturday Review*, June 12, 1976. Vincent Canby, "'Missouri Breaks,' Offbeat Western," *New York Times*, May 20, 1976. Penelope Gilliatt, *The New Yorker*, May 31, 1976, pp. 100–101, noted: "Brando's performance has a lot to do with his opulently witty sense of restoration comedy which has never been more evident than in this film," while blaming the director for misuse of "the great Brando and the unfairly overshadowed Nicholson." And a review in *TV Guide* found "a perverse joy" in the film's strangeness, concluding that "the erratic and exotic behavior of the stars is infectious" May 22–28, 1976. For DVD reviews: David Nusair, *Reel Film Reviews*, November 12, 2005, noted that Brando, "sporting an Irish accent and a series of increasingly

bizarre hats, delivers a hypnotically broad performance that often feels as though it'd be more at home in a completely different movie—yet there's no denying that Brando's off-kilter presence keeps *The Missouri Breaks* afloat during some of the more dull sequences." Tom Dawson of the BBC characterized the film as an "appealingly eccentric revisionist western [that] highlights the critical importance of violence in establishing 'civilized' society in the American wilderness," May 14, 2003. And Derek Adams of *Time Out* called it "one of the truly major Westerns of the '70's," June 24, 2006.

12 Brando quoted by Cook in *The Missouri Breaks*, p. xxv.

13 All the quotations in this discussion of *Superman* are from Brando's role as Jor-El and included in his personal copy of the *Superman Script*, in a private collection. Brando's comments about his desire to be a scientist are familiar to many who knew him. They were recalled by Ellen Adler and Avra Douglas in interviews with the author and were repeated by Brando in his interviews with Robert Lindsey for *Songs*, Brando Estate Archives.

14 Reeve wrote Brando on March 27, 1977, thanking him for a gift Brando sent to encourage him on his first day of filming. Letter reproduced in Christie's catalogue, *The Personal Property of Marlon Brando: Thursday 30 June 2005*, p. 116.

15 Betsey Sharkey, "TMI: 'Man of Steel' Needs Less Talk from Jor-El," *Los Angeles Times*, June 24, 2013. Brando's *Superman* scripts, in a private collection, display his usual revisions, the most consistent of which are cuts.

16 The poem was marked in a book in Brando's poetry collection, *One Hundred and One Famous Poems: With a Prose Supplement* (1958), compiled by Roy J. Cook, p. 39, in a private collection.

17 "Lying for a Living" Transcripts.

18 Brando's purchase of Tetiaroa in Brando Estate Archives.

19 Brando's heavily annotated copy of Baldwin's *The Fire Next Time* is in KBL, Box 45. This passage, with annotation, is on p. 112.

20 Brando's materials from the making of *Apocalypse Now* are full of articles and books about Vietnam that Brando read and annotated in preparing for the film, as well as his notes for Kurtz's dialogue and ideas about the characterization, in a private collection. For Coppola on Brando in the film's aftermath, see the *Life* magazine interview Coppola gave in June 1979, "The Private Apocalypse of Francis Ford Coppola."

21 Brando's letter to Coppola, written sometime in the fall of 1978, Brando Estate Archives.

22 This letter from Coppola to Brando, written during the summer before Brando's arrival for filming in the Philippines, was in Brando's collection of materials from the making of *Apocalypse Now*, in a private collection.

23 Cowie, *Coppola* (New York: Capo, 1994), pp. 124–25.

24 Ibid., p. 142.

25 Brando's copy of *Soldier*, by Anthony B. Herbert, Lt. Col. Ret., with James B. Wooten (New York: Holt, Rinehart, Winston, 1973), together with contemporary articles on Vietnam, and various letters from the research department, production people, are in a private collection. Included in Brando's materials from *Apocalypse Now* was a letter from the film's publicist, Debbie Fine, March 24, 1976, suggesting that Brando get in touch with Herbert, since Brando was reading the book.

26 Herbert, *Soldier*, pp. 279, 285, 339. Brando marked all of the phrases cited.

27 Ibid., pp. 240, 334. See also pp. 320, 330, which Brando marked heavily.

28 He writes, for instance, above a survey of various atrocities: "odd juxtaposition of narrative details," p. 361; and above another on civilian casualties, "WWII no flack about civil. Dresden Tokyo etc.," p. 374. The quotations in this paragraph are from *Soldier*, pp. 322, 328.

29 *Soldier*, p. 396.

30 Ibid., p. 378.

31 Ibid., pp. 215–16.

32 "In fact, the whole damned U.S. Army in Vietnam was crazy," writes Herbert in a passage Brando starred and marked. "The major leadership problem in Vietnam was the generals, and the rest of the senior officers' corps," *Soldier*, p. 240. *Apocalypse Now*, second revision of the second draft, dated June 25, 1979, collection of Mike Medavoy.

33 Willard on Kurtz—"West Point, top of his class . . . being groomed for one of the top slots in the corporation"—is from the second revision of the second draft of the *Apocalypse Now* script, June 22, 1979, Medavoy collection. The parallel description of Herbert—"proficiency in every possible military skill . . . most decorated enlisted man of the Korean War"—is from *Soldier*, book jacket.

34 Brando seems also to have drawn on previous films for his lines in *Apocalypse*. There are echoes, for instance, of a confrontation at a concentration camp from *The Young Lions* (1958); a denunciation of reality from *Last Tango in Paris* (1972); and a strategy session on outwitting guerrillas from *Burn!* (1969).

35 Brando's books on religion, anthropology, and spirituality are for the most part in KBL. His many copies of Eliot's poetry are in another private

collection. Brando's other Bibles and more of his books on religion are in two additional private collections.

36 The subtitle of this book by John Lash is "The Complete Guide to Spiritual Pathfinding," 1990. Brando referred to Hoffer's *True Believer*, a book he owned in multiples, in recordings of his houseboat conversations with Coppola, Brando Estate Archives.

37 Brando in Lindsey Interviews. See also *Songs*, pp. 428–31.

38 He mentioned it, for instance, to Lawrence Grobel. See *Conversations with Brando*, p. 100.

39 Brando quotes Conrad in *Songs*, p. 430.

40 *Apocalypse Now* script, second revision of second draft, June 22, 1979, Medavoy collection.

41 Brando: Lindsey interviews, where he also talked at length about his dismay over Coppola's public statements about his work on the film.

42 Brando marked passages in his two separate copies of Arendt's *On Violence*—one of them excerpted as a section of her *Crises of the Republic*. He marked the passage on guerrilla warfare in *On Violence* (New York: Harcourt Brace, 1970), p. 10. The other quotations in this paragraph are from passages Brando marked in his copy of *Crises of the Republic* (New York: Harcourt Brace, 1972), pp. 15, 2.

43 Tapes of Brando's speeches for Kurtz, which were not included in the film, are in Brando Estate Archives. These tapes of Brando's rich monologues for Kurtz amount to about two hours.

44 *Eichmann in Jerusalem* (New York: Viking, 1975), p. 127.

45 Unless otherwise stipulated, all quotes from *Apocalypse Now* are from the 1979 film version of Kurtz's scenes.

46 Frank Rich, "Cinema: The Making of a Quagmire," *Time*, August 27, 1979; Vincent Canby, *New York Times*, August 15, 1979; Champlin is quoted in Cowie, *Coppola*, p. 131; Dale Pollock, *Variety*, May 12, 1979; Roger Ebert, *Chicago Sun-Times*, June 1, 1979.

47 *Chicago Sun-Times*, December 23, 1980; *New York Times*, December 19, 1980.

48 Brando's August 5, 1987, letter to Mario Kassar of Carolco Pictures, turning down the role of "Soviet Colonel Zaysen" and spelling out his hopes that "raproachment" is forthcoming, as well as his disdain for the Soviet Union's "oppressive policies," is in the Brando Estate Archives.

49 Miko Brando, interviews with the author, September 21 and 23, 2012, and June 16, 2013.

50 Files on Brando's financial support of Christian, as well as letters he wrote to his son over the years, Brando Estate Archives.

51 Dodie enrolled in Yale University's summer school at the Center for Alcohol Studies, which was run by Marty Mann, during the summer of 1947. See the Marty Mann Papers, Special Collections Research Center, Syracuse University Library. Some of these details are from June Beechly interview with Brando, Tokyo, Japan, when she visited him during on-location filming of *Sayonara* in the spring of 1957, audiotape, Brando Estate Archives.

52 G. L. Harrington is credited by William Glasser as his "mentor" and quoted in *Choice Theory: A New Psychology of Personal Freedom* (New York: Harper Perennial, 1999), p. 5.

53 Brando told Robert Lindsey (Lindsey Interviews, Brando Estate Archives): "I had a lot of affairs, far too many affairs to describe me as a perfectly normal, reasonable, intelligent person."

54 Avra Douglas, interviews with the author; Miko Brando, interviews with the author. This image of Brando as "never in a hurry" is repeated by a Pakistani girlfriend in her Notes for MB Autobiography, which is discussed in the Epilogue. She writes: "Marlon you have a beautiful habit which is that you are never in a hurry. When we meet or when you telephone you have all the time in the world and it seems that you want it to continue forever," in Brando Estate Archives.

55 Brando's views of how Harrington helped him are articulated throughout the Lindsey interviews. He made similar points in an interview on *Saturday Night with Connie Chung*, October 7, 1989. He also took personality tests, one in particular at the end of Carol Pearson's *The Hero Within: Six Archetypes We Live By* (1989), where Brando's selections classified him as the "Wanderer" and the "Magician" types and reflected his high self-regard and sense of purpose.

56 Brando owned dozens of books about homebuilding and home repair and was especially attached to the Time-Life series, with specific books on advanced wiring, cabins and cottages, advanced wood-working, etc. Among his many philosophical books on being at home in the universe, he had Roderic Gorney's *The Human Agenda: How to Be at Home in the Universe without Magic* (1979), which he annotated.

57 Lindsey Interviews.

58 Ibid.

59 Michael Jackson conversation, Brando Estate Archives. All the quotations and points in the paragraph above are drawn from it.

60 David Thomson, who edited the book (published in 2005) and wrote an afterword for it, thought Brando's contributions were limited, but he

didn't have access to the Brando Estate Archives with the considerable evidence of Brando's extensive work on the project, nor did he have access to Brando's library and reading material.

61 Brando's heavily annotated copy of *Snowblind*, KBL, Box 24.

62 Tape of Brando discussing *Jericho*, in possession of Quincy Jones. Quincy Jones, interviews with the author, July 23, 2012, and June 17, 2013.

63 Fax to Brando regarding "location summary" for *Jericho*, December 3, 1987, Brando Estate Archives. People close to the production suspect that Brando himself pulled the plug.

64 Multiple versions of all of these scripts, with Brando's transcribed ideas and notes, and handwritten revisions, are in Brando Estate Archives.

65 The 1993 *Fan-Tan* screenplay, labeled "Rough Draft" with Brando's annotations throughout, was dated September 30, 1993. Brando, apparently dissatisfied with this version, took up the prospect again in 1998 with the help of the professional screenwriter with whom he had enjoyed working on *The Nightcomers*. Letter from Michael Hastings to Brando, August 19, 1998, with eight pages of notes on a possible adaptation.

66 Glenn Collins, "A Black Director Views Apartheid," *New York Times*, September 25, 1989. Director Euzhan Palcy says in this interview that she worried about working with Brando due to reports that he could be difficult with directors, but she found him easy to work with.

67 See reviews by Roger Ebert, *Chicago Sun-Times*, September 22, 1989; Rita Kempley, *Washington Post*, September 22, 1989; Peter Travers, *Rolling Stone*, September 20, 1989. Brando's three-page letter to the producers of *A Dry White Season* is in Brando Estate Archives. Brando also describes the episode in Lindsey Interviews and in *Songs*, pp. 435–39. He was nominated for an Academy Award, BAFTA, New York Film Critics Award, Golden Globe, Political Film Society, and Tokyo International Film Festival Award, all for Best Supporting Actor, and won an award in Tokyo.

68 See, for example, the interview Brando gave the *Philadelphia Daily News* on July 1, 1962, p. 32, "Brando Sharpening Up for a Comedy Role," by Joseph Finnigan. "Marlon Brando, a man not often given to smiling in pictures unless they are tinged with tragedy, is sharpening his wit for a movie comedy debut." Referring to *Teahouse of the August Moon*, Brando commented that it "was supposed to be a comedy but it turned out to be 'Anthony Adverse.'" He concluded, "I'm not a funny man and can't do gags.... But there is some kind of comedy I could do as long as it's not mugging. That's comedy where the situation contains the humor. It's farce, something a little larger than life."

69 Brando describes his experiences watching Howard's routines in New York in Lindsey Interviews and Grobel, *Conversations with Brando*, pp. 82–83. Howard's last Broadway show was *Sallie* (1948), about the comedic trials of refugee Russian nobles working as restaurant help. Of those who never received their due because they died before the television era, he laid "claim to be the king of Broadway's comedians." Frank Cullen, *Vaudeville, Old and New: An Encyclopedia of Variety Performers in America*, vol. 1 (New York: Psychology Press, 2007), pp. 535–38.

70 May Britt describes the incident with Brando at dinner in *Brando*, TCM Documentary, 2007.

71 Frances Brando Loving, Notes for MB Autobiography, Brando Estate Archives.

72 David Niven's letter of September 20, 1963, Brando Estate Archives.

73 Publicity materials for *The Freshman*, November 7, 1989, Brando Estate Archives.

74 Lindsey Interviews and *Songs*, pp. 420–22.

75 The tapes of Brando's extended critique of Lillian Hellman's script for *The Chase* (1966), discussed at length in chapter 5, are in the Brando Estate Archives.

76 Ellen Adler even sent a postcard to one of Brando's white cats, addressed to "a fortunate resident of sunny California, from a snowbound white cat in Manhattan."

77 This is confirmed by letters in Brando Estate Archives.

78 Brando recounted his struggles with the Salkinds in Lindsey Interviews and in *Songs*, pp. 440–42. Brando's materials on the film, in a private collection, also include many articles on Torquemada and the Inquisition, as well as notes to the producers with his ideas for script changes.

79 Avra Douglas, interviews with the author, February 29–March 4, June 18 and 19, 2012, and June 23 and 24, 2013. She recalled as well how much time Brando spent with Ilya Salkind, reconceptualizing and rewriting the script to accord with the history he knew.

80 The letter is in a private collection. Brando gave an interview to *Variety*, April 21, 1992, just before the release of *Christopher Columbus: The Discovery*, reiterating his outrage about the inaccurate portrayal of Columbus and the indigenous inhabitants.

81 Peter Rainer, *Los Angeles Times*, August 24, 1992.

82 Joseph Brutsman letter to Brando, January 20, 1994, in a private collection.

83 Letter to Mike Lobell, July 10, 1989, Brando Estate Archives.

84 Roger Ebert, *Chicago Sun-Times*, April 7, 1995, expressed a rare disgust with Brando's acting. Peter Travers, *Rolling Stone*, April 7, 1995; Hal Hinson and Desson Howe, *Washington Post*, April 7, 1995; and Mick LaSalle, *San Francisco Chronicle*, April 7, 1995, were all charmed by Brando's performance.

85 He added, for instance, the prediction that Don Juan would do "a flamenco number on Bill's head until it looks like a tortilla, and it's on your watch!"; complaining in the margin: "no jargon," "cliché," "lay language," and, finally, "dialogue too conventional; makes the character conventional." Brando's revisions are all on the revised script draft, December 20, 1993, pp. 16, 22, 30, 32, in a private collection.

86 A note in his files from June 26, 1989, for example, directs his assistant to "Buy Book: *Invisible Frontiers: The Race to Synthesize the Human Gene*. Published by MicroSoft in Seattle in 1988. Author is Stephen Hall." Next item: "Go to Corner of Van Nuys Bl. and Ventura and buy the June Issue of Smithsonian '89. Marlon wants 10 photocopies of the article entitled, 'A Molecular Code Links Emotion, Mind and Health.' Author is Stephen Hall." Brando Estate Archives.

87 Seventy-five-pages of Brando's transcribed conversations with Stanley date from November 17, 1994. The equally long transcribed conversations with John Frankenheimer date from August 10, 1995, Brando Estate Archives.

88 Brando's rewritten script pages for the first meeting between Dr. Moreau and the island visitor, Edward Douglas (David Thewlis), are in a private collection. All of these quotations are from this script.

89 David Page, who was Brando's costume designer for most of his late films, including *The Island of Dr. Moreau* and *The Score*, recounted this in an interview with the author, August 19, 2013.

90 Brando buddies who worked with him in theater and films over the years include (in order of association): Carlo Fiore, Sam Gilman, Philip and Marie Rhodes, Christian Marquand, George Englund, and Robert Redfield. All of them, with the exception of Gilman and Marquand, wrote books about Brando that conveyed some hostility toward him, or gave interviews to biographers who were hostile to him, but Brando could be hard on them as well.

91 Alex Ross, "Island of Lost Auteurs: What the Hell Happened to John Frankenheimer?" *Slate*, September 10, 1996.

92 Brando told Joseph Brutsman at dinner in Montreal following the wrap of *Free Money* that he "would be blamed" for whatever shortcomings were

found in the film. Joseph Brutsman interview with the author, December 1, 2012.

93 The party was held on October 21, 1995; the invitation is in a private collection. The book with its inscription is in KBL, Box 37.

94 Brando's 1995 letter to Baz Luhrmann is in Brando Estate Archives, as is the correspondence with Lynch.

95 Brando's letters to Marquez (April 16, May 28, and June 30, 1997) are in the Brando Estate Archives.

96 Brando was especially preoccupied with the Caryl Chessman case, about which he considered making a movie in the early 1960s. See chapter 4 for more on his views about and struggle against capital punishment.

97 Joseph Brutsman recalled, in interviews with the author, how Brando reflected on the situation of his son Christian, while they were touring the prison that would provide the setting for a few of his scenes in *Free Money*.

98 A boy who knew Brando in elementary school in Evanston, Illinois, remembered how he reacted "when he got 'hit' by a bullet.... He'd get plugged and he didn't just fall down.... He really knew how to die. He made a specialty of it. I mean it was *real*." Quoted in Manso, *Brando*, p. 23.

99 See writer and director's commentary in DVD of *Free Money*. All the details about behind-the-scenes developments are from there, unless otherwise noted.

100 Grobel, *Conversations with Brando*, p. 83.

101 *Chicago Sun-Times*, July 13, 2001, and *Rolling Stone*, July 13, 2001.

102 For more on *The Big Bug Man*, which was directed by Bob Bendetson and Peter Shin and never released, see Archie Thomas, "Brando's Last Role: An Evil Old Lady," *The Guardian*, July 8, 2004, and Peter Gilstrap, *LA Weekly*, "Last Tango in Drag," July 22, 2004.

103 *The Big Bug Man* script by Bob Bendetson, p. 83.

104 Marice Tobias, quoted in Gilstrap's "Last Tango in Drag."

105 Marice Tobias and Paul Doherty described their work with Brando in interviews with the author on, respectively, December 17, 2012, and March 15, 2012. I drew here also on Bob Bendetson interview with the author, June 22, 2013, and Peter Shin interview with the author, July 1, 2013.

CHAPTER EIGHT. CITIZEN OF THE PLANET

1 Brando discusses this with Robert Lindsey, Lindsey Transcripts, Brando Estate Archives.

2 Jay Kanter mentioned Brando's computers, which were upgraded yearly and sometimes even more often, in an interview, April 21, 2011. Avra Douglas, who worked as Brando's assistant from 1990 to the end of his life, described how he insisted on learning new computer programs as they came out. Avra Douglas interviews. Brando's collection of *Scientific American* and other magazines, and hundreds of books on science and technology, are in KBL.

3 Brando quoted in Grobel Interviews, Brando Estate Archives.

4 Dodie Brando quoted in "Mrs. Brando's Boy," p. 62, magazine article from 1952 in Brando Estate Archives.

5 Brando's copy of M. D. Berlitz, *Deuxième Livre: Pour l'Enseignement des Langues Modernes* (New York: Nouvelle Edition Americaine, 1924), in a private collection.

6 Brando's calendar for 1967, recording his daily appointments and travels, lists him in New York City on January 27, 28, and 29; in London from January 30 to February 10; in Cairo on February 17; Istanbul on February 18 and 19, and Hawaii on March 27. March 28 reads: "Beverly Hills: Marlon returns home from trip around the world."

7 This interview in French during filming of *The Brave* on October 14, 1996, in Los Angeles was never published, in a private collection.

8 Herman Leonard's recollection of the trip was sent in an e-mail on December 21, 2004. Herman Leonard Estate.

9 Grobel, *Conversations with Brando*, pp. 22–23.

10 Morris's chapter on Brando was called "The Godfather's Dilemma" (London: Little Books), pp. 573–80. Quotes are on pp. 576–77.

11 Tom Oppenheim recalled how surprised he was to find Brando, in the year before he died, still capable of intense anger over the way fame had hampered him. Tom Oppenheim interview, May 7, 2010.

12 Telegram from February 22, 1960, Brando Estate Archives.

13 Clurman, *All People Are Famous*, pp. 260–61.

14 This is from one of Brando's favorite quotation books: *The Great Thoughts*, compiled by George Seldes (New York: Ballantine, 1985), n.p. Brando owned two volumes of Aristotle's works: one is in KBL, one in another private collection. The volume in KBL has pencil markings throughout; the volume in the private collection has no annotations.

15 Brando's Grandmother Bess had worked for J. L. Webster, an attorney who had defended Standing Bear of the Ponca tribe in a case that paved the way for citizenship rights for American Indians. See chapter 1, and Manso, pp. 3–4, 272.

16 The Brando Estate Archives include scripts from the 1960s, but the script

by Mrs. B. R. Hill is not among them. Brando letter addressed to Mrs. Hill, Brando Estate Archives.

17 Lindsey Interviews and *Songs*, p. 384.

18 The catalog was in Brando's materials from *The Godfather* set, in a private collection. Another catalog of "Books about Indians," from the New York Museum of the American Indian, with a Congressional Research Service stamp from August 9, 1973, which also had Brando's annotations, is in a private collection. In both cases, every book marked by Brando in the catalog is in his collection. Brando even had a catalog of *Rare Out-of-Print Books on the American Indian and the Early West* by T. N. Luther Books (Kansas City, MO, 1964), in a private collection.

19 Brando's annotated copy of *The Cowboy Encyclopedia* is one of hundreds of his books on Indians purchased by an anonymous buyer at the Christie's sale. The October 25, 1957, correspondence between Marlon Brando Sr. and Marlon Brando Jr. regarding "the future of Pennebaker," Brando's film company, reveals that one possible script had strong Indian themes. Correspondence in Brando Estate Archives. These early scripts and notes for *One-Eyed Jacks* are in the *One-Eyed Jacks* collection at the Herrick Library, Beverly Hills, and in a private collection.

20 He was taken in particular by the Northwest Indian custom of potlatch, whereby the wealthy voluntarily redistributed their bounty by dispensing it publicly as gifts to the community. He queried in the margin, "Does it prevail?" See D'Arcy McNickle, *They Came Here First: The Epic of the American Indian* (Philadelphia: Lippincott, 1949), pp. 56–57. Brando's copy of McNickle's book is in a private collection. Next to a description of a "golden staircase" on a Papago reservation in Arizona leading to a cave housing possibly the mythological beginnings of many tribes, Brando wrote, "go there," and beside a reference to "the incense of sweet grass" he scrawled, "get some," pp. 31, 78. He marks, too, in another example, a passage on the precision of Indian names for things: "In the Hopi language shape and size of an object are not mentioned unless the thought is concerned with them," p. 95.

21 McNickle, *They Came Here First*, pp. 79, 83

22 Ibid., pp. 92, 127. McNickle quotes Montaigne's account of the Indians on p. 122.

23 This is acknowledged in various notes written by Brando on Indian history that are in the Brando Estate Archives: for example, "Notes on Indians, Sept. 3, 1963, Tahiti."

24 *They Came Here First*, pp. 176–78.

25 These are covered in detail in McNickle's final chapter, "Supplanting a People," pp. 188–290.

26 Lindsey Interviews and *Songs*, p. 389.

27 *They Came Here First*, pp. 100, 101, passages marked by Brando.

28 Ibid., pp. 188, 189, passages marked by Brando.

29 His copy of the *American Indian Religious Freedom Act Report*, P.L. 95–341, Federal Agencies Task Force, Chairman Cecil D. Andrus, Secretary of the Interior, August 1979, which was designed to rectify a century of efforts to stamp out tribal cultures in the name of peaceful assimilation, is in a private collection.

30 Edward H. Spicer, *Cycles of Conquest: The Impact of Spain, Mexico, and the United States on the Indians of the Southwest, 1533–1960* (Tucson: University of Arizona Press, 1974), p. 240.

31 Lindsey Interviews and *Songs*, p. 377.

32 Brando's copy of the Hearings on the Senate Joint Resolutions 170 and 171 is in a private collection. Among his comments, which are consistently critical of the lack of preparation and data on the part of the senators in making decisions about Indian rights established by mid-nineteenth-century treaties, he asks, "When was joint resolution 171 submitted to the committee and by whom? It seems that the reasons for its existence were unknown to those on the subcommittee even after it was formulated." Senate Committee Hearings, p. 22. "The Fish-in Protests at Frank's Landing," Gabriel Chrisman, *Seattle Civil Rights and Labor History Project* (HSTAA 498, Autumn 2007), www.civilrights.washington.edu.

33 From the early sixties onward, Brando was working with Jack Beck, a CBS producer on ideas for television shows about Indians. He did numerous talk shows, often accompanied by Indians—for example, *The Les Crane Show* and *The Johnny Carson Show*, where he screened slides on Indian history.

34 The Beverly Hills Fundraising Dinner for Kennedy at the Hilton Hotel is listed on Brando's calendar for 1963, Brando Estate Archives. *Songs*, pp. 291–92, and Lindsey Interviews. The encounter with Douglas is also described in *Songs*, p. 379, and in Lindsey Interviews.

35 This quotation from one of two telegrams is reproduced in the Christie's catalogue, *The Personal Property of Marlon Brando: Thursday 30 June 2005*, p. 132.

36 The quitclaim deed for the forty acres in Liberty Canyon, California, was dated December 27, 1974, and was prepared by the Law Offices of Rosenfeld, Meyer, and Susman, which handled Brando's legal affairs, in Brando

Estate Archives. The land grant was covered, somewhat snidely, by Garrick Utley on ABC News, and also on local television in Los Angeles. A collection of legal papers relating to the bequest, along with transcript notes of a speech Brando delivered at the event, are also in the Brando Estate Archives.

37 Grobel, *Conversations with Brando*, p. 111.

38 Brando's FBI file, which dates from 1946 to 2004, is #1203025-000 in the US Department of Justice, FBI, Records Management Division. Brando's work for the Irgun, in 1946, during and after his performances in Ben Hecht's *A Flag Is Born*, might have attracted the attention of the FBI in the 1940s.

39 In his concern over the issue of surveillance, Brando was again ahead of his time. Transcribed discussion with Senator Daniel Inouye of Hawaii, Brando Estate Archives.

40 For more on the Church Committee Reports, see the Assassination Archives and Research Center, http://www.aarclibrary.org/index.htm.

41 Brando's nephew Martin Asinof recalls coming out of the Mulholland Drive house with Brando in the early 1970s and seeing a man in a black suit working on the telephone pole above the house. Asked what he was doing with the phone wires, the man replied that he was from the phone company, a claim that was refuted when Brando checked directly with the company. Asinof and Brando concluded that the man had been setting up a wiretap on his phone. Martin Asinof, interview with the author, June 5, 2013, with follow-ups July and August 2013. The portion of Brando's FBI file #1203025-000 released to the author confirmed that the FBI kept watch on Brando's activities with the Indians between 1975 and 1976. It also included a letter dated December 13, 1968, from J. Edgar Hoover, regarding the December 6, 1968, incident when Brando was removed from a plane to Colombia at the Los Angeles International Airport after he jokingly asked the stewardess, who didn't recognize him, whether this was "the plane to Cuba."

42 This was noted by Bruce Cook in his piece on Brando on the set of *The Missouri Breaks* in *Crawdaddy*, December 1975: "Two gentlemen from the FBI visited me yesterday, asking me questions, and I asked *them* some. It wound up that we had a two- or three-hour conversation," Brando told him. "They were nice men. Their big question was, would I aid a man who was a fugitive from justice ... and my big question to them was, if a friend of theirs with the FBI killed someone wrongly, would they turn him in and testify against him?" (pp. 39–40).

43 These details are described on the website of the Alexian Brothers, www
.alexianbrothers.org. Brando discusses these incidents directly in *Songs*,
pp. 393–99, and in more detail in the Lindsey Interviews.

44 For example, Brando's calendar for June 23, 1963, lists "Dinner with Mr.
and Mrs. Ken MacKenzie" and "After Dinner...Film at Studio—The
Exiles." His calendar for January 24, 1964, lists "Les Crane T.V. Show
...ABC-TV With Ralph Lone Bear (Pawnee)." Brando's daily calendars
from 1963 and 1964 also feature frequent meetings with Jack Beck, visits to Indian reservations, etc., calendars and Brando's correspondence
from the early 1960s with Jack Beck concerning programs on Indians
in Brando Estate Archives. Brando notes in a passage about a Tuscarora
Indian protest at Niagara Falls in Edmund Wilson's *Apologies to the Iroquois* (New York: Farrar, Straus & Cudahy, 1960), p. 148: "Find out what
T.V. coverage there was from Jack Beck." Brando's marginal reference to
his *Johnny Carson Show* appearance is in Dee Brown and Martin Schmitt,
Fighting Indians of the West (New York: Ballantine, 1974), p. 3.

45 According to a main source, the massacre "was the worst blow ever
struck at any tribe in the whole plains region." The 700 Colorado militia
headed by Colonel John Chivington that attacked the friendly Cheyennes
in November 1864 not only killed but also mutilated their victims, taking
scalps and other body parts as trophies of battle. (Brando marks a passage
in Stan Steiner's *The New Indians*, uncorrected page proofs, p. 39, detail-
ing the eroticized savagery of Kit Carson and other soldiers toward the
Navajo and Apaches.) A few weeks later, at a Denver theater, some of these
soldiers exhibited the scalps, mostly those of women and children, accompanied by audience cheers and patriotic airs. (Notes are in Brando's copy
of *Life of George Bent: Written from His Letters* by George E. Hyde [Nor-
man: University of Oklahoma Press, 1968], p. 162.) In 1865, a congressional
committee condemned the murder "in cold blood" of "unsuspecting men,
women, and children" with "every reason to believe they were under the
protection of the United States authorities." But it took the Methodist
ministry more than a century to apologize for the un-Christian behavior
of its prominent lay preacher, Colonel Chivington. (*United States Congress
Joint Committee on the Conduct of the War, 1865*, University of Michigan
Digital Library Production Service. Accounts of the United Methodist
Church condemnation of the massacre, which resulted as well in contributions to the development of a research and learning center at the
Sand Creek Massacre Historic Site, can be found at UMC.org.) Surviving
tapes of his plot summaries for the Sand Creek Massacre series featured

Chivington and the more conciliatory Major Edward Wynkoop and wife Louisa as prominent characters. (Stan Hoig, *The Sand Creek Massacre* [Norman: University of Oklahoma Press, 1961], p. 19.) Brando annotated Hoig's book thoroughly. On a page of one source, Brando sketched an imaginary dialogue between an officer, Major Edward Wynkoop, and a friendly white trader who lived among the Indians just before the massacre: "Wynkoop would ask him how he could live without civilization. He replies, I can't that's why I live with the Cheyenne." See notes in his copy of *Life of George Bent*, p. 41.

46 Brown and Schmitt, *Fighting Indians of the West*, pp. 40–41, 23. These possibilities come up in notes and correspondence in the Brando Estate Archives.

47 Producer Frank P. Rosenberg wrote in the *New York Times*: "Every line every actor read, as well as every button on every piece of wardrobe, got Brando's concentrated attention until he was completely satisfied." "Eyeing 'Jacks': Producer Scans a Hectic Three-Year Stint with Star-Director Brando," March 26, 1961.

48 See comments, respectively, in Brando's copies of McNickle's *They Came Here First*, where he noted: "Exploitation [of the Indians] seemed not to be limited by nationality. Beginning in 1492 to the present day," p. 121; *The Old West: The Soldiers* (New York: Time-Life Books, 1973), pp. 44–45, 39, 53, 25; *Life of George Bent*, p. 195; Fey and McNickle, *Indians and Other Americans*, p. 203; Nelson Lee, *Three Years Among the Comanches* (Norman: University of Oklahoma Press, 1957), pp. 118–19; and Irvin Peithmann, *Broken Peace Pipes: A Four-Hundred-Year History of the American Indian* (Springfield, IL: Charles C. Thomas, 1964), pp. 213–14.

49 See notes in Brando's copies, respectively, of *Broken Peace Pipes*, p. 22; *Fighting Indians*, p. 19; *Indians and Other Americans*, and on the grasshopper plague, Hoig, *Sand Creek Massacre*, p. 55.

50 Elliott Arnold, *The Camp Grant Massacre* (New York: Simon and Schuster, 1976), pp. 26, 45.

51 *Life of George Bent*, pp. 180–81; Dee Brown, *Hear That Lonesome Whistle Blow: Railroads in the West* (New York: Holt, Rinehart, 1977), p. 3.

52 Notes in Brando's copy of *Hear That Lonesome Whistle Blow*, pp. 246–47.

53 Notes, respectively, in Brando's copies of Collier, *Indians of the Americas* pp. 175–76, 176–77, and Angie Debo, *Geronimo* (Norman: University of Oklahoma Press, 1986), pp. 50–53.

54 Notes in Brando's copy of Herbert Eugene Bolton, *Coronado: Knight of Pueblos and Plains* (Albuquerque: University of New Mexico Press, 1974),

p. 403; *Broken Peace Pipes*, back cover; and Edward H. Spicer, *Cycles of Conquest* (Albuquerque: University of Arizona Press, 1974), p. 240.

55 This is evident in the way Brando responded to the history of the Spanish in North America. Brando's notation on the cover of Herbert Bolton's *Coronado: Knight of Pueblos and Plains*: "Look on my work ye mighty and dispair," along with his notes inside, condemn the graphic details and Bolton's attempts to excuse them. Throughout the book, Brando wars marginally with the colonialist historian. Yet Brando still writes at the end: "I must talk to this dolt," *Coronado*, p. 323. Brando took to heart an inscription on his copy of *Indians and Other Americans*: "To Marlon Brando. In these things there are many questions and few answers. D'Arcy McNickle, August 1963." See notes in Brando's copy of McNickle, *The Indian Tribes of the United States: Ethnic and Cultural Survival*, p. 7.

56 Ever in dialogue with his friend McNickle, Brando wrote sadly in the margin of a McNickle book: "we had much to learn from the Indians." McNickle, *Indian Tribes*, p. 7.

57 He marks emphatically a statement in Steiner's *The New Indians* (uncorrected page proofs): "Like the people of Africa and Asia the Indian has now broken the silence imposed upon him by others and by himself," p. 5½.

58 The awful paradox of the Buffalo Soldiers, Brando wrote, was that "the North won the war to free the slaves/so they could use blacks for cannon foder." See notes in Brando's copy of Donnie D. Good, *The Buffalo Soldier* (Tulsa: Thomas Gilcrease Institute of American History and Art, 1970), where he is also drawn to such details as the black cavalry's charge to establish order among "Mexican bandits" and "roving Indian bands." Brando noted to himself to "use" a reference to a Spanish law applied in Mexico that allowed Spanish soldiers to enslave only Indians captured in war, a law that motivated Spaniards to provoke Indians into aggression. See Brando's copy of John Upton Terrell, *Apache Chronicle* (New York: World Publishing, 1972), p. 84.

59 These names are in John M. Carroll, ed., *The Black Military Experience in the American West* (New York: Liveright, 1971), p. 356, and Steiner's *The New Indians*, p. 1.

60 Uncorrected page proofs, Steiner's *The New Indians*, pp. 13½, 16, 16½. Brando also wrote "mud clowns" above a passage on Indian rituals that removed the taint from tribesmen who had fought for whites, p. 13. He also annotated a passage in his copy of Edmund Wilson's *Apologies to the Iroquois*, which states that Indians on reservations were refused loans authorized by the GI Bill of Rights.

61 Notes in Brando's copy of Fey and McNickle, *Indians and Other Americans*, p. 73.

62 Notes in Brando's copies of *Indians and Other Americans*, back cover, and Prucha, *American Indian Policy in the Formative Years*, back cover.

63 The Brando Estate Archives contain boxes of materials from "Vision Road" and other Indian projects, extending from the 1950s to the 1990s. The materials from *The Brave* in private collection confirm Brando's commitment to the project.

64 Brando's note on the Indian warrior is in Brown and Schmitt, *Fighting Indians of the West*, p. 41. Brando thought himself too old to play Kit Carson, but he entertained the possibility of other white figures. Grobel, *Conversations with Brando*, p. 124.

65 Baldwin's play was never made into a film. Brando's annotations on the prospective screenplay are on his copy in KBL, Box 45.

66 *Songs*, p. 296.

67 Brando recalls seeing these photographs in the newspaper as well as the incident with his fourth-grade teacher at Lincoln Elementary School in Evanston, Illinois, in his August 1983 taped conversation with Michael Jackson.

68 Brando mentions this in the August 1983 conversation with Michael Jackson; in Lindsey Interviews; and in *Songs*, pp. 26, 30–33.

69 Brando's annotations are in his copy of Baldwin's *The Fire Next Time*, pp. 18, 15, KBL, Box 45.

70 Brando's annotated copy of Baldwin, *Nobody Knows My Name* (New York: Dial, 1961), p. 13, is in KBL. This observation echoes another passage Brando highlighted, in his copy of Wilhelm Reich's *The Mass Psychology of Fascism*: "One cannot make the fascist harmless if . . . one does not look for him *in oneself*," p. xii (italics in original).

71 These quotations are from various essays by James Baldwin, in *James Baldwin: Collected Essays*, edited by Toni Morrison (New York: Library of America, 1998), p. 434. See also pp. 437–38, 439, and 450 for Baldwin's account of Brando in the civil rights movement.

72 Brando refers to the boycott, and another incident in early 1960, when black inmates at a Georgia prison protested unbearable conditions by breaking their own legs with sledgehammers, in a 1963 interview on TCM, "Marlon Brando on Civil Rights," where he describes the early days of the movement.

73 Michael Jackson conversation, August 1983.

74 An average day from Brando's 1964 calendar is similarly reflective of political commitments: January 25, for example, includes meetings with

James and Daniel Baldwin, activist reporter Drew Pearson, and black photojournalist Frank Dandridge, and an evening discussion on civil rights with a group of congressmen. The calendar is in the Brando Estate Archives.

75 These calendars, covering events, respectively, from June 11, June 25, July 12, July 14, and July 27, 1963, are in the Brando Estate Archives.

76 The Civil Rights Roundtable is widely available on YouTube and elsewhere. See www.youtube.com/watch?v=MruG888gH50.

77 Brando discusses this in his 1983 conversation with Michael Jackson and in Lindsey Interviews.

78 Brando described these experiences with the Black Panthers in Lindsey Interviews and in *Songs*, pp. 298–303.

79 Brando's notes for the eulogy he delivered at Bobby Hutton's funeral, Brando Estate Archives. In public speaking as well as on film, he improvised extensively from his notes. His notes also record some of the comments of other eulogists, such as the metaphor of the white community as the hog in the stream of humanity. Brando's eulogy, delivered on April 12, 1968, was broadcast on KTVU News in Oakland, California.

80 These quotations are from the Petition for Hearing filed by Brando's lawyers in the Supreme Court of the State of California, p. 1. See Civ. No. 35362, Court of Appeals of California, Second Appellate District, Division 5, December 10, 1970, *Samson B. Mullins, President of the Oakland Police Officers Association, et al., Plaintiffs and Appellants, v. Marlon Brando, Defendant and Respondent.* There are numerous files on the case in the Brando Estate Archives, including court briefs, many annotated by Brando's lawyers.

81 The Reverend Jesse Jackson's Operation PUSH "Excelathon" for black youth on April 21, 1979, was covered by the *Los Angeles Times*, which featured a photograph of Brando there.

82 Brando's letter to Toni Morrison, February 1, 1991. Response dated February 4, 1991, Brando Estate Archives. Brando's collection of books by Toni Morrison was sold at the Christie's sale.

83 This book—along with others on South Africa, such as Edward Feit's *South Africa: The Dynamics of the African National Congress* (1962), with Brando's marginalia—is in KBL, Box 97.

84 Gordon Allport, *The Nature of Prejudice* (New York: Doubleday, 1958), pp. 8, 11; Frantz Fanon, *Black Skin, White Masks* (New York: Grove, 1967), pp. 130, 134; Norman Mailer, *The White Negro* (San Francisco: City Lights Books, 1957), n.p. All of these books are in a private collection of Brando's books on civil rights.

85 Brando discusses this in Grobel, *Conversations with Brando*, pp. 103–4; in the Lindsey Interviews; and in the margins of his civil rights books.

86 Brando makes these comments in his conversation with Michael Jackson, August 1983 and in Robert Lindsey Interviews. The direct quotations are from the Michael Jackson tape.

87 Direct quotes are from Grobel Transcripts.

88 Lindsey Interviews and *Songs*, p. 232.

89 See, for instance, "The Private World of Bud Brando," by Don Stewart, which describes Brando's idealism, and "Brando's Search for Faith." Both articles, from the 1950s (the first from just before *Viva Zapata!*; the second from just after *The Young Lions*), are in the Brando Estate Archives, no dates available.

90 Lindsey Interviews.

91 See, for instance, Sunday, March 19, 1967, AP wire: "Brando returned from a five-day tour of the eastern India state Thursday. He said nobody outside Bihar could imagine the condition of its inhabitants." See also the press release from UNICEF, April 2, 1967, sent to "International School Students" around the world, urging them to support the children of Bihar, signed "Marlon Brando, UNICEF Ambassador at Large."

92 Brando, p. 46, in Transcriptions of Brando's taped conversations at Mulholland Drive with Stewart Brand and Jay Baldwin from 1975, Brando Estate Archives.

93 Brando described the experience in *Songs*, pp. 292–95, and at greater length in Lindsey Interviews.

94 On April 11, Brando was in New York at the UN and UNICEF offices, meeting with, among others, Henry Labouisse, executive director of UNICEF, and Hugh Downs. On April 13, he met with Downs and Mike Dann of CBS. Among the people in Hollywood to whom he showed the film were Chuck Silvers, Sherman Grinberg, Jim Real, Jack Valenti, and Shana Alexander, who was there interviewing him. On October 13 and 14, he showed the film at a UNICEF event in Helsinki, Finland, for Jack Ling, Altemur Kılıç, Henry Labouisse, and other dignitaries, as a warning for what should never be allowed to happen again. Kristin L. Ahlberg describes President Lyndon Johnson's policies in *Transplanting the Great Society: Lyndon Johnson and Food for Peace* (Columbia: University of Missouri Press, 2008), pp. 128–45.

95 These visits were listed on Brando's daily log. The marine biologists included Wallace Heath, who had helped the Lummi Indians with their aquaculture; Tap Pryor; and Edward Tarvyd; the archaeologist from the University of Hawaii was Yoshihiko Sinoto.

96 Brando's discovery and purchase of the island are described in Lindsey Interviews and in *Songs*, pp. 268–75 (quote on p. 273). The documents from his purchase of Tetiaroa, completed on March 13, 1967, are in the Brando Estate Archives. I have drawn as well on the pamphlet of the Tetiaroa Society, an organization incorporated after Brando's death to fulfill his many plans for the island. See *Tetiaroa Society: Sustainable Development for Future Generations*, http://tetiaroa.pf/about-3/.

97 Brando had multiple copies of the *Archaeology of Teti'aroa Atoll and Society Islands* in his library collection. See KBL, Box 5.

98 Transcriptions of Brando's taped conversations with Stewart Brand and Jay Baldwin from 1975, Brando Estate Archives. The strength of coconut wood was a favorite subject of Brando's. He mentioned it often in conversations with Brand and Baldwin, and he had a United Nations book (heavily annotated) on the subject, though this was from the 1980s: *Coconut Wood: Processing and Use*, Food and Agriculture Organization of the United Nations, Rome, 1985. This book is in the KBL, Box 88. Brando also owned books by Brand and by Buckminster Fuller, KBL, Boxes 83, 26, 51. *The International Book of Wood* was on the List of Books around Marlon's Bed, Brando Estate Archives. Patricia Herzog, a UCLA undergraduate in the late 1960s, remembers the day she was working in Martindale's Bookstore on Little Santa Monica Boulevard in Beverly Hills and Brando came in to buy *The Whole Earth Catalog* (personal communication). The book was not in any of the lots sold at Christie's in 2005.

99 Don Widener went so far as to clear the documentary with the UN and the US Environmental Protection Agency. These letters, from August 11 and November 15, 1972, and May 8, 1973, establishing Brando's commitment and the various negotiations with Probus productions and the news networks, are in the Stewart Brand file, Brando Estate Archives.

100 Brando–Brand–Baldwin conversations, p. 42.

101 Brando annotated his copy of Andrew Spielman and Michael D'Antonio, *Mosquito: A Natural History of Our Most Persistent and Deadly Foe* (New York: Hyperion, 2001), KBL, Box 84.

102 See the Gorilla Foundation's two-page letter, September 18, 1987, signed by Francine Patterson, trainer of the famous gorillas Koko and Michael, Brando Estate Archives. Brando also befriended Jane Goodall around this time, having read some of her books and talked to her by phone. In a handwritten letter to Brando, September 6, 1991, Goodall described her plans for "Wildlife Awareness Week" and expressed her eagerness to meet him after their conversations. This letter was found in Brando's

copy of her book, *Through a Window: Thirty Years with the Chimpanzees of Gombe* (London: Weidenfeld and Nicolson, 1990), in KBL, Box 96.

103 The original version of Brando's script for the ad, along with Brando's typed revision from February 18, 2000, which he revised from script to performance, is in the Brando Estate Archives. The ad, directed by Tony Scott, was filmed on February 22 and 23, 2000, at Anza Borrego Springs, California.

EPILOGUE. LYING FOR A LIVING

1   The first quote is from a *Time* cover story, "Cinema: A Tiger in the Reeds," October 11, 1954. The second is also from *Time*: "Cinema: New Picture, June 1, 1953."

2   One of his favorite shows was the Hasidic Chabad Telethon; he donated money to it not only because he valued the charity but also because he enjoyed the dramatic inventions of the performers (Avra Douglas interviews). Brando knew actor Jon Voigt, a devout Catholic and a regular on these Chabad shows, who appeared in 2008 on his thirteenth telethon. "Jon Voight Again Will Join Chabad's 'To Life' Telethon," *Los Angeles Times*, September 13, 2008.

3   "Marlon Brando: Notes for Book," June 22, 1992, pp. 27–28, Brando Estate Archives.

4   KBL, Boxes 86 and 92.

5   See KBL, Boxes 42 (for the article on dolphins) and 78 (for the many annotated books on religion).

6   Brando marked, for instance, Bergman's reference to "playing a role—that professional disease that has followed me mercilessly throughout my life and so often robbed or diminished my most profound experiences." *The Magic Lantern* (New York: Viking, 1988), p. 7. Brando's annotated copy is in KBL, Box 86.

7   Brando had agreed to do publicity for *Morituri* (1965), and the Maysles brothers decided to do a documentary on Brando talking to reporters about the film. The documentary is discussed in the Introduction.

8   Brando appeared on *The Dick Cavett Show* on June 12, 1973. The interview is also discussed in chapter 6.

9   The film is discussed in chapter 7.

10 There would also be a website to assist with technical problems and to provide accessories, such as scripts, instruction manuals on lighting, and dramatic techniques. These details were all discussed in "MB–Scott

Billups, Meeting of 1-10-00 re. DVD Project," transcripts in Brando Estate Archives.

11 Ibid. Brando describes *The Quiet One* on p. 40. The DVD project was linked to Billups's publications, which Brando had in his library.

12 This incident is discussed in chapter 1, in terms of Brando's difficult relationship with his father.

13 Transcripts of organizational discussions, "Lying for a Living," July 15, 2001, Brando Estate Archives. Brando was probably thinking about the project well before then.

14 Brando's fax to Clinton from December 1, 2001, is in the Brando Estate Archives. Avra Douglas remembered Brando discussing "Lying for a Living" on the phone with former president Clinton, and the fact that he was intrigued at first but then withdrew.

15 The file includes photographs with detailed accounts of the social and political functions of different African tribal masks with Brando's marks. Among the Kwele people, the "Gon" mask, fashioned in the image of a gorilla, signaled danger; the "ekuk," or antelope mask, indicated protection, Brando Estate Archives.

16 "Random Notes on Acting" and "Outline for Lying for a Living," July 11 and August 31, 2001, Brando Estate Archives.

17 The dozens of pages of notes outlining the sessions are dated July 11 and August 31, 2001. The sessions themselves were filmed from November 15 through December 12, 2001.

18 Quincy Jones, interview with the author, July 23, 2012, and June 17, 2013.

19 Philippe Petit, *Man on Wire* (New York: Skyhorse Publishing, 2008), p. 233. Petit gave Brando a copy of his 1985 book, *On the High Wire*, with an elaborately inscribed letter thanking him for the 2001 workshop: "You are an ever so rare 'Wondrous Conquistador of the Useless'... with respect, delight, gourmandize and exhaustion." KBL, Box 53. Petit's "Conquistador" is a reference to Werner Herzog's 1982 film *Fitzcarraldo*—about a manic Irishman engaged in a hopeless mission to establish a rubber factory in Peru and build an opera house in the jungle—a film he and Brando may have discussed.

20 "Here's Brando," *Collier's*, November 1, 1952, pp. 24–26.

21 Brando's statement is from his 1989 interview with Connie Chung. Friends, lovers, and family who described Brando's endlessly playful dramatic persona include Avra Douglas, Ellen Adler, Rebecca Brando, Shane Brando, Harry Dean Stanton, and Miko Brando in their interviews.

22 These Notes for MB Autobiography are in the Brando Estate Archives.

23 Brando, who advised Tom Oppenheim to "never throw out a letter," kept hundreds of letters from his many lovers. The letters from Rita Moreno are especially powerful. All are in the Brando Estate Archives. The teen-age "advice" on "how to treat women" is recounted in Bob Hoskins, Notes for MB autobiography, Brando Estate Archives.

24 Lindsey Interviews.

25 *The Actor's Duty* was entered as a possible title in "Marlon Brando: Notes for Book," June 22, 1992, p. 26, Brando Estate Archives.

26 Avra Douglas was the assistant accompanying Brando on this trip to New York at the time of the September 11, 2001, World Trade Center catastro-phe. Ellen Adler and Tom Oppenheim recounted time spent with Brando during this visit. Avra Douglas, Ellen Adler, and Tom Oppenheim, inter-views with the author.

27 Brando describes this Manhattan encounter in the early 1990s in Lindsey Interviews.

28 These recitations can be found on the website Tobiasent.com, under "The Brando Project."

PERMISSIONS

INDEX

Page numbers in italics refer to illustrations.

Academy Awards, 125, 131, 137, 143, 173, 285, 303, 324
  Brando's turning down of, 250–51, 303, 322
  Brando's winning of, 18, 403n
  Kazan honored by, 106
  On the Waterfront and, 18, 82, 106–7, 403n
accents, xxv, xxvi, 10, 29–30, 35, 53, 66, 70, 92, 100, 120, 136, 205, 260
  British, xxv, 10, 30, 120, 161, 162, 171, 214, 264, 284, 370n
  French, 232, 286
  German, xxv, 136
  Irish, xxv, 220, 258, 260, 406n
  Japanese (and Okinawan), 128
  Mexican, 92
  Southern, xx, 30, 205
  Texas, 193, 220
  Yiddish, 66, 286
Actor Prepares, An (Stanislavski), xxviii–xxix
actors, acting, xxv–xxxi, 37–41, 150, 377n, 378n
  behaving vs., xxviii
  Brando's alleged decline as, 139, 153
  Brando's attitude toward, xxiii–xxiv, xxix–xxx, 66, 249, 251
  Brando's contributions to, xxxviii, 68, 69, 70
  Brando's discovery of talent for, 29–30, 376n
  Brando Sr.'s contempt for, 18, 157
  Brando's standing among, xxiv, 117, 121, 123, 131, 136–37, 370n, 391n, 406n
  Brando's study of, xxvii, xxix, 31, 32, 37–40, 44–51, 47, 71, 123
  Brando's teaching of, xxix, 80, 232, 371n, 384n, 403n, 405n–6n
  Brando's use of objects in, xxvi–xxviii, 110–12, 135–36, 150, 188–89, 196, 202, 206–7, 208, 242–44, 247–48
  in family background, 9–11, *10*, 13, 374n
  as human survival skill, 232–33, 251

actors, acting (*continued*)
  improvisation in, xxvi–xxvii, 81,
    110, 245, 356, 389n, 423n
  instinctive, xxiii, 71, 196, 255, 405n
  Jacob Adler and, 37–41, 45, 49,
    377n, 378n
  method, 80, 255, 405n
  in *Reflections in a Golden Eye*,
    209, 210
  self brought to, 39, 40
  as slave to image, xv
  space dominated by, 261
  Stella Adler's contribution to,
    44–45
  unpredictable, 257
actor's mask, the, xxix
Actor's Mask (Klee), xxix
Actors Studio, 32, 80
Adams, Hank, 319–20, 322, 329
Adams, Marjory, 385n
addiction, 253
  see also alcohol, alcoholism
Adler, Celia, 58, 64, 65
Adler, Ellen, 41, 369n, 373n, 374n,
    379n, 380n, 407n
  Brando's correspondence with,
    119–20
  Brando's dating of, 33, 38, 40, 49,
    376n
  in Paris, 85
Adler, Jacob P., 37–41, 45, 56, 57–58,
    377n
  Brando compared with, 38–40,
    49, 378n
  makeup and, 38, 54, 381n
  marriages of, 37, 49, 380n
Adler, Luther, 58, 64
Adler, Mortimer, 192
Adler, Sara, 37, 48–49, 380n

Adler, Stella, xxiii, 33, 42–46, 80, 82,
    201, 377n
  Brando's study with, xxvii, xxix,
    xxx, 32, 37–40, 44–51, 71, 123
  The Group and, 42–44, 379n
  home gatherings of, 48–49
  Mead at dinner party with, xxiii,
    369n
affective memory exercises, 44, 51
Africa, 338
age, aging, 157
  of Brando, xxxii, xxxv, 29, 253,
    284, 302
  of "Don Corleone," 244–45
  guessing of, xv
aggression, 73, 100, 110, 233, 234
  in *Streetcar*, 74, 76, 78
alcohol, alcoholism, 205, 214, 237
  in family background, 2, 3, 5, 11,
    12, 15, 16, 17, 21–24, 30, 33, 120,
    205, 237, 253
  in *Streetcar*, 74, 78
Alexander, Shana, 249, 402n
Alexian Brothers, 325
Algeria, 227–29, 339
Allegheny River Project, 321
Allegret, Catherine, 229
Allen, Woody, 287
Allport, Gordon, 338
Alpert, Hollis, 125
ambition, 74, 240, 248
  of Brando, xxxii, 105, 123, 142,
    143, 168, 180, 218
Ambler, Eric, 161
"Ambulances" (Larkin), 293
America Challenged (Douglas),
    192–93
American Civil Liberties Union
    (ACLU), 333

American Indian Movement (AIM), 295, 322, 323–24, 325

American Indian Policy in the Formative Years (Prucha), 192, 329, 398n

American Indians, 5, 64, 293, 294, 316–30, 333
Brando's activism and, 250–51, 276, 295, 316–30, 333, 405n
Brando's prospective film about, 142, 217–18, 316, 326–29
Brando's reading about, xxii, xxxvi, 62, 85, 142, 192, 271, 317–19, 328–29, 398n–99n
in Grand Island, 2
in Mexico, 90, 91, 316, 317
treaty violations and, xviii
in West, 142, 143, 144

American Laboratory Theatre (The Lab), 41–42

American League for a Free Palestine, 59, 66

American Nazi Party, 72, 266

American Revolution, 60–61

Anderson, Maxwell, 51–52

anger (rage), 242
of Brando, 21, 22, 45, 51, 105, 284, 295
in films, 74, 76, 100, 113, 209, 210, 226

Anglo-Americans, in West, 142, 143, 150

Anhalt, Edward, 132

animals, xxxvii, 16, 45, 155, 314
Brando's books about, xxxvi
Brando's companionship with, 23
Reflections in a Golden Eye and, 201, 202, 206, 209, 210

see also cats, dogs; horses, horsemen; pets

animation, animated film, xxiv, 308–9

Anthology of Islamic Literature, xxxiv

anthropology, 169, 271, 402n, 408n

anti-Americanism, 182

anti-Communism, 89, 104–6, 182, 387n

Antigone, 26

antihero, moral and political power of, 154

antimiscegenation laws, 338

anti-Semitism, 294
Brando accused of, xxxii, 62, 382n
Holocaust and, 59–61, 63, 65–66, 117, 138, 191–92, 266, 382n

antiwar movement, 323–24

Apaches, 318

apartheid, 284

Apocalypse Now (film), xvi, xxvi, 28, 102, 163, 236, 256, 266–75, 269, 393n, 407n–8n
career materials related to, 268, 369n–70n
reviews of, 275

Apocalypse Now Redux (film), 272, 275

Appaloosa, The (film), xxv

aquaculture, 346

Archaeology of Teti'aroa Atoll and Society Islands, 344

Arcola Picture Corp., 393n

Arendt, Hannah, xvi, xxxviii, 47, 66, 73, 168, 273–74, 368n, 409n

Aristotle, 46, 316, 379n

Arizona, 156

art, xxix, 36, 208, 377n
Art of Loving, The (Fromm), 114
Ashley Book of Knots, 221
Asians:
    in West, 142, 144
    women, 129–31
Asinof, Martin, 155–56, 376n, 381n, 387n
assassins, xxv, 102, 257–62
Associated Press, 173
atom bombs, 299
audience, 47, 72, 73
    emotional participation of, xxix–xxx
    fantasy and, 261–62
    film, 69, 82, 83, 94, 99, 103, 106, 116, 123, 132, 138, 140, 149, 165, 171, 183, 197, 202, 209, 216, 224, 246, 248, 256, 261–62, 272, 383n
    Omaha, 10
    theater, 10, 39, 42, 45, 52, 58–59, 65–66, 74, 377n
    TV, 250–51
    twenty-first-century, xxxviii
Australia, 301, 311, 340
Authentic Death of Hendry Jones, The (Neider), 143–44, 146
Authentic Life of Billy the Kid, The (Garrett), 142
autogenic training, 379n
Autumn of the Patriarch (García Márquez), 303
Avedon, Richard, 19
Avery, Sid, 20

Bach, Johann Sebastian, xxii, 216, 301
Baird, Bil, 11

Baldwin, James, 35, 191, 266, 330, 331–32, 334, 337, 376n, 377n, 407n, 422n, 423n
Baldwin, Jay, 345
Bali, 119, 182, 313
Balk, Fairuza, 300
Balzac, Honoré de, 239
Bangkok, 312
Bankhead, Tallulah, 53
Banks, Dennis, 322, 324–25
Banner, Jill, 330
Barbieri, Gato, 369n
Barker, Margaret, 42
Basie, Count, 22
Battle of Algiers, The (film), 210, 211
Battle of Angels (play), 159
Beacham, Stephanie, 220
Beatles, xviii, 368n
Beaton, Cecil, 19
Beatty, Warren, 197
beauty, 155, 171, 200, 265
Beauvoir, Simone de, 114
Beck, Jack, 329
Bedtime Story (film), 28, 126, 127, 181, 286, 287, 334
Beecher, Henry Ward, 73
Beechly, June Gahan, 2–4, 3, 17, 31, 373n, 410n
bees, xxxi
Belafonte, Harry, 191, 331
Beloved (Morrison), 337
Benedict, Ruth, 133
Bergman, Andrew, 287
Bergson, Peter, 59
Bergson Group, 59, 60
Bernstein, Leonard, 48, 116–17, 369n
Bertolucci, Bernardo, 224, 330, 401n
betrayal, 106, 110, 199

Beyond Biofeedback (Green and
    Green), 374*n*
Bible, 270–71, 409*n*
Big Bug Man, The (animated film),
    xxiv, 308–9
Bihar, India, 340, 342
Bill of Rghts, 193
Billy the Kid, 142, 144
biofeedback, 5, 374*n*, 379*n*
birds, bird-watching, xxv, 159–60,
    259–60, 406*n*
Birmingham VA Hospital, 85–86, 87
bisexuality, 205
blacklisting, 105, 106, 190, 387*n*,
    398*n*
Black Panthers, 175, 211, 293, 334,
    335–36, 338
blacks, 137, 193, 240, 328, 330–39
    breaking servility image of, 208
    in *Burn!*, 211–13, 215–16, 400*n*
    Chase and, 193, 195, 197, 198
    civil rights of, 5, 96, 101, 154, 181,
        193, 198, 322, 330, 331, 333, 337
    in *Reflections in a Golden Eye*,
        208, 209
    Watts riots and, 199–200
Black Skin, White Masks (Fanon),
    338
Blake, William, 223
Blame Me on History (Modisane), 338
Bligh, William, 345
Boas, Franz, 266
Bobino (Kauffmann), 45
body, body parts, 19
    commodity status of, xiv–xv
    mind's influence on, 5, 374*n*
    see also eyes; face, facial muscles
body language:
    Brando's reading of, xiii, xv

    see also gestures
bohemianism, 157, 230
    of Brando, xvii, xxix, 237, 238
    in family background, 4, 11, 13,
        48, 237
Boleslavsky, Richard, 42
Bolivia, 176
Bonnie and Clyde (film), 197
Book Bin, 191, 398*n*
books, book collection, reading, xv–
    xvi, xx, xxii–xxiii, xxiv, xxx,
    xxxiii–xxxvi, 5, 13, 23–25, 33,
    35, 45–46, 48, 49–50, 50, 62,
    70, 71, 84–85, 86, 90–92, 96–97,
    117–18, 120, 126, 127, 139, 142,
    149, 161, 164–69, 174, 191, 192–
    93, 217, 223, 253, 256, 259–60,
    265, 268–71, 277, 279, 281, 314,
    317–19, 319, 325–29, 337–38,
    350–51, 356, 367*n*, 369*n*, 371*n*,
    372*n*, 373*n*, 376*n*, 379*n*, 382*n*,
    388*n*–89*n*, 395*n*, 396*n*, 397*n*,
    402*n*, 405*n*, 406*n*, 407*n*, 408*n*,
    409*n*, 410*n*, 415*n*, 416*n*
    annotating of, xxii, xxx, xxxiv–
        xxxvi, xxxviii, 5, 23–24, 73, 97,
        114, 116, 128, 132–33, 163, 166,
        169, 223, 268–71, 326, 369*n*,
        379*n*, 388*n*, 390*n*, 391*n*, 395*n*,
        397*n*, 406*n*, 407*n*, 408*n*, 410*n*,
        423*n*, 426*n*
    arranging of, xxx
    on Asia, 127–28, 133
    on birds, 259–60, 406*n*
    on diet, 253
    evil as subject in, 73, 166, 268–69,
        279
    on homebuilding and home
        repair, 410*n*

books (*continued*)
  on Indians, xxii, xxxvi, 62, 142,
    192, 261, 317–19, 328–29, 391n,
    398n–99n
  Jewish subjects in, 62, 382n
  poetry, xxxvi, 23–24, 270–72,
    275, 293, 407n, 408n–9n
  on politics, xxxvi
  on Polynesia, 165–66
  on psychology, xxxvi, 85, 117,
    369n, 371n
  religion, spirituality, and myth
    in, 270–71, 408n–9n
  Shakespeare in, 96, 97
  on Vietnam, 268, 406n, 407n
Boston Globe, 88, 385n
Bothers Karamazov, The (Dostoevsky), 26, 375n
Bounty Trilogy, The, 165
Bourke-White, Margaret, 19
boxing, boxers, 80, 84, 107, 384n
  see also *On the Waterfront* (film),
    "Terry Malloy" in
boycotts, 105, 181
Brain Revolution, The (Ferguson),
  369n
Brand, Stewart, 345–46
Brando, Cheyenne, 237, 291, 301,
  322, 347
  car accident of 292
  mental health of, 292
  suicide of, 293, 299
Brando, Christian, 21, 158, 174,
  175–76, 181, 289, 396n
  Brando's attention to, 237, 238,
    256, 265, 409n
  murder charges, trial, and
    imprisonment of, 256, 265,
    291–93, 292, 294, 301, 304

Brando, Dorothy Pennebaker
  (Dodie), 1–7, 9–13, 17, 20–27,
    29–34, 48, 118, 141, 191, 410n
  alcoholism of, 5, 12, 15, 16, 17,
    20–24, 30, 33, 120
  Brando's correspondence with,
    26, 27, 66, 375n
  Brando's relationship with, 12,
    26, 33, 105, 156–57
  death of, 21, 120, 156–57
  "Kowalski" portrayal criticized
    by, 73–74, 384n
  music and, 34, 376n
  in New York, 32–33
  One-Eyed Jacks and, 155
  political idealism of, 5–6, 16, 316,
    330
  as reader, 2, 5, 16, 23
  separations and reconciliations
    of, 16–17, 22, 32–33
  theater work of, 9–11, 10, 13,
    29–30, 155, 374n
Brando, Eugene, 1, 2, 17
Brando, Frances, *see* Loving, Frances Brando
Brando, Jocelyn, xx, 1–9, 22, 155,
  373n, 376n
  acting of, 24, 30–31, 105, 106n,
    190–91, 387n, 398n
  blacklisting and, 105, 106, 190,
    387n, 398n
  Brando's correspondence with,
    26
  childhood of, 6–10, 8, 13–17
  competitiveness of, 31,
    376n
  "Essences" and, 9
  ultimatum of, xxxiv
Brando, Marie Holloway, 1–2

Brando, Marlon:
actor's mask of, xxix
as actor type, xxix
adolescence of, 21–29, 34
aging of, xxxii, xxxv, 253, 284,
    292, 302
ambition of, xxxii, 105, 123, 142,
    143, 168, 180, 218
Americanness of, 1, 29, 33
anger and rage of, 21, 22, 45, 51,
    66, 105, 284, 295, 333
antics and pranks of, 28, 85
anxiety of, 33, 125, 157
arrests of, 295, 320
athleticism of, 1, 7, 18, 22, 34, 202,
    375n
authority and convention
    resisted by, xxix, 17, 23, 25,
    28–29, 46, 102–3, 105
autobiography of, see Songs My
    Mother Taught Me
awards and prizes of, 18, 51, 99,
    115, 118, 153, 233, 250–51, 255–
    56, 266, 322, 383n
in Bangkok, 312
birth of, xxix, 1
boycotts of films of, 334
branding of, xix, 368n
as camera-ready, 18–20, 19
career materials preserved by,
    xxiii, xxx, 174, 369n–70n
cats and, xxxvi, 8, 23, 242, 244,
    244, 290–91, 290, 343, 378n, 412n
causes supported by, xviii,
    xxxii, 63–64, 66–67, 83, 167,
    174–75, 250–51, 265, 276, 316–
    17, 320–26, 330–31, 333–48,
    382n, 398n
celebrity, fame, and success of,
    xv–xviii, xxxi, xxxiii, xxxviii–
    xxxix, 49, 67, 82–83, 152, 158,
    175, 180, 205, 230, 237, 254, 255,
    310, 316, 400n
chaotic personal life of, xxx, 158,
    181, 292, 301, 321
chess, passion for, 9, 20, 20, 98,
    123, 175, 213, 285, 372n
childhood of, 7–19, 8, 14, 17, 19,
    21–22, 31, 44, 53, 105, 237
civil rights involvement of, 322,
    330–39, 332
clichés and myths about, xv–xvi,
    xxxii, 367n–68n
comic work of, 126–27, 128, 286–
    88, 304–6
competitiveness of, 378n
complexity of, xxx, 368n
concentration, powers of, xxxi,
    79, 351
confidence of, xxii–xxiii, 48
contempt toward Hollywood of,
    298, 310
contract issues and, 84, 120, 125,
    161, 181, 249, 264, 393n
contradictory traits of, 24
courage of, 209
as cowboy, 19, 19
curiosity of, xxxi, 25, 169, 315,
    318, 403n
death of, xvii, xx, xxiv, xxxii,
    xxxiii, 36–37, 180, 197, 217, 344,
    367n–68n
dedication to acting of, 283–84
depression of, 293, 295
dinner parties of, xxiii, 9, 369n,
    374n
directing of, 20, 141–58, 167, 180,
    326–27, 384n

Brando, Marlon (*continued*)
  dogs of, xx, xxxvi, 8–9, 24, 32,
    120, 244, 261, 343, 354, 358,
    370*n*, 378*n*
  double-talk perfected by, 286–87
  as drummer, xx, *xxi*, 22, 30, 34,
    114
  dyslexia of, 13, 25
  early romantic interests and dat-
    ing of, 14–15, 24–25
  earnings of, xiii–xiv, 20–21, 83,
    118, 141, 153, 158, 181, 205, 256,
    261, 264, 265, 276, 294
  eating habits and dieting of, 128,
    253, 261, 267, 321, 405*n*
  eccentricity of, xvi, 24, 29, 34, 49
  education of, xxii, xxxii, xxxix,
    13–16, *14*, 23, 25–32, 90, 96, 207,
    263, 374*n*, 375*n*; *see also* actors,
    acting, Brando's study of
  energy and vigor of, xvi, 1, 50, 86,
    202, 218, 256, 401*n*
  expulsion from military school
    of, 28–29, 30
  eyes of, xxix, 33, 121, 160, 370*n*
  family background of, 1–7, 50,
    237, 373*n*
  Far East tour of, 311–12
  as father, 21, 174, 176–77, 181,
    237–38, 256, 265, 289, 292, 297,
    396*n*, 401*n*
  FBI file of, 323, 324, 334
  film role preparations of, xxiii,
    85–86, *86*, *87*, 90–92, 118, 120,
    182–84, 192–93, 255, 256, 268–
    71, 407*n*, 408*n*
  financial carelessness of, 67, 84,
    158, 181
  freedom of, xv, 83, 126, 196, 265

genius of, xiii, 21, 34, 45, 70, 81,
    217, 376*n*
  gift giving of, 46, 369*n*, 407*n*
  gifts received by, xxxiv–xxxv
  as grandfather, xxxi
  greatness of, xv, 58, 137
  guilt of, 66, 292
  health issues of, 29, 253, 296–97,
    400*n*, 405*n*
  hiking of, 15–16
  historical afterlife, iconic longev-
    ity, and wide-ranging appeal
    of, xv, xvi–xvii, xxiv, 101–2, 219,
    234, 236, 255–56, 287–90
  honesty of, xxxviii–xxxix,
    44–45, 138
  humanitarianism of, 16, 67, 68,
    322, 339–48
  humor of, xxxiv, xxxvii–xxxviii,
    8, 15, 33, 41, 48, 53, 71, 72, 81, 85,
    97, 126–27, 147, 155, 187, 188, 221,
    261, 276, 286–88, 296, 304–6,
    331, 411*n*
  idealism of, 103, 117–19, 158, 179,
    180, 214, 264, 265, 275, 391*n*
  image of, xv, xviii, xxii, 174, 253
  imagination and creativity of, 44,
    70, 78–79, 95, 160, 217, 276
  imitative skills of, xxv, 24–25,
    29–30, 45, 124, 287, 380*n*
  improvisation and, xxvi–xxvii,
    81, 110, 187, 245, 356, 389*n*
  independent thinking of, xvi, 66,
    331
  individuality, nonconformity and
    subversive streak of, xxxiv, 1, 28,
    29, 82, 84, 105, 125, 320
  instincts of, xxiii, 71, 196, 255,
    405*n*

intellect, hunger for knowledge, and "life of the mind" of, xv–xvi, xxii, xxxv, xxxviii, 15, 50, 103, 164, 256, 310, 327

interviews of, xviii, xxiii, xxxviii, 99, 286, 336, 339–40, 346

language skills and interests of, xv, xxxiv, xxxv, xxxvi–xxxvii, 15, 25, 26–27, 36, 49, 71, 96–99, 117, 127, 128, 129, 149, 165, 182, 243, 282–83, 296, 314, 318, 319, 326, 331, 348, 350–51, 371n–72n, 380n, 386n, 396n, 413n

legal wrangling and libel suit of, xxx, 158, 174, 265, 336, 396n

Liberty Canyon acreage donated by, 322, 323

lists as passion of, 26, 149, 391n

loneliness of, xx, 23, 44, 53

loyalty and, 32, 38, 62, 180, 238, 299

lying and fabrications of, xix, 24, 46, 82, 230–32

makeup of, xxv, 54–56, 54, 55, 121, 123, 126, 128, 235, 334, 356, 381n

marginalia by, xxii, xxx, xxxiv–xxxvi, 97, 163, 166, 169, 184, 317–19, 319, 326–29, 337, 338, 369n, 379n, 397n, 400n, 416n, 419n, 421n, 422n, 423n, 424n

marriages and divorces of, xxx, 92, 131, 158

masks, interest in and uses of, xxix, 216, 225, 307, 356, 359, 362, 427n

materialism of, xxxii, 177, 264, 378n

memory of, 26, 96, 386n

as Midwesterner, xxxix, 1–31, 237

modesty of, xxxii, 128

motivations of, xxx, xxxviii, 179, 232, 265

as observant, xiii, xv, xx, xxxvii, 25, 33, 39, 45, 70–71, 80, 121, 255, 287

on-location filming of, 314

parody interviews of, xix, 249–50

passions of, xx–xxiv, xxi, 217

phone tapping of, 324

physical appeal of, xv, xvi, xxxii, 23, 33, 368n

physique of, 75, 108, 121

political views and activities of, xvii, xxxii, 89–90, 105, 106, 118, 139, 180–83, 191–92, 215, 250–51, 256, 293, 295, 304, 310, 320–22, 324, 325, 329, 333, 398n; see also political films

poor spelling of, 15, 15, 26, 398n

privacy and secrecy of, xxxii–xxxiii, 82, 175–76, 224, 238, 291

psychiatry and therapy of, xxxiv, 105, 253, 296

and realism about racism, 338–39

scripts written and rewritten by, xxiii, xxxvi–xxxvii, 79, 83, 109–10, 129–30, 132, 136, 147–49, 148, 151, 161–65, 183–88, 189, 195, 198, 201, 215, 221, 267–68, 283, 298, 390n, 394n, 398n, 399n, 407n

seductiveness of, 15, 124, 169

self-reflection of, 256

sense of fairness in, 315–16

sensitivity and empathy of, 16, 21, 23, 29, 36, 39, 53, 66, 86, 92, 121, 201–2, 209, 315, 318, 378n

Brando, Marlon (*continued*)
  sexism experienced by, xv–xvi,
    368*n*
  sexuality, promiscuity, and
    womanizing of, xvi, xxix, xxx,
    xxxiii, xxxv, 12–13, 32, 62, 70,
    75, 92, 125, 169, 219, 237, 238,
    253, 256, 378*n*
  sidekicks of, 299–300
  singing of, 124–26
  skepticism of, xxii, 267, 269–70,
    317–18
  smiles discussed by, xiii–xv, 177,
    327, 362
  social conscience of, 58, 63–64,
    66, 85, 140, 315, 316, 331–32
  as social outcast, 331–32
  and suffering, xxxvii, 16, 35, 38,
    62, 157, 197, 251, 281, 310, 315,
    322, 336, 340
  talent of, 29–30, 123, 154–55, 157,
    180, 181, 185, 215, 255, 376*n*
  technique of, xxvi–xxix, 70–75,
    123–24, 298
  theater career of, xviii, xix, xxxii,
    20, 24, 28, 30, 31, 45, 49, 51–81,
    230, 310, 380*n*, 384*n*
  touch of, 5, 373*n*
  as traveler, 311–16, 330, 340
  types of roles played by, xiv,
    xvi–xvii, xxv–xxvi, 28, 38–39,
    83–84, 117, 139, 234, 253–54,
    256, 265–66, 370*n*
  unhurried and patient image of,
    149–50, 279, 410*n*
  vision of, 131, 146, 156–57,
    218
  voice of, 160, 285, 308
  vulnerability of, 44, 379*n*
    zeal for order and habits of, xxii,
      xxx–xxxi, 371*n*
    see also specific films and plays
Brando, Marlon, Sr., 1–2, 6–7, 10–13,
    18, 23–26, 30, 31, 291, *291*, 373*n*,
    384*n*
  Brando's correspondence with,
    26, 27, 66, 141, 375*n*, 398*n*
  Brando's relationship with,
    17–22, *20*, 26, 105, 141, 154–56,
    221
  death of, 21, 156
  drinking of, 11, 23
  education of, 6, 25, 31
  Pennebaker work of, 20–21, 141,
    154
  photography of, 18–19
  ranch of, 141, 391*n*
  separations and reconciliations
    of, 16–17, 22, 32–33
  violence of, 12, 21, 35, 141, 376*n*
  womanizing of, 12, 16, 23, 24
Brando, Miko, 92, 174, 176–77, 181,
    238, 396*n*
Brando, Myles Jonathan, 373*n*
Brando, Ninna, 297
Brando, Rebecca, 92, 238, 396*n*
Brando, Teihotu, 174, 177, 367*n*, 396*n*
Brando, Timothy Gahan, 373*n*
"Brando" (Hodenfield), 261
Brando Estate, sale of, *see* Christie's
Braudy, Leo, 388*n*
Brave, The (film), 329
Breen Office, 81
"Bridge of Sighs, The" (Hood), 293
Brink, André, 284
British Academy of Film and Televi-
    sion Arts (BAFTA), 99, 181, 222
British Board of Film Censors, 102

Britt, May, 135, 286–87
Britton, Edgar, 11
Broadway, xix, 20, 51, 103, 126, 158
    Brando's debut on, 45
    Brando's departure from, xxxii, 83
    Brando's fame on, xv, 24, 230
    commercialism and, 83
    see also specific plays
Broderick, Matthew, 289
Brooklyn, courts in, xv, 40
Brooks, Stanley, 380n
Brown, Barbara, 374n
Brown, Dee, 326
Brown, Harrison, 182–83
Brown, Norman O., 169
Brutsman, Joseph, 296, 303, 305–6
Brynner, Yul, 140
Buddhism, 128, 271
Buffalo Soldiers, 328
Bull Boy (script), 283
Burdick, Eugene, 167, 182, 184, 397n
Burn! (film), xxv, 140, 181, 210–17,
    213, 381n, 400n–401n, 408n
Burton, Richard, xix, 140
Byron, George Gordon, Lord, 262

Caan, James, 94, 239, 242
California, 119, 144, 167, 193
California Supreme Court, 175
Cambodia, 272
camera, 160, 163, 196, 261
    On the Waterfront and, 112–13
    Streetcar and, 78, 79, 81
Campbell, Joseph, 271
Camp Grant Massacre, The (novel),
    327
Camus, Albert, 113–14, 229–30,
    386n, 388n, 402n
Canby, Vincent, 216, 234, 275

Candida (Shaw), xix, 52–53, 368n,
    380n
Candy (film), xxv, 126, 140, 285, 286,
    330
capitalism (free enterprise), 144, 177,
    238–39, 240, 264, 265
capital punishment, 167, 304,
    394n–95n
Capone, Al, 24
Capote, Truman, xviii, xxix, 232,
    403n
Captain Bligh and Mr. Christian
    (Hough), 164
Carey, Norman, 330
Caribbean, 211–13
Carnovsky, Morris, 42, 104
Carroll, Diahann, 333
Cartagena, 212–13, 213, 400n
Castaneda, Movita, 92, 174, 181, 314,
    338
caste, 166, 192, 340, 342
cats, xxxvi, 8, 23, 41, 81, 242, 244,
    244, 290–91, 290, 343, 378n,
    412n
Catholic Church, Catholicism, 90,
    238, 325
    censorship and, 81–82
    in On the Waterfront, 107, 116
Cat on a Hot Tin Roof (Williams),
    283
Cavett, Dick, 252
celebrities and fame, xiii–xx, xxxi–
    xxxiii, 26, 125, 152, 173, 230,
    254, 297, 308
    Brando's views of, xiii–xx, xxxi–
    xxxiii, 82, 83, 84, 230, 254, 297,
    310, 314–16, 345, 403n
    see also Brando, Marlon, celeb-
    rity, fame, and success of

Cell 2455, Death Row (Chessman),
    167
censorship, 81–82, 102, 384*n*
    self-, 208
Central High School, 6
Champlin, Charles, 275
Chaplin, Charlie, xxvi, 126, 140
characterization, 147, 163, 188, 256,
    398*n*
    in *Apocalypse Now*, 259, 407*n*
    Brando's technique of, xxvi–
    xxviii, 70–75, 79, 92–93, 123,
    209, 215
    in *Godfather*, 236
    in *Last Tango in Paris*, 231–33
    in *Missouri Breaks*, 257, 406*n*
charisma and magnetism, 72–75,
    121, 154, 185, 220, 256
Chase, Borden, 161
Chase, The (film), xxii, xxv, xxxviii,
    127, 140, 181, 191–201, *194*, 289,
    370*n*, 399*n*
    improvisation in, 196, 399*n*
    innovative portrayal of violence
    in, 197–99
    makeup for, 54
    Reflections in a Golden Eye com-
    pared with, 200, 201
    slow-motion beating scene in,
    197–98
Chekhov, Anton, 68–69
chess, 9, 20, *20*, *98*, 123, *175*, *213*, 285,
    372*n*
Chessman, Caryl, 167
Cheyenne Indians, 326
Chicago, Ill., 13, 24
Chicago Art Institute, 36, 377*n*
Chicago Sun-Times, 275
child actors, 246–48, *247*, 404*n*

Childer, James Saxon, 182, 387*n*
children:
    Brando's attention to, 237–38, 256
    in *Godfather*, 238, 239, 240, 244,
    246–48, *247*, 404*n*
    legitimizing of, xxx, 92
    play for, 45
Chinese culture, 177–78
Chivington, John, 326
Christianity, Christians, 39, 85, 103,
    271
    see also specific sects
Christian Science, 5, 17, 33, 191, 237,
    271, 374*n*
Christie's, xxxiii, 96, 368*n*, 396*n*–
    70*n*, 371*n*, 374*n*, 375*n*, 382*n*,
    386*n*, 393*n*
*Christopher Columbus: The Discov-
    ery* (film), 293–95
Chrysanthemum and the Sword, The
    (Benedict), 133
Church, Frank, 320, 323
Church, Sandra, 18
Church, Thomas Haden, 303
Church Committee Reports, 323
CIA, 271, 324
cinema-face, 225, 367*n*, 402*n*
citizenship, 91
civil rights, xviii, 214, 240, 283, 320,
    324, 330–39, *332*, 398*n*
    of blacks, 5, 96, 101, 154, 181, 193,
    198, 322, 330, 331, 333, 337
    of immigrants, 5
Civil Rights Roundtable, 191–92
Clark, Edward, 20
class, xxiv, 90, 135, 192, 219
    Brando's characterization of,
    38–39
    in *Chase*, 193, 195

in *Last Tango in Paris*, 224, 227, 228

in *Mutiny on the Bounty*, 161–62, 171–73

Nightcomers and, 220–22

in *On the Waterfront*, 110, 113, 116

Cleaver, Eldridge, 211, 334, 335

Clift, Montgomery, 68–70, 132, 200, 204–5

Clinton, Bill, 368n

clothes and costumes, 56, 266, 301, 306–7, 326, 356, 358

glasses, 188, 276, 398n

gloves, 39, 110, 135, 309, 387n

in *Godfather*, 243–44, 244

hats, xxvii, 150, 406n–7n

in *Last Tango in Paris*, 225, 229

in *Missouri Breaks*, 258, 260, 406n

Club Saint-Germain, *xxi*

Clurman, Harold, 48

on Brando, 79, 315–16, 371n–72n, 378n

The Group and, 41, 42, 43

Truckline Café and, 51–52, 380n

Cobb, Lee J., 107

Cocteau, Jean, 53

Cold War, 104, 118, 186

Cole, Nat King, 126

Coleridge, Samuel Taylor, 226, 393n

Colon, Miriam, 303

colonialism, 117, 127, 211, 227–28, 327

in Mexico, 90, 91

Columbus, Christopher, 295

Columbus (film), 256

comedy, comedians, 126–27, 128, 286–87, 304–5, 306

Brando's ideas about, 305–6

risk in, 288

Come Out Fighting (TV show), 80, 108

Coming of Age in Samoa (Mead), xxiii

communication, nonverbal, 149, 150

see also gestures; silence; words vs.

Communism, 47, 73, 88–91, 103–6, 114, 182, 183, 189, 192, 387n

community, 116, 161, 166, 199

Community of Fear (Brown and Real), 382–83, 397n

competition, sexual, 199

computers, xxxvi, 238, 372n

concentration camps, 136, 138, 408n

conformity, 102, 192

Congress, U.S., 182

Congress for Racial Equality (CORE), 200, 333, 335

Congressional Record, 320

conquest, of Mexico, 90, 91

Conrad, Joseph, xxii, 266, 271–72

Constitution, U.S., 192

Convis, David R., 405n

Cook, Bruce, 262, 406n

Coolidge, Calvin, 42

Copland, Aaron, 47, 48, 81

Coppola, Francis Ford, 94, 209–10, 297, 330, 386n

Apocalypse Now and, 267–68, 270–72, 275, 407n–8n, 409n

Godfather and, 235, 239, 246, 403n, 404n

Cornell, Katharine, 52, 141

Corridan, John, 108

corruption, 198, 248

Costner, Kevin, 218

Cottman, Herman Stuart, 30

Countess from Hong Kong, A (film), xxvi

courts, xv, 39, 40, 175
Covarrubias, Miguel, 90–91, 317
Cowboy Encyclopedia, 317
Cox, Wally, 15–16, 26, 31, 149
    Brando's correspondence with,
        36, 377n
    death of, 36–37
    in New York, 35–36
Crawdaddy, 262
Crawford, Cheryl, 42
crime, criminals, xv, 24, 168, 197,
    230, 285, 306
    in *One-Eyed Jacks*, 142, 144
    in *On the Waterfront*, 107–13, 116
    organized, *see* mob, Mafia
    war, 268, 274
"Crime on the Waterfront" (John-
    son), 107
Crises of the Republic (Arendt), 273,
    409n
Crist, Judith, 262
cross-cultural understanding, 118,
    128–31
Crowe, Russell, 264
Crowther, Bosley, 153
Cuba, 103, 192, 397n
cultural politics, 219
culture, xxiv, xxxviii, xxxix, 12, 25,
    168
    American, 99, 103, 119, 127, 248,
        267
    Asian, 117–18, 128, 129, 130
    Brando's roles and, xxv, 117
    Chinese, 177–78
    clash of, 163, 193, 216
    diversity and differences of, 116,
        118, 133, 141, 142, 166, 169, 171,
        227
    emotion and, xiii

hierarchy and, 214
Holocaust and, 117
humor and, xxxiv, 126
Jews and, 62, 382n
rituals and, 171, 226–27
standardization of, 119
storytelling and, xxix
Tahitian and Polynesian, 163,
    165, 175
transformations of, 68
Curtis, Michael, 169

Dacascos, Mark, 300
dance, 34, 169, 177, 283
Dances with Wolves (film), 218
Davis, Miles, xxii, 114, 369n
Davis, Ossie, 331
Davis, Sammy, Jr., 333
Dawn, Robert, 406n
Dawson, Tom, 407n
Dean, James, 123–24, 378n
death, 94–95, 160, 173, 198, 223
    in *Apocalypse Now*, 273
    in *Godfather*, 93–95, 244–49, *248*,
        404n
    in *Last Tango in Paris*, 2, 25, 223,
        224, 226–28, 231
    mass, 116
    in *Missouri Breaks*, 257
    in *On the Waterfront*, 107, 110–13,
        116
death penalty, 167, 394n–95n
Death Valley, 37, 142
deception, in *One-Eyed Jacks*, 145,
    154, 157
Dee, Ruby, 331
de Gaulle, Charles, 228
de la Rosa, Nelson, 299, *300*, 301
Deloria, Vine, 320, 322, 326

democracy, 73, 89, 91, 102, 164, 165, 177, 182, 186, 192, 193
Democrats, 321
De Niro, Robert, 209, 306, 307–8
Dennis, Marsha S., 373n
Depp, Johnny, 295–96, 329, 368n, 385n
desert, 136, 142, 143, 145, 155
desire, 223, 226, 248
  in *On the Waterfront*, 108
  in *Streetcar*, 75, 81
Désirée (film), xxv, 28, 120–24, *122*, 126, 389n, 404n
developing countries, Brando's trips to, 181–82
dialogue, 163, 169, 188, 196, 216, 256, 393n
  brevity of, xxxvii, 257
  in *Godfather*, 241–43
  in *One-Eyed Jacks*, 147, 149, 157
Diaz, Porfiro, 91, 93
Dick Cavett Show, The (TV show), 250–51, 253, 322, 346, 352–53, 353, 405n
Dickinson, Angie, 196, 399n, 400n
Dickinson, Emily, xxxi, 23–24, 375n
diet, dieting, 4, 128, 253, 405n
diplomacy, U.S., 181–90, 192
  Brando's film about, 118, 388n
Diplomat (Thayer), 182
disguises, 258, 406n
Dmytryk, Edward, 381n
Doctor in Spite of Himself, The (Moliere), 30
dogfight, staged, 24–25
dogs, xxxvi, xxxvii, 8–9, 23, 32, 94, 95, 120, 212, 261, 343, 358, 370n, 378n
  in *Last Tango in Paris*, 227, 228

dominance, 74, 75, 154, 168
  of actors, 261
  in *Godfather*, 236, 255–56
  in *Last Tango in Paris*, 226–27, 230
  in *Nightcomers*, 220
Donaldson Award, 51
Donat, Robert, 14, 374n
Don Juan DeMarco (film), 256, 291, 296–97
Doran, Marjorie, 343–44, 347
Dostoevsky, Fyodor, 26, 375n
double-talk, 286–87
Douglas, Avra, 283, 396n, 407n
Douglas, Guy, 261
Douglas, William O., 192–93, 321, 399n
dramatic authenticity, 183–84, 198, 215
dramatic theory, Stanislavski, xxviii–xxix, 40, 44, 50
Drinnon, Richard, 167
Driscoll, William L., 161
Drollet, Dag, 291, 293, 301
drugs, 204–5, 240, 245
drums, drumming, xx, *xxi*, 22, 30, 34, 114, 123, 331
Dry White Season, A (Brink), 284
Dry White Season, A (film), xxv, 55–56, 256, 265, 276, 284–86, 337, 398n
  rebellion in, 102
Dudar, Helen, 367n
Dunaway, Faye, 197, 297
Dunham, Katherine, 34–35, 331
Duvall, Robert, xxviii, 196, 241, 270

Eagle Has Two Heads, The (Cocteau), 53
Eastern religion and philosophy, 50

Eastwood, Clint, 153

Ebert, Roger, 210, 234, 275, 276, 307, 400n

Ebony, 193

eccentricity and strangeness:
    of Brando, xvi, 24, 29, 34, 49
    in family background, 2, 6

École Normale, 345

Eddy, Mary Baker, 5

Edelstein (Jewish boarder), 4

Ed Sullivan Show, The, 30

education, 61, 73
    of Brando's children, 237–38
    see also actors, acting, Brando's study of; Brando, Marlon, education of; *specific schools*

Egypt, 311

Eichmann, Adolf, 168

Eichmann in Jerusalem (Arendt), 168, 273–74

Einstein, Albert, 63, 250

election of 2008, xxiv

Eliot, T. S., 270–71, 275, 408n–9n

Elkies, Cathy, 371n

Ellington, Duke, 22

Ellis, Christopher, 220

Emergency Food Assistance to India (1967), 342

Emmy Award, 266, 383n

emotion, xiii, 234
    concealment of, xiii
    evoking of, xxviii–xxix, 43–45
    The Men and, 86–87
    in *Streetcar*, 76, 78, 79
    in *Wild One*, 102

empathy and sympathy, xxxvii, 39, 74, 398n
    of audience, 116, 136, 183, 266, 350
    humor and, 126

England, 99, 220, 311

Englund, George, 185, 189, 311, 313, 376n, 388n

Engstead, John, 20

environment, 165
    Brando's commitment to, xxxvi, 165, 310, 321, 339–47, 359
    of character, xxviii, 44, 70, 201

epic mode, 139–79, 425n
    see also Fugitive Kind, The; *Mutiny on the Bounty*; *One-Eyed Jacks*

Erdrich, Louise, 325–26

Ermi (governess), 12–13

Eskimos, 345

"Essences" (form of charades), 9

ethnicity, 68
    Brando's romances and, 13
    diversity of, 143
    see also specific groups

Euripides, 46

Evans, Robert, 403n

Evanston, Ill., 11–23, *12*, 29, 48, 374n–75n

Evers, Medgar, 333

extras, 86, 161, 213

eyes, 108, 129–30, 142, 169
    of Brando, xxix, 33, 121, 160, 370n
    of Celia Adler, 64
    of Napoleon, 120, 121
    as storyteller, 79
    in *Viva Zapata!*, 93

face, facial muscles, xiii, xxvi, 68, 70, 79, 225, 367n
    of Brando, xvi, 18, 19, 71, 160, 216
    in film, 79
    as stage, 79
    see also eyes

Fall, The (Camus), 229–30, 402*n*
fame, *see* celebrities and fame
family:
    Brando's valuing of, 237–38
    Godfather and, xxiv, 237–39, 248,
        256
    Last Tango in Paris and, 226
    see also fathers; father-son
        relationships
Fanon, Frantz, 338
fans, xviii, xxxii
    letters from, 88, 131, 137–38, 262,
        385*n*
Fan-Tan (Brando and Cammell),
    276, 283
fantasy, 124–25, 155, 225, 226, 240,
    261–62, 296,
Far East, Brando's tour of, 311–12
Faribault, Minn., 304
Farmer, James, 335
fascism, 46, 47, 73, 90, 91, 116, 128,
    131–38, 240, 390*n*, 422*n*
    in Latin America, 90, 91
    see also Germany, Nazi
fathers, 124
    Brando's roles as, 246, 263–65,
        301, 404*n*
father-son relationships, 141
    in *Nightcomers*, 221–22
    in *One-Eyed Jacks*, 144–47, 150–
        51, 154–58
Faulkner, William, 85
FBI, 24, 295, 325
    Brando file of, 323–25, 334, 418*n*,
    counterintelligence campaign of,
        323–24
    in *Free Money*, 304, 305, 306
Federalist Papers, The (Hamilton,
    Jay, and Madison), 192

*Federal Power Commission v. Tusca-
    rora Indian Nation*, 321
Fellini, Frederico, 184
femininity, 206–7, 378*n*
feminism, 226, 240, 402*n*
Ferguson, Jeff, 15
Ferguson, Marilyn, 369*n*
Ferlinghetti, Lawrence, 167
Fey, Harold E., 398*n*–99*n*
Field Elementary School, 13
Fields, W. C., 126
film:
    Brando as himself on, 224, 230–
        32, 234, 402*n*
    Brando's contribution to, xxii–
        xxiv, xxv–xxxi, xxxvi–xxxix
    Brando's cynicism toward, 276
    Brando's notes on, xxxviii–xxxix
    Brando's sabbatical from, 276–83
    in Evanston, 14
    fabricating power of, 225
    of Muni, 57
    reviews of, *see* reviews, film
    scores for, xxii, 369*n*
    see also specific films
film editing, 147, 153–54, 196, 382*n*
film industry:
    Brando's exploitation of, xxxii,
        264
    mindlessness and, 73
    "power of Jews" in, 62
Fine, Debbie, 408*n*
Fiore, Carlo, 392*n*
Fire Next Time, The (Baldwin), 35,
    266, 331–32, 377*n*, 407*n*
First Amendment, 175–76, 182
fish, fishing, 160, 171, 251
    entitlements, 320
    "fish-ins," 320–21, *320*

Fitz, Foster, 30
Flag Is Born, A (Hecht), xix, 57–66, 61, 65, 83, 310, 368n, 382n
Fonda, Henry, 10, 92
Fonda, Jane, 140, 195, 196, 197
Foote, Horton, 201
Ford, Glenn, 54, 127
foreign languages, 96, 165, 182, 186
  see also specific languages
foreign policy, U.S., 181–91
Foreman, Carl, 84
Foreman, John, 329
Forman, Milos, 287
Formula, The (film), xxv, 276, 398n
Forrest, Frederic, 406n
Forster, Robert, 205
Four on a Heath (Fitz), 30
Fox, James, 195, 196
Fraenkel, Heinrich, 168
France, 85, 114, 176, 227–28, 311
  see also Paris
Franco, Francisco, 211
Frankenheimer, John, 298
Fraser, Brendan, 308–9
Frazer, James, 270–71, 275
freedom, 116, 155, 164, 165, 193, 251, 262
  acting and, 70, 81, 257
  of Brando, xv, 17, 83, 126, 196, 265
  Burn! and, 212, 215–16
  of Mexico, 91
  in Paris, 114
  of press, 182
  of speech, 174–76, 396n
Freedom Walkers, 333
Free Money (film), 126, 202, 256, 286, 296, 297, 298, 303–6, 381n
French language, xxxvi, 165, 237, 388n
Frenke, Gene, 396n–97n

Freshman, The (film), 54, 256, 284, 286, 287–91, 292, 296, 381n
Freud, Sigmund, 63, 85, 168, 250
Freudian theory, 40
Friedhofer, Hugo, 140, 143, 369n
Friedkin, William, 330
Fromm, Erich, 114
Fuchs, Leo, 20
Fugitive Kind, The (film), xviii, xxv, 140, 158–60
Fulbright, William, 182, 397n
Fuller, Buckminster, 345
Future: Tense (documentary), 345

Gable, Clark, 161, 162, 385n
Gabler, Neal, 62
Gahan, Bess, *see* Myers, Elizabeth Gahan (Bess)
Gahan, Julia Watts, 2–4
Gahan, June, *see* Beechly, June Gahan
Gahan, Myles (great-grandfather), 316
Gahan, Myles Joseph, Jr., 2
Gahan, Myles Joseph, Sr., 2–4
Gahan, Uncle Jay, 2
Gahan, Vine, 2, 17
gait, xxvi, 70, 108, 214
Gambon, Michael, 284
games, 9, 29, 50, 248, 315
  chess, 9, 20, 20, 98, 123, 175, 213, 285, 372n
Gannett Center for Media Studies, 174
Garbo, Greta, xvi
García Márquez, Gabriel, 303
gardens, gardening, xxxvi, xxxvii, 19, 129, 220–21, 223, 275, 276, 279, 297

in *Godfather*, 94, 244, 246–48, 247, 249
Garrett, Pat, 142
Gatti, Marcello, 210
Genet, Jean, 114, 388n
genetic engineering, 256
genocide, 64, 192, 295, 334
  see also Holocaust
German language, xxxvi, 262
Germany, 176
Germany, Nazi, 59, 63, 128, 191–92, 382n
  in *Young Lions*, 132–38
gestures, xxvi, 68, 70, 80, 92, 111, 128, 150, 196, 214
  in *Godfather*, 93, 236, 242, 244, 245–46
  in *Last Tango in Paris*, 225, 233
  in *Streetcar*, 72, 76, 79, 80
  in *Ugly American*, 188, 190
  in *Viva Zapata!*, 92, 93
Giancana, Sam, 24
Gielgud, John, 99, 276
Gill, Brendan, 190
Gilliatt, Penelope, 406n
Gilman, Sam, 20, 146
Girotti, Massimo, 224
Glasser, William, 410n
Godfather, The (film), xxiv, xxv, 93–95, 102, 219, 234–56, 287–88, 301, 322
  afterlife of, 249–54
  awards and, 219, 222, 223, 233, 250–51, 255–56
  as Brando's rejuvenation, 139, 254, 255
  cat in, 242, 244, 244
  "Don Corleone" in, 93–95, 123, 196, 222, 234, 235–50, 244, 247, 253, 255–56, 381n
  family ideal and, xxiv, 237–39, 248, 256
  as novelty in Brando's career, 246
Godfather, The (Puzo), 235, 239
Golden Globe, 115
Goldman, Emma, xxxv
Goldwyn, Samuel, 125
Golffing, Francis, 167
Goodall, Jane, xxxvi, *xxxvii*
Gorney, Roderic, 410n
gossip, gossip columnists, xxxiii, 152–53, 176, 250
Go Tell It on the Mountain (Baldwin), 35, 376n
Gotti, John, 288
Gounaris, Anthony, 246–48, 404n
Graham, Sheilah, 163, 392n
Grand Island, Nebr., 2, 4, 11, 322
Gray, Dorothy, 333
Graziano, Rocky, 80
Great Britain, the British, 66
  in *Burn!*, 211, 212, 214, 215, 216
Great Depression, 7, 41, 92
Great Thoughts, The, 73
Greco, Juliette, 114, 388n
Greece, 340
Green, Alyce, 374n
Green, Elmer, 374n
Green, Nina, 33
Green, Paul, 42–43
Green, Walon, 298
Gresham, Wisc., 325
grief, 2, 23, 112, 120, 156–57, 245
Group Theatre, *see* The Group Theatre
Grusin, Dave, 140, 284–85, 369n
Guam, 182, 192

guerrilla fighters, 211–12, 272, 273,
    408n, 409n
guilt, 66, 165, 206, 215, 230
guns, xxvii–xxviii, 94, 109, 110–11,
    135, 142, 143, 145, 146, 150, 154,
    195, 197, 202, 212, 228, 237, 239,
    245, 249, 260, 261, 266, 305, 324,
    324, 335
Guys and Dolls (film), xviii, 124–26,
    286, 370n

Haiti, 34, 96, 192, 334, 395n
Haley, Alex, 72, 265–66, 337
Hall, Helen, 371n
Hall, James Norman, 165
Halsman, Philippe, 20
Hamilton, Alexander, 192
Hammarskjold, Dag, 270
Hammerstein, Oscar, 49
Hanmer, Don, 26, 33, 375n
happiness, 14, 164, 168, 177, 207
Harlem, xx, 90, 283, 331, 334–35
    Brando in, 334–35
Harrington, G. L., 296
Harris, Richard, 396n
Harvey, Verna, 220
Hastings, Michael, 222, 283
Hawaii, University of, 345
Heart of Darkness (Conrad), 266,
    271–72
Heath, Wally, 346
Hebrew, 262
Hecht, Ben, 57–61, 310, 382n
Hefner, O. O., 4
Hellman, Lillian, 69, 140, 196, 198,
    201, 399n
Hemingway, Ernest, 160, 388n,
    392n, 393n
Henning, Pat, 107

Herbert, Anthony B., 268–70, 408n
heroes, heroism, 60, 68, 72–73, 90,
    102, 140, 143, 165, 261
    existential, 229–30
    of Westerns, 237, 240
    Zapata as, 91, 93
Hero Within, The (Pearson), 410n
hero worship, 123
Herr, Michael, 268, 298
Heston, Charlton, 191
Hill, Mrs. B. R., 316
Hill, Norman, 215
Hinduism, 271
Hird, Thora, 220
Hispanic women, 131
historical change, 214
history, xxiv, xxxvi, 50, 59, 103, 121,
    133, 150, 163, 165, 166, 168, 174,
    207, 211, 262, 291, 351, 356, 373n,
    382n, 412n
    American Indian, 85, 251, 316–19,
    325–29, 412n, 417n, 419n–20n,
    421n
    Asian, 117, 118, 281
    Black American, 331, 337–38,
    422n
    film, 108, 110, 196, 197, 230, 231,
    282
    Jewish, 60, 62–63, 382n
    Latin American, 26, 89, 90, 91–92,
    421n
History of Capital Punishment, A
    (Laurence), 167
History of Philosophy Eastern and
    Western (Radhakrishnan), 133
Hitler, Adolf, 127, 135, 294
Hoboken, N.J., 106
Hodenfield, Chris, 261
Hoffer, Eric, 73, 211, 409n

Hofschneider, Marco, 300
Hollister, Calif., 99
Hollywood, 42, 58, 96, 107, 131 164,
    217, 231, 235, 237, 248, 250–51,
    257, 265, 278, 319, 360, 381n
  Brando's ambivalence and dis-
    dain for, 34, 46, 83, 118, 119, 124,
    125, 153, 157, 158, 180, 298, 310
  Brando's contract negotiations in,
    84, 120, 125, 161, 181, 264, 393n
  Brando's introduction to, 82–88
  Brando's move to, xxx, xxxii, 231
  censorship in, 81, 89, 202–5, 210,
    384n
  HUAC and, 104–6, 108, 116
  Jews in, 62
  Kazan as pariah in, 104–5
  Kazan's relationship with, 103, 104
  marketability in, xii–xiv, 139–40,
    349
  racism in, 333, 360
Hollywood Reporter, 153
Hollywood Variety, 153, 392n
Holocaust, 59–61, 63, 65–66, 117, 138,
    191–92, 266, 382n
homebuilding and home repair, 410n
homophobia, 176, 202–5, 208, 209,
    400n
homosexuals, homoeroticism, xxvi,
    157, 176, 200–210
Hong Kong, 119, 182
Hood, Thomas, 293
Hook, Sidney, 102–3, 166
Horney, Karen, 85, 402n
horses, horsemen, 12, 19, 23, 93, 145,
    151, 200, 201, 206, 209, 210, 215,
    221, 222, 257–62, 282, 314
  in Missouri Breaks, 258–62
  in Nightcomers, 221–22
  in Reflections in a Golden Eye,
    201, 206, 209, 210
Hough, Richard, 164
Houseman, John, 96
House of Connelly, The (Green),
    42–43, 44
House Un-American Activities
  Committee (HUAC), 88, 90,
    104–6, 108, 114, 116, 386n
Howard, Trevor, 162, 396n
Howard, Willie, 286
human ambiguity, 72
human experience, xxxix, 45
Human Face, The (Picard), 225,
    367n, 402n
humanitarianism, 68, 339–48
human nature, 57, 103, 168
humor, xxxvii–xxxviii, 36, 72, 86,
    126–27, 233, 276
  of Brando, xxxvii–xxxviii, 8, 15,
    33, 41, 53, 71, 85, 97, 126–27, 221,
    261, 276, 286–88, 296, 304–6,
    331, 411n
  culture and, xxxiv, 126
  in family background, 5, 8, 17
  One-Eyed Jacks and, 147, 153, 155
  Streetcar and, 81, 126
  in Ugly American, 187, 188
Hungary, 103
Hunter, Kim, 25, 75
Hussein, Saddam, 250
Huston, John, 90, 140, 153, 330
  Reflections in a Golden Eye and,
    204, 205, 208, 210
Hutton, Bobby, 175, 335–36, 396n,
    423n

Iain Johnstone Show (TV show), 322
idealism, 96, 103, 240, 266

idealism (*continued*)
  of Brando, 103, 117–19, 158, 179,
    180, 214, 264, 265, 275, 391*n*
  in family background, 2
idolatry, Brando's view of, xvii
image:
  actor's enslavement to, xv
  of Brando, xv, xviii, xxii, 174, 253
  recognition of, xviii
imagination, 223
immigrants:
  civil rights for, 5
  illegal, 195
imperialism, 185–86, 211
improvisation, xxvi–xxvii, 81, 110,
    147, 187, 245, 255, 262, 298, 305,
    356, 389*n*, 423*n*
  for *Apocalypse Now*, 274
  for *Chase*, 196, 399*n*
  for *Godfather*, 243, 245
In Cold Blood (Capote), 403*n*
India, xxv, xxxvi, 133, 340
  caste in, 192, 340, 342
Indians and Other Americans (Fey
    and McNickle), 328, 398*n*–99*n*
*Indian Tribes of the United States,
    The* (McNickle), xxii, 369*n*
Indonesia, 339
Infinite Jest (Wallace), xxvi, 370*n*
In-Laws, The (film), 287
innovation, 257, 265
  Brando and, xxxvi, 125, 153, 165,
    310, 347–48, 372*n*, 415*n*
  in *Chase*, 197–98, 399*n*
  color movies and, 106
  see also technology
Inouye, Daniel, 323
interracial romance and marriage,
    117, 128–31, 169, 338, 360

In the Minds of Men (Murphy), 133
Ireland, 311, 316
I Remember Mama (Van Druten),
    xix, 49, 51, 368*n*
irony, 97, 127, 224, 235, 241, 404*n*
Isabella, Queen of Spain, 294
Islam, 266, 271
Island of Dr. Moreau, The (film), 102,
    256, 297, 298, 299–303, *300*, 311,
    381*n*, 398*n*
Island of Lost Souls (film), 302
Israel, 58–59, 63–64, 66, 168, 382*n*
Istanbul, 311
Italian language, xxxvi
"It's better to die on your feet than
    to live on your knees," 93, 386*n*

Jackson, Anne, 52, 380*n*
Jackson, Henry, 320
Jackson, Jesse, 336
Jackson, Michael, xvi, 21, 33, 331,
    375*n*, 376*n*, 383*n*
James, Henry, xxii, 220
Japan, xxxvi, 133, 339, 373*n*
  Brando in, 119, 127–31, 311, 410*n*
Japanese language, xxxvi, 128, 129,
    389*n*
Jaques, Ronny, 20
Java, 119
Javits, Jacob, 64, 382*n*
Jay, John, 192
jazz, 71, 90, 331
jazz clubs, xx, 114, 369*n*, 376*n*
Jericho (script), 276, 283, 296
Jews, Judaism, 4, 35, 45, 131, 210,
    271, 294, 334
  Brando's views on, xxxii, 48,
    62–64, 382*n*
  Flag Is Born and, 58–66, 310

at New School, 46, 48

"Shylock," 38–39, 377n

Jimi Hendrix: Electric Gypsy (Shapiro and Glebbeek), xxxv

job discrimination, 200

Joey Bishop Show, The (TV show), 336

Johnson, Ben, 27, 146

Johnson, Lyndon, 334

Johnson, Malcolm, 107–8

Johnston, Robert M., 120

Jones, Quincy, xx, 114, 283, 296, 331, 369n

Juarez, Benito, 91

Julius Caesar (film), 82, 95–99, *98*, 131, 387n

"Mark Antony" in, 28, 96–99, 245, 351n

Jumping Bull, 295

Jung, Carl, 85

justice, 218, 250, 256

Kael, Pauline, 213–24, 234, 240, 380n

Kanter, Jay, 284, 329, 370n, 372n, 398n

Kaplan, E. Ann, 402n

Kashfi, Anna, 92, 131, 158, 174, 181, 338

Kassar, Mario, 309n

Kastner, Elliott, 283

Kauffmann, Stanley, 45, 137

Kaufman, Boris, 159, 160

Kazan, Elia, 40–41, 51, 80–81, 123, 376n, 380n

as Brando's ideal director, 71, 81

HUAC and, 104–6, 108, 114, 116, 386n

On the Waterfront and, 103–6, 108, 110, 113, 116, 387n

Streetcar (movie) and, 69, 81

Streetcar (play) and, 67–72, 74, 75

Viva Zapata! and, 69, 88–90, 92, 93, 94, 386n

Keaton, Diane, 239

Keesing, Felix, 128

Keith, Brian, 207

Kennedy, John F., 182, 183, 321

Kerr, Deborah, 131

Kiliç, Altemur, 342

Kilmer, Joyce, 264, 407n

King, Alan, 380n

King, Coretta Scott, 336

King, Martin Luther, Jr., 191, *332*, 333, 334

King Rat (film), 287

Kitt, Eartha, 333

Klee, Paul, xxix

knots, 220, 221, 401n

KNXT, 315

Koster, Henry, 120

"Kowalski, Stanley," 28, 67, 69, 71–79, *77*, 82, 124, 138, 384n

humor of, 81, 126

Kramer, Stanley, 83–84, 99

Krishnamurti, 50, *50*, 271

Kubrick, Stanley, 151

Kunstler, William, 291, 322

Ladysmith Black Mambazo, 284

Lake Zurich Playhouse, 24, 25, 31

L'Amour, Louis, 143, 144

landscape, 260

Lane, Mark, 322

Lang, Charles, 143

language, 25, 26–27, 57, 243, 314, 396n

in *Fugitive Kind*, 159–60

in *Mutiny on the Bounty*, 162

invention of, 15, 149

language (*continued*)
in *Julius Caesar*, 95–99
in *Mutiny on the Bounty*, 163, 165, 393*n*
in *One-Eyed Jacks*, 149, 150
in *Streetcar*, 71
in *Wild One*, 95, 96, 99–101
words vs. silence and, 5, 79, 94, 110, 111, 136, 169
see also accents; *specific foreign languages*
Lao Tzu, 270
Larkin, Philip, 293
Larry King Live, 382*n*
Lash, John, 490*n*
Last Tango in Paris (film), xiv, 78, 219, 223–34, *229*, *231*, 255, 256, 305, 408*n*
Algerian connection in, 227–29
Lathrop Junior High School, 22, 375*n*
Latin America:
history of, 26, 90
music of, 34–35
Laughton, Charles, 161, 162, 302
Laurel and Hardy, 126
Laurence, John, 167
Lawrence, T. E., 160–61
Lawrence of Arabia (film), 160–61, 314
Lean, David, 160–61
Léaud, Jean-Pierre, 224
Lebanon, 340
Lederer, Charles, 161
Lederer, William, 182, 184, 397*n*
Legion of Decency, 82
Leigh, Vivien, 76
Leonard, Herman, 311, 313
Leone, Sergio, 153
Leventhal, Larry, 322

Lewis, Robert, 42, 43, 123, 379*n*
Lewis, Robert E., 393*n*
libel, 174, 176, 396*n*
Liberty Canyon, 322, *323*
Libertyville, Ill., 22–25
Libertyville Township High School, 23, 25
libraries, 388*n*–89*n*
Life, 84–85, 232, 239–40, 249, 402*n*, 407*n*
Life on the Stage, A (J. Adler), 38
Light in August (Faulkner), 85
Lincoln Elementary School, 13–16, *14*, 374*n*
Lindsay, John, 334–35
Lindsey, Robert, 382*n*, 383*n*, 407*n*, 410*n*
lists, Brando's passion for, 26, 149, 391*n*
literature, 96
see also poetry, poets; *specific authors and books*
Littlefeather, Sacheen, 250–52, 322, 324, 405*n*
Lives of a Cell (Thomas), xxxiv–xxxv, 372*n*
Living My Life (Goldman), xxxv
Lloyd, Kathleen, *259*
Logan, Joshua, 129
loneliness:
of Brando, xx, 23, 44, 53
in films, 108, 154, 202, 207
Lopez, Miguel, 300
Loren, Sophia, 140
Los Angeles, Calif., 15–16, 92, 119, 237, 369*n*
Mulholland house in, xxxiii–xxxiv, *xxxvii*, 16, 235, 265, 276, 277, 370*n*, 375*n*

Watts riots in, 199–200
  see also Hollywood
Los Angeles Herald Examiner, 210
Los Angeles Police Department, 175
Los Angeles Times, 174, 275
love, 21, 39, 49, 169, 202
  in Mutiny on the Bounty, 165, 171, 395n
  in One-Eyed Jacks, 146, 151, 154
  in On the Waterfront, 107, 108, 109
  in plays, 52, 53
  in Sayonara, 129–31
  in Ugly American, 187–88
Love Medicine (Erdrich), 325–26
Loving, Frances Brando, 287, 373n, 377n
  childhood of, 6–9, 8, 11, 12, 13–17
  education of, 31
  inscription of, 16, 374n
  in New York, 31, 32, 33, 36
Loving, Julie, 155–56
Loving, Richard, 36, 377n
Luhrmann, Baz, 303
Lumet, Sidney, 158
Lummi Indians, 346
Lunt, Alfred, 69
lying and fabrications, 154, 251
  of Brando, xix, 24, 46, 82, 230–32
"Lying for a Living" (acting classes), 232, 355–56, 371n, 384n, 406n
Lynch, David, 303
lynching, 105, 330–31

Mabley, Moms, 306
MacArthur, Charles, 59
Madison, James, 192
magazines, 174, 176, 248–49
  see also specific magazines
Magnani, Anna, 140, 158–59

Mailer, Norman, 35, 377n
makeup, 38, 54–56, 54, 55, 121, 123, 128, 235, 381n
Malcolm X, 338
Malden, Karl, 107, 108
  One-Eyed Jacks and, 144, 146, 147, 154, 155
Malinowski, Bronislaw, 169, 271, 395n
Mankiewicz, Joseph M., 96, 191
Mann, Abby, 326, 329
Mann, Marty, 410n
Man of Steel (film), 264
Manso, Peter, 396n
Manvell, Roger, 168
Mao Tse-tung, 183, 397n
Marchak, Alice, 382n, 404n
"March on Washington," 336
Marquand, Christian, 285
Marquez, Evaristo, 211
Marrakech, 313–14
marriage, interracial, 129–31
Marshall, E. G., 196
Marshall Islands, 192
Martha Raye Show, The (TV show), 384n
Martin, Dean, 132
Marvin, Lee, 100
Marx, Karl, 63
Marxism, 40, 214
masculinity, 227, 378n
  American norms of, 248
  of Brando's characters, xiv, xv, 68, 74–76, 78, 154, 171, 201, 207, 208, 233, 240, 244, 248
masks, xxix, 225
Maslin, Janet, 276
Mason, Jackie, 287
Mass Psychology of Fascism, The (Reich), 132–33, 390n

"Masterson, Sky," 124–25

materialism, 177, 240

Maysles brothers, xviii–xix, 368n

McCain, John, xxiv, 370n

McCarthy, Joe, 73, 102, 383n

McCarthy era, 73

McClintic, Guthrie, 52

McCullers, Carson, xxii, 140, 201, 208

McGuane, Thomas, 406n

McLiam, John, 258

McNamara, Robert, 273

McNickle, D'Arcy, xxii, 317–18, 319, *319*, 320, 328, 369n, 391n, 398n–99n

Mead, Margaret, xxiii, 47, 345, 369n, 402n

Means, Russell, 322, 324–25

Medavoy, Mike, 303

media, 174, 203, 230–31, 250, 261, 396n

  political role of, 174

  see also press; television; *specific publications and shows*

Meet Marlon Brando (documentary), xviii–xix

Meisner, Sanford, 42

Melanesia, 169

Mellen, Joan, 216

Men, The (film), *11*, 28, 83–88, *86, 87*

Mencken, H. L., 326

Menominee, Wisc., 295

Menominee Indians, 325

Merkin, Daphne, xvi

Merton, Thomas, 260

Message from Khufu, A (Cottman), 30

Mexicans:

  Chase and, 193, 195

  in West, 142–46, 150, 155

Mexico, xxv, 90–92, 316, 317

Mexico City, 303

Mexico South (Covarrubias), 90, 91, 317

MGM, 88, 96, 161, 286, 387n

Michener, James, 128, 129

Michi, Maria, 224

Milar, Mildred, 16, 374n

Milestone, Lewis, 173

military:

  in *Last Tango in Paris*, 227–28

  see also paraplegic war veterans; Shattuck Military Academy

Miller, Arthur, 70, 75, 141

mind, 5, 374n, 403n

mindlessness, 73

ministry, 230

misogyny, 207, 208

Missouri Breaks, The (film), xxv, 202, 252, 257–63, *258, 259*, 283, 325, 416n

Mittelmann, Bela, 105

mob, Mafia:

  as diabolical mirror for established institutions, 239–40, 249

  in *Godfather*, 235–49

  in *On the Waterfront*, 107–13, 116

Modisane, Bloke, 337–38

Mokae, Zakes, 284

Moliere, 30

Mona Lisa, with card, 150, *152*

Monaster, Nate, 333

Monroe, Marilyn, xvi

Montana, 257, 262

Montevecchi, Liliane, 135, 136–37

Montgomery Bus Boycott, 333

morality, 73, 100, 114, 132, 139, 141, 193, 199, 216, 258

Moreno, Rita, xxiii
Morituri (film), xviii–xix, xxv, 396*n*
Mormonism, 271
Morricone, Ennio, 140
Morris, Desmond, 315
Morrison, Temuera, 300
Morrison, Toni, 283, 337
Moscow Art Theatre (MAT), 42
Motion Picture Association of
    America, 205, 400*n*
Motley, Mary, 137–38
motorcycling, 99–102, 123, 136
Mr. Peepers (TV show), 36
multiculturalism, xxiv, 71, 130, 193
mumbling, 88, 385*n*
Mundelein, Ill., 377*n*
Muni, Paul, 35, 54, 56–61, 64, 65,
    376*n*, 379*n*, 381*n*
murder, 167, 202, 204, 209, 266
    in *Chase*, 198, 199
    Christian and, 265
    in *Godfather*, 238, 239, 250
    in *Julius Caesar*, 97
    in *Last Tango in Paris*, 226, 231
    in *Missouri Breaks*, 102
    in *On the Waterfront*, 107, 111, 112,
        113
Murphy, Gardner, 133
Murphy, Mary, xxvi–xxvii
Murrow, Edward R., 18, 73, 291, *291*,
    383*n*
music, xxx, 216, 234
    Brando's knowledge of, xx–xxii,
        xxi, 22, 34–35, 369*n*, 376*n*
    Dodie and, 34, 376*n*
    Fugitive Kind and, 158–59
    jazz clubs, xx, 114, 369*n*, 376*n*
    Latin American, 34–35
    for plays, 58, 377*n*

scores, xxii, 71, 116, 127, 140, 369*n*
musicals, 125–26
mustache, 56, *56*, 381*n*
"Mutiny of Marlon Brando, The,"
    173–74
Mutiny on the Bounty (film), xiv, xxv,
    xxvii, xxxviii, 28, 160–79, *170*,
    314, 343, 393*n*–98*n*
    Bounty ship in, *166*, *172*, 174, *175*
    expense of, 173, 395*n*
    "Fletcher Christian" in., 28,
        160–65, 169–73, 214, 388*n*, 393*n*,
        394*n*, 398*n*
    major consequences of, 174–77
    1935 version of, 92, 161, 162
    On the Waterfront compared
        with, 114, 388*n*
    Pitcairn Island sequence in, 139,
        161–64, 168
    research for, 161, 165–69, 393*n*
    reviews of, 88, 385*n*
Myers, Betty, 7, 17, 31, 84–85
Myers, Elizabeth Gahan (Bess), 2–8,
    8, *11*, 16–17, 31, 84, 191
    Brando's correspondence with,
        26, 27–28, 50, 375*n*
    marriages of, 4, 5
Myers, Frank, 5, 6, 7
My Life in Art (Stanislavski), 381*n*

NAACP, 322
Napoleon (Johnston), 120
Napoleon I, Emperor of France, 28,
    117, 120–24, *122*, 404*n*
Napoleon's Victories (Parquin), 120
National Congress of American
    Indians (NCAI), 321
National Geographic, 311
National Guard, U.S., 295, 325

National Indian Youth Council, 319–20, 330

nationalism, 227–28, 240

National Theater for the Deaf, 79

Nation of Islam, 266

Nation on the Flying Trapeze, The (Childer), 182, 397*n*

Native Peoples of the Pacific World (Keesing), 128

nature, 200
    Brando's feeling at home in, 15–16, 19, 301
    Dodie and, 155, 156
    state of, 226

Nature of Prejudice, The (Allport), 338

Navajo, 156

Nazis, 274
    Brando's portrayal of, 68, 72, 117, 126–27, 132–38
    humanizing of, 68, 126–27, 132–38
    see also Germany, Nazi

Nebraska, 316

Neider, Charles, 143–44, 146

Neusom, Tom, 333

New Republic, 137

New School for Social Research, 32, 37, 44–50, 54, 96, 331

newspapers, 176
    see also specific newspapers

Newsweek, 232

New York, N.Y., 4, 30–83, *252*
    attention attracted by Brando in, xviii
    Brando's book buying in, xxxiii, 161, 166, 371*n*
    Brando's girlfriends and dating in, 32, 33, 38, 39–40, 49, 376*n*
    Brando's move to, 30–31
    Carnegie Hall apartment in, xxiii, 369*n*
    jazz clubs in, xx, 269*n*, 331
    Stonewall riots in, 202–3, 204
    see also Broadway

New York Daily News, 153

New Yorker, 153, 168, 173, 174, 190, 216, 232, 240

New York Post, 210

New York *Sun*, 107

New York Times, 59, 105, 153, 173, 189–90, 251, 263, 270, 275

New York Times Magazine, 367*n*–68*n*

Nicholson, Jack, 257, *259*, 262, 416*n*

Nicomachean Ethics (Aristotle), 316

Niel, André, 168–69

Nightcomers, The (film), xxv, 181, 219–23, 253, 258, 283, 401*n*, 404*n*

Night of the Following Day, The (film), xxiii, xxv

Niven, David, 127, 287

Nobody Knows My Name (Baldwin), 332

nonconformity, *Wild One* and, 99–100

nonviolent protest, 333

Nordhoff, Charles, 165

North, Alex, 369*n*

Norton, Ed, 306, 307

Notes for his Autobiography (NFA), xxxviii–xxxix, 373*n*

"Notes on Indians" (Brando), 142

nuclear arms, 183, 276, 299

nudity, 12, 34, 221
    in *Reflections in a Golden Eye*, 202, 205, 206

Obama, Barack, xxiv, 370n
objects, Brando's work with, xxvi–
xxviii, 39, 45, 150, 196
O'Brien, Frederick, 166
Odets, Clifford, 42, 43, 104
Okinawa, xxv, 126, 127, 192
Old Man and the Sea, The (Hemingway), 160
Oliver, Douglas, 166
Oliver, Edith, 153
Olivier, Laurence, xvi, 79, 117, 121,
123, 400n
Olympia, Wash., 320
Omaha, Nebr., 1, 4–13, 8, 23, 48, 64
Omaha Community Playhouse, 9–11,
10, 13
One-Eyed Jacks (film), xxv, xxvii–
xxviii, xxxvii, 91, 139–58, 148,
193, 217, 317, 329
Brando's directing of, 20, 141–58,
180, 326, 384n
Chase compared with, 193, 200
chess playing on set of, 20, 20
dramatic saloon entrances in, 150
earnings of, 151, 153
family screening of, 155–56
handshake in, 147, 150, 151
influence of, 151–53
marginality in, 142–43, 150
Mona Lisa with card in, 150, 152
plot of, 141, 145–46
psychological implications and,
144–45, 151, 154–57
scene in Spanish in, 149,
391n–92n
sources for, 143–45
title of, 151
On Guerrilla Warfare (Mao Tse-
tung), 183

On the Waterfront (film), xiv, xxv,
38–39, 69, 82, 103–17, 115, 387n,
390n
Brando's alterations to, 109–10
makeup for, 54, 55, 55
and passing of an era, 106
pigeons in, 111–12, 113
renowned lines in, 108–9
success of, 116–17
"Terry Malloy" in, 107–14, 116,
388n
On Violence (Arendt), 409n
Open End (TV show), 176–77
Operation PUSH, 336
Oppenheim, Tom, 405n
Optima Cigar Store, xv
Orkin, Ruth, 20
Orpheus Descending (Williams), 158,
159
Orpheus myth, 158–59
Osborn, Paul, 129
Oswald, Lee Harvey, 199
Ouspenskaya, Maria, 42
outcasts and marginality, 157
in Fugitive Kind, 159–60
in One-Eyed Jacks, 142–43, 150
Texas and, 193, 195
outrage, 66, 75, 284, 333
Outsider, The (Wilson), 114, 388n
Oz, Frank, 307

Pacino, Al, 239, 404n
Page, David, 306
Paglia, Camille, xvi
"Pain No More Party," 302
Palcy, Euzhan, 284
Palestine, Palestinians, 61, 63, 64,
66, 382n
Panama, 192

Paramount, 146, 153, 154, 390*n*–91*n*, 392*n*

paraplegic war veterans, 84–88, *86*, *87*

Paris, 135, 136
  Brando in, *xxi*, 105, 114, 133–34, *134*, 311
  Ellen Adler in, 85
  Les Deux Magots in, 114
  Stella Adler in, xxvii, 44

Parker, Gitta, 370*n*

parody, xix, 249–50

Parqui, C., 120

Partisan Review, 167

Pat (Irish wolfhound), 8, 374*n*

patriarchy, xxiv, 145, 158, 264, 381*n*
  in *Godfather*, 236–37, 240

patriotism, 311

Pauling, Linus, 167

Peace Corps, 183

Pearson, Carol, 410*n*

Peavine Frenzy (horse), 19, 23

Peck, Anthony, 303

Pellicer, Pina, 391*n*

Penn, Arthur, xxviii, 140, 196, 197–98, 200, 399*n*
  Missouri Breaks and, 257, 261, 406*n*

Penn, Sean, 303, 325–26, 368*n*

Pennebaker, Dorothy, *see* Brando, Dorothy Pennebaker

Pennebaker, William John, 4, 9, 272*n*

Pennebaker Productions, 118, 179, 181, 313
  Brando Sr.'s work for, 20–21, 141, 154
  purpose of, 140–41, 391*n*
  see also One-Eyed Jacks

Pentagon Papers, 273

personality, emotion and, xiii

personality tests, 410*n*

Person to Person, 291, *291*

Peters, Jean, 93

pets, xxxvi, 8–9, 23, 291, 370*n*, 374*n*
  childhood, 8

Philippines, 119, 182, 267, 269, 399*n*, 408*n*

philosophy, 25, 50, 117, 166, 410*n*
  existentialism, 114, 229–30
  non-Western, 4
  political, 192–93

physicality, 108, 244
  of Ermi, 12–13

Picard, Max, 2, 25, 367*n*, 402*n*

Picasso, Pablo, 208

pigeons, 111–12, *113*

Piscator, Erwin, 37, 96

playbills, fabricated biographies in, xix, 368*n*

Playboy, 266

Pocket Book of Verse, 293

poetry, poets, xx, xxxv, xxxvi, 46, 96, 159, 293
  Dickinson, xxxi, 23–24, 375*n*
  Eliot, 270–71, 275, 408*n*–9*n*
  Kilmer, 264, 407*n*

Poitier, Sidney, 191

political films, 180–219, 325–26, 337
  see also Burn!; Chase, The; Reflections in a Golden Eye; Ugly American, The

political philosophy, 192–93

Political Power and Personal Freedom (Hook), 102–3, 166

political science, 396*n*

politics, 53, 66, 85, 117, 165, 166, 168, 240, 267

Brando's books about, xxxvi
Kazan and, 88–90, 104
in Mexico, 90–93
sexual, *see* sexual politics
Pollock, Dale, 275
pollution, 310
Polynesia, 311
Pomare I, King, 345
Pomare V, King, 343
Pontecorvo, Gillo, 140, 210–18, 330,
    400*n*, 401*n*
Pope, Carmelita, 24–25, 31
Portugal, 211–13
poverty, 315
power, 70, 72, 73, 78, 93–94, 123,
    234, 262
of acting, 157, 225, 249
American, 61
Brando's contempt for, 28–29, 315
of film, 225
in *Godfather*, 234, 237
of Hollywood Jews, 62
moral, 154
in *Mutiny on the Bounty*, 171–73
natural, 296
political, 154
of rhetoric, 95, 97–99
of seduction, 124
Zapata's distrust of, 90
prejudice, 129–31, 137–38, 140, 192,
    315
homophobic, 176, 203–4, 400*n*
see also race, racism
Preminger, Otto, 137
Prescott, William H., 92
press, 82, 263, 403*n*
freedom of, 182
merchandising aspect of, xix
primates, xxxvi, 8, 347, 425*n*, 427*n*

Progoff, Ira, 191
Prohibition, 11
Prophet, The (Gibran), 46
Protestants, 214, 237, 239
Prucha, Francis Paul, 192, 329, 398*n*
Pryor, Richard, 306
psychiatrist, psychiatry, xxxiv, 124
psychoanalysis, 85
psychology, 216, 402*n*
of character, 44
mass, 73, 132–33, 390*n*
One-Eyed Jacks and, 144–45, 151,
    154–57
psychology books, xxxvi, 85, 117,
    369*n*, 371*n*
psychotherapy, 191
publicity, 173, 175, 210, 216
Brando's disdain for, xviii–xx,
    xxxii–xxxiii, 82, 125–26, 251,
    382*n*
Puente, Tito, 34
punishment, 162, 206, 226, 236
capital, 167, 394*n*–95*n*
puppies, in *Viva Zapata!*, 94, 95*n*
Puyallup River, 320
Puzo, Mario, 235, 239

Quinn, Anthony, 94, 386*n*
quotes, quotation books, 26, 149

race, racism, 35, 71, 84, 117, 129, 166,
    191–92, 199, 200, 211, 266, 294
against blacks, 66, 208, 209, 331,
    333, 338
Brando's realism about, 338–39
in Hollywood, 333
in *Last Tango in Paris*, 227, 228
Zionism as, 63
racial intermarriage, 68

Radhakrishnan, Sarvepalli, 133
Rafelson, Bob, 330
railroads, 327
Rains, Claude, 120
Rambo III (film), 276, 409n
Random House, xix, 379n, 403n
"Random Notes on the Script"
    (Brando), 193, 197
rape, 204, 230, 402n
    Streetcar and, 76, 78, 81, 384n
    Wild One and, 100–101
Real, James, 183n
reality, theater vs., 248
Rebel, The (Camus), 113–14, 116, 386n
rebels, rebellion, 227–28, 270
    Brando and, 28–29, 40, 46, 101–3,
        114, 166
    in *Burn!*, 211–12, 216
    in *Godfather*, 236
    On the Waterfront and, 112–14
    Wild One and, 99–102
    see also guerrilla fighters
Redford, Robert, 140, 195, 196
Reed, Carol, 167, 173
Reeve, Christopher, 264, 407n
Reflections in a Golden Eye (film),
    xxv, xxvi, 28, 140, 181, 200–210,
    203, *204*, 272
    distribution problems of, 210, 216
    influence of, 209, 400n
    mirrors in, 209, 206, 400n
Reflections in a Golden Eye (McCul-
    lers), 208
Reich, Wilhelm, 132–33, 390n
religion, 117, 230, 237
    Brando's reading about, 50,
        117, 270–71, 351, 372n, 395n,
        408n–9n
    non-Western, 4, 50, 128

    see also specific religions
Republicans, xxiv, 321
reviews:
    film, 87, 88, 137, 139, 153, 173,
        189–90, 195, 210, 216, 222, 230,
        234, 249, 261–64, 275, 276, 302,
        307, 385n, 395n, 406n–7n
    theater, 49, 53, 66, 73–74, 380n,
        384n
Rexroth, Kenneth, 167
rhetoric, 95, 97–99, 264
Rhetoric (Aristotle), 46
Rhodes, Philip, *300*
Rich, Frank, 275
Richardson, Samuel, 27
Rickles, Don, 306
riots, 199–200, 202–3, 204
rituals, 84, 171, 226–27
Robertson, Cliff, 158
Robinson, Edward G., 59
Rockwell, George Lincoln, 72, 266
Rodgers, Richard, 49
Rodriguez, Tito, 34
roles:
    Brando's types of, *see* Brando,
        Marlon, types of roles played by
        mumbling in, 79
Rolling Stone, 261
Romeo and Juliet (film; 1996), 303
Roosevelt, Eleanor, 61
Roosevelt, Franklin D., 59, 382n
Roots (TV show), 72, 80, 265–66, 337
Rosellini, Albert D., 320
Rosenberg, Frank, 149, 382n
Rota, Nino, 369n
Ruby, Jack, 199
Ruddy, Al, 235, 403n
Ruiz, Christina, 297, 401n
Rumshinsky, Joseph, 377n

Runyon, Damon, 125
Russell, Bertrand, 25
Russian theater, 42, 45, 54

sacrifice, sacrificial characters, xxiv,
68, 110, 115–17, 167, 197, 216, 322
Apocalypse Now and, 273, 275
sadomasochism:
in *Last Tango in Paris*, 225–26
in *Nightcomers*, 219, 220, 223
Saint, Eva Marie, 107, 287n
Salisbury, J. H., 4
Salkind, Alexander, 293, 294, 295
Salkind, Ilya, 293, 294–95
Salvatori, Renato, 211
Sand Creek Massacre, 326
Santa Ana, Calif., 16–17
Sarandon, Susan, 284
Sartre, Jean-Paul, 114, 338, 388n
Satiacum, Robert, *320*
Saturday Evening Post, 173–74
Saturday Night with Connie Chung,
286
Saturday Review, 125
Sayonara (film), xxv, 28, 68, 126,
128–31, 373n, 410n
Schary, Dore, 63–64, 126, 382n
Schell, Maximilian, 135
Schneider, Maria, 223
Schoenbrun, David, 134, 390n
Schulberg, Budd, 106, 107, 108, 110,
111, 113
science, xxxi, xxxvi, 102, 256, 263,
265, 407n
Science and Health (Eddy), 5
Score, The (film), xiv, 297–98, 306–8,
307
Scorsese, Martin, 153, 330, 400n
Scott, George C., 276

scripts, xxx, 121, 276
for *Apocalypse Now*, 267–72, 409n
Brando's rewriting and writing
of, xxiii, xxxvi–xxxvii, 20, 79,
83, 109–10, 129–30, 132, 136, 143,
147–49, *148*, 151, 161–65, 183–88,
189, 195, 198, 201, 215, 221,
240–46, 267–68, 271–72, 283,
298, 390n, 394n, 398n, 399n,
403n–4n, 407n
for *Chase*, 195, 196, 198, 201, 399n
for *Godfather*, 235, 240–46,
403n–4n
Jericho, 276
for *Mutiny on the Bounty*, 161–65,
174, 394n
for *One-Eyed Jacks*, 141, 143
for *On the Waterfront*, 107–10, 241
for *Reflections in a Golden Eye*,
201, 205, 209
for *Sayonara*, 129–30
for *Ugly American*, 183–88, *189*,
398n
Seagull, The (Chekhov), 68–69
Seale, Bobby, 101, 211, 334, 400n
seductiveness, 202, 220, 232–33, 248
of Brando, 15, 124, 169
Segal, Ronald, 192
Selected Poems of Emily Dickinson,
23–24, 375n
self-knowledge, 224, 402n
Senate, U.S., 182, 185, 187, 197, 320,
323
sensitivity, 68, 76, 108, 124
see also Brando, Marlon, sensitivity and empathy of
sex, sexuality, 53
post-1972 films subordination of,
219

sex, sexuality (*continued*)
  in *Streetcar*, 74–75, 76, 78, 81
  as ultimate stage, 230
  see also Brando, Marlon, sexuality, promiscuity, and womanizing of; sadomasochism
Sex and Repression in Savage Society (Malinowski), 169
sexism, xv–xvi, 368n
sexual dysfunction, in *The Men*, 84, 86
sexual fantasy, 224, 225
sexual politics, 219–34
  see also Last Tango in Paris; *Nightcomers, The*
Shabalala, Joseph, 284
Shakespeare, William, 57, 204, 207, 260
  Brando's memorizing of, 26, 386n
  Brando's reading of, 25
  Jacob Adler's playing of, 38–39
shame, 93, 104
Shapiro, Robert, 291
Shattuck Military Academy, 6, 25–30, 90, 96, 207, 375n, 376n
Shaw, George Bernard, 52–53
Shaw, Irwin, 128, 131–34, *134*
Sheen, Charlie, 303, 305
Sheen, Martin, 163, 270, 305
Shin, Peter, 308, *309*
"Shylock," 38–39, 377n
Signoret, Simone, 229
silence, 107, 233
  Holocaust and, 60
  words vs., xxxvii, 5, 68, 79, 88, 94, 110–12, 136, 169, 233, 350
Silko, Leslie, 326
Simmons, Jean, 124, 125
Simoneau, Yves, 303, 305–6

Simpson, Alan, 320
Sinatra, Frank, xvi
Singapore, 119
Sinoto, Yosihiko H., 344
Sioux Indians, 324
Sixtus IV, Pope, 294
Sketches of Spain (Davis), xxii, 369n
slavery, 178, 211–13, 328, 330
smiles, xiii–xv, 97, 101, 142, 150, 156, 177, 205, 222, 232, 243, 260, 301, 308, 327, 357, 362
  earning power and, xiii–xiv
  as indices of vulnerability and manipulation, xiv
Smith, Kenneth J., 230
social change, 101
socialism, Socialists, 46, 240
social science, 117
sodomy, 225–26, 233
Soldier (Herbert), 268–70, 408n
Solinas, Franco, 211
Songs My Mother Taught Me (Brando), xix, 9, 376n, 382n, 388n, 403n, 405n–6n
  fan letters in, 385n
  Hamlet's advice used in, 79
  Jewish experience in, 62–63
  notes for, xxxviii–xxxix, 373n
  photographs in, 55–56, 381n
  promotion of, 249
Sorvino, Mira, 303–4, 305
South, U.S., 105, 181, 199, 200
South Africa, 102, 192, 337
  apartheid in, 284
Southeast Asia, 118, 127, 141, 178, 183, 188–89, 197
Southern, Terry, 285
South Pacific, xxxvi
South Sea Story, A (script), 283

Soviet Union, 102–3, 104, 176, 192, 276, 409n

Spain, 211, 294

Spanish, xxxvi, 149, 193, 195, 391n–92n

Spanish Inquisition, 294

Spiegel, Sam, 105, 108, 196, 387n, 390n

Spingarn Medal, 322

spirituality, 2, 4, 128, 143, 237
    Brando's reading about, 270–71, 408n–9n

Standing Bear, 5

Stanislavski, Constantin, xxiii, 42, 381n
    Adler's work with, xxvii, 44
    dramatic theory of, xxviii–xxix, 40, 44, 50

Stanley, Richard, 298

Stanton, Harry Dean, 258, 259

Stapleton, Maureen, xviii, 69, 158

Stark, Ray, 205, 210

stars, 250, 264, 265
    multitalented, 125

Steiger, Rod, 107

Steinbeck, John, xxii, 88, 89, 91, 93, 385n

Stern, Stewart, 185, 187, 311, 313, 388n

Stevenson, Adlai, xviii

Stillman's Gym, 80

Stone, I. F., 73, 383n

Stonewall riots, 202–3, 204

stories, storytelling, xxix, 125, 160, 222
    for Apocalypse Now, 267
    eyes and, 79

"Strabler, Johnny," 124

Strasberg, Lee, 41–44, 80
    The Group and, 42, 43, 44, 379n

Strasberg, Paula, 104

Strauss, Theodore, 84–85

Streetcar Named Desire, A (film), xiv, 69, 74, 76, 78, 79, 81–82, 126, 310
    baby in, 81, 384n

Streetcar Named Desire, A (play), xviii, 25, 28, 67–80, 77, 230, 311, 378n, 384n
    photographs for, 76, 77
    reviews of, 73–74, 384n
    voice in, 74–75

Stress and the Art of Biofeedback (Brown), 374n

student activism, 240

studio-contract system, 83

Suddenly Last Summer (film), 200

suffering, 136, 154, 157, 167, 197
    Brando and, 16, 35, 38, 62, 157, 197, 251, 281, 310, 315, 340
    HUAC and, 106
    of Indians, 251
    of Jews, 63
    in On the Waterfront, 107, 116, 117
    in Reflections in a Golden Eye, 206, 209

Sugar Cane Alley (film), 284

Sullivan, Ed, 30

Sunday Morning Address (Smith), 230

Superman (film), 263–66, 294, 396n, 404n

Supreme Court, California, 336

surveillance, 282, 323–24, 418n

Survival of American Indians Association (SAIA), 321, 322

Susskind, David, 176–77, 396n

Sutherland, Donald, 284, 285, 303, 305

symbolic castration, 154

symbolism, 142, 169, 188, 197, 206, 207, 228, 240
Szold, Bernard, 11, 48
Szold, Betty, 11, 48

taboos, 226
Tahiti, Tahitians, xxxvi, 131, 142, 160–79, *178*, 180, 237, 253, 265, 299, 311, 339, 340, 344–45, 370*n*, 373*n*, 393*n*, 396*n*
    see also Tetiaroa
Tahitian language, xxxvi, 165, 171
talent:
    of Brando, xxii, xxiv, 29–30, 37, 51, 76, 123, 150, 154–55, 157, 180, 181, 185, 210, 215, 255, 358, 279, 357, 370*n*, 376*n*, 397*n*
    Brando as magnet for, xxii, 139–40, 264, 369*n*
talk shows, xviii, 30, 174–78, 203–4, 208, 232, 250–53, *252*, 286, 322, 336, 346, 351, 352–54, *353*, 396*n*, 405*n*, 410*n*, 417*n*, 427*n*
Talmudic wisdom, xvii, 43, 62–63,
Tandy, Jessica, 76
Tao Te Ching, 16, 374*n*
Tarantino, Quentin, 153
Taxi Driver (film), 209, 400*n*
Taylor, Elizabeth, xix, 69–70, 140, 173
    Reflections in a Golden Eye and, 201, *203*, 205, 210
Teahouse of the August Moon, The (film), xxv, 126–28, 286, 311
    makeup for, 54, *54*, 126
technology, xxiv, 178–79, 185, 197–98, 265, 346, 348, 354, 415*n*
teeth, xiv, xv, 9, 177, 260, 276, 301
Telecom Italia, 347–48

telegraph lines, 327
television, 106
    Brando's interviews on, xviii, 30, 174–78, 203–4, 208, 232, 250–53, *252*, 286, 322, 336, 346, 352–54, *353*, 396*n*, 405*n*, 410*n*, 417*n*, 427*n*
    Brando's work for, 80, 108, 265–66
Teriipaia, Tarita, 169, 174, 177
Tetiaroa, 177, *178*, 179, 180, 276, 293, 299, 311, 313, 330, 343–48, *344*, 396*n*
    marae of, 343, 345
Tetiaroa Society, 347
Tetiaroa University, 347
Tex and Jinx Show, The, 351, 405*n*
Texas, 192, 193, 195
Thailand, 119, 182, *341*
Thayer, Charles W., 182
theater, 51–81
    Brando's contribution to, xxiv
    in Lake Zurich, 24, 25, 31
    in Omaha, 9–11, *10*, 13
    reviews of, 49, 53, 66, 73–74, 380*n*
    Russian, 42, 45, 54
    scores for, xxii, 369*n*
    Yiddish, xxvii, 37–39, 41, 54, 377*n*
    see also Broadway; Yiddish theater; Yiddish Theatre; *specific plays*
Theatre Guild, 41, 42, 159
theft, xxxiv, 167, 221
    in *One-Eyed Jacks*, 145, 157
    of roast, 9, 374*n*
The Group Theatre (The Group), 37, 40–44, 58, 80, 103, 104, 379*n*
therapy, 105, 253

They Came Here First (McNickle), 317–18, *319*

thinking, independent, xvi, 66, 368*n*

Thomas, Lewis, xxxiv–xxxv, 372*n*

Thomson, David, 410*n*–11*n*

Tim and His Friends (script), 283

Time, 176, 203–4, 232, 275, 400*n*, 402*n*

Tjorkorda Agung Sukawati, Prince, 313

Today Show, 175–76, 203–4, 208, 396*n*, 400*n*

Tomlin, Lily, 306

Tone, Franchot, 42, 92

Torrance, Calif., 333

totalitarianism, 47, 102–3

To Tame a Land (L'Amour), 143, 144

Toto (St. Bernard), 8–9, 358, 374*n*

Towne, Michael, 246

Towne, Robert, 246

travel, 22, 90, 118, 127–31, 140, 169, 180, 181–82, 192, 311–16, 330, 340

Travers, Peter, 307

"Trees" (Kilmer), 264, 407*n*

Trosper, Guy, 144

Truckline Café (Anderson), 28, 49, 51 52, 371*n*, 380*n*

True Believer, The (Hoffer), 73, 271, 409*n*

truth, 46
Brando's stretching of, 82
about other people, 223, 224–25
sense of, 44–45, 79–80

Tucker, Mel, 189

Turn of the Screw, The (James), 220

TV Guide, 406*n*

Twain, Mark, 143–44

Twelfth Night (Shakespeare), 96

Ugly American, The (Burdick and Lederer), 167, 182, 184, 397*n*

Ugly American, The (film), 28, 118, 127, 140–41, 179–92, 200, 397*n*–98*n*
Brando's preparations for, 182–84
Chase compared with, 191, 192, 195, 196–97
gestures in, 188, *190*
makeup for, 56, *56*
script for, 183–88, *189*, 398*n*

"Ugly Americanism," 176

UNESCO, 133

"Unfinished Oscar Speech, That" (Brando), 251

United Artists, 216

United Nations, 118, 339, 340, 347, 388*n*

United Nations International Children's Emergency Fund (UNICEF), 181–82, 311, 340–41, 342, *343*

United States, 114, 116, 276
diplomacy of, 118, 181–90, 192, 388*n*
foreign policy of, 181–91
Japan's relations with, 128–30
Mafia as diabolical mirror and, 239–40
technical superiority and, 273

Universal Studios, 181

UN World Food Programme, 342

US Savings Bond Program, 118

utopia, 167–68, 177, 208

values, 114, 257
American, 154
Brando's promotion of, 83, 117, 265

values (*continued*)
  in *Godfather*, 237–39
  political, 215
Van Cleve, Edith, 53, 83
Van Druten, John, 49
Van Vechten, Carl, 19–20
Variety, 173, 190, 275, 396*n*
veterans, 28, 84–88, *86, 87*
victims, victimization, 68, 101, 143,
  154, 197
Vietnam War, 118, 154, 189, 240,
  266–75, 407*n*, 408*n*
villains, 72, 126–27, 202, 255–63,
  265–66, 383*n*
violence, 84, 141, 192, 250
  in *Apocalypse Now*, 275
  in *Bonnie and Clyde*, 197
  in *Burn!*, 211, 212, 214, 215, 216
  in *Chase*, 195, 197–200
  of fathers and father figures, 12,
    21, 35, 146, 376*n*
  and film history, 197–99
  in *Godfather*, 94, 236–46, 248,
    404*n*
  in *Last Tango in Paris*, 227, 228,
    231
  in *Missouri Breaks*, 257–62, 407*n*
  in *Nightcomers*, 220, 222
  in *One-Eyed Jacks*, 146, 149, 154,
    155–56
  in *On the Waterfront*, 107, 111, 116,
    387*n*
  in Palestine, 61
  in *Reflections in a Golden Eye*,
    200, 201, 206, 209
  sexual, 200; *see also* rape
  in *Streetcar*, 74–75, 76, 78, 81
  in *Ugly American*, 200
  Wild One and, 99–102

of Zapata, 91, 94
  see also guns; murder; riots
virtue, 124, 248, 256
"Vision Road" (TV series), 326
Viva Zapata! (film), xvii, xxiv, xxv,
  28, 82, 88–95, 317, 385*n*
  Brando's preparation for, 90–92
  Godfather compared with, 93–95
  puppies in, 94, *95*
voting rights, 5
voyeurism, 224, 272
vulnerability, 44, 56, 154, 222, 379*n*

Wagner, Duke, 27, 28, 30, 96, 376*n*
walking sticks, 16, 374*n*
Wallace, David Foster, xxvi, 370*n*
Walsh, Raoul, 153
war and its aftermath, 28
Warner Brothers, 76, 129, 210
Warren Court, 321
Warrior, Clyde, 319, 322
warriors, 95, 228
Washington (state), 320
*Watching: Encounters with Humans
  and Other Animals* (Morris), 315
Watts riots, 199–200
We Americans (play), 57
Webb, Celia, 32
Webster, J. L., 5
Weill, Kurt, 48, 369*n*
Welles, Orson, 96
Wells, H. G., xxii, 256, 298
Westerns, 139–57, 237, 240
  Brando's stretching of limits of,
    142–45
  revisionist, 257–63, 407*n*
  see also One-Eyed Jacks
Westley, Helen, 379*n*
We Will Never Die (1943 pageant), 59

white supremacy, 198

Whole Earth Catalog, The (Brand), 345

Widener, Don, 346

Wiesel, Elie, 64, 382*n*

Wild One, The (film), xxiii, xxv, xxvi–xxvii, 55, 69, 99–102

language as preoccupation in, 95, 96, 99–101

Wilkensen, Mr., 375*n*

Williams, Johnston Walter, 343

Williams, Tennessee, xxii, 15, 28, 71, 72, 74, 81, 140, 158–60, 383*n*

on Brando, 67, 78, 208, 376*n*, 400*n*

and film version of *Streetcar*, 76, 78

Time's prejudice against, 176, 203–4, 400*n*

Willingham, Calder, 144

Wilson, Colin, 114, 388*n*

Winner, Michael, 222–23, 330, 401*n*

Wisconsin, 29–30

women, xxx, xxxiii, xxxv, 5, 32, 50, 124, 157, 169, 201, 203, 226, 258, 314

Brando's problem of commitment with, 62, 105, 217, 238, 256, 296, 316

Brando's taste in, 13, 131

in *Godfather*, 239, 240

Japanese, 129–31

in *Last Tango*, 226, 227, 228, 229, 230, 233

in *One-Eyed Jacks*, 143, 145, 146, 149, 151, 154

Wood, Robin, 196, 199, 399*n*

working class, workers, 6, 38, 107, 110, 113, 116, 171

World Summit on Sustainable Development, 347

World War II, xviii, 29, 104, 116, 132–38, 192, 240, 268, 328

Wounded Knee, 324–25

Wylie, Anita Kong, 402*n*

Yale, 16, 40, 374*n*, 410*n*

Yiddish, xviii, xxxiv, xxxvi, 48, 49, 62, 66, 286, 357, 377*n*, 380*n*

kibitz, 71, 383*n*

Yiddish Theatre, xxvii, 37–40, 41, 48–49, 54, 56, 57, 58, 352, 377*n*, 378*n*, 379*n*, 381*n*

Young Lions, The (film), xxv, 28, 55, 128, 131–38, 286, 408*n*

Nazi character in, 68, 126–27, 132–38

youth, American, 99–102

Zanuck, Darryl, 88–89, 106, 116, 120

Zapata, Emiliano, 28, 88–95, *89*, 123, 192, 314, 316

Zapata, Eufemio, 93, 94

Zeiger, Henry, 168

Zinkin, Taya, 192

Zinnemann, Fred, 84

Zionism, 58–61, 63–64